Accommodation
Services

For Colin. Thank you. Thank you. Thank you.

And for Bryce and Willem. Thank you for your understanding and support.

For Robyn and Adrienne. Thank you for all your help and for reading the manuscript.

A special thank you to Achdan Harris and the team at Micros Fidelio for your assistance in putting together the screen pages.

Accommoda
Services

VIVIENNE O'SHANNESSY
SHERYL HABY
PANIA RICHMOND

Pearson Education Australia
Unit 4, Level 2
14 Aquatic Drive
Frenchs Forest NSW 2086

Publisher: Matthew Coxhill
Project Editor: Jane Roy
Copy Editor: Loretta Barnard, Sonnet Editorial
Illustrations by: Jacinta Young
Cover and text designed by Ramsay Macfarlane Design, Surry Hills, NSW
Typeset by Midland Typesetters

Printed in Malaysia, VVP

5 05

National Library of Australia
Cataloguing-in-Publication data

O'Shannessy, Vivienne, 1962–
Accommodation Services

   ISBN 1 74009 558 8.

   1. Hotel management. I. Haby, Sheryl. II. Richmond, Pania.
   III. Title.

647.94

An imprint of Pearson Education Australia

Contents

CHAPTER 13   **DEALING WITH CONFLICT SITUATIONS**

GLOSSARY

INDEX

Introduction to Accommodation Services

LEARNING OUTCOMES

On completion of this chapter you will be able to:

▷ describe the scope of the hospitality industry;

▷ define who a guest is (target market);

▷ identify the target markets each hospitality sector may attract;

▷ describe the structure of accommodation venues and the services they may offer;

▷ correctly identify the stages of the cycle of service and the importance of services to guest satisfaction;

▷ explain the property management systems used to help control accommodation services operations; and

▷ identify the desirable attributes of accommodation services staff.

Introduction

During the last two decades of the 20th century, dramatic changes occurred in the way we do business, whether in a hospitality environment or in any other type of business, whether in Australia or overseas. Mainly driven by changing consumer needs and wants, the changes have led to a more customer-centred approach in the provision of goods and services. Facilitated by factors such as technological advances, improved transportation and globalisation, the changes have also increased competition, contributed to more efficient and effective ways of doing business and encouraged a proactive approach to staff training, enabling greater customer satisfaction and better business outcomes.

Perhaps nowhere is this customer focus and competitive environment in the provision of services more evident than in the hospitality industry. The hospitality industry is:

▷ *built entirely on providing service to customers;*
▷ *committed to meeting the needs and wants of its various markets in a dynamic and challenging way; and*
▷ *providing career opportunities in a range of sectors.*

*Throughout this book we aim to provide you with an understanding of the dynamics of the industry, specifically in **accommodation services**, and the skills required to build your career in this field. We aim to give you the confidence and underlying knowledge and skills that will enable you to make every guest's experience of the hospitality industry a positive one. We will provide you with a greater understanding of the roles and responsibilities in the accommodation services division of a hospitality venue, and with the necessary tools to help you achieve the organisation's goals, as well as your own personal career goals.*

Scope of the hospitality industry

Scope of hospitality industry refers to the range of businesses that provide goods, services and facilities to travellers, including accommodation, food, beverages, gaming and entertainment.

The scope of the hospitality industry comprises the range of businesses that provide services and facilities such as accommodation, food, beverages, entertainment, gaming and related products to people while travelling away from home.

For many, the hospitality industry appears to consist of only five star hotels and fancy restaurants and the services offered by these venues. But this belief ignores the wider scope of the industry. Today, the industry boasts multiple sectors; it offers significant career opportunities and generates substantial economic benefits in the wider community.

Those of you who choose to establish a career in hospitality are building on a profession that is centuries old, and contributing substantially to the enjoyment of travellers' experiences. Whether in a five star hotel, up-market restaurant or any other type of venue, hospitality professionals have within them the power to influence the extent of the enjoyment experienced by each of their guests. And the first opportunity to do this in accommodation venues rests with the accommodation services staff.

For example, imagine a couple on their honeymoon. They are booked into a fine hotel in a strange city. While excited after the wedding celebrations, they are tired and a bit unsure of their surroundings. On arrival the porter warmly greets them. They are quickly registered and then escorted to their room. During this process, the reception staff and porters offer assistance and advice about things they may like to do while staying here and where they can get additional information if needed. After this initial experience, they feel confident and relaxed about their choice of venue.

THE LINK WITH THE TOURISM INDUSTRY

The hospitality industry is a sector of the broader tourism industry. **Tourism** usually implies people travelling away from home for pleasure, either for a day, a night, a week or even longer. Hospitality venues however, cater not only to the tourism markets but also to other markets requiring hospitality services, such as business people.

When travelling away from home (whether for business or pleasure), we need a variety of facilities and services to meet our needs. These facilities and services may include transport, accommodation, food and beverages, tours, entertainment and information, to name a few. Each of these services and facilities potentially represents a sector of the tourism industry.

For example, you are planning a winter holiday in the snowfields. You need to arrange to get there, book a place to stay and buy ski equipment—all before you leave home. When you get there, you need to arrange your ski pass, think about where you are going to eat and what entertainment is available after a long day of skiing. Each of the services and facilities you need and use for your ski holiday is potentially provided by different businesses, and potentially linked to the tourism industry.

To give you a clearer picture of how this works, Table 1.1 lists some of the services and facilities a traveller may need or want, and which sector of the tourism industry is able to meet that need.

Tourism is an essential ingredient to the economic well-being of many regions in Australia. This means that tourism is also vital to the economic well-being of most hospitality

Tourism refers to people travelling away from home for pleasure, for a day, a night or longer (not for business).

Business travellers are not included in the definition of tourism because they are travelling for business, not pleasure.

The **hospitality industry** is a sector of the tourism industry.

Table 1.1 ▷ **Tourism sectors and services**

SECTORS	SERVICES
Travel agencies	• Tour bookings • Transport arrangements • Accommodation bookings
Hospitality establishments	• Accommodation • Food • Beverages • Entertainment and gaming • Conventions/functions
Transportation	• Rail and coach companies • Rental vehicles • Cruise ships • Airline flights • Tours (including accommodation arrangements) • Package holidays
Convention centres/meeting organisers	• Conventions • Seminars • Trade shows
Tour operators	• Short and long term group and individual tours (including accommodation arrangements)
Attractions	• Purpose built (for example, SeaWorld, Sydney Harbour Bridge) • Natural (Uluru, fairy penguins)

establishments. It offers employment opportunities and a flow of spending through the community (multiplier effect) that sustains other businesses and industries. It generates infrastructure development and attracts foreign currency into the country. These factors contribute to the overall economic importance of tourism to Australia.

Without tourism, many communities may not survive, and indeed some communities rely mainly on attracting tourists for their survival. To meet the needs and wants of the tourists that it attracts, the community needs to have in place facilities such as accommodation venues, tourist attractions (natural and man-made), and entertainment and retail outlets specifically catering to the tourism market. An example of this is Queensland's Gold Coast. Many of the businesses there are linked to the tourism industry, which substantially sustains the local economy.

HOSPITALITY SECTORS

Commercial venues—hospitality establishments in business to make money and hence a profit.

To fully understand the scope of the hospitality industry, it is important to recognise that hospitality itself is comprised of several sectors. The various sectors of hospitality are classified as either **commercial** or **non-commercial**. Commercial venues are those establishments that are in business to make a profit. Table 1.2 lists the commercial sectors of the hospitality industry and provides examples of the types of venues operating in those sectors and the possible services offered.

Non-commercial businesses—establishments providing hospitality services but not for profit.

Non-commercial establishments do not generally function to make a profit. These establishments provide services such as institutional catering in hospitals and schools, emergency services catering and institutional accommodation, such as student residential facilities, prisons and hostels. In this book, we focus only on commercial venues, and more specifically, the role of accommodation services in these venues.

Table 1.2 ▷ **Hospitality sectors and services**

SECTOR	TYPES	SERVICES AVAILABLE
Hotels	• 1–5 star • Residential • Pubs and taverns	• Accommodation • Food and beverage • Entertainment and gaming • Retail outlets • Recreational facilities
Motels and Motor Inns	• 1–4 star	• Accommodation • Food and beverage • Entertainment • Recreational facilities
Restaurants	• Fine dining • Casual dining • Cafes • Sandwich bars	• Food and beverage • Entertainment
Clubs	• Private • RSL (Returned Services League) • RAC (Royal Automobile Club) • Sports	• Accommodation • Food and beverage • Entertainment and gaming • Recreational facilities
Caravan parks	• Basic and luxury	• Accommodation • Cooking facilities • Entertainment

Table 1.2 ▷ *(continued)*

SECTOR	TYPES	SERVICES AVAILABLE
Bed and breakfast	• Basic and luxury	• Accommodation
		• Food
Hostels	• Backpacker	• Accommodation
	• Student	• Cooking facilities
Fast food outlets	• McDonalds	• Food and beverage
	• Pizza Hut	• Kids' playground
	• Red Rooster	
	• Burger King	
	• KFC	
Resorts	• 3–5 star	• Accommodation
	• Beach	• Food and beverage
	• Country	• Entertainment
		• Retail outlets
		• Recreational facilities
Convention and conference venues	• Basic and luxury	• Food and beverage
Serviced apartments	• Basic and luxury	• Accommodation
		• Self-catering
Entertainment/sporting venues	• Corporate facilities	• Food and beverage
		• Entertainment
Casino complexes	• Entertainment	• Accommodation
		• Food and beverage
		• Entertainment
		• Gambling
		• Retail outlets
Road houses		• Food and beverage
Private catering		• Food and beverage
Cruise ships	• Basic and luxury	• Accommodation
	• Passenger ferries	• Food and beverage
		• Entertainment
		• Gambling
		• Activities
		• Retail outlets

Simply by studying this table it is easy to build a picture of the scope of hospitality. Of course, there is great diversification between even similar categories within the same sector. For example, compare a two star hotel on the fringe of a city with a five star hotel in the central business district of a city. The five star city venue will provide more services and facilities, such as 24-hour room service and laundry services, and at a greater cost than the two star hotel.

What every hospitality venue, irrespective of its sectors, has in common however, is the need for some form of reception. Each venue needs someone to greet guests on arrival, act as a provider of information and ensure that customers receive the standard of hospitality they expect and deserve.

What is critically important for every venue is the need for well-trained staff who are able to identify and meet the differing needs and expectations of the customers who use the services offered by them.

APPLY YOUR KNOWLEDGE

Research the facilities and attractions in your area that are likely to be related to the tourism industry. For example, what attractions are there? What accommodation options are available? Where do visitors eat? How do people travel to your area? What entertainment is available?

SKILLS FOCUS

The hospitality industry is comprised of a number of businesses that provide services and facilities such as accommodation, food, beverages, entertainment and related products to people travelling away from home. It is a sector of the broader tourism industry, but within hospitality itself there are numerous other sectors.

Hospitality sectors are either commercial (make a profit) or non-commercial (not for profit) establishments. Commercial venues provide a range of facilities and services to meet the needs of their various guests, and include hotels, clubs, restaurants, hostels and resorts. Non-commercial venues provide services such as institutional catering in hospitals and schools, emergency services catering and catering in prisons.

FOCUS REVIEW

▷ *What is meant by the scope of the hospitality industry?*
▷ *Why do you think a definition of tourism excludes people travelling for business?*
▷ *Which tourism sectors are potentially linked to the hospitality industry?*
▷ *What impact does tourism have on hospitality?*
▷ *Distinguish between commercial and non-commercial establishments.*
▷ *What does every hospitality venue have in common?*

Defining hospitality guests

Guests are the customers of the hospitality industry. Guests are the people who pay for the services and facilities provided by hospitality establishments. As you would provide hospitality to a guest in your home, so too would you provide hospitality to a guest in your workplace. The difference of course is that we don't present a bill to our house guests when they leave!

Each guest is different. It may be easy to think of every guest having the same wants, needs and expectations but this is not the case. Differences such as age, gender, cultural background, reasons for travelling and a range of other influences, will combine to form the differing wants and needs of guests. Typically, these wants and needs influence the types of hospitality establishments they visit, their expectations of services and standards, the amount of money they are willing to spend, and the reason for their stay.

Guests may be local residents, interstate or intrastate visitors or international tourists. The hospitality industry attracts guests from various backgrounds both international (**inbound**

Inbound tourists— visitors to Australia whose main place of residence is outside Australia.

tourists) and domestic (**intrastate** and **interstate**). One of the only things you can usually generalise about guest requirements is their basic need for accommodation and food. They will differ in almost every other way.

For example, a woman travelling for business may choose to stay in a five star hotel because her needs include secretarial services, 24-hour room service, valet parking and a laundry service, which the venue is able to provide. She expects a very high standard of service and attention to detail, and is prepared to pay for it.

On the other hand, a young couple with children may choose to holiday at the beach. They may drive there and hire a caravan instead of staying in a motel or hotel. This allows them to cook all their own meals, thereby saving money on food costs. Their expectations will be far different to the businesswoman staying in the five star hotel because their needs are different and the reason for travel is different.

While the expectations of the young family are different from the businesswoman's, they are still entitled to hospitality. The two examples show different **target markets** (the market segment an establishment promotes its products to). What is important to note is that many hospitality sectors and even the various categories within each sector, are aiming to attract different **market segments** (a category of customers with similar traits, needs and wants).

Table 1.3 shows some of the typical markets various hospitality sectors are likely to attract.

Most hospitality establishments specifically design their products and services to cater to a particular type of customer. That is, they cater to a particular market segment, and that

Intrastate tourists—visitors who live in Australia travelling within their home state.

Interstate tourists—visitors who live in Australia travelling outside their home state.

Target market—the market segment an establishment markets its products to.

Market segment—a category of customers with similar traits, needs and wants.

Table 1.3 ▷ **Hospitality sectors and their target markets**

SECTOR	MARKET
Hotels 3–5 star	• Business people • Weekend packages • Honeymoon couples • Conference and tour groups
Hotels 1–2 star	• Business people • Budget travellers • Families
Motels and Motor Inns	• Some business travellers • Families on holidays • Travellers travelling by car • Tour groups
Bed and breakfast	• Weekend getaways • Independent travellers
Resorts	• Couples • Families • Honeymoon couples • Singles
Clubs	• Business people • Club members and their guests
Caravan parks	• Families • School groups • Budget travellers
Fast food outlets	• Almost anyone!
Serviced apartments	• Business travellers • Families

market segment becomes their target market. The businessperson is one segment, a family is another segment. The five star city hotel is not likely to market its services and facilities to a family looking for a budget beach holiday. Similarly, the caravan park is not likely to attract the businessperson travelling for business purposes. Both establishments are unlikely to be able to simultaneously meet the wants and needs of both these market segments.

With a basic understanding of the various market segments, the wants and needs of the target markets and the hospitality sector to which they may be attracted, it is easier to understand how to provide the standard of service expected and the facilities desired.

How establishments market their services and facilities to the relevant target markets is discussed in the next chapter.

SKILLS FOCUS

Customers are the people who use and pay for a venue's services and facilities. In hospitality we refer to customers as guests. Our guests are drawn from various markets depending on what they need and want and what the venue offers. The needs and wants of the guest influence the type of establishments they visit, their expectations and the amount of money they spend. Hospitality establishments market their products to the market segments they have identified as needing and wanting their specific product features.

FOCUS REVIEW

▷ *What influences the types of hospitality establishments a traveller may visit?*
▷ *What factors do you think might influence a person's decision to stay at a resort rather than at a serviced apartment?*
▷ *What is meant by 'market segment'? How does this differ from 'target market'?*
▷ *Do you think it is important for hospitality venues to market their products only to their target market? Why? Why not?*
▷. *How is having an understanding of the various target markets useful?*

APPLY YOUR KNOWLEDGE

Arrange to visit a five star hotel, a bed and breakfast venue and a small motel. Identify:

▷ *the services and facilities offered;*
▷ *the target market they are likely to attract;*
▷ *how the services available would influence the target market's expectations.*

Talking to staff and reading printed material about the venue will help you to identify the target markets, services offered and how these services may influence target market expectations.

Structure of accommodation venues

As we have seen, there are numerous types of hospitality establishments in various sectors—hotels, motels, bed and breakfasts, resorts, clubs and caravan parks. Each establishment, irrespective of its sector, is **structured** to enable it to best meet the needs and expectations of its target markets.

By structure we mean how the different services and facilities are organised within the venue. The functions and activities that take place in a hospitality establishment are grouped according to the nature of the service. For example, food and beverage services are grouped into a department (and frequently sub-divided further into outlets). Accommodation-related activities are grouped into a department, as are all the other activities that take place, such as the human resources functions, sales and marketing functions, and general administration functions.

This grouping into a structure of departments allows a better control of the services available. Grouping into departments is also useful for staff. It helps them to clearly identify their roles and responsibilities and allows them to see where they fit into the overall structure of the establishment.

Typically, hospitality venues have the following departments:

▷ accommodation services
▷ food and beverage
▷ maintenance and engineering
▷ sales and marketing
▷ human resources
▷ financial control
▷ general administration.

An **organisational chart** can be used to show the structure of a venue. It shows each department, the division of labour, levels of authority and lines of communication. Figure 1.1 shows an organisational chart for a large hospitality venue. At the top of the chart is the general manager. Descending unbroken lines indicate the various management and staff levels and reporting lines.

A position on the chart directly below another position with a connecting unbroken line, reports to the position directly above.

The bigger an establishment is, the more staff it is likely to have and the more structured it is likely to be. In other words, the larger the venue, the more clearly defined are its departments and staff roles and responsibilities.

In this section we describe each department in more detail. Our focus is on a reasonably large hotel as this will help provide an overall picture of an accommodation venue and why it is structured the way it is. In smaller venues, roles tend to overlap and responsibilities become less distinguishable.

ACCOMMODATION SERVICES

The term 'accommodation services' is just one of many given to the broader definition of the departments responsible for selling and maintaining guest rooms and associated services. The other popular industry name used is 'rooms division'. As both names suggest, the primary concerns of this department are guest rooms and the services available to guests staying in the venue.

Organisational structure refers to how the services and facilities of a venue are organised and grouped in order to conduct its business so as to meet guests' needs and expectations.

An **organisational chart** is a graphical representation of the division of labour, levels of authority and lines of communication in a business.

Accommodation services comprise:
• front and back office operations
• concierge
• housekeeping.

Figure 1.1 ▷ **Organisational chart of structure of a venue**

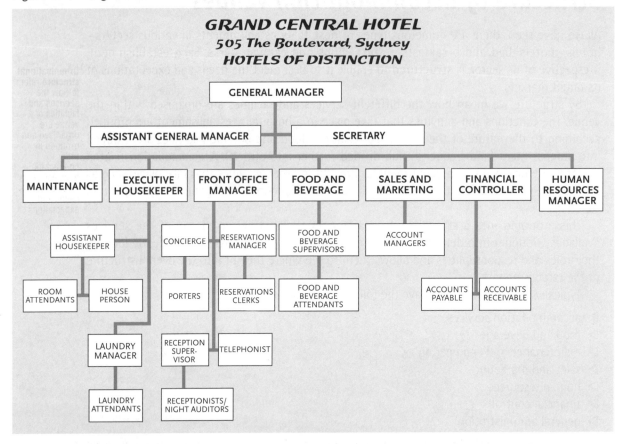

Accommodation services usually encompass three distinct areas of control: front and back office operations, housekeeping and concierge.

Front office

Front office roles:
• receptionist
• cashier
• night auditor
• FOM

The **front office** is the 'face' of the hotel. It is also the heart of the hotel, if not physically, then certainly operationally. The front office usually generates the greatest amount of revenue for an accommodation venue and every guest at some point must pass through the front office. The term 'front office' is frequently used to imply both front office and back office operations.

On a physical level, the front office does not resemble our usual image of an office. The reception desk is strategically placed in the entry foyer of the hotel. Both the foyer and reception desk are designed to give a positive, welcoming first impression of the venue.

The front office is responsible for a variety of functions and activities. These include checking-in the guest on arrival, organising services during the guest's stay and checking the guest out. Front office tasks may be undertaken by all staff, or divided among the staff, depending on the size of the venue. Table 1.4 shows the various tasks and the role, or position, most likely to be responsible for completing each activity.

Back office

A **reservation** is a booking for accommodation in a hospitality venue.

The function of the **back office** is to provide support for front office services. It also provides that crucial first contact with a venue for many guests—the **reservation**. The back office is

Table 1.4 ▷ **Roles and responsibilities of the front office**

POSITION	ACTIVITY OR TASK
Receptionist	• Greet guests on arrival • Check guests in and out • Handle guest requests • Post guests' charges
Cashier	• Post guests' charges • Maintain guests' accounts • Finalise guests' accounts
Night auditor	• Balance all financial transactions that occurred that day in the venue • Manage the switchboard at night • Perform reception duties at night
Supervisor	• Oversee the activities at the front office during each shift
Front office manager (FOM) or Rooms division manager	• The most senior person in the department oversees all front and back office activities. Develops: • rosters • departmental budgets and forecasts • policies and procedures • rate structures • training schedules • service standards guidelines

usually physically located directly behind the front office because of the integral link between these two functional areas. While the front office staff has face-to-face contact with guests, back office staff frequently liaise with guests by other means such as over the telephone or via written communication.

Among other things, the back office is mainly responsible for reservation bookings and maintenance, guest correspondence, the generation of reports and receiving and transferring telephone calls. The extent of these roles will vary depending on the size of the venue. Table 1.5 shows the back office roles most likely to be found in a large accommodation venue.

Table 1.5 ▷ **Back office roles and responsibilities**

POSITION	ACTIVITIES
Reservation clerk	• Process and maintain all individual and group reservations • Actively sell and promote the venue • Process reservation deposits • Allocate rooms
Telephonist	• Manage switchboard • Receive incoming calls • Transfer calls • Make calls • Take messages
Reservations manager	• Manage room yield • Supervise reservation activities

Cross-training—training in more than one job or department in a hospitality venue.

In most venues, front and back office staff are regularly **cross-trained**. Another commonly used termed for cross-training is multi-skilling. Being multi-skilled means you have skills in more than one area. Cross-training means that staff are trained to perform in more than one role, which allows for greater flexibility in the roles each staff member is able to undertake. This tends to eliminate the possibility of a staff member not being able to fulfil a guest's request where that request is not part of their normal duties.

Concierge

The **concierge** (or **porters'**) department is frequently the first physical point of contact a guest may have with an establishment. The concierge role includes guest liaison, providing services and information relating to services and facilities offered by the establishment, and services, facilities, attractions and activities that are available outside the establishment. The positions in the concierge department may include porters, door attendants, valets and bellhops.

The role of the porter is discussed in greater detail in Chapter 9.

Housekeeping

Public areas are those areas in a hospitality venue to which the public has general access (for example, a bar, restaurant, or foyer).

The primary function of **housekeeping** is maintaining the cleanliness of the guest rooms and **public areas** of the establishment. Housekeeping and front office work closely together and it is therefore critical for staff in these two functional areas to be familiar with the services and functions that each performs. The roles and responsibilities in housekeeping are discussed in Chapters 10, 11 and 12.

Many of the larger establishments also cross-train their front and back office staff in both concierge and housekeeping duties. This helps staff to better understand the various roles and responsibilities of their colleagues. They are also able to gain first hand experience meeting a larger number of guests' needs and in the servicing of guest rooms. An additional benefit of cross-training in housekeeping is that staff gain an appreciation of the fixtures and fittings and layout of each room type in the venue.

FOOD AND BEVERAGE

A **food and beverage manager**, or director, usually oversees the food and beverage department (or division). This person's role is to manage all food and beverage operations within the venue including:

Occupancy refers to the number of rooms booked in the venue. It is usually expressed as a percentage of the total number of rooms available in the venue.

▷ kitchens
▷ restaurants
▷ bars
▷ banquets, functions and conferences, and
▷ room service.

Each of these sections or outlets usually has a separate manager reporting directly to the food and beverage director. Their role is to manage the day-to-day activities of their outlet in line with the overall goals of the department.

The front (and back) office and the food and beverage department need to maintain regular and timely communication with each other. Each food and beverage outlet must know the level of **occupancy** in the establishment at any given time, any specific requirements of guests, the number of arrivals and check-outs, group bookings, **meal plans**, and any other information generated by front office that may affect their operations.

Staffing levels—the number of staff required to serve the expected number of guests.

From this information, food and beverage outlets are able to plan **staffing levels** (and roster staff accordingly), order food and beverages, set up functions and conferences, arrange equipment and coordinate a number of other activities.

Group bookings indicates that a booking is for a group of people.

MAINTENANCE AND ENGINEERING

Most venues employ one or more maintenance people or engineers to manage the day-to-day maintenance problems that arise. Large establishments are likely to have a number of staff in this department who are able to fix most things such as a hot water system, a broken chair or chipped plaster.

As most maintenance problems are reported to accommodation services staff (front and back office, housekeeping and concierge) constant and timely communication must take place between these departments.

SALES AND MARKETING

Sales and marketing specialists are often employed by larger venues to promote the venue's services and facilities. The sales and marketing department is responsible for identifying marketing opportunities and establishing strategies and tactics to take advantage of those opportunities in line with the overall objectives of the establishment.

However, accommodation services staff also have a large role to play in promoting the venue, simply because of their regular and constant contact with all guests. The sales and marketing department and accommodation services department work closely to develop strategies and promotional activities.

In the next chapter we concentrate on the activities involved in promoting the venue and its services and facilities to potential guests.

HUMAN RESOURCES

Most large hospitality establishments employ a **human resources manager** to manage a range of staff-related issues including:

▷ recruitment
▷ staffing related policies and procedures
▷ induction and training
▷ position descriptions
▷ personal development programs
▷ reward systems
▷ performance appraisals
▷ conducting exit interviews.

The human resources manager works closely with each department to determine its specific needs.

FINANCIAL CONTROL

Financial control, in simple terms, refers to the management of revenue received and expenses incurred by the venue. Revenue and expenses are the result of financial transactions that occur on a daily basis. The financial controller is employed to check that all transactions are accurately recorded. Often referred to as the accounts department, financial control is necessary to ensure that all moneys received and expended by the venue are accounted for.

In Chapter 7 we discuss the responsibilities for financial control that accommodation services staff have in relation to guest accounts.

GENERAL ADMINISTRATION

Larger establishments frequently employ staff to perform general administrative duties. These staff are often considered as being in a support role for management. These administrative or clerical duties might include:

▷ written correspondence
▷ filing
▷ report generation, and
▷ miscellaneous clerical support for other departments.

Clerical procedures are discussed in greater detail in Chapter 5.

MANAGEMENT

All accommodation venues need a manager. The size and structure of the venue will often determine how many managers are needed and each manager's title. For example, a large five star venue will have a **general manager** who is responsible for the entire operation. In addition, the establishment is likely to have a manager, or department head, in charge of each department and a supervisor, or **assistant manager** responsible for an outlet, shift or subsection of the department. Many large venues also appoint duty managers. A duty manager's role is that of acting manager-in-charge, in the absence of a more senior manager.

In a small venue, there may be a general manager and an assistant manager and supervisors for each department or outlet.

SKILLS FOCUS

Accommodation venues are organisationally structured by grouping similar activities into separate departments or functional areas to allow better control of those activities. Each department is represented graphically on an organisational chart that also shows levels of authority and communication channels. By structuring the establishment into related activities, staff are better able to identify their roles and responsibilities and determine how they fit into the overall structure of the venue.

The accommodation services department, also referred to as the rooms division, includes front and back office, housekeeping and concierge activities. The food and beverage department includes the kitchen, restaurants, bars, banquets and functions, and room service. Other departments include human resources, sales and marketing, financial control and maintenance. General administration activities provide clerical support usually to management but frequently to other departments as well.

FOCUS REVIEW

▷ *What is the purpose of an organisational chart?*
▷ *Why is grouping similar activities into departments or divisions useful?*
▷ *What are the main differences between the front and back offices in terms of guest contact?*
▷ *What benefits arise from cross-training in all accommodation services areas?*
▷ *Why is it important for front office staff to maintain timely and constant communication with other departments?*

ACCOMMODATION SERVICES AND GUEST SATISFACTION

The accommodation services department plays an important role in the guest's level of satisfaction. Throughout the guest's stay, every service used, every product purchased and every transaction undertaken, affects the accommodation services division. From the first point of contact where a guest enquires about available accommodation, through to servicing the room and finally, the guest's departure, the staff working in the front and back office, housekeeping and concierge are all potentially involved. Each of these events takes place within the framework of the **cycle of service**.

The cycle of service

The cycle of service represents the four stages of the guest's experience with the venue—pre-arrival, arrival, occupancy and departure. Figure 1.2 shows how each of the stages works.

Cycle of service—four stages of the guest's contact with the venue:
• pre-arrival
• arrival
• occupancy
• departure.

PRE-ARRIVAL

The **pre-arrival** stage occurs before the guest stays at the venue. Back office, housekeeping and concierge are all potentially involved in the pre-arrival stage. A guest makes telephone or face-to-face enquiries about availability and cost and potentially a reservation; once a reservation has been made, housekeeping will check that the room is ready to be occupied and the porter may arrange a variety of services, such as luggage storage and car parking, all before the guest arrives. Some guests may even visit the venue prior to booking to allow them to determine first hand if the venue offers what they are looking for.

Figure 1.2 ▷ **The Cycle of Service**

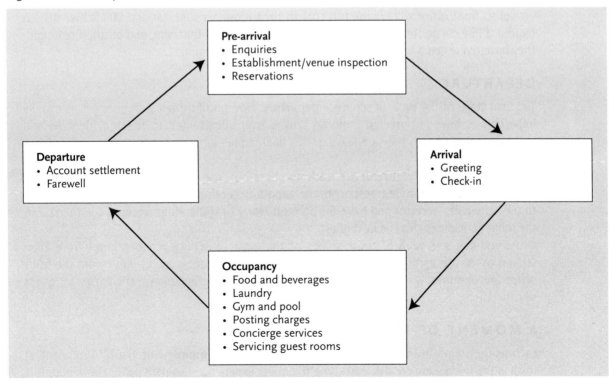

For example, Mr and Mrs Schwerdt are visiting Perth for the first time. They call the Hotel Grand requesting accommodation in a double room for three nights and would like a cot set up in their room. Because they are arriving before the usual check-in time, they have requested their luggage be stored so that they can go sight seeing for the day unhindered with luggage. A reservations clerk takes the booking and enters the details into the computer. They advise housekeeping that a cot needs to be set up on the day of arrival. The porters are also advised that the Schwerdts will require luggage storage the morning of arrival.

ARRIVAL

The **arrival** stage of the cycle of service is most often the first opportunity to greet and welcome the guests face-to-face, unless a pre-arrival inspection has taken place.

When Mr and Mrs Schwerdt arrive, George, the porter, will meet them at the door. He will store their luggage for them until they are able to check into their room (they have arrived before the usual check-in time). When their room is ready, a porter will take the luggage to the room. Milly, the receptionist will check them into the room and advise them of the other services available in the venue.

OCCUPANCY

Occupancy refers to the actual stay or period of time spent in the venue. During occupancy, the guests may use a range of services: they may, for example, dine in the restaurant or request information or transportation. Housekeeping will service the room each day the guests are **in-house**.

In-house refers to a guest who is currently staying in the venue.

For example, Mr and Mrs Schwerdt have breakfast each morning in the hotel's cafe. Breakfast is not included in the room rate (rate charged per night per room to stay in the venue) so front office will charge this cost to their room account. Mr and Mrs Schwerdt also request a hire car for one day, which the porter will arrange for them, and on the final night, they have requested a baby sitter which housekeeping will arrange.

DEPARTURE

The final stage of the cycle of service is **departure**. How you farewell your guests is as equally important as how you greeted them on arrival. Your guests want to feel that they are still important even though they are leaving. This final impression, this last 'moment of truth', is a permanent one.

When Mr and Mrs Schwerdt are ready to check out, the porter will collect their luggage from the room and arrange transport to the airport. Reception will have posted all the charges to the Schwerdts' account and have the account ready to settle. Housekeeping will then clean the room in readiness for the next guest.

As you can see, each of these stages of the cycle of service requires input from each section of the accommodation services department. Every stage requires input from the front office and requires that procedures be followed to ensure accuracy, efficiency and guest satisfaction.

A MOMENT OF TRUTH

Each of the stages in the cycle of service also represents a **'moment of truth'**. A moment of truth is the impression created each time the guest experiences 'something' in the venue. This 'something' may be the guest's first impression of the building, the way they were greeted on arrival, the way a complaint was handled or the cleanliness of their room.

Moment of truth—the impression created by each experience the guest has in the venue. It may be positive, negative or neutral.

Each of these experiences will result in either a positive, negative or neutral impression. If the impression is either positive or negative, the guest will take these experiences away with them and tell others about it. A neutral experience is perhaps worst of all. It means that no lasting impression was made and if asked about that experience, the guest probably won't be able to recall how they felt or what they thought about that experience.

Positive moment of truth

A positive moment of truth occurs when a good impression has been made. It may be how clean the surrounds of the establishment are, or it may be how welcome the guest felt on arrival. A positive moment of truth contributes to the guest's overall feeling of satisfaction with the establishment. One positive moment of truth is not sufficient to satisfy the guest entirely. If the reservation was a positive experience and the check-in process a negative experience, the guest is most likely to remember only the last moment of truth. In this case, a bad experience.

Negative moment of truth

A negative moment of truth occurs when a bad impression is left on the guest. This experience may be about how a complaint was handled or how poorly the guest was treated on departure, or when the guest's room service food order was cold! Once a bad moment of truth has been experienced what happens next is crucial to the overall experience the guest will take away with them. For example, if a poor moment of truth is compounded by another poor moment of truth, this guest will probably not focus on any of the good things about the venue.

It requires great skills to turn around a bad experience and achieve a positive outcome. You will need to be able to show empathy, diplomacy and sympathy. You will need to be understanding, caring and interested. You will need to work very hard to make the guest believe that the negative experience is not the usual standard of service at your venue. In Chapter 13, we discuss how to manage conflict and the skills required to change a bad impression into a good one.

Neutral moment of truth

The neutral moment of truth fails to make any impression at all. If the guest can't recall the name of the venue they stayed in, for example, it is impossible for them to recommend it to others or return themselves! It is difficult to determine when a neutral impression has occurred. The guest is unlikely to provide any feedback on the experience because they have no or few feelings about it.

YOUR ROLE

Understanding how the cycle of service works and its relationship to your role is important for ensuring that you provide your guests with positive moments of truth throughout their stay. This in turn will contribute to the overall success of the establishment and thus continued employment for you in the long term.

Your role is to ensure that guests leave with a positive impression and to do this you need to meet their expectations. To meet their expectations you will need to know:

▷ how to do your job
▷ the expectations of the guests in the sector you work in

▷ how to meet the needs of individual guests
▷ the expectations of you by your employer
▷ all the facilities and services available in your venue.

Each of the chapters in this book represent stages in the cycle of service and provides you with the skills to create positive moments of truth every time you have contact with a guest.

SKILLS FOCUS

A guest's satisfaction with an establishment is directly linked to how accommodation services staff perform their roles. This is because every service and facility used by the guest affects this department. The guest's experience with the venue can be represented in the four stages of the cycle of service, which in turn provides opportunities for you to create positive moments of truth.

FOCUS REVIEW

▷ *How is it that everything a guest does in an accommodation venue affects the accommodation services department (particularly front office)?*
▷ *In your own words, explain the cycle of service.*
▷ *During occupancy, list four things a porter might help a guest with and four things a room attendant might help a guest with.*
▷ *During departure, why is the last moment of truth important?*
▷ *What is your role in satisfying guests' expectations of the venue? What do you need to know?*

Property Management Systems

A **Property Management System** (PMS) is a system that helps coordinate the flow of information required to control the transactions and activities that take place in a hospitality establishment. For example, an accommodation venue needs to keep track of its reservations, monitor its levels of occupancy, know who is registered, expected to arrive and depart, control and account for all financial transactions, determine how much money has been earned, expended and is payable, and regulate many other activities that relate to the guest and non-guest activities. The PMS provides a reporting facility for all the activities that take place in the venue that in turn can assist the establishment with operational decisions. In other words, a PMS is a means of collecting, storing and manipulating data relating to the activities of the venue and its guests.

Property Management Systems—
manual, semi-automated or automated.

The PMS used must be able to provide adequate and timely information because this is essential if a venue is to operate successfully. Whether the establishment uses a manual, semi-automated or fully automated (computerised) PMS depends on its size, turnover and control needs. Throughout this book, references to a PMS are for a computerised system.

MANUAL SYSTEMS

In a **manual system** all tasks relating to guest and venue activities are completed by hand or in written form. The only automation is possibly a typewriter and a calculator. The most common system is known as the *Whitney system*. This system uses booking diaries and conventional charts to keep track of reservations, colour-coded room racks to keep track of room types, room status and room occupancy, and other equipment that are today built into PMS computer programs. A completely manual system incorporates the use of a **tabular ledger** for recording financial transactions.

Small establishments, such as a four-roomed bed and breakfast, are likely to operate a manual system. However, they are also not likely to use a Whitney system but simply maintain a reservation book to keep track of their bookings and may even handwrite receipts.

SEMI-AUTOMATED SYSTEMS

A **semi-automated system** is one in which the data is processed manually but there is some automation in the accounting area of front office. For example, using a cash register, an account posting machine and a calculator. This equipment is often used in conjunction with a Whitney system. Tabular ledgers are used to control and balance financial transactions. An account-posting machine is a machine that allows you to record the financial transactions of each guest's account and keeps track of the totals charged for each service available in the venue.

AUTOMATED SYSTEMS

Automated systems use a minimal amount of handwritten information. Rather, information is entered into a computer where it is compiled and processed.

A computerised PMS can perform almost all the tasks previously undertaken manually. It is generally a more efficient and reliable system than a manual or semi-automated system and is able to process data far more rapidly than ever before.

There are many different front office software packages available that are designed to meet the various needs of individual establishments. Examples include, but are not limited to:

▷ Micros Fidelio
▷ Landmark
▷ Qantel
▷ Hotel XL
▷ HIS.

The PMS you will learn and use will depend on where you work. However, most systems are able to perform essentially the same tasks and they include:

▷ reservation maintenance
▷ guest account maintenance
▷ guest history maintenance
▷ report generation and statistical analysis
▷ housekeeping functions
▷ maintenance control
▷ non-guest financial control.

Table 1.6 lists some of the accommodation services duties performed by the various PMSs available. All of the duties are discussed in detail in their relevant chapters.

Table 1.6 △ Comparisons of Property Management Systems

FUNCTION	MANUAL	SEMI-AUTOMATED	COMPUTERISED
Reservations	• Handwritten reservation form	• Handwritten reservation form	• Handwritten reservation form • Entered into computer • Maintained on computer
Check-in	• Handwritten onto conventional chart • Changes manually managed • Typed or handwritten reservation slip; guest signs • Room rack manually adjusted; signed registration card placed in room rack	• Handwritten onto conventional chart • Changes manually managed • Typed or handwritten reservation slip; guest signs • Room rack manually adjusted; signed registration card placed in room rack	• Computer generated reservation slip; guest signs • Check-in registered on computer (opens guest account) • Room rack automatically updated
Posting charges	• Guest account on cards or a ledger—hand entered	• Guest account on cards or a ledger—posted on an account posting machine	• Entered on guest's account in computer
Account balancing	• Tabular ledgers	• Tabular ledgers	• Computer keeps track of all financial transactions by guest, department, method of payment
Check-out	• Account settlement entered manually to guest account	• Account settlement posted on account posting machine	• Account settlement entered onto computer, which generates receipt and closes account
Room status change	• Manually changed on room rack	• Manually changed on room rack	• Automatically updated at check-out • Updated by housekeeping when room cleaned
Report generation	• Manual collation of data from records maintained	• Manual collation of data from records maintained • Some report generation from account posting machine	• Automatically generated by computer, which compiles information entered into the system according to codes and other identifiers
Shift balance	• Manual tabular ledger entries	• Manual tabular ledger entries • Account posting machine will generate some financial tallies	• Automatically calculated and balanced by computer. However, must also complete a manual balance to ensure both (manual and computer) balances

Attributes for success in accommodation services

We conclude this chapter with a brief look at the personal attributes that hospitality establishments look for when recruiting accommodation services staff. While front and back office, housekeeping and concierge have varying degrees of contact with the guests and perform different tasks in meeting guests' needs, there are a few attributes that all staff in these positions should possess. These include:

▷ high standard of personal hygiene and grooming
▷ excellent knowledge and understanding of the venue and the services and facilities available
▷ excellent interpersonal skills
▷ a willingness to help and serve guests
▷ ability to perform a range of tasks related to their area of expertise
▷ a willingness to learn new tasks
▷ ability to learn the systems and procedures in place in the workplace
▷ good general knowledge of the local environment and attractions.

FOCUS REVIEW

▷ Why do you think we have included knowledge of the local environment and attractions as an important attribute of accommodation services staff?

▷ List 10 attractions or features in your local area.

▷ What other attributes do you think are necessary for success in accommodation services? Why?

PUT YOUR KNOWLEDGE TO THE TEST

At the end of her first day on the job, Robyn changed out of her uniform and reflected on her good fortune. She felt confident she would live up to the expectations of her employers as a management trainee at the Grand Central Hotel, a new five star venue in the heart of the city.

When she applied for the position, Robyn knew she was up against some of the best in the industry. But she knew that her personal attributes, including her willingness to learn and her formal qualifications, were in her favour. She had told the human resources manager that her goal was to be a front office manager within five years and that she understood that cross-training provided her with a better understanding of the overall operation.

During induction Robyn's trainer had stressed the importance of creating a positive impression every time she dealt with a guest. Robyn had not heard the term 'moment of truth' before but quickly realised the importance of this concept. She had within her the power to influence how a guest felt about their experience. With this power came responsibility for the guest's satisfaction with the venue and the services she provided.

Robyn was to spend a year in training in the accommodation services division before she would be considered for a supervisory role. During this time she would gain valuable experience in all areas of the front and back office, housekeeping and portering. At the end of the first day, she knew that this was going to be a hard job but immensely satisfying.

1. List 10 facilities and services the Grand Central Hotel may offer.

2. What target market(s) do you think this hotel is likely to attract?

3. Do you think it is more or less likely that roles and responsibilities in this venue will be clearly defined? Why?

4. What expectations do you think the Grand Central Hotel has of its trainee managers?

5. What attributes do you think Robyn demonstrated during the recruitment process that helped her be selected?

6. What value will cross-training be to Robyn in achieving her goal as a front office manager?

7. What responsibility do you think Robyn meant when she talked about the power to influence the guests' satisfaction with the venue?

Promoting Products and Services to Customers

LEARNING OUTCOMES

On completion of this chapter you will be able to:

▷ develop product and service knowledge using research techniques and list services and products available in hospitality venues;

▷ develop products and services to meet target market requirements;

▷ accurately describe a range of promotional tools and their use in a service industry;

▷ accurately describe the personal skills and techniques used to promote products and services; and

▷ describe the role of legislation for fair trade practices.

Introduction

Hospitality is a service industry offering a range of services, products and facilities to a vast array of people. You learned in the last chapter that the services, products and facilities offered by hospitality establishments include among other things accommodation, food and beverages, entertainment and information. As a hospitality professional you have a responsibility to help your guests make the best, most informed decisions about what services, products and facilities they want to buy in your venue. To do this you need the ability to paint a picture in your guest's mind about the features of the products and services available. And to be able to do this you need a number of skills and industry related knowledge.

There are tools and techniques that help you in this important role. By suggesting options and then describing the features of those options, you are providing a valuable service to your guests and fulfilling an important function for your employer—promoting its products and services.

For example, your venue may have standard double rooms and suites available. When a potential guest asks for information about your rooms, you could simply say 'We have available a deluxe double room for $220.00 a night or a suite for $265.00.' But so does the venue across the road. To persuade a guest to stay at your venue, you could say 'We have available a deluxe double room with an ocean view and a balcony, queen size bed and a spa bath for only $220.00. Or, for only $45.00 extra, we have a suite available with a king size bed, separate lounge area, free in-room video access and a choice of either ocean or city views.'

Essentially, you have given the guest the same information. But by describing in greater detail the features and facilities in the room types available, the guest has a clearer picture of what you have to offer beyond knowing that you simply have double rooms and suites. The guest is more likely to book your venue because of your helpfulness and ability to be specific about what is available.

All roles in accommodation services—reservations, reception, telephonist, concierge and housekeeping—are involved in selling the venue's products and services. But selling the venue's products and services is not meant to be a 'hard sell'. The guest has already made the decision to 'buy' accommodation (or other products); your role is to assist them in making the decision to buy your product, rather than your competitor's. And whether you are promoting the food and beverage outlets or suggesting the guest use the venue's limousine service, you will need both the product knowledge and the skill to sell confidently.

In this chapter you will learn how to develop **product knowledge** *and the necessary skills to achieve effective results in promoting your venue's services and products. You will also learn about the basic marketing activities that take place to attract and retain guests.*

Developing product and service knowledge

The importance of developing product and service knowledge rests with understanding each guest's wants and needs.

The importance of developing product and service knowledge rests with understanding each guest's wants and needs. Guests do not know as much about the venue or the industry as you do and therefore expect you to be able to provide them with the information they need to make their buying decisions.

When you first start a new job, your main concern is learning the routine aspects of the role, such as how to check a guest in, how to clean a room or how to answer the telephone. Equally as important is learning what products and services the venue offers and keeping up to date with industry trends that influence guest preferences. Sometimes you will learn this on the job; sometimes you will already have prior knowledge. Most of the time you will need to carry out some form of research.

FORMAL RESEARCH

Formal research involves systematically gathering and analysing information from primary and secondary sources relating to a product or service or even the industry in general. **Primary source** information is information collected through interviewing (one-on-one or group sessions) or questionnaires (for example, from the guest) or even chatting to colleagues. **Secondary source** information is information gathered from already published data.

While this may seem a little tedious, formal research can assist you in getting a job in the first place. For example, at the interview stage of recruitment, it is useful to know something about the organisation you are applying to (such as the venue's target market and star rating). A little research will provide the information you need.

Following are a few examples of secondary source formal research options you may like to use.

The Internet

The **World Wide Web** can give you a 'virtual' tour of many hospitality venues. By accessing a venue's website, you can find information relating to the size, location, features, services and prices of many establishments. Some venues today also have an option on their site that allows anybody to book a room directly via the Web using their e-mail link.

Libraries

A public library can provide you with access to the Internet as well as to printed reference material about the hospitality industry. The library is likely to stock a range of reference books and a selection of hospitality trade or related magazines.

Promotional material

Promotional material is printed information about the venue such as brochures and leaflets. Most of the formal research in promotional material has been done for you, but by studying these you are able to develop a bigger picture of individual venues, the image each is attempting to portray and the type of guests they are trying to attract.

INFORMAL RESEARCH

Informal research is not as structured or time-consuming as formal research. It involves the collection of information from sources that have already formally researched the products and services (secondary sources). This could include reading the menus and wine lists used in the venue, or reading a brochure on other accommodation venues in the chain of venues.

Other forms of informal research include:

▷ attending orientation and training sessions (including cross-training)
▷ talking with colleagues
▷ reading the staff hand book
▷ reading general media articles
▷ using the venue's facilities (such as dining in the restaurant)
▷ visiting competitors' venues
▷ personal observation.

It takes time to develop a high level of product knowledge and as there is a lot to know it is important that you take time to familiarise yourself with all aspects of the products and services available in the venues you work in. Ask questions if you are not sure, as you never know when a guest may ask you the same question. The higher the level of product knowledge, the greater your confidence and the higher the level of service you can offer your guests.

THE PRODUCTS AND SERVICES AVAILABLE

The products and services available in hospitality venues are as diverse as the industry itself. Because of your front-line role in the establishment, there is an expectation that you possess *all* of the establishment-related knowledge and much of the other knowledge a guest may enquire about.

Establishment-related knowledge

The sort of information that is useful to know about the venue you work in includes:

▷ accommodation options (number and types of rooms, room layouts, views and features)
▷ conference and convention facilities (number and size of rooms, room configuration options)
▷ function and banquet facilities (number and size of rooms, menu options, additional services such as decorations and entertainment)
▷ in-house entertainment (videos, swimming pool, sauna, gaming)
▷ food and beverage outlets (bars, restaurants, room service)
▷ front office services (currency exchange, secretarial, safety deposit, information service)
▷ concierge services (luggage handling, transport arrangements, general information)
▷ special offers (such as packages, special rates etc), and
▷ cost of all services and facilities offered at the venue.

CROSS-TRAINING

In Chapter 1 we said that cross-training was useful for all accommodation services staff as an aid to understanding the roles and responsibilities of their colleagues. Cross-training in different areas can also lead to increased product and services knowledge. It provides you with an opportunity to view—first hand—the services offered by other departments. And it will help you understand why things are done the way they are and ultimately provide better service to your guests. For example, if you work in reception, but spend some time learning the room attendant's role, you are better able to 'sell' rooms to guests and confidently advise your guests on the services offered by housekeeping (such as the availability of cots, rollaway beds and laundry).

No matter where you work in an organisation it is important to know what happens in other areas of the venue as no guest ever wants to hear 'that's not my department' or 'I don't know'.

External knowledge

Your guests also rely on you to provide information about, and arrange for, services and products that may not be related to the venue at all. Examples include:

▷ tours and travel information
▷ transport options
▷ entertainment
▷ medical services

▷ activities and attractions
▷ shopping services
▷ local events and festivals
▷ local area directions
▷ banking hours, post office services.

APPLY YOUR KNOWLEDGE

If you are currently working in an accommodation venue, use the following questions as a guide to how much product knowledge you have. If you are not currently working, select a local hospitality venue and call them to see how much product knowledge the person you speak to has about the venue. Ask questions from the following lists.

Accommodation
▷ *How many floors of accommodation are there?*
▷ *What is the bedding configuration in a twin room?*
▷ *Are there family rooms?*
▷ *What is the maximum amount of people to a room?*
▷ *When was the establishment built? Refurbished?*
▷ *Do you have non-smoking rooms/floors?*
▷ *What room numbers are near the elevators?*
▷ *Are there child facilities?*

Food and beverage outlets
▷ *How many outlets are in the establishment?*
▷ *Can you order a restaurant meal and eat it in the bar or guest room?*
▷ *What are the hours when room service operates?*
▷ *How many and which types of milk are available?*
▷ *What are the hours of operation for food and beverage outlets?*
▷ *Are vegetarian meals available?*
▷ *What is the average price of a main meal in the restaurant?*

General
▷ *What are the operating hours of the pool/spa/sauna/gym?*
▷ *Where is the nearest ATM/chemist/grocer?*
▷ *How much do movies cost in the room?*
▷ *How does the air-conditioning work in the room?*
▷ *How much does car-parking cost for guests? Conference attendees?*
▷ *What is the quickest way a guest can get a suit cleaned?*
▷ *What methods of transportation are available between the establishment and the airport and what is the approximate cost?*
▷ *Where is the nearest railway station?*
▷ *Where can I book a tour?*

How many did you or the venue get right? Check your answers and then correct those you didn't know or got wrong. If you had to call a venue, hopefully they could answer all your questions! While at the venue, ask for copies of their promotional material such as brochures. Would this information entice you to stay?

The marketing process

In its simplest form, **marketing** comprises all of the activities carried out by the establishment that are aimed at identifying its target market and promoting the venue to attract that target market. The target markets are the venue's potential guests—the people who buy the venue's products and services.

When a venue has identified its target markets, it implements a range of marketing strategies that involve **positioning** itself in the market place. This is the process of communicating the benefits of its products and services to its potential and existing guests, and developing products and services so that they are desirable for potential and existing guests. Once the venue has decided on the products and services it will offer, it is then potentially in a position to *differentiate* its products, services or prices. The venue is then able to develop its **marketing mix**. Finally, of course, the venue needs to measure the extent of success of its marketing strategies.

Thus, the venue:

▷ clearly identifies its target markets
▷ develops marketing strategies to meet the needs of potential and existing guests
▷ measures the success of its marketing efforts.

Identifying target markets

To be able to fit the product to the market, organisations must know who their target markets are. A target market is a category of people with similar characteristics and buying habits that the venue wants to attract. The target markets can be further distinguished as market segments. A market segment is a group of customers, or guests, with similar traits, needs and wants. Market segment characteristics help the venue in a number of ways. The venue can determine which products and services to make available based on each of the market segments. For example, a venue trying to attract families on holiday may offer interconnecting rooms, self-contained apartments and a child's menu in the restaurant. A venue wanting to attract business people might offer business centre facilities, express check-in and check-out facilities, and a same day laundry service.

By identifying their target markets and tailoring their products and services to meet each of the market's specific needs, a venue is better able to attract its potential market categories and consistently achieve the standard of quality expected by those markets. An example of a venue's market segment is shown in Table 2.1 on the next page.

In general terms, accommodation venues categorise their markets as:

▷ FITs (Free/Fully Independent Travellers)
▷ corporate/business
▷ government personnel
▷ travel agents
▷ airlines
▷ groups
▷ special occasion functions.

The importance of recognising the characteristics of each market group helps you in promoting the venue's products and services and has implications for reservations (we look at reservations in Chapter 5).

FREE INDEPENDENT TRAVELLERS (FITS)

Free or fully independent travellers are those guests who make reservations directly with the accommodation venue, are not part of a group, and make their own travel arrangements. These guests are usually travelling for leisure and can be further segmented according to the purpose of travel.

Leisure

Those classified in the leisure market include people travelling on holiday, visiting friends or relatives, taking a short break, such as a weekend getaway or long term visitors such as backpackers. The leisure market can include young people or the elderly, families, singles or couples. Leisure travellers may be locals, intrastate, interstate or inbound tourists. These guests may stay any time of the year and their individual needs vary.

Holiday makers

Most holiday makers do not want to think about cooking, cleaning or struggling to have a good time. They expect all the ease and familiarity of home with the convenience of activities, transport and accessibility to attractions at their doorstep. Their prime objective is recreation and relaxation.

Visiting friends and relatives

This segment's prime concern is to catch up with friends or relatives. For many, the purpose of the accommodation venue is a safe and comfortable place to sleep. They may want food and beverage services and a few ancillary services (for example, dry cleaning) and may even request information about the external environment.

Table 2.1 ▷ Market segment report

For Wednesday, 15 November 2000

	DAY					MONTH					YEAR				
	Rooms	Room Rev	ARR	%ROCC	Pers	Rooms	Room Rev	ARR	%ROCC	Pers	Rooms	Room Rev	ARR	%ROCC	Pers
**CORPORATE															
Corp. contract	1	120.00	120.00	0.7	1	1	120.00	120.00	0.0	1	1	120.00	120.00	0.0	1
Corp. no contract	0	0.00	0.00	0.0	0	0	0.00	0.00	0.0	0	0	0.00	0.00	0.0	0
Corporate Meetings	0	0.00	0.00	0.0	0	0	0.00	0.00	0.0	0	0	0.00	0.00	0.0	0
Meetings & Conferences	0	0.00	0.00	0.0	0	0	0.00	0.00	0.0	0	0	0.00	0.00	0.0	0
Subtotal	1	120.00	120.00	0.7	1	1	120.00	120.00	0.0	1	1	120.00	120.00	0.0	1
**INDIVIDUAL															
Banquet only	0	0.00	0.00	0.0	0	0	0.00	0.00	0.0	0	0	0.00	0.00	0.0	0
Catering only	0	0.00	0.00	0.0	0	0	0.00	0.00	0.0	0	0	0.00	0.00	0.0	0
Packages	0	0.00	0.00	0.0	0	0	0.00	0.00	0.0	0	0	0.00	0.00	0.0	0
Rack Business Room	0	0.00	0.00	0.0	0	0	0.00	0.00	0.0	0	0	0.00	0.00	0.0	0
Rack	7	2,700.00	385.71	5.1	7	7	2,700.00	385.71	0.3	7	7	2,700.00	385.71	0.0	7
Rack Deluxe Room	0	0.00	0.00	0.0	0	0	0.00	0.00	0.0	0	0	0.00	0.00	0.0	0
Rack Executive Room	0	0.00	0.00	0.0	0	0	0.00	0.00	0.0	0	0	0.00	0.00	0.0	0
Waitlist	0	0.00	0.00	0.0	0	0	0.00	0.00	0.0	0	0	0.00	0.00	0.0	0
Subtotal	7	2,700.00	385.71	5.1	7	7	2,700.00	385.71	0.3	7	7	2,700.00	385.71	0.0	7
**GROUP															
Airline Crew	0	0.00	0.00	0.0	0	0	0.00	0.00	0.0	0	0	0.00	0.00	0.0	0

Table 2.1 ▷ *(continued)*

For Wednesday, 15 November 2000

	DAY					MONTH					YEAR				
	Rooms	Room Rev	ARR	%ROCC	Pers	Rooms	Room Rev	ARR	%ROCC	Pers	Rooms	Room Rev	ARR	%ROCC	Pers
Group association	0	0.00	0.00	0.0	0	0	0.00	0.00	0.0	0	0	0.00	0.00	0.0	0
Group corporate	0	0.00	0.00	0.0	0	0	0.00	0.00	0.0	0	0	0.00	0.00	0.0	0
Group leisure	0	0.00	0.00	0.0	0	0	0.00	0.00	0.0	0	0	0.00	0.00	0.0	0
Tour One Off	0	0.00	0.00	0.0	0	0	0.00	0.00	0.0	0	0	0.00	0.00	0.0	0
Tour Series	0	0.00	0.00	0.0	0	0	0.00	0.00	0.0	0	0	0.00	0.00	0.0	0
Tour Series	0	0.00	0.00	0.0	0	0	0.00	0.00	0.0	0	0	0.00	0.00	0.0	0
Wholesale/FIT	0	0.00	0.00	0.0	0	0	0.00	0.00	0.0	0	0	0.00	0.00	0.0	0
Subtotal	0	0.00	0.00	0.0	0	0	0.00	0.00	0.0	0	0	0.00	0.00	0.0	0
**COMPLIMENTARY															
Complimentary	0	0.00	0.00	0.0	0	0	0.00	0.00	0.0	0	0	0.00	0.00	0.0	0
House use	0	0.00	0.00	0.0	0	0	0.00	0.00	0.0	0	0	0.00	0.00	0.0	0
Subtotal	0	0.00	0.00	0.0	0	0	0.00	0.00	0.0	0	0	0.00	0.00	0.0	0
** **ACCOUNTS**															
Accounts Receivable	0	0.00	0.00	0.0	0	0	0.00	0.00	0.0	0	0	0.00	0.00	0.0	0
Subtotal	0	0.00	0.00	0.0	0	0	0.00	0.00	0.0	0	0	0.00	0.00	0.0	0
GRAND TOTAL	8	2,820.00	352.50	5.8	8	8	2,820.00	352.50	0.4	8	8	2,820.00	352.50	0.0	8

ARR = Average Room Rate   %ROCC = % Rooms Occupied

Families

What a family needs and expects will be influenced greatly by their budget (how much they can afford to spend), the age and number of children, activities and services available at or near the venue, and their mode of transport. For example, families may require interconnecting rooms, a cot, high chair, information on local attractions, children's meals and a baby sitting service.

Weekenders

Many weekenders are couples taking a short break or maybe weekenders are a few friends snow skiing or sunning themselves at a beach resort. Many weekenders don't want to work too hard at enjoying themselves, so will look for convenience and suitability to their requirements. For example, if they are planning on snow skiing, ski equipment hire and access to the mountain should be easy, and a good hot meal (and probably a bar) is wanted at the end of the day. A couple on a romantic weekend probably aren't planning to cook their own meals and may not want too many interruptions to their day. It's best not to swamp these people with lots of information about the bird watching expedition planned for the next day (unless this is the purpose of the visit!).

Backpackers

The backpacker market is usually looking for budget accommodation, cheap transport options and the opportunity to see and do as much as possible in the time available to them. They are not likely to want or need 'luxuries' and generally have more money to spend and more time to spend it than other categories of travellers (however, they spend less *per day* than other categories of travellers). They are likely to be prepared to cook their own meals.

CORPORATE/BUSINESS

Corporate clients are guests who are employed by companies that require their employees to travel as part of their work. A guest travelling for business likes familiarity when away from home, so will often stay at the same venue. In addition to this, they usually stay in the same type of room and even the same room. Their stay is frequently short and usually only during the working week.

Room night— the occupancy of one room for one night.

Many companies tend to be loyal to one hotel chain so they have the ability to negotiate better rates. For example, a company that books a thousand **room nights** a year may receive a better corporate rate than a company that books only 300 room nights a year.

Gender and place of origin frequently influence a business traveller's needs; however there are commonalties, such as the requirement of:

▷ Internet access
▷ business centre access
▷ shaving/make-up mirrors
▷ in-room facsimile machine
▷ express check-out facility
▷ direct dial telephone
▷ breakfast included in rate.

An international business traveller may require all of the above as well as:

▷ foreign exchange facility
▷ information on rental cars/directions/tours

▷ an interpreter service

▷ possible dietary considerations.

A female corporate traveller may require, in addition to the above:

▷ adequate lighting in the bathroom

▷ additional hangers in the wardrobe

▷ a room close to the elevator

▷ a chain and secure locks on the doors

▷ a full-length mirror.

GOVERNMENT PERSONNEL

Government employees, such as military personnel, often receive a discount rate at many venues. The main reasons for this are that this market segment represents a potentially large customer base and also because they often have only a limited travel allowance, which has been set by the government.

The government rate will vary between venues and between cities and country areas because of the different allowances granted to the various categories of government workers. For example, a government worker staying in Adelaide may receive a different allowance from one staying in Sydney, where hotel rates are higher.

TRAVEL AGENTS

Individuals, companies and groups often use the services of a travel agent to make their reservations for them. Many people prefer a travel agent when making accommodation arrangements because the travel agent is able to coordinate all their travel arrangements at once. Travel agents do not technically constitute a market segment, but as they represent potential guests within various target markets they should be looked after just as well as any other market segments. Don't forget that they recommend your venue to their clients.

While rates will vary depending on the venue and the travel agent, it will vary also because of the volume of business transacted between each venue and the travel agent. Similar to corporate arrangements, a travel agency's volume of business can influence the rate they can attract for their clients.

AIRLINES

Reservations received from airlines are similar to reservations received from travel agents, although airlines often have **allotments** held with accommodation venues which they can either fill or release (usually seven days) before the day of arrival. An allotment is an agreed number of rooms allocated to the airline on specified dates. The hotel cannot sell these rooms to anyone else before the release back date. For example, Qantas may have five rooms allotted every day at The Park Hotel which they either confirm by sending through to the venue a rooming list or release one week out from the arrival date.

Allotment—an agreed number of rooms allocated on specified dates. The hotel cannot sell these rooms to anyone else before the release back date.

Some tour operators and travel agencies also negotiate allotment arrangements with individual establishments.

GROUPS

Groups come in all shapes and sizes and may originate from overseas, locally, intrastate or interstate. A group may be travelling for pleasure and on an inclusive package, be a special interest tour or part of a conference.

Many of the accommodation requirements, meals (some or all), tours and other activities are pre-planned (and frequently pre-paid) and most groups are on a tight schedule. All details such as wake up calls and breakfast times and costs are pre-arranged with the venue.

Group Inclusive Tours (GITs)

Group Inclusive Tour—group of people travelling together on a package arrangement.

Group inclusive tours are groups of people travelling together on a package arrangement. This means their transport, accommodation, meals (some or all) and side trips are usually included in the price paid. Everyone will arrive together, eat together and check-out together.

Conference Groups

Many guests are part of a conference group, whether the conference is held in the accommodation venue or elsewhere.

The conference delegates are likely to require those services frequently needed by most business travellers, such as Internet access, laundry services and mini-bar.

Special Interest Tours (SITs)

Special Interest Tour—a group of people travelling together because of a mutual interest.

These tours consist of groups of people travelling because of a mutual special interest. For example, the tour may be specifically designed to visit Aboriginal sacred sites in the Northern Territory. Other examples include a group touring art galleries, or end of season sports club holidays.

Other features of SITs are the same as GITs.

SPECIAL OCCASION FUNCTIONS

Many accommodation venues cater to an ever increasing market of special occasion functions. Examples of these include weddings, 21st birthday parties, graduation balls, debutante balls, Christmas parties, launch parties and New Year's Eve celebrations, among others. While the focus of the event is food, beverage and entertainment, it is common to attract room bookings from many of the guests attending the function.

SKILLS FOCUS

Market segment characteristics are useful to an individual venue as they enable identification of the specific accommodation and other hospitality related needs of each market segment. They also help the venue design the services and facilities available thus maximising its potential to attract its target markets.

There are a number of target markets that venues identify as potentially requiring their services and products: FITs, corporate guests, government personnel and groups among others. Each of these markets has clearly identifiable needs and wants.

FOCUS REVIEW

▷ *Why is it useful to clearly identify market segments?*
▷ *How does a market segment differ from a target market?*
▷ *What is the difference between an individual booking and a group booking?*

> How may the needs of a female corporate guest differ from those of a male corporate guest? Why is it important to recognise that they may have different needs?
> What is the definition of a 'room night'?
> How may the number of room nights booked affect a corporate guest's rate?
> What advantage, if any, is there to booking accommodation with a travel agent?
> What is an allotment? Who is likely to arrange an allotment with a venue?
> What do the following acronyms stand for? FIT, GIT, SIT.

APPLY YOUR KNOWLEDGE

What special requirements do you think the following target markets may have and why?

> *young families*
> *weekend leisure groups*
> *American businessmen*
> *female corporate traveller.*

What venues in your local area may attract each of these markets? Is the venue's promotional material targeted at all or selected segments?

KEEPING UP TO DATE

By discovering who their target markets are, accommodation venues are able to adapt their products and services to meet those markets' requirements. However, trends in the market place, cultural factors, lifestyle preferences and consumer demographics can influence guests' preferences over time.

For these reasons it is important—and indeed necessary—to keep up to date with changes that influence preferences and to adapt products and services accordingly. For example, 20 years ago it would have been difficult to find a non-smoking room. Today, almost all establishments cater to this requirement.

To help venues keep in touch with what influences their guests' preferences, they undertake a number of activities such as **market research**.

MARKET RESEARCH

In order to know what the target market wants, and to identify opportunities in the market place, especially effective ways to promote the venue, sales and marketing staff carry out research. There are various ways organisations can research what trends are emerging, what customer preferences are and what the competition is offering, including:

> searching Internet sites
> subscribing to (and reading) trade magazines
> researching industry trends and figures (such as those available from the Bureau of Tourism or the Australian Bureau of Statistics)
> using mystery customers (described below)
> conducting site inspections
> visiting and participating in trade shows

- ▷ conducting surveys
- ▷ asking for customer feedback
- ▷ asking for staff feedback.

Internet sites

As we said earlier, many large hospitality organisations have a website. Potential guests can log on to the websites of different venues and compare how each venue looks and the rates that are available. Venues in direct competition can also see what the guest can see, so by regularly looking at other venues' Internet sites, sales departments can keep up with the specials that are being offered by their competitors and thus increase their competitive knowledge.

Trade magazines

There are a variety of local and international hospitality industry magazines available to help keep the industry up to date with new technology, innovative service and product ideas, staff movements, food and beverage preferences and other industry trends.

Industry trends and figures

Many venues regularly exchange figures such as occupancy, average rates and spending trends in the market place. This is another important source of information about what the competition is doing and what the market wants and expects. From this information, the venue is able to plan necessary adjustments to meet the changing trends. For example, if you don't know that a new venue is opening down the road and it is offering a special opening rate of $75.00 per night, you are likely to be left wondering what has happened to your business as people choose the new venue over yours in order to take advantage of the cheaper rates.

Seasonal influences (or trends) include major one-off and recurring events, such as the 2000 Olympic Games, the Australian Grand Prix, Mardi Gras and the AFL Grand Final. These events represent peak demand and an opportunity for establishments to maximise revenue.

Mystery customers

Many venues use mystery customers to determine what their competitors are doing and also, to check on the standards of their own operations. The customer stays at a venue, uses the services and products, and reports on their findings. This information can be used to adjust services and facilities offered and improve standards.

Site inspections

A site inspection is not unlike a mystery customer, although it is less covert. The site inspection is designed to identify what the competition is doing differently or better than your venue, or to identify what you are doing, or not doing well and make the necessary adjustments that may help attract increased guest numbers.

Trade shows

A trade show provides the opportunity for establishments to highlight and promote their products and services to prospective customers alongside other establishments and sectors of the industry. For example, the trade show could be designed for the convention and conference market, or it could be attempting to catch the leisure market at a holiday show.

Most shows have a theme, and when participating in trade shows it is important to tailor the product to match the theme. There is no use advertising a corporate business club with the latest technology available at a leisure show when the potential guest is more interested in whether or not the venue has a pool and provides leisure-related activities.

Surveys

Surveys are one way of obtaining existing and potential guests' views on the venue as well as identifying specific guest needs. Many venues use in-room questionnaires for this purpose. An example of an accommodation venue in-room survey is shown in Figure 2.1. Other ways of determining preferences, trends and opportunities is to conduct surveys of groups of people either over the telephone, face-to-face or by using a mail out survey.

With the exception of in-room questionnaires, this type of research is relatively time-consuming and expensive. And unless the people chosen to complete the survey are first identified as potential target markets and appropriately selected for suitability, the information gained from the surveys may be misleading or skewed.

Figure 2.1 ▷ **Example of a guest questionnaire**

GRAND CENTRAL HOTEL
505 The Boulevard, Sydney
HOTELS OF DISTINCTION

GUEST QUESTIONNAIRE

Please tick the box under the heading that best describes your experience with the Grand Central Hotel, Sydney.

Why did you choose to stay at our hotel?
- ☐ Previous visit
- ☐ Personal recommendation
- ☐ Visit at other Grand Central
- ☐ Company Choice
- ☐ Travel Agent Recommendation
- ☐ Advertising
- ☐ Other _____

Do you have any other comments or suggestions?
_____
_____
_____
_____
_____
_____
_____

	Excellent	Average	Below average	Did not use
Service on arrival	☐	☐	☐	☐
Service at check-in	☐	☐	☐	☐
General Services				
• Reservations	☐	☐	☐	☐
• Reception	☐	☐	☐	☐
• Telephonist	☐	☐	☐	☐
• Concierge	☐	☐	☐	☐
• Laundry	☐	☐	☐	☐
• Gym/pool facilities	☐	☐	☐	☐
Your room				
• Cleanliness	☐	☐	☐	☐
• Facilities	☐	☐	☐	☐
• Amenities	☐	☐	☐	☐
The Bistro				
• Food	☐	☐	☐	☐
• Beverage	☐	☐	☐	☐
• Service	☐	☐	☐	☐

Please name any staff member who you felt offered outstanding service:
Name: _____
Department: _____

Would you like to be sent information about our other hotels?
Yes ☐ No ☐

Your Name: _____
Company: _____
Address: _____
_____

Room No.: _____
Visit:
☐ Business ☐ Pleasure ☐ Group tour

Dates of stay: Arrival _____
Departure _____

Date of Birth: _____

Customer feedback

Accommodation venues rely heavily on customer feedback and word of mouth. It is a generally accepted fact that a guest who is happy with an accommodation venue will tell around four to six people. But if a guest receives bad service or has had a bad experience they will report the incident to eight or ten people. So every venue needs to work hard to combat the negatives.

Not all feedback can be positive, as different people experience, and therefore react to, the same things differently. So what may have been an unacceptable experience for one guest may have been great for another guest depending on their expectations and perceptions of the situation. For example, a guest from the country may find a room in a city hotel quite noisy because of the traffic, while a city person staying in the same venue may not even notice the traffic noise.

Venues and their staff need also to attempt to rectify any negative feedback or conflict at the earliest moment. This allows you the opportunity to turn the experience around and create a good impression for both the guest's benefit and the venue's. If the guest has already departed then telephoning the guest or writing a letter can be a good public relations exercise to try to win the guest back. We deal with conflict resolution in more detail in Chapter 13.

Around 3 per cent of all guests fill in an in-room questionnaire and although these can be very valuable feedback for management, customer feedback needs to be collected also by talking directly with the guest, such as at check-out. Often the guest has a suggestion for improving a service or highlights a maintenance problem. Mentioning of staff names in both positive and negative ways can also give management a feel for how well staff are performing. Some establishments offer staff incentives when their name is mentioned in a positive way in a guest questionnaire as they are obviously giving the establishment a good name.

Staff feedback

Another source of valuable information is staff feedback. Guests frequently make comments to staff about services, products and expectations. They indicate their changes in preferences, their need or desire for particular products and services and their ongoing satisfaction with aspects of the venue. Many guests are more comfortable doing this face-to-face with staff rather than completing the venue's more formal questionnaire.

All research is potentially valuable to the venue and to you and it should be ongoing. A venue can use this information to plan future promotional activities and adjust existing products and services to meet emerging and existing preferences. You can use this information to better serve your guests.

Developing marketing strategies

Once the venue has identified its target markets and conducted research to determine changes in preferences and industry trends, it is able to develop its **marketing strategies**. Marketing strategies are those activities the venue undertakes to attract potential guests, and include positioning its products and services in the market place, developing products and services, and developing the marketing mix.

POSITIONING

Establishments need to determine where they fit in the market place and they do this in conjunction with the communicating of the benefits of their products and services. This is called positioning. Positioning relates to how guests perceive the product in relation to similar products in the market place.

For example, the Hyatt and Sheraton hotel groups are both regarded as five star establishments. The primary target markets of these venues are the upper end of the leisure market and the corporate market. In the potential guest's mind, one venue may be better in terms of suitability to their individual needs and wants than the other, or the guest may perceive one as the market leader and the other as a follower. In the target market's mind, one venue may convey a greater image of luxury than the other and the venue can use this perception to attract those market segments for which luxury is important.

Thus, the venue (or hotel chain) attempts to influence the perceptions of potential guests by the way in which it positions itself (communicates the benefits of its products and services) in the market place.

To help service industries position themselves, they frequently use 'brand' names to promote their products to various market segments. For example, Grand Hyatt and Park Hyatt hotels are both brands of the Hyatt group but are attempting to attract slightly different market segments. Similarly, a Holiday Inn and a Park Plaza hotel both belong to the Bass Hotels and Resorts group but each 'brand' attempts to attract different market segments.

While one venue may position itself as the most luxurious available, another venue may position itself as being in the best location in the city or as being 'affordable' or as 'your home away from home'.

Positioning— the determination of where a venue fits in the market place in relation to its competitors and in conjunction with communicating the benefits of their products and services to their guests.

PRODUCT AND SERVICES DEVELOPMENT

As you have learned, preferences and needs change over time. Venues can either adapt their products and services to meet the emerging trends in guests' needs and wants, or risk losing business to the competition. So product and services development must be ongoing for the establishment to remain attractive and to effectively compete in the market place. This requires a constant identification of the factors that influence preferences, such as **demographics**, lifestyles, economic climate, new technologies and legal and regulatory changes.

Factors influencing guest preferences:
• demographics
• lifestyles
• economic climate
• new technologies
• legal and regulatory influences.

Demographics is the term used to describe characteristics of potential guests such as their age, education, income, occupation, marital status and where they live. This in turn can have an impact on lifestyle, which refers to the potential guests' preferences for the way they live their life, including the activities they participate in, their eating habits and their general interests.

The economic climate is linked to the level of spending by potential guests. If the economy is healthy, there is greater spending and increased leisure dollars available for tourism and hospitality-related activities.

New technologies refers to developments that help not only how the venue can better serve its guests, but the growing expectation of guests that the venue is able to better meet their needs through the use of technology.

Legal and regulatory influences affect how the venue operates *and* the guest expectations. For example, the restriction of smoking in restaurants in some states is legally imposed while in other states it is self-imposed (that is, the venue decides whether or not to provide non-smoking areas).

Thus product and services development in hospitality environments will focus on these factors with an overall goal of generating increased revenue.

Most of the time, increased revenue for accommodation venues will come from selling rooms. So an accommodation venue is most likely to develop products and services that feature a guest room as part of the package, for example:

▷ bed and breakfast rates
▷ bed, breakfast and theatre tickets
▷ romantic weekend getaway package (bed, breakfast, champagne on arrival, valet parking)
▷ conference package that includes conference facilities, three meals per day and accommodation
▷ group discount
▷ special event function room discounts.

Depending on the target market, the venue may also promote the fact that it is a non-smoking venue, caters to a range of dietary requirements, is able to accommodate children, offers a range of activities included in the price and is fully serviced by the latest technology.

Product and services development may relate also to the more tangible, physical attributes of the venue, such as:

▷ a refurbishment (to gain a higher star rating)
▷ differentiation (of product, price or service)
▷ a new concept in the restaurant (from formal to casual, for example, or a new style of cuisine)
▷ introduction of additional benefits to regular guests (such as a loyalty program)
▷ introduction of additional services such as Internet access, laundry facilities, butler service, late check-out, earlier check-in, activities, complimentary fruit and others.

There are any number of other things that are intended to continue to attract guests. What is important to remember is that product and services development must be ongoing and reflect the needs and wants of the target markets, as well as take account of emerging trends.

DIFFERENTIATION

Knowing your target market helps you to identify what your guests value. Hospitality is a very competitive industry. There are literally hundreds of alternatives available in each sector from which guests can make a choice. When a guest is searching for accommodation, they usually don't call all the options in that sector. They are likely to know their requirements and search for a venue that fits their needs, such as location, price, availability, room size and other services available.

When the potential guest compares several venues that all essentially meet their criteria, they are likely to make their choice based on:

▷ product differentiation
▷ service differentiation
▷ price differentiation.

Product differentiation

Product differentiation— occurs when a guest chooses a product based on the comparison between two similar products.

Product differentiation refers to the features or characteristics of a product that distinguish it from other similar products. Product differentiation for a guest occurs when a product is chosen based on the comparison between two similar products. The service and the price may be the same but the difference is between the two products. For example, a guest may choose to stay at the Windsor Hotel in Melbourne instead of the Hotel Como. Both are five star hotels with excellent standards and facilities but the Windsor is a classic English style venue, whereas the Hotel Como has an art deco modern style. The Windsor is located in the heart of the city, while the Hotel Como is located on the outskirts of the city.

Service differentiation

Service differentiation refers to the features and characteristics of the services offered by a venue that distinguishes it from similar services offered by other venues. Some guests for example, are more comfortable with a five star level of service which can be very formal, while other guests feel more at ease with the relaxed atmosphere of the four star level of service. Another guest may choose to stay at one five star hotel and not another, as the first hotel has personal butler service and the other doesn't.

Service differentiation —when a guest chooses a venue based on the difference in service standards or services offered.

But even between similarly rated venues, service differentiation has the potential to offer a venue a competitive edge. Today's guests demand a higher level of professionalism than ever before and failing to meet this demand potentially means losing business.

Price differentiation

Price differentiation occurs when the same product and service are offered by otherwise similar venues but the price differs. Some target markets are very price conscious so they may choose to stay on the weekend when prices drop by $25 instead of on a weekday when the rate is higher.

Price differentiation —when the same product or service is offered by otherwise similar venues but the price differs.

If you know what your competition is offering, you are better placed to compete based on price differentiation. If a guest tells you that your competition is offering the same product at a lower price, it is worthwhile asking your supervisor if you can match that price or better it.

THE MARKETING MIX

The marketing mix is a combination of strategies that are selected to achieve the establishment's marketing goals (attract targeted markets). The sales and marketing team use a combination of the 'four Ps of marketing'—product, promotion, price and place—to influence their potential guests to buy its products or services.

Product

Product refers to managing products and services (or an organisation) so that they are beneficial and desirable to the guest. For example, as non-smoking rooms have increased in preference in Australia, more and more venues make available non-smoking rooms and floors. In some other countries, such as in France, for example, where smoking is more widely accepted, it is not as important for establishments to have non-smoking rooms.

In other words, products are designed to meet the expectations and needs of the target market. If your venue is designed to attract business people, then it is appropriate to make available services and products that business people want and need. These may include having an up to date business centre and a secretary available for guests, or installing a gym with a spa and sauna so that guests are able to relax after a busy day at work.

Promotion

Promotion is how the market is informed about the product. This can be achieved through advertising, or by staff selling the products when talking to guests, public relations activities, or promotional material distribution. Promotional activities are influenced by the budget allowed for promotion, the skills and ability of the staff employed to communicate the promotional message, and the ability of the venue to meet guests' expectations which have been created by the promotional message.

What promotional activities work best for each establishment is fairly subjective. One venue may decide to place an advertisement in a national newspaper or glossy magazine while another may send a sales letter to all previous guests on their mailing list. Both options may work and generally, experience is the best guide. We discuss promotional activities in detail later in the chapter.

Price

Price refers to pricing the product according to the targeted market. Too high or too low a price will eliminate some potential guests. An example of this would be a three star venue charging the same price for their rooms as the five star venue nearby. Guests expect to pay less in a three star hotel, as they are theoretically receiving a lower standard of service and product (for example they may have to carry their own bags or park their own car).

Guests in a five star establishment pay more for the privileges offered by this standard of establishment. The rooms are usually more extravagantly furnished and there are other services available not found in a three star venue (such as 24-hour room service, valet parking or secretarial support).

Place

Place refers to distribution of the product. In the case of an accommodation venue, place relates more to how accessible the establishment is to the guest. For example, if a guest needs to be in the city, then they usually won't plan to stay at a venue that is located in the outer suburbs. It makes sense to be close to where they want to be.

When promoting the establishment, venues frequently use location as a benefit or they promote the ease of access to the venue or nearby attractions ('In the centre of the city', 'Away from all the hustle and bustle').

Another aspect of Place is ensuring that the targeted markets have access to the establishment's promotional material. For example, distribution of information about the venue may not only be to clearly identified target markets. It may also be distributed to a more general market such as anyone interested in visiting that location. So a small, family-run motel, for example, may not have the budget to place colourful advertisements in magazines, but it may produce a brochure and distribute these through the region's visitor information centre.

MEASURING THE SUCCESS OF MARKETING ACTIVITIES

For most venues, the greatest measure of success lies with the bottom line, that is, how much money it has made. For example, if revenue is up 10 per cent, the venue may conclude that this was because of its marketing activities. However, revenue may be up because prices were increased and associated costs were reduced. The increase in profit needs to be measured in context with the other activities that take place in the venue.

The measure of success is usually gained by seeking feedback from the guests. The venue needs to find out if the installation of an Internet service is part of the reason for an increase in room nights or if the introduction of the loyalty program has contributed. The venue needs to find out the opinion of its guests in terms of standard of service offered, facilities available, their reaction to products and services offered, rates charged and a number of other things that help identify the relative success of the marketing activities.

The only way to find this information is to ask. Both potential and existing guests need to be asked for their opinions, and their intention to use the venue based on their reactions to the actual products and services provided and used and the marketing strategies implemented. For example, did the guest decide to book the venue because they saw an advertisement in a magazine, and what was it about the advertisement that made them decide to stay?

This feedback in turn helps the venue identify what it is doing well, or not so well, and to make adjustments to both the products and services offered and the marketing mix.

SKILLS FOCUS

Positioning refers to how guests perceive a venue in relation to similar venues in the market place. A venue will develop its range of services and products and market itself according to where it wants to position itself in the market place.

Product and service development begins with the identification of a venue's target market. Research is conducted to help identify preferences. Individual venues can then develop their products and services to meet the needs of their target markets and later adapt their products and services to meet the emerging trends in preferences, or they can risk losing business to the competition. This requires a constant identification of the factors that influence preferences such as lifestyles, the social environment, economic climate, new technologies, and legal and regulation changes, among others.

Product and services development in hospitality environments will focus on generating increased revenue usually from selling rooms. So an accommodation venue is most likely to develop products and services that feature a guest room as part of the package.

Product and services development also may relate to the more tangible, physical attributes of the venue such as a refurbishment, or rewards for frequent user guests.

A venue can differentiate itself in a number of ways: service, product or price. Service differentiation refers to the features or characteristics of the services offered by a venue that distinguishes it from those offered by similar venues. Product differentiation refers to the features or characteristics of a product that distinguishes it from other similar products. Price differentiation occurs when similar products and services are offered by otherwise similar venues but the price differs.

The marketing mix is a combination of strategies used by the venue to attract its potential markets. A combination of the 'four Ps of marketing'—product, promotion, price and place—is used. Product refers to the products and services offered by the venue. Price refers to the pricing structure of those products and services designed to meet the targeted markets. Promotion refers to how the market is informed about the products and services, and place refers to how the products and services (or information about them) are distributed.

An important aspect of marketing the venue is measuring its success. Measuring the marketing activities' success helps the venue determine the value of the strategies employed and whether or not to continue to use those strategies or to change them.

FOCUS REVIEW

▷ *What purpose does market research serve?*

▷ *Explain the different information that can be obtained between a trade magazine and trade show.*

▷ *Do you think customer feedback is important? Why? Why not?*

▷ *What value, if any, is there in gaining staff feedback?*

▷ *What are the factors that can influence market preferences?*

▷ *Why is it important to keep up to date with changes in guest preferences?*

▷ *What is the difference between service, product and price differentiation? Give an example of each.*

▷ *What are the 'four Ps of marketing'?*

▷ *How does a venue use the marketing mix to attract its targeted market?*

▷ *Explain what 'positioning' means.*

▷ *Do you think this is an important concern for a hospitality venue? Why? Why not?*

▷ *Why is feedback on marketing activities important?*

Promotional tools and their uses

The marketing mix is developed to deliver the products and services to the market place using several marketing and promotional tools. All businesses that have a product or service to sell need to carry out some form of promotional and marketing activities and use a variety of strategies to achieve the organisation's promotional focus which is generally in line with the organisation's overall goals—to make a profit.

The promotional focus may vary. For example, the venue may want to promote one aspect of the business or the whole business or a new product or service. The overall goal of the activity is usually product or service awareness and increased guest satisfaction, leading to greater profit.

Services— items that cannot be touched, seen or felt. Services have the potential to lack consistency and demonstrate a great potential for variability.

The difficulty in promoting hospitality establishments lies mainly in the nature of the industry. It is a service industry and it therefore promotes an *image*, or its **services**, rather than a tangible product. Because of this image, it is important for venues to establish standards in the level of service they provide. This in turn can provide a venue with the opportunity to focus on its staff, who provide the services, as the tangible aspect of the product.

Of course, once a guest arrives at the venue, the actual guest room and some features in the venue are tangible products, that is, products that can be touched and seen. But they are not tangible products in the sense that the guest can take the product away. They can only *use* the product while in the venue. However, there is greater potential for consistency and less variability in these products than in the provision of a service.

What is fundamental to the success of a venue is attracting the potential guest into the venue in the first place to take advantage of both the tangible and intangible aspects on offer. This brings us back to the image and selling of an intangible service. While we have already stressed that all staff play a role in promoting the venue, there are other tools used to attract potential guests.

ACCOUNT MANAGERS

Larger hospitality establishments employ account managers, or sales and marketing professionals, but this does not eliminate the important role all employees have for following through with sales activities. Account managers are responsible for developing a range of approaches to promoting the venue. This will usually take the form of a marketing plan, which will include:

▷ identifying marketing opportunities for the venue
▷ defining the target market
▷ identifying the competition and threats to the establishment
▷ identifying the strengths and weakness of the establishment
▷ developing strategies to reach the venue's target markets
▷ developing a marketing mix
▷ measuring marketing activity success.

Account managers also maintain constant and regular contact with potential guests either by visiting, calling or writing to target markets. One of their objectives is to increase the occupancy of the venue (and therefore revenue) and promoting all the features of the establishment. They do this by designing package deals (accommodation combined with other services for a set price) to meet individual guest needs. They also negotiate rates for corporate and group clients, design advertising campaigns, conduct marketing research and a range of other activities aimed at attracting more people to the establishment.

PROMOTIONAL MATERIAL

Promotional material includes any printed matter produced for the venue promoting its products and services. Promotional materials are usually used in conjunction with other marketing tools, although some small establishments may limit their marketing activities to the production of promotional materials only. Examples of promotional materials include:

▷ brochures
▷ leaflets
▷ menus and wine lists
▷ sales letters
▷ in-house displays (for example, promotional posters in the lift)
▷ business cards.

These materials are designed to present the establishment in the best possible light and create an expectation in the guest. For example, a well designed brochure, menu or business card can influence the guest's perceptions of the venue and hence the decision to use certain services or facilities.

ADVERTISING

Advertising is any paid promotion of the establishment in the mass media, such as television, radio and print mediums. The establishment is attempting to 'sell' the service or product to the targeted market via:

▷ daily newspapers
▷ local newspapers
▷ selected magazines (according to the target market sought)

▷ trade magazines
▷ selected radio stations (according to the target market sought)
▷ television.

Advertising communicates information about the establishment (or more commonly about a 'brand' of venues or group of venues, such as Sheraton, Hyatt, Marriott, Best Western, Holiday Inn, Rydges) and the services it offers. The primary objective of advertising is usually to create an awareness of the venue. It is also designed to influence potential guests to buy and to help keep the image of the venue in the potential guest's mind. Because of the high cost of advertising, establishments are very selective about when and where they advertise.

Radio and television advertising

Most venues that use radio or television advertise in the low season (when the venue is likely to have low occupancy) because of the high cost involved. There is little point in advertising when an establishment is full or likely to be full not only because of the cost involved but because when the guest calls they are unable to get a room!

Magazine and newspaper advertising

Venues advertise in magazines where the specific target market can potentially be reached. For example, corporate guests are reached through business and in-flight magazines, often with an offer of bonus points in the airline loyalty program. For example, a stay at any Hyatt hotel or resort in August may attract an additional 1000 bonus points. Business papers are also a good place to reach corporate guests.

Leisure guests are targeted in holiday magazines or auto club magazines, often with special rates offered if mentioning the advertisement.

PUBLIC RELATIONS

Public relations—activities designed to promote the venue in a positive light through publicity.

Publicity—free communication to the public about the venue (services) in the media.

Public relations involve a range of activities designed to promote the venue in a positive light through 'publicity'. **Publicity** usually implies gaining time on the radio, in a news broadcast or a mention in the newspaper for free or minimal cost. For example, when a venue introduces a new product or service, a promotional event (or events) may be arranged to promote the product to those people most likely to use it. The media will be invited in the hope that they write about the product. An example of this may be the introduction of a loyalty program by the venue. The loyalty program is targeted at those guests who frequently need accommodation in the area. There are several ways this new product can be promoted. We look at some below.

Launch party

A launch party is a special event or party specifically designed to 'launch' a new product or service. The purpose of the party is to create awareness of the product or service. A venue may invite all corporate guests on its mailing list as well as the local media. At the party, the product is 'launched' and the guests invited to use the product. The media are frequently given a promotional pack containing information about the product. While the party will cost money to host, the benefits gained by attracting potential new guests and free publicity often outweighs this expense.

Media release

To coincide with the launch of a new product or to announce an event of importance within the venue (such as the appointment of a new general manager, a merger with another company) a media release may be sent to all relevant print (and sometimes radio) media. A **media release** is an informative, newsworthy article usually written by the sales department (or Public Relations Department if the venue has one) promoting the new service or product. The style in which it is written meets exactly that of the media in which publication is sought. It is also written in such a way so that it can be inserted into the print media with minimal changes.

As the establishment writes the release, the information is very controlled. It doesn't express the opinion of an outsider, usually includes a quote from an authority figure (for example, the general manager) and is always positive. It is intended to gain publicity, free advertising for the venue, and in this case, for the new product.

SALES CALLS

Sales calls, also referred to as **personal selling**, are face-to-face promotional activities designed to inform targeted markets of the venue or new products and influence them to buy the service. Sales calls launching a new product are specifically designed to communicate details of the new product to existing and potential guests.

> **Sales calls—**
> personal selling strategy.

Because services are intangible, sales calls are an important promotional activity for the venue. They provide an opportunity for the potential guest to put a 'face' to the service (which can influence the decision to buy) and allow the service sale to be tailored to meet the individual guests' needs.

MAIL OUT

A mail out is the term used to describe a sales letter (usually standardised) sent to a large number of existing or potential guests on the venue's mailing list. Included with the letter may be a selection of brochures or other promotional materials. It is a relatively inexpensive (compared with advertising), although an impersonal way (compared with personal selling), to promote a service or product.

> Promotional tools:
> • sales staff
> • promotional materials
> • advertising
> • public relations
> • sales calls
> • mail outs
> • loyalty programs.

The mail out may be designed to invite guests to a launch party (if there is one), advise them of the features of the new service or simply to keep guests up to date with what is happening at the venue. Mail outs are often used during the low season. Special discounted rates are offered to encourage guests to stay when business is traditionally slow. For example, corporate venues will discount rates over the Christmas and January period, where corporate trade is usually slower, to encourage more leisure business and increase occupancy. Snowfield resorts reduce their rates during off peak (summer) to encourage guests at this time. They also promote other activities during this time, such as hiking and bush walking.

LOYALTY PROGRAMS

Many venues, especially those belonging to a chain, offer loyalty programs to regular guests to encourage them to return. Guests who have stayed a number of times are invited to join the loyalty program (often at little or no cost) and receive a variety of benefits. Some of these benefits may include:

▷ complimentary room upgrades (subject to availability)
▷ invitation to a club floor for drinks and appetisers

▷ free use of a business centre facility
▷ late check-out
▷ express check-out
▷ club gift on arrival (such as wine/luggage tags/umbrella)
▷ extra frequent flyer points.

Members of loyalty programs are usually given a membership card which they present at check-in. This helps reception identify and record specific details about each guest particularly as it relates to the guest's stays.

Loyalty programs benefit both the guest and the venue. The venue attracts repeat business and word of mouth promotion from its guests. Guests not only receive rewards for their membership and loyalty but are also made to feel their value to the venue.

WORD OF MOUTH

Of course, it is helpful when guests are so impressed with the venue that they recommend it to family, friends, and colleagues. Guests are only likely to do this if they are certain that the venue can consistently live up to the high standards they have come to expect. This is another reason why venues are concerned with establishing a service standard and using this as a promotional tool.

YOUR ROLE

With all this activity going on around you, it's not hard to believe that the venue will be inundated with demands for its products and services. You need to be aware of what promotional activities are planned and being implemented because it is also up to you to meet the guests' expectations created by any promotion. This means that you need a range of skills and product knowledge to follow through on the service standards promised in the marketing activities. We discuss the skills and knowledge you require in the next section of this chapter.

SKILLS FOCUS

Accommodation venues use a variety of methods to promote their products or services to achieve their goals of attracting guests and increasing profits. The tools frequently used include advertising, personal selling, mail outs and public relations activities. As a service industry, hospitality venues are promoting intangible items. This means that frequently, they must promote an 'image' as opposed to an actual, tangible product.

FOCUS REVIEW

▷ *Distinguish between promotional materials and advertising. What value do you think each has to a venue?*
▷ *Why is it important for venues to establish standards in the level of service they provide? How does this help the promotional activities of the establishment?*
▷ *Describe four ways a venue can promote a new product or service. Which do you think will be the most effective? Why?*

> ▷ The primary objective of advertising is to promote awareness of the establishment. What other purposes does advertising serve?
> ▷ Your venue has recently introduced a range of packages that include accommodation, dinner and drinks, for the Christmas and New Year period. You are a small venue with limited funds available for promotional activities. What recommendations would you make for promoting the packages? What might influence who is attracted by the packages offered?

Encouraging guests to use and buy products and services

So far we have provided you with a lot of information about who your guests are, how to find out what your guests want and what establishments can do to attract more guests, and at the beginning of this chapter we introduced you to the importance of developing product knowledge. Now that you have developed your product knowledge, you need to learn how to use this information to encourage your guests to buy and use your services and products.

PERSONAL SKILLS NEEDED TO PROMOTE PRODUCTS AND SERVICES

For most people selling doesn't come naturally. If you're one of these people who think selling is hard work, consider this—most of the skills you need to promote products, you already have. You have them because these skills are not unlike the skills you need to be a hospitality professional:

▷ excellent interpersonal skills (communication skills, questioning, listening, interacting)
▷ enthusiasm
▷ attention to detail
▷ a desire to please your guests
▷ motivation
▷ self-confidence
▷ product knowledge
▷ market knowledge.

These skills help you do your job. They also help you 'sell' the venue and its services and facilities. We have already discussed developing product and market knowledge, but two of the other important criteria on this list need further explanation.

Motivation

Motivation is the force that induces you to do something. You are motivated to finish this course successfully so that you can get a good job; you are motivated to cook dinner so that you have something to eat. At work, you are motivated to give the guest the best possible service. This means being good at your job, which includes being able to supply the correct information in a courteous and helpful manner so that guests can make an informed decision about their options.

Motivation is that force that induces you to do certain things.

For example, if a guest calls the front desk and wants to know where they can eat dinner and is only offered room service, that guest could well be disappointed the next day to find out that the establishment has both a bistro and fine dining room. It is necessary for you to not only know that other options are available but also be motivated to share this information.

Motivation in the workplace is frequently linked to rewards. For example, you may be motivated to go to work because you are paid for your services (*extrinsic motivation*). You may be motivated to do your job well because of the satisfaction it gives you (*intrinsic motivation*). From the perspective of promoting products and services, motivation can be either extrinsic or intrinsic.

Extrinsic motivation

Extrinsic
motivators:
• pay
• bonuses
• job security
• employment
  benefits.

Extrinsic motivation is related to the receiving of rewards. For example, if you reach a sales target, say 80 per cent occupancy for a month, you might receive a $100.00 bonus. However, this form of motivation is only useful if you perceive that the $100.00 reward is valuable. If the reward was only $5.00, you may not see that the effort required in achieving the sales target is worthwhile.

In the workplace, other extrinsic motivators include being paid, job security, employment benefits such as annual leave, and other 'rewards' that 'pay' you for your efforts. Employers however, frequently rely on your intrinsic motivation to do your job well and promote the venue.

Intrinsic motivation

Intrinsic
motivators:
• job
  satisfaction
• guest
  compliment.

Intrinsic motivation relates to your personal satisfaction at having achieved something. For example, the motivation to reach a target of six upgrades in one shift for personal satisfaction is intrinsic. It is a desire to do well, purely for the pleasure. You won't get more money or a promotion for intrinsic motivation, but you will feel you have done a good job. You may receive acknowledgment from management and your colleagues for doing a good job and you will feel satisfied that six more guests have had their expectations of you and the venue met.

No one can force you to be motivated; it comes from within. However, you can be tempted with motivators, such as rewards, but only when you perceive the reward is worth the effort. The effort will seem much easier for most when targets are set and goals are realistic, as then you have a tangible aim.

APPLY YOUR KNOWLEDGE

Look at the following rewards and state if they are intrinsic or extrinsic.

▷ *wage increase*
▷ *job satisfaction*
▷ *employee of the month*
▷ *promotion to reception supervisor*
▷ *guest compliment.*

As we have seen, hospitality venues have a common motivating goal—to make a profit. By making a profit, the establishment stays in business. Front-line staff contribute to the organisation's goal by offering good service to the guests. By promoting the venue's products and services our personal goals are linked to the establishment's because as long as the venue stays in business, you potentially have employment.

Confidence

Confidence is a major contributing factor in being a good sales person. It develops over time with good training and product knowledge. Confidence comes with believing you can sell and believing in the products you are selling.

Imagine you work in reception and the guest wants to know that if he sends a shirt to the dry cleaners tomorrow morning, will it be back the same day? The guest expects an instant reply. He doesn't expect the receptionist to say 'I'm not sure' or 'The instructions are on the laundry bag'. This is not helpful and you have potentially lost a guest (or at least potential revenue from the laundry service). Finding out for the guest whether or not the required service is available provides you with the confidence and knowledge for future reference, the establishment with increased revenue, and the guest with met needs.

SELLING SKILLS

Selling skills are important if you are to be successful in promoting the venue. As we said, you have the knowledge, now you need to know how to pass this information on in a useful way.

Selling is only successful when other people accept your ideas. You are not a successful sales person if no one accepts what you are selling! The same principle applies to accommodation venues; if you only offer standard rooms and no one ever stays in the suites except when given a complimentary upgrade, then you are an order taker, not a sales person. To help guests decide what services and products they would like, there are a variety of methods that can be used including:

▷ suggestive selling
▷ upselling
▷ downselling
▷ personal selling
▷ add ons or extras.

Suggestive selling

Suggestive selling is the selling of products or services by suggesting alternatives in a way that creates desire. To create a desire, we need to describe the item to conjure up a mental picture or to advise the buyer of the features available. For example, Mr Hobbs calls requesting a standard room. Rachael, the reservations clerk, suggests that there is a room with a spa available if Mr Hobbs prefers. Mr Hobbs has had a long day at the office and thinks that a spa would be nice and relaxing, so he books that room. Mr Hobbs's original intention was to book a standard room not thinking about a spa until Rachael suggested it to him. Rachael has potentially increased revenue and Mr Hobbs's decision will contribute to a more enjoyable stay.

Suggestive selling—selling by suggesting alternatives and describing features.

Suggestive selling doesn't force a guest into a sale but offers them alternatives they may not have thought of before. For example, Mrs Bolt calls to book two interconnecting rooms for the weekend and Adrienne, the reservations clerk, offers her a family suite with two bedrooms and a lounge area. It is more expensive than the two interconnecting rooms, but offers the advantage of a central lounge, sitting area and a small kitchenette. Mrs Bolt is happy as the children now have somewhere to play and she has the option of preparing meals herself.

Suggestive selling is a proven successful technique for fast food outlets such as McDonald's where all staff are trained to ask each customer if they 'Would like fries or a drink with that?'. The same concepts for accommodation venues can apply.

Upselling

Upselling—
a selling technique that starts at the lowest priced product or service and progressively moves up the price and quality levels.

Upselling is a technique regularly used by reservation staff to sell accommodation. The reservations clerk starts at the lowest priced room and then sells up to the next level and then the next, until the guest chooses the level and price of accommodation they require based on the features described and the perceived value. For example, Mrs Armitage calls requesting a room for her wedding anniversary. You already know that this is a special occasion, so you can use this information to upsell your accommodation. For example, 'Mrs Armitage, we have a standard room available for $120.00 but for only an extra $50.00 we can offer you a king room with a king size bed, spa bath and an ocean view. We also have an executive suite available for only $220.00 which has a king size bed, separate living room and a spa bath'.

Mrs Armitage can now make a decision based on the information provided. To help her make the decision, you may need to offer more information or simply ask 'Which room would you like me to book for you?'.

Downselling

Downselling—
a selling technique that begins by suggesting the highest priced item and working down through the price and quality levels.

Downselling is when the reservations clerk starts at the most expensive room and works down to the lowest price until the guest chooses the accommodation they require. This means beginning with the executive suite and then working down to the king room and then the standard room.

For example, when Mrs Armitage says she is looking for a room for her and her husband for their wedding anniversary, you can say 'Mrs Armitage, we have a lovely executive suite, which has a king size bed, separate living room and a spa bath, for $220.00. We also have a king room, with a king size bed and spa bath for $170.00 and we have a standard room for $120.00'.

Personal selling

Using personal selling techniques or the questioning method is presenting the guest with all the options available to them along with the benefits and attributes, and asking the potential guest what, if anything, they specifically require from the venue. Personal selling takes the form of an oral presentation usually face-to-face. However, the presentation can take place over the telephone in the form of a sales call.

The questioning technique requires using open-ended questions that make a yes or no answer difficult. Open-ended questions assume the guest is going to purchase and usually begin with *why, which, how, what* and *who*. For example, which room type do you prefer, a double or a king?

Closed questions usually begin with *would* and make it easy for a guest to say yes or no. For example, 'Would you like me to reserve the room for you?'. The open-ended question assumes that the guest is going to make a booking while the closed question gives the guest the opportunity to say 'no' to making any reservation.

Add ons or extras

Add ons or extras (also sometimes referred to as cross-selling) are what we can attach to the product to make it more desirable and to promote the use of other areas in the venue. A very common example is adding breakfast to the price of the room. The guest has breakfast, and revenue is increased. For example, a corporate rate could be $150.00 for a room but if breakfast is included as part of a package, then the rate may be increased to $165.00. This is perceived as good value to the guest as breakfast in the restaurant would normally be $22.50, but by including this in the rate, they save money and also the restaurant has guaranteed customers for breakfast.

Other examples of extras include:

▷ A bottle of champagne or wine in the room for special occasions ('Mrs Armitage, would you like me to arrange a bottle of champagne or wine for you on arrival, for your anniversary?')

▷ Massage ('Mr Hobbs, I see on previous visits you have used our masseur, would you like me to book a massage for you now?')

▷ Dinner package ('Mr Caulfield, on that weekend I can offer you a romance package which includes dinner for two in our restaurant.')

▷ Airport transfers.

Add ons and extras— a selling technique used to persuade a potential guest to buy additional products and services.

Add ons are attached to the price of the product and are seen to represent value for the guest.

These sales techniques can be used in a variety of combinations and it is important to practise using all of them. Sales methods are interchangeable depending on the situation and the customer.

APPLY YOUR KNOWLEDGE

Look at the following examples and determine which selling techniques you would use to offer better service to the customer. What products or services would you recommend and why?

▷ *couple spending the weekend*
▷ *family staying overnight*
▷ *businessman away from home at Christmas.*

Now imagine you are travelling to Brisbane for the first time and you called both of the following establishments. Where would you stay and why?

Venue 1

Julie:	Reservations, this is Julie.
Colin:	Hello, I'm looking for a room for two people next week.
Julie:	Yes, we have a room for $120 a night.
Colin:	Can you please tell me about the room as I've never been there.
Julie:	Yes, it has a queen size bed and a private bathroom.
Colin:	Does that include breakfast?
Julie:	No.
Colin:	OK, well I'll call you if I want the room.
Julie:	OK, bye.

Venue 2

Simone:	Good morning, reservations, this is Simone, how may I help you?
Colin:	Hello, I'm looking for a room for two people next week.
Simone:	Certainly. We have two types of room available. One is a queen room with private ensuite and lovely views overlooking the ocean for $130 a night. The other room

available is a king suite, it has a separate bedroom and lounge room with a double spa in the bathroom. The lounge and bedroom have views overlooking the pool. This room is $220 per night.

Colin: That sounds nice. Do those rates include breakfast?

Simone: No, but for only $15 more per person I can include a full buffet breakfast each morning in the bistro. Which room would you like to book sir?

Colin: Well I need to ask my wife which room she'll prefer but I'll call you soon. Bye.

Simone: If you would like, I can book a room for you now and you can confirm later today which room you prefer.

Colin: OK. Can you book the suite for me?

Simone: Certainly sir (then records guest's details).

Colin: Thank you for your help.

Simone: You're welcome. I look forward to hearing from you. Good-bye.

Simone is obviously more confident in her role as a sales person and knows her product very well. She also appears more interested in her job! When Colin was talking to Julie, she also knew what was in the room and the tariff but wasn't confident—or motivated—to do more than just offer the basic information to the potential guest. This illustrates for us two important factors for establishments to be able to successfully sell their products: staff must be both *motivated and confident* (which comes from training and experience) to be a good sales person.

SKILLS FOCUS

You already possess most of the skills you need to be successful in promoting your venue's products and services—excellent interpersonal skills, enthusiasm, a desire to please your guests, self-confidence and product knowledge. Motivation refers to the force that induces us to do something, for example, to do your job well. Extrinsic motivation is related to the receiving of rewards for the success in achieving or doing something well. Intrinsic motivation relates to your personal satisfaction from having achieved something or having done something well. Promoting your venue's products and services can result in both types of motivation.

The selling techniques used by many venues include suggestive selling, upselling, downselling and personal selling. Add ons and extras can be used to cross-sell other products and services in the establishment, which helps increase revenue.

Suggestive selling refers to the promotion of a product or service by offering alternatives and describing features. Upselling is a technique that involves promoting products beginning at the lowest price available and progressively suggesting higher priced items. Downselling is the reverse of this. Personal selling is a form of oral presentation, usually face-to-face, to promote a product or service. Extras or add ons refer to the promotion of additional services or products to the original product purchased.

FOCUS REVIEW

▷ List four skills needed for a sales person to be successful. Which of these do you think you have? Which do you think you need to develop?
▷ Why is motivation so important for a sales person?
▷ Explain the difference between intrinsic and extrinsic motivation.
▷ What is the difference between suggestive selling and personal selling?
▷ When do you think it is appropriate to use upselling techniques? Downselling techniques? Why?

Principles of successful selling

So far we have looked at what makes a successful sales person and discussed various techniques that can be used to sell the product, but what are the principles of successful selling? How can we get a customer to first listen to what our product is, and then make sure the sale is completed?

Principles of successful selling include:

▷ product knowledge
▷ capturing attention
▷ maintaining their interest
▷ creating a desire
▷ reading buying signals
▷ closing the sale.

PRODUCT KNOWLEDGE

The better we know the product the easier it is to sell that product. We have confidence in what we are doing and we are better able to describe the features of the product. As we saw with Julie and Simone, they both appeared to know their product but Simone's knowledge was of a greater depth and this was evident in her ability to sell the room. She also demonstrated greater confidence and seemed motivated to provide good service.

CAPTURING ATTENTION

When selling a room, or any product or service, we usually have a captive audience. This means that the guest has sought out our products and services. This is particularly true once the guest is in-house. The guest needs to eat, for example, and the most convenient location for them to do this is in the venue where they are staying.

However, you need to *capture* the guest's interest and create a desire for your products (as opposed to your competitors'). The guest needs to believe that you are offering them the best possible options. The guest needs to believe that you are interested in their specific needs and you can demonstrate this by being enthusiastic and knowledgeable.

MAINTAINING THEIR INTEREST

Once you have captured the guest's interest, you need to hold it. The guest will soon lose interest if you lose interest. Looking the guest in the eye (if face-to-face) or keeping a smile in your voice if talking over the phone, are just two ways we can maintain the guest's interest. Questioning the guest to find out what they really want and responding appropriately will help maintain their interest.

By being enthusiastic and telling the potential guest what you have to offer, you are able to maintain the guest's interest. If a guest telephones a venue and has to work hard to get information they will probably not be interested in staying at the establishment. If they then call a venue that displays interest and is helpful, they are more likely to stay there.

Look at the following examples of two places which are both fully booked:

Venue 1: Sorry we don't have any rooms next Tuesday, we're fully booked.

Venue 2: I'm sorry, we're currently full next Tuesday, but I can place you on the waiting list and call you in two days to let you know if any rooms become available?

Both venues are fully booked but Venue 2 is more helpful and even if the guest can't stay on this occasion, they will remember the helpfulness of the receptionist and call again.

CREATING A DESIRE

As we discussed in suggestive selling techniques, we need to create a desire so the guest feels that they want the product and its extra services. Offering views, spa baths, king size beds and swimming pool facilities can create a desire in the guest just by power of suggestion. If a view of the park was never mentioned then the guest may never have known that they wanted it!

READING BUYING SIGNALS

A good sales person is able to read the 'buying signals' coming from a guest. Buying signals are the unintentional signs that customers give to signal their interest but they need you to help them make a decision. Buying signals can be the spoken word or body language.

For example, when Mrs Armitage called requesting accommodation, she said it was her wedding anniversary. This is a buying signal. She has implied that because it is her anniversary, she wants to stay at a hotel (or other accommodation venue) so whether it is your venue or another, she will book somewhere. It is also likely that you will be able to sell other products and services to Mrs Armitage, such as champagne, dinner in the restaurant, breakfast in bed.

When promoting your products and services face-to-face it is easy to recognise buying signals indicated by body language. For example:

▷ guest maintaining eye contact
▷ guest not leaving the reception desk
▷ guest bringing out their purse or wallet
▷ looking at an item (for example, promotional material).

If you are selling over the telephone, buying signals usually take the form of questions, for example:

▷ 'What else do you have?' (more information needed)
▷ 'It's a bit more than I planned to spend' (they want to buy, just not at this price)
▷ 'I'm not really sure' (describe more features or downsell).

By listening to or observing the buying signals we can offer the customer more information or options. Often they are hesitant over the price and this is a good chance to use the downselling method. For example, 'Mr Hedger, we also have an executive room without a spa bath but it does have the same view as the suite and it is only $180.00 per night.'

CLOSING THE SALE

After all the effort put into making the sale for the customer it is important to make sure that the sale is closed correctly. By closing a sale, we mean getting the guest to buy the product or service. When closing a sale you need to use open-ended questions as we discussed earlier. After going through all the options available, you need to assume that the guest is going to buy one option or the other. Close the sale by asking which option the guest would prefer. For example:

▷ 'Which date would you like me to book the room for?'
▷ 'Which room would you like me to book for you?'
▷ 'We have the king room available on the date you asked for; can I take down your details and book that now for you?'

By following the principles of successful selling and using the selling techniques previously discussed at every opportunity you are well equipped to become a successful sales person in the hospitality industry.

SKILLS FOCUS

Engaging the principles of successful selling contributes to being a better sales person. The key principles to remember are: product knowledge, capture the guest's attention, maintain their interest, create a desire, watch for buying signals then close the sale.

FOCUS REVIEW

▷ *Why is it important to capture the guests' attention when promoting products and services?*
▷ *How do you maintain their interest during the sales process?*
▷ *What is a buying signal? Why is it important to recognise buying signals?*
▷ *List two examples of an open-ended question and two examples of a closed question that can be used when closing a sale.*
▷ *Why is it important to 'close a sale' correctly?*

The role of legislation

This chapter concludes with a brief look at the legal implications of sales and marketing activities undertaken by your venue.

Accommodation venues, like all businesses, have an ethical and legal responsibility to supply what they are promoting and what the guest is paying for. This can sometimes be a bit tricky when selling accommodation services and products. Remember that a lot of what you are selling is an 'image', an intangible product. For example, a guest may book a room in your venue based on a picture seen in a brochure and the information provided by a reservation clerk or sales representative. These promotional activities (advertising and personal selling) create an *image* of the venue in the guest's mind and this image creates certain expectations. To accurately meet the guest's expectations, the venue is responsible for ensuring that it is able to provide the services, products and standards promoted.

Unfortunately, this does not always happen. Sometimes, the venue misrepresents itself. If the venue is unable to live up to the expectations of the guest there may be potential legal issues. It becomes a legal issue if the venue attempted to deliberately mislead this guest.

All hospitality enterprises (and indeed, all businesses) must operate competitively and fairly. The principles of competition and fair trading are contained in the Commonwealth *Trade Practices Act 1974* and are generally mirrored by state or territory fair trading legislation, which applies to businesses not covered by Commonwealth legislation.

TRADE PRACTICES ACT 1974

The *Trade Practices Act* regulates business dealings between consumers, competitors and suppliers operating in the Australian market place. The Act's main aims are to:

▷ prevent anti-competitive behaviour
▷ promote fair trading, and
▷ protect consumers.

Anti-competitive behaviour

Anti-competitive behaviour refers to the behaviour of businesses to reduce competition in the market place. This reduction in competition may be because of the actions of certain venues in dealings with their competitors or in dealings with suppliers and purchasers.

Dealing with competitors

Competition in the market place is generally considered good for business and good for consumers (your guests). For example, when several venues are offering similar services and a similar standard of service, and operate in the same locality, their promotional activities and pricing structures are designed to attract as big a portion of the market share to maintain their profit level and retain guest loyalty.

A *lack* of competition may also be good for some businesses but certainly not good for consumers. For example, where there is little or no competition, a business is able to increase prices (therefore profits) but decrease the quality of the goods and services offered.

Anti-competitive conduct can also take place when two or more competitors fix their prices for goods and services between themselves. This is referred to as **price fixing** and occurs when a business enters into an agreement with a competitor to fix the price, for example, two hotels in the same town agree to set the price of their rooms at the same rate.

Price fixing— when a business enters into an agreement with its competitor(s) to fix the price of a good or service.

Anti competitive agreements are arrangements (or contracts) that are likely to reduce, or have the purpose of, reducing competition In the market place. An anti-competitive agreement may be an arrangement between two venues not to sell to each other's customers, such as two five star hotels agreeing not to make rooms available to each other's corporate guests.

Unfair trading

Unfair trading refers to the behaviour of businesses that may mislead or deceive consumers or be dishonest or unfair. It relates particularly to the advertising and promoting of the venue's products and services and applies regardless of how the promotion took place (over the telephone, in a brochure, a paid advertisement or some other means).

All hospitality venues have a legal obligation to ensure that their promotional material and activities are not misleading or dishonest. In this sense, misleading means that the venue cannot create an impression about itself that is essentially false. For example, a venue cannot say that 'every room is luxuriously appointed and has panoramic views' when in fact only rooms on the top floor have the advantage of the views. Misleading conduct does not have to be intentional. There may still be a breach of the Act even if the conduct was simply carelessness or a mistake on the part of the venue.

A venue may be guilty of misleading or deceptive conduct by:

▷ lying to someone
▷ leading someone to believe something that is not strictly true
▷ creating a false impression
▷ leaving out relevant information, or
▷ making false claims.

False representations

False representations are any claims or representations a venue makes about the price, benefits, standard, quality, value or grade of goods or services, among others, that may unfairly influence its guests' purchasing decisions. For example, a venue claiming to be a five star establishment places certain expectations in the guest's mind and may influence their decision to stay there. When the guest arrives and finds that the venue's services and facilities are not that of a five star venue, then it can be said that the venue falsely represented itself.

Under unfair trading, it is also illegal for venues to make false representations about:

▷ uses or benefits of goods or services
▷ the venue's sponsorship, approval or affiliation
▷ full cash price
▷ gifts and prizes on offer
▷ conditions, warranties and guarantees
▷ the nature or characteristics of services.

There are quite possibly several examples of each of these unfair practices you may have encountered or heard about. Here is a list of the most common sorts of claims that may be considered unfair:

▷ Advertisements claiming the venue is 'Only minutes away from the snow fields/beach' when in fact it is a 30 minute bus ride to get there.
▷ Linking the venue to a well known organisation when in fact no association exists.
▷ Offering a package that includes services or goods that in fact are at additional cost.
▷ Offering gifts or prizes that are not intended to be awarded, or so limited in availability or difficult to achieve that it is unlikely that many people can receive the gift or prize.
▷ A claim stating you will 'look 10 years younger after a weekend at our health resort'.
▷ Advertising a package that includes for example, a particular room type, and then make a few only available at the special rate, making it almost impossible to secure a room unless you work in the print room where the promotional material was printed!
▷ Offering services or products that it cannot reasonably expect to provide.
▷ Selling a product as one thing, when it is really something else. For example, put eye fillet steak on the menu, when it is really scotch fillet, or sell Johnny Walker Red Scotch, that is really a cheap whiskey poured into a Johnny Walker bottle.
▷ Verbally guaranteeing that 'this will be the best romantic weekend package you'll ever have'.

And this is only a small selection! Not only is this 'ripping off' the guest and illegal, but it is bad for business. Even if the guest doesn't complain they will never come back and the establishment loses a potential future guest (not to mention all the people he told).

WHOSE RESPONSIBILITY?

In complying with legislation, whether Commonwealth or at the state or territory level, it is important that all people who may be affected by the legislation be aware of their legal responsibilities. Anyone in the organisation, whether it is the owners of the business or their staff, can be held liable for any contravention of the legislation. The primary responsibility for compliance with the Act lies with those people in charge of the business.

Companies

The company may be a large organisation or a small family owned entity, but it can be held liable for not only its own corporate actions but also those of its employees and other parties who act on their behalf. For example, the company may be responsible for the actions of the marketing manager who falsely represented the venue in promotional activities.

Employees

As an employee, you have an obligation to your employer to behave in a manner that does not contravene any laws. You can be personally liable if your actions do break a law—whether you know it or not. For example, as the front office manager, you agree with your counterpart at the hotel down the road to fix room prices, refer all their corporate guests back to that hotel, and not accept those guests yourself.

PENALTIES

Penalties vary depending on who breached the Act and the type of breach. A company may be liable to pay up to $10 million for a breach of the Act's competition provisions and up to $200,000 for a breach of the unfair trading provisions. Individuals (directors or employees) may be liable for up to $500,000 and $40,000 respectively.

In addition, a court order may direct that:

▷ compensation be paid
▷ corrective measures be taken
▷ conduct be ceased.

AUSTRALIAN COMPETITION AND CONSUMER COMMISSION

If a guest has a complaint about the way a venue has conducted its business that they feel is not adequately addressed by the venue, they can take their complaint to the Australian Competition and Consumer Commission (ACCC). It is also important to note that it is not only a guest who may make a complaint about your venue; a competitor may, a current or ex-employee may, or any number of other 'concerned' bodies may.

The ACCC is the main regulatory body responsible for overseeing compliance with the *Trade Practices Act*. The Commission has the authority to investigate complaints made under the relevant legislation relating to the way business is conducted and the way products and services are promoted.

There is no fee for making a complaint and a Commission office is located in each state. And while the Commission cannot give legal advice in the same way a solicitor can to the person making the complaint, it can explain the underlying principles of the Act and a business's obligations under the Act.

When a complaint is received, the Commission determines whether the complaint is covered by the Act and will take action accordingly. The action that is likely to be taken begins with an investigation of the complaint. During this investigation, the Commission may or may not tell the business it is being investigated. The Commission may choose to interview a number of people connected to the business such as the owners, management, employees, competition and consumers. From the evidence collected, the Commission then decides whether or not to take action against the business through the court system.

SKILLS FOCUS

Legislation exists to protect both the consumer and businesses from unfair and misleading trading practices. Unfair practices may also represent unethical practices, but strictly speaking, unethical practices may not necessarily have legal implications.

The principles of competition and fair trading are contained in the Commonwealth Trade Practices Act 1974. *The Act regulates business dealings between consumers, competitors and suppliers and its main aims are to prevent anti-competitive behaviour, promote fair trading and protect consumers. The responsibility for compliance with legislation lies mainly with the owners of the business. Employees however, also have a legal responsibility to ensure compliance. Penalties apply for non-compliance.*

Anti-competitive behaviour refers to the behaviour of businesses to reduce competition in the market place.

Price fixing occurs when a business enters into an agreement with its competitors to fix the price of a good or service.

Anti-competitive agreements are arrangements that are likely to reduce, or have the purpose of reducing, competition.

Unfair trading refers to the behaviour of a business that may mislead or deceive consumers, and does not have to be intentional to be a breach of the Act.

False representations are any claims made about the price, benefits, standard, quality, value, or grade of goods or services that may unfairly influence a consumer's purchasing decision.

The ACCC is the main regulatory body responsible for overseeing compliance with the Trade Practices Act.

FOCUS REVIEW

▷ *Briefly explain the primary aims of the* Trade Practices Act.
▷ *Apart from legal requirements, why should an organisation deliver the product they promised to sell to the guest?*
▷ *List three practices you consider unethical. Explain why.*
▷ *What is anti-competitive behaviour? Give an example.*
▷ *Explain price fixing. Do you agree/disagree that this practice should be illegal. Explain your answer.*

▷ In a small town with only two accommodation venues, do you think an anti-competitive agreement may be useful (for the venues)? Why? Why not?

▷ How do the principles of unfair trading affect how the venue represents itself in its promotional activities?

▷ What responsibility do you have, as an employee, to ensure compliance with the Trade Practices Act?

▷ What is the role of the ACCC? Do you think a regulatory body such as the ACCC is really necessary? Why? Why not?

PUT YOUR KNOWLEDGE TO THE TEST

Robyn sifted through all the promotional materials she could find on the Grand Central Hotel. There wasn't much to go on as the venue was quite new and had undertaken only select promotional activities. So far, they had been targeting business people and most of their guests were from interstate.

The ads the hotel had been running were placed mainly in the business magazines. There were a couple of different brochures sent to potential guests and the venue maintained a website.

While during the week the hotel was maintaining good occupancy at around 80 per cent, by the weekend the place was all but deserted. Robyn had suggested there must be something the venue could do, such as design accommodation packages and target other market segments, to attract weekend trade. The front office manager thought this was a good idea so asked Robyn and another trainee, Cordelia, to develop a few ideas.

Cordelia thought that the local, higher income market was a good target and that packages could be designed around an 'escape' theme. Robyn agreed but thought there must be other markets they could also attract but that they would need to do some research before they could plan the packages and design the promotional campaign.

1. Do you think Cordelia's idea is a good one? Why? Why not?

2. What kind of research would they need to undertake? Where would they get the information needed to identify potential target markets?

3. Identify other potential markets Cordelia and Robyn could target.

4. Keeping in mind the star rating of the venue and the facilities and services it is likely to offer (identified in Chapter 1):

   (a) Design a package (or several) to attract the potential target markets (identified in question 3) to the venue at the weekend.

   (b) Justify your inclusion of items in the package (for example, explain why you would include champagne if you do).

   (c) Price the package(s).

(d) Write up a list of promotional activities you would undertake to attract each of the target markets you have identified as suitable.

5. Write a sales letter designed to attract one of the target markets you have identified. Remember that you are trying to encourage this market to make a booking so the wording must be enticing. Check with a colleague to ensure that it complies with legislation.

CHAPTER

3

Performing Clerical Duties

LEARNING OUTCOMES

On completion of this chapter, you will be able to:

▷ process a range of office documents;

▷ identify and use office equipment;

▷ manage equipment malfunctions;

▷ produce a range of office documents;

▷ maintain correct filing and storage systems for front office information following enterprise security procedures.

Introduction

When we think about the front or back office of an accommodation venue, we mainly associate these areas with reservations, greeting guests, guest check-in and check-out and meeting a range of guest requests during their stay. We sometimes forget that the word 'office', in an accommodation venue, also means that the venue undertakes a range of clerical and administrative tasks more commonly associated with the conventional meaning of the word 'office'.

Essentially, you become an office worker when working in either front or back office (or both). So it is important to have a thorough understanding of the **clerical and administrative tasks** to be completed to meet both the needs of the organisation and its guests. Clerical and administrative tasks refer to those aspects of the job that require you to process a range of documents and maintain document filing systems.

To be able to do this, you also need to know how to operate a variety of office equipment, such as the computer or facsimile machine, compose a range of documents, such as business letters, internal memos and operational reports, and handle administrative tasks related to the guest's stay, such as maintain reservations and accounts. And you will need to be able to do all of this to the venue's standards following the venue's procedures.

The main purpose of this chapter therefore, is to provide you with the basic skills and knowledge required to effectively perform the clerical and administrative tasks associated with the front and back office.

Processing office documents

The front and back office operations of a hospitality venue differ from other business offices in that it is usually a 24-hour, seven day a week function. Different people work the various shifts required to maintain the various office-related tasks. Communication among the staff is vitally important as it isn't always possible to complete all tasks during an eight hour shift and information needs to be passed on from one shift to the next, from one day to the next and even from week to week. Also, several staff are likely to process documents at different times. So it is critical to put systems in place to control the flow of information and to make sure that all staff are familiar with the systems and follow correct operating procedures. To achieve this continuity in the flow of information and communication, various office documents are produced and processed.

We begin by looking at the types of documents you are likely to encounter in a front or back office situation and what each is most commonly used for.

Documents used in accommodation services

The type of documents used in accommodation services may vary in layout and size, but you will find that they perform essentially the same purpose. For example, a reservation slip used in one venue may look slightly different from the one used in another venue. The format used for writing a letter of confirmation to a guest may vary between venues, but the letter is likely to contain the same basic information. The examples used here therefore are representative of the types of documents used: they are not the only versions you are likely to encounter.

Documents may be produced manually or by a computer, and they may be for **internal** use or **external** use.

INTERNAL USE DOCUMENTS

Internal use documents are those documents used within the venue. There are a number of internal use documents, and these are discussed below.

Internal use documents— those documents used within the venue.

Front office diary

All front office operations use a diary (it may also be referred to as a 'log book') to facilitate communication between staff. The diary is used to record information about the daily activities in the venue as they relate to the front office. It is also used to record information that needs to be passed on to your colleagues and that may need to be acted upon. It is usually kept in a central location for easy access. The diary is likely to include messages about guests, events in the establishment, unusual occurrences, changed procedures—in fact just about anything else that the next shift may need to be aware of and which is relevant to the front office. Figure 3.1 shows the entries for the morning shift for one day.

It is standard practice for all staff to read the diary at the start of their shift. The diary is a more reliable communication tool than your memory. Important information can be forgotten or incorrectly conveyed if memory alone is relied on.

Having read the entries for the day, staff should sign the bottom of the diary to acknowledge that they have read it.

Daily running sheet

Many venues use a daily running sheet. This document is a form of checklist for, and reminder about, the duties to be completed on a particular shift in the front office. When each task is completed, it is marked off. It can also be used to record events that have happened throughout the day, often in response to diary entries. For example, a diary entry may have recorded that the television in Room 1145 is not working. Not only does this indicate that a guest should not be checked into this room until the television is fixed, but you can record, on the daily running sheet, that it was fixed during your shift. An example of a typical daily running sheet is shown in Figure 3.2.

Daily running sheet—a form of checklist of the duties to be completed on a particular shift in the front office.

The daily running sheets are filed at the end of the day. This is so it can be referred to later if need be, such as in the event of a complaint or if something needs to be followed up from that day.

Guest request sheets

Guest requests are frequently written down so that they are not forgotten. The request may come directly from the guest (either at the front desk or via the telephone from their room) or through another department. An example is shown in Figure 3.3.

The request sheet will detail:

▷ the guest's name and room number
▷ time the request was made
▷ what the request is
▷ name of the person who took the request.

Figure 3.1 ▷ **Diary entries**

7.30	
8.00	**28** WEDNESDAY 209—156 WEEK 30 JULY
8.30	
9.00	Pool closed tomorrow between 11am & 3pm for cleaning FOM
9.30	
10.00	
10.30	Mr Singh booked on Penguin Parade tour leaving at 3pm from front of hotel—tomorrow—please let him know tonight. Jenny
11.00	
11.30	
12.00	
12.30	Weekend rate has now increased Please see memo on back wall for details FOM
1.00	
1.30	
2.00	Paula from Sales not in today.
2.30	
3.00	
3.30	
4.00	
4.30	
5.00	
5.30	
EVENING	MEMO

	JULY							AUGUST							SEPTEMBER							OCTOBER							NOVEMBER							DECEMBER					
S	M	T	W	T	F	S	S	M	T	W	T	F	S	S	M	T	W	T	F	S	S	M	T	W	T	F	S	S	M	T	W	T	F	S	S	M	T	W	T	F	S
				1	2	3	1	2	3	4	5	6	7				1	2	3	4						1	2		1	2	3	4	5	6				1	2	3	4
4	5	6	7	8	9	10	8	9	10	11	12	13	14	5	6	7	8	9	10	11	3	4	5	6	7	8	9	7	8	9	10	11	12	13	5	6	7	8	9	10	11
11	12	13	14	15	16	17	15	16	17	18	19	20	21	12	13	14	15	16	17	18	10	11	12	13	14	15	16	14	15	16	17	18	19	20	12	13	14	15	16	17	18
18	19	20	21	22	23	24	22	23	24	25	26	27	28	19	20	21	22	23	24	25	17	18	19	20	21	22	23	21	22	23	24	25	26	27	19	20	21	22	23	24	25
25	26	27	28	29	30	31	29	30	31					26	27	28	29	30			24	25	26	27	28	29	30	28	29	30					26	27	28	29	30	31	
																					31																				

Figure 3.2 ▷ **Example of a daily running sheet**

GRAND CENTRAL HOTEL
505 The Boulevard, Sydney
HOTELS OF DISTINCTION

Daily Running Sheet: 'A' Shift

Completed	Task
_____	Read diary
_____	Count front float $500.00
_____	Count back-up float $2000.00
_____	Check departures report
_____	Check flag report and action all requests
_____	Make sure all arrivals with special requests are allocated
_____	Inform housekeeping of any late departures and special requests for arrivals
_____	Post all breakfast dockets from the restaurant
_____	Inform maintenance of any maintenance issues

Notes: _____
_____

Figure 3.3 ▷ **Example of a guest request sheet**

GRAND CENTRAL HOTEL
505 The Boulevard, Sydney
HOTELS OF DISTINCTION

GUEST REQUEST SHEET

Date: _____

Guest name/ room number	Request	Completed by: (name & time)
Smyth 1047	car to reception	John 10:55
Hunt 2035	bags down	Shane 11:02
Hedger 1048	iron & board to room	

The request is completed either by the person who took the request, or, if it is the responsibility of another department, it is passed on accordingly. Larger venues often use a follow-up sheet to make sure that requests are completed in a reasonable time frame.

Examples of guest requests made at front office include:

▷ valet parking
▷ bags to be collected
▷ iron and board to the room
▷ gift vouchers
▷ fresh towels
▷ tour to be booked
▷ newspapers.

Guest mail

Although this is not strictly an internal use document, mail for guests does arrive at accommodation venues. Any personal mail arriving for a guest is forwarded to the guest's room. If the guest has already departed, the mail is forwarded to the guest's home address, according to the information contained on the reservation slip.

Reservation slip

When guests and potential guests call the venue to make a reservation, their details are recorded on a pre-printed reservation slip. How these are processed is discussed in Chapter 5.

Registration cards

When a guest registers at an accommodation venue, their personal details and information relating to their stay is recorded on a registration card which the guest is required to sign as part of the check-in procedure. How registration cards are processed is discussed in Chapter 6.

Guest profiles

A guest profile is a detailed record about all guests who stay at the venue. It contains personal information about the guest including name and contact details, likes and dislikes, favourite room, previous stays and future bookings (if linked to a reservation).

Guest profiles may be maintained manually or in the computer. If maintained manually, all the relevant information is written onto file cards which are then filed alphabetically. Each time the guest visits, the card is removed form the file and manually updated. Computerised guest profiles can be automatically updated every time a guest makes a reservation and/or checks-out. Guest profiles are discussed in detail in Chapter 6.

Financial control documentation

Several documents are used in an accommodation venue to help maintain control of the financial transactions that take place. These documents and how to process them are discussed in later chapters.

Source documents

The most common document you will need to process is a source document. A source document is the record of charges incurred by guests. For example, a guest dining in the restaurant receives a bill at the end of their meal. The bill, or docket, records the details of what the guest ate and drank, the charge, their room number and their name. The guest signs the bill as acknowledgement of accepting the charges and the information contained on the bill is used to record the charge to the guest's account.

Wake up call sheets

Many guests, although supplied with an alarm clock in the room, prefer a wake up call from the staff. A wake up call is a telephone call placed by the telephonist or receptionist to a guest's room (at the guest's request) to wake up the guest. An example is shown in Figure 3.4.

The details relating to the call are recorded on the wake up call sheet including:

▷ guest name and room number
▷ time the call is required
▷ requests (such as a taxi booking).

Wake up calls must be made at the exact time requested. If the guest doesn't answer the telephone wake up call, a staff member is sent up to the room to investigate.

The wake up call sheet is usually kept next to the switchboard and an alarm clock is set to remind the receptionist that it is time for the wake up call to be placed. Alternatively, the venue's switchboard may be programmed to make the call.

Figure 3.4 ▷ **Example of a wake up call sheet**

GRAND CENTRAL HOTEL
505 The Boulevard, Sydney
HOTELS OF DISTINCTION

WAKE-UP CALL SHEET

Date: _21 May_

TIME	ROOM NUMBER/NAME
5:30	475 Mr Smith
5:45	
6:00	
6:15	
6:30	219 Mr Habery
6:45	112 Ms Ho
7:00	
7:15	
7:30	
7:45	
8:00	341 Mr Dade
8:15	
misc	

Notes: _7.15—taxi for RM 219_
7.30—knock on door—RM 716 Mrs Jenkins phone out of order

Completed: _____ Signed: _____

Telephone message pads

Many venues (indeed many businesses) use pre-printed telephone message pads. Many incoming calls are received by a venue every day and it is often necessary to record a message for the caller. You may need to record a message for a guest, colleague or management. A pre-printed message pad allows you to record all the relevant information by prompting you at each stage.

The pad is usually in duplicate. The top copy is passed onto the person who the message is for; the duplicate copy stays in the message pad. A duplicate copy is retained in the event that the original gets lost. Recording of telephone messages is discussed in Chapter 4.

Venue policies and procedures

Policy—a statement about the venue's position on an issue.

Procedure—a step-by-step guide to performing a task.

Venue policies and procedures are developed for internal staff use but may relate to issues and staff behaviour in relation to guest service. A **policy** is a statement about the venue's position on an issue. For example, the venue may have a policy that states that theft by employees is a dismissible offence. It may have another policy that states that during an evacuation the priority of all staff is guest safety.

A **procedure** is a step-by-step guide to performing a task. For example, each task you perform in the front or back office (recording reservations, registering a guest, recording charges) is performed in a specific way each time you undertake the task.

Memorandums

Memo—internal use document for communicating a brief message to many people (staff) at once.

A memorandum, or **memo**, is an internal document used for communicating a brief message to a lot of people at once, such as changes to, or introduction of, a policy, notification of upcoming events or important decisions that have been made that may affect staff and/or guests. How memos are structured and processed is discussed in detail later in this chapter.

Reports

The front and back office generate various reports on a daily, weekly, monthly or other period basis. These reports relate to the multitude of activities that take place in the venue and are discussed in detail throughout this text. In addition, there are a number of reports generated as required. Examples of these types of reports are incident or accident reports.

The layout and design of a report depends on the requirements of the user (the person who reads the report) and the venue itself.

Minutes

Minutes—the record of a meeting.

Agenda—the list of the points or topics to be discussed at a meeting.

Minutes is the record of a meeting, that is, what was discussed and by whom, what decisions were made, date the meeting was held, who was in attendance and who wasn't and anything else relevant to the particular meeting to which the minutes relate.

Minutes are distributed to those in attendance and anyone who may be affected by the information contained in the minutes. All minutes are filed after being read and actioned. How this is completed will depend on the policies and procedures in place in the venue. For example, minutes for meetings attended by the front office staff may be distributed to all accommodation services staff and a copy kept on file in the front office for future reference if need be.

Agenda

An agenda is a list of the points or topics to be discussed at a meeting. An agenda is usually distributed before the commencement of the meeting to allow the attendees time to prepare for the meeting. Most agendas follow a standard format. An example is shown in Figure 3.5.

Figure 3.5 ▷ **Example of an agenda for a meeting**

GRAND CENTRAL HOTEL
505 The Boulevard, Sydney
HOTELS OF DISTINCTION

Agenda

Location:	The boardroom
Attendees:	Andrew, Ling, Melanie, Robert, Graham, Felicity, Willem, Robyn, Damien, Brett, Adrian, Colin, Finn, Nick, Kendelle, Darcy
Apologies:	David, Thomas
Chair:	Samantha Shoreham, Front Office Manager
Minutes:	Merinda More
Date:	10 November 2001
Time:	3 pm

Items for discussion

1. Minutes of previous meeting
2. Front office trainees
3. New uniforms
4. Mr Daw's complaint letter
5. Christmas planning
   - Rosters
   - Annual leave
   - Swing shift
   - Occupancy targets
6. Other business

EXTERNAL USE DOCUMENTS

External documents refer to those documents that are coming into or being sent out of the venue. External use documents may be seen and used only by staff or may be seen and used by guests.

External use documents—those documents that are coming into or being sent out of the venue.

Correspondence

Correspondence refers to written communication between the venue and external entities (for example guests and suppliers).

Incoming correspondence includes:

▷ requests for and confirmation of reservations
▷ sales letters (usually from suppliers)
▷ charge authorities from companies
▷ requests for information

$\triangleright$ letters of complaint

$\triangleright$ job applications

$\triangleright$ requests for payment.

Outgoing correspondence includes:

$\triangleright$ confirmation of reservations

$\triangleright$ guests' accounts

$\triangleright$ purchase orders

$\triangleright$ responding to letters of complaint

$\triangleright$ sales or promotional letters

$\triangleright$ letters requesting payment of an account.

Correspon- dence—written communication between the venue and external entities.

Correspondence may be received in a number of ways:

$\triangleright$ written letter

$\triangleright$ facsimile

$\triangleright$ e-mail.

Invoices

Invoice—a request for payment for the services or goods supplied. It provides a detailed account of actual goods or services bought, date supplied, cost per unit and settlement details.

Invoices are received by the venue on a daily basis. An invoice is a request for payment for the services or goods supplied and provides a detailed account of the actual goods or services bought by the venue, date supplied, cost per unit and settlement details. These documents are usually forwarded to the venue's accounts department for processing.

Receipts

Receipts are issued in exchange for a payment. For example, a guest paying his or her account will be issued a receipt. Most receipts are computer-generated. Receipts are also received by the venue for the supplies they purchase and have paid for.

Gift vouchers

Most accommodation venues will sell gift vouchers. A gift voucher can be issued for the use of almost any service provided by the venue. For example, a gift voucher may be for a night's accommodation, or dinner in the restaurant, or a package that includes room and breakfast. Gift vouchers are used not only as gifts, but also often purchased to give as a prize. They may also be used as a reward to loyal guests or for an outstanding employee. An example is shown in Figure 3.6.

Each of the documents discussed must be managed and processed in a way that is logical and complies with the venue's procedures. How you physically process these documents is discussed later. First, you need to know what equipment is available to you to help with processing documents.

Types of office equipment

For most accommodation venues to function effectively, there are a number of pieces of equipment it must have:

$\triangleright$ switchboard

$\triangleright$ facsimile machine

Figure 3.6 ▷ **Example of a gift voucher**

GRAND CENTRAL HOTEL
505 The Boulevard, Sydney
HOTELS OF DISTINCTION

Awarded to Melinda and Matthew

Please present this voucher for two nights' accommodation, including a three course set-menu dinner in The Bistro one night, room service breakfast for two both mornings and complimentary valet parking.

Please call Sandra on 03 9555 4441 to make your reservation.

Voucher valid until 31 December 2002 (not available for Saturday nights)
Ref: GV000106

▷ photocopier
▷ computer (various software)
▷ printer(s)
▷ franking machine
▷ calculator
▷ binders
▷ filing cabinets
▷ paging system
▷ stamps
▷ stationery items.

Even the smallest of operations today needs most of the above items. Whatever equipment is available in your venue, the idea is to help you do your job more effectively and efficiently. For most documents you produce, you need to be able to create it, copy it, store it and retrieve it. The equipment available to you will help this process.

But of course, not every venue will have the latest, fastest, biggest, most recent version of each piece of equipment so a brief overview only of their capabilities is provided. How you actually use each brand or style of equipment you will learn on the job.

SWITCHBOARD

A switchboard is the piece of equipment that enables a venue to manage several telephone lines and multiple extensions. You may be familiar with the term PABX (private automatic branch exchange), an older style of switchboard. A modern switchboard is capable of:

▷ receiving several calls at once
▷ making several calls at once
▷ recording messages to extensions
▷ interfacing with the venue's PMS to record calls made and associated charges
▷ place calls on hold
▷ transfer calls
▷ play on-hold music.

Of course most of these functions require some operator input. Telephone operations are discussed in Chapter 4.

FACSIMILE MACHINE

The word facsimile means an exact copy. A facsimile machine, or fax, reproduces written documents received from or sent to external locations by electronically scanning and transmitting the document via a telephone line. A fax allows you to send or receive the documents within minutes of transmission. The fax machine will process only one single-sided page at a time (although all modern machines allow you to load several pages at once) and you are usually restricted to a maximum A4 page size. A fax machine will not process stapled pages; staples will jam the machine. An alternative to faxing a document is to send it by post. By fax, you are most likely to receive requests for accommodation, rooming lists and charge authorities. You are likely to send, by fax, letters of confirmation, quotes and purchase orders.

PHOTOCOPIER

A photocopier, similarly to a fax machine, will produce an exact copy of a document. It enables you to reproduce documents without the need to retype or reprint them. The difference however, between a fax machine and a photocopier is that the photocopier produces copies for the person using the machine; the document is not transmitted anywhere. Photocopiers have multiple capabilities including:

▷ rapidly copying several one or two sided pages
▷ sorting and collating documents being copied
▷ stapling collated documents
▷ reducing or increasing the size of the copied document
▷ reproducing in colour or black and white
▷ producing overhead transparencies.

Photocopiers can achieve a high quality of reproduction in a relatively short time. Many of the documents you use will need to be copied. In addition, many of your guests request that you copy documents for them.

COMPUTER (VARIOUS SOFTWARE)

Today, the majority of accommodation venues maintain some form of automation of the front and back office administrative and clerical tasks by using a computer. Indeed, there are likely to be several computers. Those located at the front desk will be programmed with the venue's PMS, those located in the back office area are likely to be programmed with the venue's PMS and a word processing package.

Depending on the software applications installed, the computer should enable you to:

▷ produce, save and store a range of internal and external use documents, such as letters, memos, procedures and minutes
▷ produce accurate and timely financial records
▷ maintain the venue's accounting systems
▷ record and maintain reservations
▷ register and check-out guests
▷ maintain and generate reports relevant to the operational needs of the venue
▷ access the Internet
▷ send and receive e-mail.

Using this technology requires training. And because of the variations and capabilities of the software available, it is possible that you will require training on several systems, depending on your place of work.

E-mail

The term 'e-mail' means electronic mail. It is a more recent communication tool that allows you to send and receive information electronically, through the computer, via a telephone line. E-mail allows you and your guests to correspond with each other without delay as e-mails transmit within minutes of being sent. A guest, for example, can send a message requesting accommodation; you will receive the message within minutes and can respond equally as fast.

PRINTER(S)

Maintaining a computer system that can process all the above information and perform the necessary functions to manage accommodation services is only really useful if the information can also be printed. Despite modern technology making our working lives easier, a hard copy (print-out) of most of the information you need is still required. The quality of the printed copy of information will depend on the printer quality and your needs. For example, a copy of correspondence to a guest should be of a high quality.

FRANKING MACHINE

A franking machine is a machine that allows you to stamp literally hundreds of envelopes quickly and efficiently by printing the correct amount of postage required and date on the envelope according to the envelope's weight and size. For those venues that generate large quantities of correspondence to be sent by post, a franking machine is an excellent alternative to buying stamps at the post office and stamping each envelope individually.

The franking machine records the totals of all stamps issued. At the end of the week or month or other agreed time, the amount of postage used is paid to the supplier along with a lease fee for the product.

CALCULATOR

A calculator is used frequently by the front and back office staff to calculate foreign exchange, tally source documents, and to calculate commissions. Some computer systems have a calculator function. Most venues will have several calculators available for staff use.

BINDERS

Binders are used to bind large documents. They allow you to hole-punch entire documents at once, thus holding documents together. An alternative to using a binding machine is to place large documents in a ring binder or other file.

FILING CABINETS

Filing cabinets (and filing systems) are maintained for the storage of hard copies of both internal and external use documents. Filing systems are discussed later in the chapter. Filing cabinets and storage facilities come in a range of sizes and colours.

PAGING SYSTEM

A paging system is an internal communication tool. It is used to maintain contact with staff, such as porters, maintenance, house persons and heads of department, whose place of work is not in one location. They allow these staff to be readily located at all times while on duty.

The 'control' panel remains in the front or back office and may or may not be a function of the switchboard. When a staff member carrying a pager is required, a text message is sent to the pager number, advising the pager holder of what is required of them.

At the commencement of their shift, those staff required to carry a pager log their pager 'out' and log it 'in' at the end of their shift. The reason a pager is logged out and in is so that the venue is able to account for each individual pager and to regularly check when batteries are required.

STAMPS

A variety of stamps are used in the front and back office. These include:

▷ time stamp
▷ date stamp which is used to indicate the date a document was received or processed
▷ faxed stamp. When an item is sent by fax, it is stamped as 'faxed'
▷ received stamp. The received stamp is stamped on documents the day they are received. The date is written in the space provided to indicate the arrival date of the document.

These are important tools for processing documents coming into and out of the venue.

STATIONERY ITEMS

Finally, every office requires a supply of stationery items and sundry equipment. These are required to help you process documents and manage your office. These items include:

▷ staplers
▷ hole punches
▷ binding machine
▷ answering machine
▷ desks and chairs
▷ clips (paper, bull dog)
▷ disks (for backing up computer work)
▷ manila folders
▷ envelopes
▷ letterhead
▷ folders/binders (for filing items)
▷ pens, paper, pencils.

How do you process documents?

Now that you are familiar with the types of documents you are likely to manage in accommodation services and the equipment used, you need to understand how to process each document. Processing of documents may involve handling the document only once or perhaps several times. It may require you to create, collate, modify, save, store, bind, retrieve or distribute the document, or perform only one of these tasks. Whatever your role is, you need to know how to process all documents.

Table 3.1 lists some of the documents discussed earlier and how to process each using the equipment available. Those that are fully explained later in this chapter, such as memos

Table 3.1 ▷ **Processing documents**

TYPE OF DOCUMENT	HOW TO PROCESS
Front office diary	Fill in the diary as important information arises (relevant to guest and venue activities). This will then be communicated to your colleagues.
Daily running sheet	As you complete each task listed on the running sheet, mark it as completed. At the end of your shift, file it by date in the daily running sheet file.
Guest request sheet	Enter the request details on the sheet for each guest request. Pass the request on to the relevant department for completion.
Guest mail	Stamp the envelope with the date of arrival. Pass guest mail on to in-house guests the same day or, re-address the letter and forward to the guest.
Wake up call sheet	As guests call to request a wake up call, complete the details on the form. Place the form next to the switchboard.
Telephone message pad	Record guest and colleague messages on the telephone message pad. Write clearly and legibly. Pass the original copy to the guest or colleague for whom the message is intended.
Policy manual	Read all policies and store in the policy file. New policies should be read, signed as acknowledgement as having been read, and then filed.
Procedures	Follow the same steps as for policies.
Minutes	Minutes are recorded first by hand at meetings and later typed (on to a computer file). The minutes are printed, copied and distributed to all staff in attendance at the meeting or anyone who needs to be aware of the information recorded in the minutes. A copy of the minutes is also filed.
Agenda	Type the agenda and distribute to those required to be in attendance at the meeting. File a copy of the agenda after the meeting.
Requests for reservations	Date stamp the request and pass on to the reservations department.
Incoming sales letters	Date stamp the letter and pass onto the department most relevant to the letter (for example, a sales letter about kitchen supplies would be passed onto the chef).
Charge authorities from companies	This is a letter detailing those charges that can be made by a guest that a company will pay for. Date stamp the letter and pass on to reservations. These are discussed in detail in Chapter 6.
Requests for information	Date stamp the request and pass the letter onto the sales and marketing department.
Letters of complaint	Date stamp the letter and pass onto the department head most suited to deal with the complaint. For example, a complaint about the restaurant is passed to the food and beverage manager. A complaint about a room is passed onto the front office manager.
Responding to letters of complaint	The person who dealt with the complaint writes these. A copy is held on file with the letter of complaint (usually in a complaints file). The letter is likely to be passed to front office for stamping and mailing.
Job applications	Date stamp the letter and pass on to the human resources department.
Requests for payments	Date stamp the request and pass on to the accounts department.
Confirmation of reservations	Usually completed by the reservations department. A standard letter is used with dates and names entered accordingly. A copy of every letter of confirmation is held on file with the guest's reservation slip.
Guest accounts	Guests who have pre-established credit with the venue are sent accounts each month. The accounts department is responsible for generating the request but may pass the letter to front office for stamping and posting.
Purchase orders	These are orders for supplies needed by the venue. Either the purchasing officer, accounts department or department head will write the purchase order but may pass the order to front office to fax or mail.
Sales and promotional letters	These are written by the sales and marketing department. They are usually processed (stamped and mailed) through front office because of the quantity.
Requests for payment from account holders	Written by the accounts department but may be processed by the front office.

and reports, or in other chapters, such as reservation slips and registration forms, are not included in this list.

Managing equipment malfunctions

A good rule of thumb when considering what can go wrong with any equipment is to assume that the greater the level of sophistication, the more that can go wrong. Front and back office equipment represents an enormous capital outlay for accommodation venues. As employees of the venue and users of the equipment, it is important that you learn the correct way to use each piece of equipment, to use it as it was intended to be used and to report malfunctions immediately. Without a lot of the equipment most of us now take for granted, your job would be a lot harder, take longer to complete and often be quite tedious. Remember also, that a lot of your guests also rely on the venue's equipment; imagine if you had to explain to a guest that the only way he could fax a document was if you took it to the post office!

Most equipment has an estimable life span; after this period it begins to get tired, may break down more frequently or is simply no longer able to perform the tasks for which it is intended. In other instances, some equipment simply becomes obsolete. Computers are a good example, of this. Most computers (hardware) are upgraded every two years. The actual operating system and software however, is likely to be outdated within six to 12 months.

For large and complex equipment—computers, facsimile, photocopier and franking machine—it is common for venues to enter into maintenance and upgrade contracts with the supplier. The contract, for a fee, ensures that the equipment is regularly maintained, quickly replaced if broken and frequently updated as newer technology emerges or as the venue's needs change. The maintenance contract for this equipment is voided if you or the venue's maintenance department attempt to fix the equipment. Apart from fixing paper jams and replacing a cartridge, it is best to leave it to the experts.

If equipment breaks down or you notice that it is not functioning, as it should:

▷ stop using the equipment
▷ place a sign on it to say it is out of order
▷ report the problem to your supervisor.

SKILLS FOCUS

Many of the tasks performed in front and back offices are administrative and clerical in nature. This means that in order for you to work efficiently and effectively in these areas you need to be able to process all of the many documents that pass through these functional areas. The types of documents you will manage include internal use (used within the venue) and external use (incoming or outgoing correspondence) and include the daily running sheet, reservation slips, general correspondence, registration forms, guest request sheets, financial control documents and memos, among others.

To process these documents, offices are equipped with a range of equipment such as computers, facsimile machine, photocopier and printers. Modern technology assists greatly when performing tasks in any office, but due to the variety of styles and complexities of equipment available, training on how to operate each piece of equipment should first be undertaken.

> *Installing equipment in an office represents an enormous financial outlay. Equipment needs to be maintained to achieve the best results from it. So only use equipment you are trained to use, use equipment as it is intended to be used and report malfunctions.*

FOCUS REVIEW

▷ *What are clerical and administrative tasks?*
▷ *What types of administrative tasks are performed in the front and back office?*
▷ *Explain the difference between internal and external use documents.*
▷ *What use is a front office diary?*
▷ *How does a front office diary differ from the daily running sheet?*
▷ *Why use a guest request sheet?*
▷ *When you have recorded a guest request, how should you process the request?*
▷ *Why is a telephone message pad in duplicate?*
▷ *How do you process requests for information? Letters of complaint?*
▷ *What is the difference between a facsimile machine and a photocopier?*
▷ *What is a franking machine? What is it used for?*
▷ *Explain how a paging system works.*
▷ *How should equipment malfunctions be managed?*
▷ *What is a maintenance contract? What benefit do you think such a contract offers?*

Writing correspondence

Many of the documents you have just learned about you are going to need to write. Some you will produce manually, that is handwritten, others you need to produce on the computer, that is typed.

Most venues have standard formats for the layout and style of the documents you produce and here you will learn just one of those standard formats and layouts for each type of document you are likely to produce. And whether you are writing a formal letter and sending it by mail, fax or e-mail, or writing an informal message and communicating it by memo, in the front office diary or by other means, there are a few 'rules' to keep in mind when writing these documents.

A FEW RULES OF GOOD WRITING

Adhering to the rules of writing results in both improving the quality of what you write and maintaining a level of consistency in your writing. The rules are not hard to remember, but they are essential for success when writing just about anything. Complicated writing is difficult both for the writer and for the reader. The sender achieves effective communication when the receiver understands the message as intended. You may like to keep in mind that many of your colleagues, your supervisors and your guests make assessments and a judgment about you based on how effective your writing is.

Keep it simple

To keep it simple means that you are concise and get to the point. Write only what is necessary to make the message easy to understand. Do not use unnecessary elaboration.

Don't use slang or jargon

Not everyone who reads what you write will have the same level of understanding of all the words you use. If the reader doesn't understand what you are staying, then effective communication has not taken place. Slang (colloquialisms and idioms) and jargon (industry-specific words) are also inappropriate in most forms of communication, so avoid slang and jargon in all written correspondence.

Use simple words

The use of simple words does not imply that your reader isn't as clever as you; it just ensures that the message is easier to understand.

Be clear

Whatever the form of written communication, it must convey the intended message in a way that is easily understood by the receiver. Imagine writing to a business seeking information about their products and in return, you receive a letter that uses a lot of jargon, does not flow logically and never gets to the point. Think about the impression this has made on you. Would you go ahead and buy the products anyway? Probably not. Your guests, colleagues and supervisors want and appreciate clarity when you communicate with them. They don't have time to wade through a lot of irrelevant, confusing and misleading information to get to the important and relevant details.

Use the right tone

The tone of what is said refers to how the information sounds. It expresses the feelings of the writer (or speaker). If you think you would take offence at receiving a document in the tone you have written, then it's probable the receiver will also take offence. The tone should encourage the desired reaction from the receiver. For example, if you write a memo that requires certain action, the tone should encourage that action. If the tone of the memo is aggressive or offensive, it is unlikely to achieve the desired outcome.

Be accurate

Accuracy is another important feature of written communication. The information you convey may be relied upon at a future date. For example, if you state in a sales letter that a deluxe suite is available every Saturday night for $120, and you neglect to mention that this rate only applies for every Saturday in the month of July, then the information is misleading. It is also inaccurate because the word 'every' implies all Saturday nights, not just those in July.

If you write a report about an incident that occurred with a guest, management needs to be confident that you have reported the details accurately. It is not very helpful to remember half the information three days later or exaggerate the exact nature of the incident. Before distributing your document, check that all the information is correct.

Be logical

Check that what you write flows and is in a logical order. If necessary, jot down a list of the points you wish to make and then decide what the order of those points will be. The information should flow logically as this makes writing the document easier and means that your readers will gain a clear understanding of what you are conveying.

Check your spelling and grammar

An important component of any written communication is correct spelling and grammar. The English language is such that the same word can have a different spelling for a different meaning. If you are not sure if the word you wish to use is the right one, look the word up in a dictionary, or find an alternative word to use.

Grammar refers to the structure of your sentences, that is, how you put the words together. We use punctuation in writing to help express our meaning. Punctuation provides the flow to a document. When people read your document, they must know when to pause, how long the pause should be and when a thought ends. If the punctuation is poor, it is difficult to understand the meaning of the sentence.

Check your sentence structure

Short simple sentences are easier to understand. Long sentences, with several thoughts and ideas separated by commas, are more difficult to read and understand. Try to construct your sentences with only one main thought.

Proofread your document

Before distributing any document, proofread it. Proofreading means reading the document carefully, looking for errors and then correcting them. You are looking for:

▷ clarity
▷ accuracy
▷ jargon and slang
▷ spelling and grammatical errors.

If you don't think it is clear, it is not likely the reader will either. If you think it is inaccurate, you are likely to mislead the reader. If you find jargon or slang used in the document, substitute these words with more appropriate words. And if there are spelling and grammatical errors, fix these.

Most word processing packages have a spelling and grammar checker. And while these are useful, they are not entirely reliable. The main reason is that the word you have typed may in fact be spelt correctly but be the wrong word to use!

Types of written correspondence

Now that you understand the rules, you can start to produce a range of correspondence.
Mostly you will need to write:

▷ business letters
▷ facsimiles
▷ memorandums
▷ reports
▷ guest messages from the venue.

BUSINESS LETTERS

Business letters are written forms of communication between businesses, between a business and an individual, and between individuals. The most common business letters you will produce are:

▷ letters of confirmation
▷ responses to inquiries
▷ responses to complaints
▷ guest welcome letters.

Business letters from your venue and those received by your venue from other businesses are printed on letterhead. Letterhead is pre-printed stationery with the company's logo and address details.

Business letter layout

Throughout the business community, there is general uniformity in the layout of a business letter. Layout is the way in which information in the letter is presented on the page. Uniformity in layout is useful because it helps maintain consistency and maximise readability. It is helpful for producing and reading similar document types if information is located in the same place. Figure 3.7 shows one layout commonly used when writing business letters.

Parts of the letter

The letter in Figure 3.7 indicates the various parts that are standard for most letters you will write.

1. Venue's name and address
All correspondence from the venue is written on the businesses letterhead—Grand Central Hotel. This should include the name and address of the venue.

2. Inside address
An inside address includes the name, title and address of the recipient of the letter.

3. Today's date
Always date your correspondence in a standard format.

4. Greeting
A greeting or salutation is always included. Use the formal title of the recipient and precede it with 'Dear'.

5. Body of the letter
Now type the body of the letter. The contents of business letters should flow logically. After the greeting:

▷ in the first paragraph, introduce the reason you are writing
▷ in the second (and third) paragraph explain the details
▷ in the final paragraph explain what action you will take or you expect the reader to take.

6. Close
How you close your letter will depend on the greeting:

▷ If the letter is addressed to a specific individual, such as Ms Cresto, then the close is 'Yours sincerely'.

Figure 3.7 ▷ **Example of a business letter layout**

GRAND CENTRAL HOTEL *505 The Boulevard, Sydney* **HOTELS OF DISTINCTION**	1. Venue's name and address
Ms Angelina Cresto Director Cresto Consulting Pty Ltd PO Box 290 EDMONSTON QLD 4567	2. Inside address
12 May 2001	3. Today's date
Dear Ms Cresto	4. Greeting
Please find enclosed the requested gift voucher for Matthew and Melinda. The voucher is valid until 31 December 2002 for any night except a Saturday. The voucher includes: • Two nights' accommodation in a deluxe double room with ocean view, • Dinner for two in The Bistro on one night, • Room service breakfast for two, both mornings, and • Complimentary valet parking. Your Visa card has been debited $450.00. A receipt is enclosed. Thank you for choosing the Grand Central Hotel. We look forward to welcoming Matthew and Melinda to the Grand Central.	5. Body of the letter
Yours sincerely	6. Close
S. Shoreham	7. Signature
Samantha Shoreham Front Office Manager	8. Writer's name and title
Enc	9. Enclosure

▷ If the letter is not addressed to a specific person, for example, Dear Sir or Madam, then the close is 'Yours faithfully'.

7. Signature
Always sign your correspondence.

8. Writer's name and title
Type your name here and full title underneath.

9. Enclosure
When you need to include items in addition to the letter, type the word 'enc' at the bottom of the page. This alerts the reader to the fact that there should be attachments to this letter. In

the example given, the enclosures included the gift voucher and the receipt. Do not use 'enc' if no enclosures are included.

STANDARD LETTERS AND TEMPLATES

Because many of the business letters you will write contain essentially the same information and follow the same layout, to save time, a **standard letter** can be developed and stored in the word processing software in your computer. A standard letter saves time because all the basic information required in the letter already exists; you need only to add the personal details of the person for whom the letter is intended and the information specific to this person.

Standard letters are used when the same information needs to be conveyed to several people. For example, a sales letter to be sent to 500 people does not need to be retyped 500 times. One letter is typed and can be personalised with the addition of each recipient's name and personal details. Of course, you could enter each person's name separately 500 times or, use the mail merge function in the word processing package. An example of a standard letter is shown in Figure 3.8.

Standard letters are used when the same information needs to be conveyed to several people.

Figure 3.8 ▷ **Example of a standard letter**

GRAND CENTRAL HOTEL
505 The Boulevard, Sydney
HOTELS OF DISTINCTION

{Type name and inside address here}
{Address}
{Address}
{Address}

{Date}

Dear {recipient's name}

Thank you for choosing to stay at the Grand Central Hotel. We are pleased to confirm your reservation details as follows:

Guest name:	{insert}
Date of arrival:	{insert}
Date of departure:	{insert}
Room type:	{insert}
Room rate:	{insert}

Your reservation has been guaranteed with your {insert   } Card.

We look forward to welcoming you.

Yours sincerely

Samantha Shoreham
Front Office Manager

A **template** is a blueprint for text (fonts, type sizes), graphics or layout, or a combination of all three. Many of the documents you produce contain a number of elements, or pre-defined styles, that remain essentially the same: letterhead, insertion of date, insertion of inside address, salutation and the close, font and type size, and other attributes. These documents also follow the same layout each time they are produced. Instead of reproducing the same layout and elements each time, it is possible to set up a template that facilitates the process and therefore makes your job that much easier.

A **template** is a blueprint for text, graphics or layout, or a combination of all three.

As well as making your job easier, the benefits of using templates include faster performance time, the avoidance of repetition and routine in letter writing, and the maintaining of consistency in the way in which information is presented.

Templates can be designed and customised to best suit the user's needs. Most word processing packages include pre-designed templates but also allow you to modify these or create your own.

How it works

The template has the basic elements and layout already in place. When you open a template on your computer, your input includes filling in the 'blank' spaces. For example, the template indicates where the date should be and how it should be written. You can also set up the template to automatically insert today's date. You then fill in the rest of the information required as you would for any other business letter:

▷ inside address
▷ salutation
▷ body of the letter
▷ close
▷ signature.

Once you have created your document using a template, it is saved according to the standard save and file procedures in your venue. Whatever name you give your document and whichever file you save it to in the computer, will not affect the original template structure. Thus, if you need to, you can use the exact same template time and again.

Templates are not limited to business letters. Templates can be created for any other type of document you use frequently, such as:

▷ memos
▷ facsimiles
▷ reports
▷ publications
▷ order forms
▷ invoices
▷ agendas
▷ minutes
▷ procedures
▷ policies
▷ e-mails
▷ time sheets.

An example of a business letter template is shown in Figure 3.9.

Figure 3.9 ▷ **Example of a business letter template**

GRAND CENTRAL HOTEL
505 The Boulevard, Sydney
HOTELS OF DISTINCTION

{Type name and inside address here}
{Address}
{Address}
{Address}

{Date}

Dear {recipient's name}

{body of the letter}

{Close}

{Writer's name}
{Writer's title}

Mail merge

Almost all accommodation venues maintain records of their guests' name and address. This information is stored in the venue's database in a standardised manner. It is useful to have this information for a number of reasons:

▷ it helps keep track of and locate your guests
▷ it facilitates the reservation process, and
▷ it allows mail merge with standard letters.

Mail merge allows you to use your guest details (name and address) to personalise standard letters. You can also use the mail merge function to print labels and envelopes. Mail merge involves merging the standard documents you create with the database of names and addresses. The database contains the information needed to personalise each standard letter, which contains the same information that every addressee will receive. When you create your standard letter, you instruct the computer (program) where to insert the merge fields that will be used when you use the merge function. Thus, if you were to mail merge the standard document shown in Figure 3.8, it would now look like the document shown in Figure 3.10.

FACSIMILES

Facsimiles are written in a standardised format and usually created from a template. A facsimile is usually a less formal form of communication than a business letter but it contains many similar elements, only presented differently. An example is shown in Figure 3.11.

Depending on the level of formality you want to achieve your fax can be typed or hand written.

A fax is usually sent when information is needed quickly and contains information that is better written than communicated orally.

Figure 3.10 ▷ **Example of a merged standard letter**

GRAND CENTRAL HOTEL
505 The Boulevard, Sydney
HOTELS OF DISTINCTION

Ms Andrea Hislop
46 Anaconda Drive
SNAKE BEND NSW 2301

24 November 2001

Dear Ms Hislop

Thank you for choosing to stay at the Grand Central Hotel. We are pleased to confirm your reservation details as follows:

Guest name: Ms Hislop
Date of arrival: 23 March 2002
Date of departure: 26 March 2002
Room type: Central Suite
Room rate: $285 per night

Your reservation has been guaranteed with your American Express Card.

We look forward to welcoming you.

Yours sincerely

S. Shoreham

Samantha Shoreham
Front Office Manager

MEMORANDUMS

Memos are written when you need to communicate the same information to several people, usually at once. It is an internal use document (for staff only), and more effective than trying to communicate the same information verbally. Memos are used to convey information that affects the workplace. For example, you may need to write a memo about an upcoming event, a new or changed policy, changes to work procedures, or a request for something, or almost anything else.

To get the response you need from those who receive your memos, always show the same courtesy you would in any business correspondence.

Memo layout

Memos follow a standard layout, although you are likely to encounter variations in this. In general, all memos follow the layout as shown in Figure 3.12. From the example, you can see that the memo follows a less formal approach than a business letter; it does not have a salutation or a

Figure 3.11 ▷ **Example of a facsimile**

GRAND CENTRAL HOTEL
505 The Boulevard, Sydney
HOTELS OF DISTINCTION

Facsimile Transmission

To: Adriatic Travel Services   **Fax No.:** 02 9202 6444
Attention: Liz   **From:** Susan
Date: 25 July 2001   **Total pages:** 1

Message

Dear Liz

We have double rooms available as follows:

—16 Dec (10 only)
—24 Dec (2 only)
—25 Dec (2 only)
—31 Dec (4 only)

If your clients wish to confirm these dates, please let me know as soon as possible.

Regards

Susan

---

close. It is brief and to the point. You do not need to type your name at the bottom of the memo because it is entered at the top. However, the person who wrote it signs the memo.

Parts of the memo

As with a business letter, there are standard parts to memos that help maintain consistency and aid readability. When writing memos:

▷ try to keep it to one page
▷ the first paragraph should introduce the topic
▷ the second paragraph should provide details of the topic
▷ the final paragraph should state what action, if any, is required.

REPORTS

Apart from the reports that are produced as a consequence of the daily activities undertaken by most accommodation services staff (occupancy reports, financial reports, etc) and that are mostly computer-generated, you may need to write a report as a result of an accident or other incident. Many workplaces have standard report forms for you to use. This saves you time and ensures information is not overlooked. You need to complete the blank spaces on the form in as much detail as possible.

Figure 3.12 ▷ **Example of a memo**

Memorandum

To:	All front office staff	**Type recipient's name(s) or position here**
From:	Front Office Manager	**Type your name or position here**
Date:	14 May 2001	**Type today's date here**
Subject:	New staff uniforms	**Type the subject or topic here**

Type the body of the memo here

The new staff uniforms have finally arrived.

I would like everyone to be fitted for their uniform by Friday 18 May to allow time for adjustments, if necessary, and everyone in their new uniform on Monday 28 May.

Please contact the laundry to arrange for your fitting between 2pm and 5pm on Wednesday or Thursday this week.

Samantha

Sign the memo at the bottom

If you need to write a simple report, there are guidelines to follow:

▷ always type your report
▷ number the pages
▷ date your report
▷ introduce the report with a brief background of the event
▷ provide specific details of the incident or event including:
  – what happened
  – who was involved
  – when it happened
  – how it happened
  – where it happened
  – what action was taken
▷ make recommendations (to prevent the incident occurring again)
▷ sign the report.

The report is then handed directly to the person who requested it, or it may be accompanied by a memo explaining that a report has been written and why. Attach the report to the memo. A simple report layout is shown in Figure 3.13.

Always keep a copy of your reports. They are frequently referred to at a later date.

As you can see, the simple report shown in Figure 3.13 follows a similar layout and structure to a memorandum. However, it is likely to extend to several pages.

Finally, all reports should:

▷ be easy to read and understand
▷ be written in a rational and objective manner
▷ follow a logical sequence

Figure 3.13 ▷ **Example of an incident report**

GRAND CENTRAL HOTEL
505 The Boulevard, Sydney
HOTELS OF DISTINCTION

Incident Report

To: Ms Benson
             General Manager

From: Samantha Shoreham
             Front Office Manager

Date: 3 August 2001

Introduce the report with a brief background of the event.

Provide specific details of the incident or event:

• What happened
• Who was involved
• When it happened
• How it happened
• Where it happened
• What action was taken

Make recommendations (to prevent the incident occurring again).

Sign the report.

▷ be written in a concise and lively style
▷ draw valid and logical conclusions
▷ be proofed.

GUEST MESSAGES FROM THE VENUE

Guest messages from the venue may be for one guest, a few guests, or all guests. Guest messages should be typed on the venue's letterhead and follow a similar layout to business letters. Because the guest is in-house, instead of inserting an inside address, the guest's room number is inserted.

For guest messages that are to be sent to all or several guests (such as a welcome letter), then a standard letter or template can be used. A copy of the message is then filed, usually according to subject. For messages that are for only one guest, file a copy of the message with the guest's reservation details. A copy of a guest message is shown in Figure 3.14.

Messages are usually placed in an envelope with the guest's name and room number typed on the front and delivered to the guest's room. The message is usually slipped under the guest room door.

If the message for the guest is a telephone message, then these are handwritten, usually on standard telephone message pads. The message may be handed to the guest at reception (when they collect their room key, for example) or slipped under their door. Alternatively, for those venues whose room telephones have a message display light, this is switched on to let the guest know there is a message for them to collect.

Figure 3.14 ▷ **Example of a guest message**

GRAND CENTRAL HOTEL
505 The Boulevard, Sydney
HOTELS OF DISTINCTION

Mr Gerard
Room 1206

28 September 2001

Dear Mr Gerard

Please be advised that on Thursday 30 September, the hot water system in the hotel will be out of use between 11am and 1pm.

We sincerely apologise for any inconvenience this may cause you.

Yours sincerely

S. Shoreham

Samantha Shoreham
Front Office Manager

APPLY YOUR KNOWLEDGE

Write a welcome letter for your guests at the Grand Central Hotel following a business letter layout. Include the following information:

▷ *departure date*
▷ *important venue phone numbers your guest may like to know*
▷ *outlet opening times and current specials*
▷ *any other information you think your guest may like to know.*

Make up the details you need.

SKILLS FOCUS

Most venues use standard formats for the layout and style of the documents you will produce. Use of standard formats helps you do your job and maintain consistency in the way information is presented. It also helps the reader to locate information. Whatever type of document you are writing, there are a few rules that help with the communication process: keep it simple, don't use slang, use the right tone, be clear, concise and accurate and always check your spelling and grammar.

The types of documents you are likely to produce are business letters, facsimiles, memorandums, reports, and guest messages. Follow the standard layout used for each of these to meet the venue's standards.

A standard letter is used when essentially the same information in the body of the letter is to be conveyed to a number of recipients. A template is a blueprint for text, graphics and layout used for many business documents and can save you time in producing these documents. A template also makes your job easier, avoids repetition, and maintains consistency in the way information is presented.

FOCUS REVIEW

▷ List five rules to remember for successful writing.
▷ Why are the rules important?
▷ Why shouldn't you use slang or jargon when writing?
▷ Name four types of correspondence you may be asked to write when working in a front office.
▷ What is letterhead? Why do you think businesses send out letters on letterhead?
▷ What types of correspondence might you use a standard letter for?
▷ What are the advantages of using a template?
▷ When would you mail merge?
▷ Why would you send staff a memo? List three examples of things you would write a memo about.
▷ Why is it important to keep the tone of a memo polite?
▷ What does each paragraph in a memo discuss?
▷ Why might you need to know how to write a report when working in the front office?
▷ Explain two different ways that guest messages can be handled.
▷ Write a message to all guests at the Grand Central Hotel from the food and beverage manager explaining that the restaurant will be closed for lunch tomorrow while the carpets are being steamed cleaned. Let the guests know that lunch will be served in the bar and that room service is available.
▷ Mr Fowler's wife called and she will meet him in the cocktail bar at 6.00 pm. Write him a message and explain how this will get to him.

Maintaining filing and storage systems

Accommodation venues generate large quantities of printed and manual documentation. And whether the documentation is in current use (active) or theoretically finished with (inactive), it needs to be filed and stored.

Active documents (documents that relate to current events, ongoing events, in-house guests or reservations) are filed where they are readily accessed—in the front and back office. **Inactive documents** (documents that have no immediate use) are filed in a central location where they are readily accessed but out of the way—in a storage cupboard or similar facility.

Much of the documentation is kept for a number of years. Some of the documents are kept as reference material, for example, internal memos, purchase orders, and menus. Other documents are kept for legal reasons, such as tax invoices and copies of guest accounts and payment method, for tax auditing purposes. Documents can be filed manually and some can be filed electronically. Whatever the reason for keeping records, and however it is managed (manually or electronically) it is important that documents be filed and stored logically for both ease of reference and security.

> **Active documents**—documents in current use.
>
> **Inactive documents**—documents not in current use.

WHAT IS FILING?

Filing is the process of arranging and storing documents according to a particular classification. Printed documents, such as reservation slips, reports, memos, correspondence, and guest accounts, are filed manually. This information can also be filed electronically. For example, the details of a reservation recorded manually is later entered into the PMS and filed in the computer. Details of a deposit received for a reservation are recorded in the PMS and a receipt printed. A copy of the receipt is sent to the guest and another filed with the guest's reservation.

> **Filing** is the process of arranging and storing documents according to a particular classification.

Filing can be classified, or indexed, into five categories:

1. alphabetically
2. numerically
3. geographically
4. by subject
5. chronologically.

Filing alphabetically

Documents filed alphabetically are filed according to the first, and subsequent, letter of the sender's or receiver's name, or according to the type of document, such as policies and procedures. For example, employee files are filed according to the employee's surname. Group reservation files may be filed first under 'groups' and then by group name. A letter requesting information may be held in a 'pending' file by guest name. Guest profiles are maintained alphabetically.

Filing numerically

Filing numerically means your documents are filed according to a number, such as a room number, account number, invoice number, or other numerical identifier, such as a procedure number. For example, procedures for all the front office tasks may be allocated a procedure number and filed together numerically. All in-house guest registration cards are filed numerically (by room number).

Filing geographically

Filing geographically means the filing is done according to a location or designated area. For example, Victoria, western region, or southern district. This type of information can be useful for the sales and marketing department because it helps the department to identify regions where the venue's guests (target markets) live.

Filing by subject

Some documents cannot be filed any other way except by their subject matter. Examples of files filed by subject include complaint letters (filed under 'complaints'), menus (filed under 'menus'), training, quotes, wine lists etc.

Filing chronologically

Documents filed chronologically are filed in date or time order. For example, when a reservation has been entered into the PMS, the manual reservation record is filed according to date of arrival.

Classifications within classifications

Many of the filing examples used above are filed in more than one way under a main heading. For example, reservations are filed under 'reservations' and then by date order. Groups are filed under 'groups' and then alphabetically. Similarly, many other documents can be filed in this way. For example, menus can be filed under 'menus' then according to type of menu or the food outlet (restaurant menus, room service menus).

MANUAL FILING

Despite predictions of a paperless office with increased computer technology, most offices maintain a paper-based filing system. There are several reasons for this (computer breakdown, for example) but for accommodation venues, the most compelling reason is the need for a hard copy of all information that may be stored on the computer. For example, a guest needs to sign a registration form as part of the check-in process. On departure, the guest needs to see a copy of his or her account so that the contents can be verified.

File preparation

Before filing any documents, there are a number of tasks to be completed:
▷ collecting all relevant documents
▷ inspecting the quality of the documents
▷ cross-referencing your files
▷ coding the files
▷ sorting the files, then
▷ filing the documents.

Collecting all relevant documents

Before filing documents, check that all details are included in the one file. For example, if filing a reservation slip with a deposit, check that there is a copy of the deposit slip, the method and amount of payment is listed and that the original reservation slip and any changes made are attached, along with a copy of the confirmation letter. If there happens to be a query about the reservation or deposit at any time, then it will be easy to check all relevant details because they have been collected and filed together.

Inspecting the quality of the paperwork

Paper is easily damaged and, over time, can deteriorate through constant handling. Before filing your documents, check the quality of the items. Is the paper torn? Does it need to be photocopied and replaced? Is there an excess of staples and paper clips to be removed? Make sure that all the paperwork is straightened and neat before placing in the file.

Cross-referencing your files

Cross-referencing means linking one file, or information in a file, to another relevant file. For example, a group file, filed under 'groups' (alphabetically) is cross-referenced with the reservations file (filed chronologically, by date).

Coding the files

To code a document means to give it a reference number or name, that is, what is the file to be called? A code is often required as you may have more than one file with the same name. For example, Southern Pacific Tours make several group bookings with your venue each year. You may have several groups booked for the coming months. If you filed them all under 'Southern Pacific', how are you going to know to which group the information belongs. By allocating a code, you have a distinctive identifier. For example, the code may be the group name (or abbreviation) and the arrival date, thus SouthPac2010 and SouthPac1012. The first Southern Pacific group is arriving on 20 October and the second group is arriving on 10 December.

Sorting the files

Sorting simply requires you to put like files with like files. For example, put all reservation files together, group files together, guest profiles together, etc. This is useful because often the file storage facility for each of the different files is located in various areas. Instead of moving backwards and forwards between the various filing cabinets and locations, you are able to first file all of one type of files, then the next and so on.

Filing the documents

Once you have everything together, cross-referenced, coded and sorted, you are now ready to file. Documents can be filed in filing cabinets, A4 folders, index boxes or shelving, depending on the equipment and filing system used by the venue.

Whatever system is used, follow the established system (alphabetical, numerical, etc) and place the documents in the correct location in the file. A misplaced or incorrectly filed document can create problems at a later stage.

APPLY YOUR KNOWLEDGE

The table below lists a range of documents that need filing. On the right, indicate how you would file each document. For example, a reservation slip is filed chronologically (by date of arrival). Indicate which, if any, you would cross-reference and to which file you would cross-reference it.

Document	File Classification
Fax requesting information on rates	
Memo about new staff uniforms	
Sales letter to be sent to all residents in a particular suburb	
A new policy about staff leave entitlements	
A variation to the emergency evacuation procedure	
Incident report	
Menus and wine lists	
Letter of complaint	
Letter to a guest confirming their reservation	

ELECTRONIC FILING

Some information is filed and stored electronically. An example of electronic only storing is the guest's account while in-house. Venues do not keep a manual tally of the guest's account. However, each charge and payment recorded to a guest's account can be traced manually. Every transaction entered on the guest's account is accompanied by a corresponding source document, which is filed by room number during the guest's stay.

Information collated and filed onto a computer reduces the need for a lot of physical filing storage space. The storage medium is either the hard drive (the computer 'memory') of the computer or a diskette. What was previously stored in a three-drawer filing cabinet can now be stored on several diskettes, which are in turned filed. The disk is removed from the computer after use. When you need to retrieve and access the information stored on the disk, it can be reloaded onto almost any computer (operating the same system in which it originally saved information).

Apart from its portability, the advantages of saving data to disk are:

▷ reduced filing space
▷ reduced filing time
▷ easy access and document modification
▷ document changes readily traced.

Filing documents on disk

Just as it is important to have an organised manual filing system, it is also important to maintain an organised electronic filing system. Similarly to manual filing, your documents must be first named and/or coded and then filed according to a logical classification. For example, to file your documents electronically, you may decide to create 'folders' into which you place each file. A folder name should clearly identify its contents. For example, 'memos', 'complaints', 'welcome letters', and so on. Within these folders you then place the file; for example, you have just written a memo to all front office staff about the introduction of a new computer system. The memo is given a name and filed in the 'memos' folder.

So to organise your electronic filing efficiently:

▷ Label files in an easily recognisable and logical manner. Depending on the recency of the word processing package in use, most file names can have in excess of 200 characters.
▷ File documents to folders.
▷ Always back up your files to disk. In other words, save the document on the computer hard drive and on a disk. If the computer crashes, or the file is deleted from the computer, you will still have a copy.
▷ Label and keep secure all disks (as you would your filing cabinets).
▷ Treat your disks with care. A broken or damaged disk may lose literally hundreds of hours of work and multiple documents.

Use of electronic files in accommodation services

Most of the work you perform in reception or reservations is processed electronically—guest reservations, registration and departure, recording of transactions, account balancing, and guest profiles, among others. You are able to perform these functions because the computer is programmed to 'file' the subsequent data you entered. You are then able to retrieve or access information in a number of ways, by:

▷ guest name
▷ room number
▷ account number
▷ transaction type, or
▷ arrival date.

For example, most venues maintain their guest profiles electronically, and you can retrieve this file any time by entering the guest's name. You can also link a new reservation for this guest to their profile. And because the profile contains many of the elements required to process a reservation, by linking the two you are able also to save time (because you do not need to re-record relevant information).

RECORD MAINTENANCE

Once a document is filed, it may need to be updated and maintained. For example, a manually maintained guest profile needs updating after each visit to the venue by the guest. When you handle files in this way, follow the procedures for file preparation making sure that the files are always kept neat and clean and in an orderly fashion. At other times, you may need to access files and make changes to it (record utilisation) and on other occasions you need to remove a file altogether (archiving).

Record utilisation and transmission

From time to time, you need to access files to change or refer to its contents. This means you need to physically remove a paper-based file from its storage facility or retrieve an electronic file on the computer, for example, when a reservation you processed needs to be changed (at the guest's request). You need to remove the reservation slip from the file, and retrieve the reservation in the computer, make the changes on the slip and in the computer record, then re-file the reservation slip and save the change in the computer. This is a frequent occurrence with group reservations.

If you retrieve other types of documents (such as a letter or memo) that are saved to disk (or the hard drive of a computer), when you retrieve it, adjust it, and then close it again, the computer remembers where to file it. The computer is also able to automatically record the date the file was last accessed, and which computer terminal accessed the file.

When removing a file from the manual filing system it is important that there is a record of the movement. The record should indicate the date the file was removed, by whom and where it has gone. This helps keep track of files and reduces the likelihood of lost files. Also, if someone else needs to access the file, they will know where to find it. Figure 3.15 shows an example of a file movement marker used for this purpose. The movement marker is placed into the filing cabinet in place of the original file. An alternative to this is a file movement book. It records essentially the same information but in a logbook.

Archiving

Archiving—the practice of removing a file or record from everyday use and storing it in another location.

Archiving is the practice of removing a file or record from everyday use and storing it in another location. The file is not disposed of but transferred to where it is still accessible, but not as easily. Documents are archived:

▷ to make room (there is limited storage space in an office environment)
▷ because they are not used as often as they were, and
▷ because most records must be kept (by law) for a minimum of five years.

Most archives are located in the basement or a storage facility away from the office (it may even be away from the venue). Wherever you archive your documents, the area must be dry and clean. A damp environment will cause deterioration of your documents; it will cause mould and mildew and potentially attract pests such as silverfish.

When a document is archived is subjective. Most venues archive when the filing cabinet is full! Others are quite methodical about their archiving. They may archive some documents after three months, such as reservation slips, and others at the end of the financial year, such as financial reports. When archiving your documents label them clearly and store them in date order.

Figure 3.15 ▷ **Example of a file movement marker**

```
File Name: _____
Removed by: _____
Date: _____
Returned Date: _____
```

Due to the vast quantity of documents produced in accommodation venues, documents must be filed and stored. Active files (those in current use) are filed in an easily accessible location. Those that are inactive (not in current use) are archived.

Filing is the process of arranging and sorting documents according to a particular classification. Documents may be filed alphabetically, numerically, geographically, by subject or chronologically.

Filing may be undertaken manually or electronically. When manual filing, collect all relevant documents belonging to the one file, inspect the quality of the documents, cross-reference the file where applicable, code the files, sort them and then file them.

Electronic filing refers to those files maintained on a computer or computer disk. In a front office environment, much of the work you process will be completed on a computer, such as guest reservations, registration and departure, account transactions and the like. This information is then stored on the computer by guest name, room number, account number or some other identifier.

Record maintenance is the process of accessing, utilising and re-filing documents. Archiving is the practice of removing a file or record from everyday use and storing it in another location.

FOCUS REVIEW

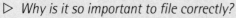

▷ What is the difference between active and inactive files? Give two examples of front office documents that may be regarded as active or inactive. When might documents become inactive? What do you then do with them?

▷ Why is it so important to file correctly?

▷ List the five different ways in which files can be arranged. Briefly explain each.

▷ What would be the best way to file a complaint letter? A checked-out guest registration card?

▷ What tasks need to be completed to prepare a document for filing?

▷ Why would you cross-reference a file? Give an example of a file that may be cross-referenced.

▷ What is the difference between manual and electronic filing?

▷ Why should you always back up documents to disks?

▷ Describe the advantages of using a movement marker when removing a document from a file.

▷ What is archiving?

▷ Where is the best place to store the archived documents? What conditions should archives be stored in? Why?

PUT YOUR KNOWLEDGE TO THE TEST

Robyn was spending a month producing and processing front office correspondence, working closely with Adrienne, the front office manager. A great portion of Adrienne's day is spent sorting through all the different correspondence that comes across her desk and responding to it. She is also responsible for writing the agendas of the meetings she holds, developing policies and procedures for her staff and communicating with everyone often by memo.

With Robyn trained in much of the work, Adrienne now relied on her to carry out many of these tasks.

Robyn sat at her desk, looked at the pile of documents, and decided first to sort through them, prioritise the important tasks, and then get on with the job. Robyn is required to complete all the following tasks today.

1. *Susan, the reservations manager, needs a confirmation letter requesting a deposit for the following booking: Ms Tinnam has a three-night booking for a non-smoking family room for two adults and three children. The room rate is $180.00 per night, which includes breakfast. They also require a cot. The deposit required is one night's accommodation. After writing this letter, where would Robyn file the information?*

2. *Mr Porter had called reception to say he had misplaced his account and needs a faxed copy of it today. Write a facsimile to accompany the account.*

3. *Ms Spirit has written to the hotel asking for room availability and prices for New Year's Eve. Write a letter of response. Make up the details you think you need. Where would Robyn now file this letter?*

4. *Raphael, the executive chef, wants a memo written informing staff that staff meal times have now changed. Lunch is now available between 11.30 am and 1.30 pm and dinner is now available between 5 pm and 7 pm. Who should sign this memo? Why? Where would Robyn file this memo?*

5. *Serge, the restaurant manager, asks Robyn to fax Madame Pink the Christmas menus and brochures. Write a covering fax to accompany the menu. Make up the details you think are necessary. Who should sign this fax? Why?*

6. *Bruce from maintenance informs Adrienne that the pool will be closed for two hours tomorrow morning from 9 am to 11 am. Robyn needs to write a message to all guests explaining this. Who should sign this letter? What kind of letter would Robyn use for this message?*

7. *Write a message for Mr Simpson advising him that the airline called and they have found his luggage and will send it to the hotel. Where would Robyn then file this letter?*

8. *A guest slipped over in the foyer and sustained a broken arm. Write a simple report for Adrienne. The report should not be more than three pages long. Make up whatever details you think are necessary.*

9. *From the above work, which written correspondence do you think needs to be kept and filed? Why is some of it not kept?*

Communicating on the Telephone

LEARNING OUTCOMES

On completion of this chapter you will be able to:

▷ describe the role and responsibilities of a telephonist;

▷ describe a range of telephone systems;

▷ demonstrate your ability to use the telephone system in the workplace;

▷ promptly and correctly respond to incoming calls;

▷ accurately record requests and messages and pass them on to the appropriate department/person;

▷ identify appropriate occasions to promote features and facilities of the establishment;

▷ manage threatening or suspicious calls in accordance to set emergency procedures;

▷ make outgoing calls.

Introduction

The telephone is a communication tool that all businesses must and do have. In a hospitality environment, the telephone, when used correctly, allows you to communicate both internally and externally with guests and potential guests, your colleagues and employers, suppliers, associates, and the competition, among others, in a timely and efficient manner. To communicate effectively using the telephone requires both skill in using the telephone system as well as knowledge of the procedures in place.

In an accommodation venue the telephone system must be able to meet the needs of all users—staff and guests. The telephone procedures in place must be able to meet the standards expected of the venue and provide consistency as well as help you do your job.

All of you will have used the telephone before, probably at home. Think for a moment how you behave when responding to various telephone calls—you respond one way to calls that are for you, another way to calls that are for someone else and a different way again to calls that are of a business nature. There is possibly even some consistency in the way you respond to each of these different calls. And while it is likely that you do not have procedures in the home for receiving and making calls, you do know how to use the telephone equipment.

Throughout this chapter we aim to help you develop the skills and knowledge required to manage a telephone system in a professional manner. This requires you becoming familiar with the telephone system in the workplace and the role of the telephonist. It will also require you to develop skills for managing a range of tasks performed on the telephone and identifying the various functions most telephone systems in hospitality environments are able to perform.

The role and responsibilities of the telephonist

The telephonist is the person who operates and manages the telephone system in the back office. This is where most incoming calls are received. The telephonist's primary role is to receive all **incoming calls** and redirect the calls as required.

There are two types of incoming calls—calls received from external sources and calls received from internal sources. External sources are calls from outside the venue, such as a potential guest or a supplier. Internal calls are calls from inside the venue, such as from colleagues and in-house guests.

HOURS

The telephones in a large venue need to be answered 24 hours a day, every day of the year. It is therefore likely that, in a large venue, several telephonists are employed and the shifts the telephonist is likely to work are usually the same as a receptionist:

▷ 7.00 am–3.30 pm
▷ 3.00 pm–11.30 pm
▷ 11.00 pm–7.30 am.

Depending on the size of the venue a swing swift may also operate. On the weekends there are usually fewer external incoming calls because there are fewer inquiries and business-related calls, so there are usually fewer telephonists rostered to work at that time. When a telephonist does not manage telephones, it is common to find that the reception staff takes care of the telephone functions.

The telephonist has a responsibility for ensuring that all calls are:

▷ promptly and professionally answered, and
▷ correctly transferred, placed on hold or screened according to established procedures.

To be able to do this, the telephonist must:

▷ correctly and efficiently operate the venue's telephone system
▷ have an in depth knowledge of the various activities taking place within the venue
▷ have an in depth knowledge of all departments and employee roles in the venue and their various extension numbers
▷ be organised, friendly and professional
▷ accurately record messages
▷ demonstrate an appropriate telephone manner
▷ have an in depth knowledge of the products and services available in the venue.

However, it is not only the telephonist who carries these responsibilities. All accommodation services staff are required to develop proficient telephone skills. While perhaps not to the extent of the telephonist, you do need to be able to use the telephone system in place, follow standard procedures for managing telephone communication and you need to demonstrate appropriate telephone etiquette.

SKILLS FOCUS

To communicate effectively using the telephone requires skill and knowledge of the system in place. Because of the importance of the telephone as a communication tool within the establishment, all staff should be able to demonstrate effective telephone skills.

The role of the telephonist is to proficiently operate and manage the telephone system in place in the venue. The telephonist is required to perform a range of telephone-related tasks (operating the switchboard) following established procedures.

The telephonist must answer all calls promptly and professionally, and be able to correctly transfer, place on hold and screen calls. To be able to do this, the telephonist must be able to operate the switchboard, have an in depth knowledge of the activities that take place in the venue and the roles of the various staff, be organised, friendly and professional and be able to demonstrate appropriate telephone behaviour.

FOCUS REVIEW

▷ *What is required to effectively communicate on the telephone?*
▷ *What is the telephonist's primary role?*
▷ *What is meant by 'incoming' calls? Explain the types of incoming calls the telephonist is likely to manage.*
▷ *What must a telephonist be able to do to ensure that calls are managed promptly and professionally?*
▷ *Who else in a hospitality environment needs efficient telephone skills? Why?*

Telephone and switchboard equipment

Every day, a number of activities take place over the telephone, such as reservations, credit card authorisations, the ordering of supplies and equipment, confirmation of bookings and general enquiries. To ensure that the needs of both the venue and the guests are met, several calls must be able to be made simultaneously. This means that at any one time, several people may be calling the venue: to make a reservation or a restaurant booking, confirm supply orders with the kitchen or housekeeping, to speak to an in-house guest or enquire about conference facilities. In addition, staff and in-house guests may need to make calls from the venue to external and internal sources.

An appropriate telephone system must be in place for this to happen. This means that the venue's telephone system must be capable of receiving and making multiple calls at one time. This doesn't mean that the venue has a separate telephone line for every department and every guest room. What the venue does have is one main telephone line with multiple extensions.

However, the venue may also have several other telephone lines used exclusively by specific departments, such as sales and marketing and finance, because these departments must use the telephone frequently. But even these telephone lines will be linked to the main telephone line through the use of an extension. The venue is likely also to operate separate telephone lines for its facsimile machines and e-mail and toll free reservation number—all services made possible via a telephone line.

FREE CALL LINE

Toll free line— telephone line whereby the venue pays for the cost of the incoming call. It is usually only available for long distance calls.

Direct dial telephone—a telephone that allows the user to make calls without the assistance of an operator

Many accommodation venues offer a free call line or toll free line to encourage potential guests to call them for a booking. It can be expensive for Mr Bartlett in Perth to call Melbourne looking for accommodation. By dialing the free call line the venue picks up the cost of the call and Mr Bartlett can enquire about accommodation at no cost to himself or his business.

These numbers are usually 1800 or 1300 numbers and are intended for long distance reservation bookings (calls outside the venue's local call range). For example, Ms Chong, who lives in Brisbane, is unable to call the Brisbane Hilton using the venue's toll free line, as she is calling from the same city in which the hotel is located. However, if Ms Chong was to call the Adelaide Hilton from Brisbane, she is able to use the toll free line for that hotel because it is an interstate call.

Free call lines are treated in the same professional manner as any other incoming call.

Table 4.1 lists the types of services that may be required by guests and the venue via a telephone line.

Table 4.1 ▷ **Telephone services**

GUEST REQUIREMENTS	VENUE REQUIREMENTS
In-room direct dial telephone (local, STD, IDD) for incoming and outgoing calls	Multiple lines for incoming and outgoing calls
Facsimile access	Multiple extensions
Internet access	Facsimile access
E-mail access	Internet access
Modem	E-mail access

Large, corporate venues failing to provide these facilities are potentially failing to meet the increasingly high demand for these services by their guests. This in turn can lead to a loss of business, as guests increasingly search for the best value and service for their money.

SWITCHBOARDS

It is not practical or possible to use a single telephone to coordinate and manage all the telephone lines and extensions required in an accommodation venue. Instead, a switchboard is used. A switchboard is the piece of equipment that allows a venue to connect all the telephone lines and extensions. All calls coming into or being made from the venue pass through the switchboard.

However, this does not mean that a switchboard operator needs to connect all calls. Most calls can be made directly from a telephone handset. For example, Mrs Karabatsis calls Danni in banquets to enquire about a wedding reception. Bruce the telephonist takes the message at the switchboard and passes the message onto Danni. Danni can then dial direct to Mrs Karabatsis from the telephone handset on her desk without going through Bruce. After Danni and Mrs Karabatsis have made contact, then Danni can give Mrs Karabatsis her direct line (if one is in place in the banquets office) and further calls to Danni from Mrs Karabatsis can be placed directly to the banquets office, bypassing the switchboard.

A switchboard can be said to be the 'brain' of the telephone system in place. Not only does it allow the use of several lines and extensions at once, it can also allow you and other users to perform a range of other functions. Table 4.2 lists the functions the switchboard should be able to perform and the reasons why.

The correct operating of a switchboard has greatly improved customer service. The ability to handle a number of calls at one time, connect internal and external calls to correct extensions, and assist guests with calls, gives the establishment a reputation of service excellence and professionalism.

Parts of the switchboard

All switchboards have essentially the same parts. What may vary are the number of extensions that it is able to operate, and the extent of the functions it is able to perform. Figure 4.1 on page 109 shows a diagram of a switchboard indicating its various parts. Let's look at them:

▷ working system—this is the actual switchboard equipment. Its capabilities and size will be determined by the needs of the venue
▷ handpiece—for making and receiving calls
▷ headpiece—this can replace the handpiece and is often preferred to a handpiece, as it allows the operator to work more efficiently as it leaves both hands free. It is also better for the telephonist's posture reducing the incidence of sore necks resulting from holding the handpiece to the ear
▷ key pad—numbered key pad and function keypad
▷ indicator/display panel—this indicates the number (or extension) called and incoming numbers. This display panel can often show the department called or the name of the guest for more efficient guest service. For example, a system whose display panel only shows a number (either a room number or extension) means that the telephonist must look up the computer for the guest's name. A system whose display panel shows both the number and the department or guest's name is far more helpful and allows for a more personalised level of service as the operator is able to answer 'Good evening switchboard, this is Stacey, how may I help you, Mr Stewart?'

Table 4.2 ▷ **Switchboard functions**

SWITCHBOARD FUNCTION	REASON
Monitor all incoming and outgoing calls	It is useful to determine where calls are coming from and going to, as the venue can use this information to better manage its telephone system and therefore improve services offered via the telephone.
Receive and make several calls at once	More than one person is likely to want to call the venue or to make a call from the venue at any one time.
Place calls on hold	Even with the potential to receive many calls at once, it is important to remember that often only one or two people may operate the switchboard at a time. This means that sometimes it is necessary to place a call on hold until the call can be properly dealt with. At other times, if the requested extension is busy, it may be necessary to place a call on hold until the extension is no longer busy.
	Most switchboards also have the capability to play either music or a recorded advertising message while the caller is on hold. The advertising message is usually about packages offered by, or features of, the venue.
Time all calls	When guests use the telephone in their rooms, they pay for the call. To accurately charge the guest for the call, it must be timed. Calls made by staff may also be timed. This is to determine how much of the working day is spent on the telephone.
Interface with the computerised PMS	This means that the telephone system is directly linked to the computerised property management system and allows all call charges to be directly applied to individual guest and departmental accounts.
Cost all calls and automatically direct the charge to the guest's account	All call costs, whether made by staff or a guest, are charged according to the number of units (of time) or pulses used. For guest use, the charge is made directly to the guest's account, which reduces the likelihood of errors that can occur when posted manually.
	For internal (staff) use the call charge is registered against each department (where the call originated) and allows the venue to keep track of the cost of all calls made by staff.
Record messages	When a requested extension (guest room or department) is unmanned, some telephone systems allow the caller to record a message.
Direct dialing for both staff and guests—local, STD (Subscriber Trunk Dialing) and IDD (International Direct Dialing)	This means that calls can be made without the assistance of the telephonist.
Transfer calls (to departmental extensions and guest rooms)	When the telephonist receives incoming calls, the caller usually requests to speak to an in-house guest or a department. Connecting the caller to the requested person is referred to as transferring the call.
Re-dial the last number called (from the switchboard)	The telephonist is often required to re-dial the same number several times (for example, when the called number is engaged). Rather than enter the number each time, the re-dial function allows the telephonist to call the required number by pressing only one key.
Divert calls to other extensions	Most venues do not have a telephonist on duty 24 hours a day. So when the switchboard is unmanned, it can be programmed to automatically redirect incoming calls to another telephone (extension), usually reception.
Dial hands free	Most telephone systems used in accommodation venues allow you to dial hands free. This means that by pressing a key on the panel, you can dial the required number without lifting a handset.
Place wake up calls	Many guests request a wake up call. These can be programmed into the telephone system and placed automatically at the requested time. If the guest does not answer the call, the system will recall after a preprogrammed time.

Figure 4.1 ▷ **Parts of a switchboard**

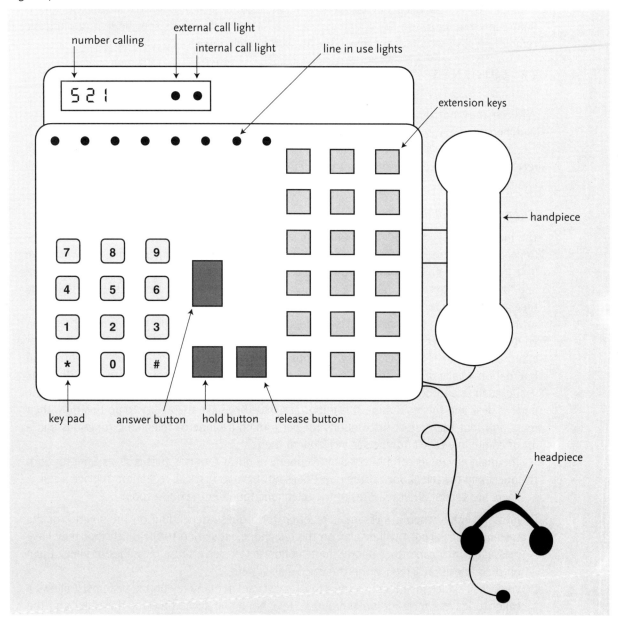

Whichever system is installed, it must be not only able to meet the venue's tele-communications needs, but also be:

▷ user friendly and easy to operate
▷ compact enough so it doesn't take up too much room (perhaps be able to install two boards: one as an extra or emergency board)
▷ cost effective for the venue
▷ easy to maintain (with a good maintenance agreement).

Training is required no matter what the system in place. Training is usually provided when you start work as a telephonist or in any other role that requires you to use the telephone system; training is also needed when a new telephone system is installed. Additional training is required to meet the telephone etiquette standards and procedures in place in your workplace. Before attempting to use the telephone, familiarise yourself with its specific features and the establishment's procedures for telephone answering techniques.

TELEPHONES

The telephone is the actual handset that allows you (and the guest) to make and receive calls. While it may not be essential for you to learn all the features and capabilities of the switchboard, it is essential for you to be able to use all the features of the telephone handset. Like a switchboard, a telephone allows you to perform a range of functions, such as make and receive calls, place calls on hold and transfer calls, but unlike a switchboard, for only one call at a time.

Guest room telephones

The majority of accommodation venues place at least one telephone in their guest rooms. Depending on the size of the room and the quality of the establishment, there may be more (one in the bedroom, one in the bathroom, another in the lounge). There may also be an extra line for Internet access or facsimile machine, so the telephone can be accessed at the same time as the computer.

The telephone in the guest rooms will usually be a standard handset not unlike the one in your home. It allows guests to dial directly out of the accommodation room internally or externally and to receive calls as well. Your guests may want to make local, national and international calls directly from their room. They may want to call an extension within the venue, such as another guest's room or a department, such as room service, housekeeping, the porter's desk and the restaurant. It is important that they have the ability to do this from their room and that the correct instructions for performing a range of telephone functions and a list of commonly called numbers is available to them.

The main advantage of a direct dial telephone in guest rooms is that is saves time for both the guest and the telephonist if the guest does not have to first call reception to place a call.

There are several other features of the telephone found in the guest room:

▷ message light—when a message is received for a guest, depending on the abilities of the system, a special light will display on the telephone, indicating to the guest that they have messages. They can either phone the telephonist to receive these messages or check them on their television screen, or on the voice mail system.

▷ voice mail—voice mail technology is today available on many telephone systems. It allows a caller to leave a message on the guest's telephone and saves time for the caller and the telephonist. Rather than the person leaving a message with the operator, a message can be recorded directly onto the telephone, like an answering machine. A light goes on to let the guest know there are messages waiting to be heard.

▷ direct dial—this is a very efficient feature for both the guest and the establishment. The guest can simply dial whatever number they require (just like dialling a number from home) and get straight through. The other option is for the guest to call the telephonist who places the call and then calls the guest back to take the call when it is connected. As you can imagine, this is time-consuming for both the guest and the telephonist.

Receiving telephone calls

Before you can begin to receive and transfer calls, you need to learn the correct way to use the telephone. This will depend on the system in place. How you physically answer the telephone, transfer a call or place a call, varies from one system to another and often from one venue to another.

To operate a switchboard you need to press one button to answer a call, another to place it on hold and another to dial a number to transfer a call or disconnect the call. This is the essential first step to developing your telephone skills—knowing how to operate the equipment you are using. Even standard telephone sets can be programmed to perform these functions (receive and make calls, put calls on hold, transfer calls) and you need to be able to perform these functions.

A telephone (single handset) requires you to pick up the handpiece to receive or make a call. You then need to press a button to place a call on hold and dial an extension to transfer the call. To disconnect the telephone, simply hang up the handpiece.

Most venues will provide you with the necessary skills to operate the telephone system in the workplace. The telephone techniques and procedures may vary but here we provide you with a few techniques to get you started.

TELEPHONE TECHNIQUE

The telephone is so familiar to most of us that sometimes it's easy to fall into bad and sloppy telephone habits that may give your caller a bad impression of the establishment (and you). Remember, when you are speaking on the telephone, you have chosen to be a representative of the establishment. There are several things to be learned that ensure your behaviour on the telephone is a reflection of your professionalism.

Preparing to use the telephone

Having learned how to operate the telephone, the next important step is preparing to use the telephone. Preparation means doing all the necessary things in order for you to efficiently and confidently receive and make telephone calls:

▷ put a smile on your face—this will reflect in your voice when you are talking
▷ have paper and pen ready to record information
▷ have a list of in-house extensions by the phone. An example is shown in Table 4.3
▷ know where and how to direct each enquiry
▷ sit upright (it helps you breathe better)
▷ have a sound knowledge of STD and IDD operator connected calls, and directory assistance procedures.

In-house extensions—telephone extension numbers used within the venue.

Table 4.3 ▷ **Example of a telephone extension list**

Grand Central Hotel Telephone Extension List

POSITION	EXTENSION	PAGER NO
General Manager	100	
GM's personal assistant	110	
Front Office Manager	500	
	Mobile: 0418 555 555	1
Reception	550	
Reservations	555	
Porter's desk	560	
Food and Beverage Manager	650	
	Mobile: 0418 555 554	2
Oscar's Bar and Grill	300	
The Grand Cocktail Bar	350	
Executive Housekeeper	400	3
Laundry	450	
Chef's office	655	4
Kitchen	670	
Purchasing office	700	5
Banquet Sales	850	
Sales and Marketing	800	
	Mobile: 0418 555 553	
Maintenance	900	6

USING THE TELEPHONE

Once you have prepared to use the telephone, you can now actually use it. Again, there are a few techniques to be observed (apart from the procedures, which we will look at later).

Answer promptly

Simply because you can't see the caller doesn't mean that person should be treated less professionally than when a guest is standing in front of you. Don't let the phone ring on and on. *All* calls are important to the establishment. This may be the first opportunity to make a first good impression. And a first impression is lasting!

Most establishments maintain a three-ring policy. This means that all incoming calls should be answered by the third ring. Continuous ringing of a telephone is distracting to other work colleagues and can be annoying to a caller. If you have both an external and internal call ringing at the same time it is important to prioritise which to answer first. Many venues train their staff to answer external calls first. This is because external calls can usually be diverted more quickly and also because internal callers are already in the venue and have (hopefully received) many good impressions. However, calls should be answered in order of how they are received.

Using the telephone:
- answer within three rings
- speak distinctly
- speak into the mouthpiece
- concentrate
- follow procedures.

Speak distinctly

All of us have different sounding voices: some are deep with the sound of authority, while others are meek and frail. Some voices can sound pleasant or annoying, and still others are easy to decipher or can be unintelligible. The voice you project is determined by four factors:

1. **Energy:** This reflects your attitude and enthusiasm. If your voice appears to lack energy, this may be interpreted as lack of interest in what you are doing.
2. **Rate of speech:** Make sure it's not too fast, not too slow. The normal rate of speech is 125 words a minute and speaking any faster may create problems.
3. **Pitch:** Speaking in a monotone in a low or high pitch can create an undesirable effect. Vary your tone and inflection.
4. **Quality:** Using the above three techniques correctly will give a good quality of voice.

To produce a more desirable speaking voice there are a number of exercises that you can do:

▷ warm up your vocal cords by humming a song, as this will help to deepen the sound of your voice

▷ practise your pitch and control by recording a message onto an answering machine or voice mail, listen to the play back and critique yourself

▷ role-play with a friend and record the conversation. Review the recording for tone, and rate of speech.

The easiest way to produce a desirable voice is to 'put a smile into your voice'; it's easy to do and produces the best effect. Just remember to smile when you answer the telephone and your voice will naturally sound friendly to your caller.

APPLY YOUR KNOWLEDGE

Rate your voice using the following self-evaluation—1 is poor, 5 is good. Check those characteristics that apply to you, and then ask a friend or colleague to help evaluate your responses.

My Voice

Desirable traits		Undesirable traits	
Is pleasant sounding	_____	Nasally sounding	_____
Has pitch variations	_____	Sounds throaty	_____
Has normal rate	_____	Is raspy	_____
Varies in volume	_____	Sometimes squeaky	_____
Has distinct articulation	_____	Has a boring monotone	_____
Sounds like I am smiling	_____	Is too weak	_____
Has ample force	_____	Is too loud	_____
Stresses proper accents	_____	Has too many pauses	_____
Conveys a smile	_____	Does not convey a smile	_____

If you rated less than a 3 for any trait in the first column, or higher than a 3 for any traits in the second column, you should begin work on correcting them to achieve a balanced telephone voice.

Speak into the mouthpiece

The caller is best able to understand you if you speak directly into the mouthpiece. If your head is cocked at an angle, with the mouthpiece hovering somewhere under your chin, not only is your voice distorted, but also it is difficult for the caller to hear what you are saying. If you are wearing a head set, check that the microphone is pointed near your mouth and not facing away at an angle, as this will make your voice seem distant.

Concentrate

Don't be distracted! As you would with face-to-face contact, give your full attention to the caller. Stop anything else you may be doing and pay attention. Your caller knows when other things distract you.

Follow procedures

Every time you make or receive a telephone call you need to follow a procedure. Each procedure helps maintain a professional standard by ensuring consistency in the way telephone calls are managed. Procedures usually exist for:

▷ responding to incoming calls
▷ transferring calls
▷ placing calls on hold
▷ screening calls
▷ taking messages.

Responding to incoming telephone calls

As you know calls are received from external and internal sources. These are all incoming calls and there is a standard procedure for responding to these calls.

ACCEPTING EXTERNAL INCOMING TELEPHONE CALLS

Calls to the venue are for any number of reasons:

▷ guests wanting to make a reservation
▷ suppliers calling about orders
▷ potential guests enquiring about the venue's facilities
▷ people wanting to speak with guests
▷ people wanting to speak with staff.

These are all examples of external calls. The standard procedure for responding to incoming external calls is:

▷ greet the caller
▷ identify the establishment
▷ identify yourself
▷ offer assistance.

'Good morning/afternoon/evening, Taylor's Townhouse, this is Jim, how may I help you?'

The use of the standard greeting identifies your establishment so the guest knows they have called the right place. By identifying yourself, the caller is able to put a name to the voice they are speaking to for future reference and it personalises the call. By asking how you may help the caller, you are able to quickly establish the purpose of the call. When a telephonist receives the call, the caller will most likely be transferred to a department or a guest. The telephonist is unlikely to respond to requests for information. For this reason, it is important that whoever answers the telephone concentrates on what the caller is saying so that the caller can be transferred to the right person efficiently.

The other benefit of using a standard procedure when receiving incoming calls is that it provides consistency. Also, if you know the caller's name, use it, as it makes the caller feel important and that you are paying attention to them.

Example 1
'Good morning, Taylor's Townhouse, this is Samantha, how may I help you?'
'It's Mrs Jones calling, I'd like to speak to my husband Mr Mitchell Jones in Room 312, please.'
'Certainly, Mrs Jones, transferring you now.'

When connecting calls to guest extensions ensure the caller knows the guest's name. Don't connect a call when the caller only gives a room number, without first asking for and receiving the guest's full name. You must ensure that the caller has requested the correct extension. This minimises the likelihood of disrupting the wrong guest, and maximises the likelihood of transferring the caller to the right guest.

Example 2
'Good evening, Calamity House Hotel, this is Sean, how may I help you?'
'Room 602, please.'
'Sir, may I have the guest's name please?'
'Ms Dwyer.'
'Thank you sir, I'm connecting you now.'

You will remember earlier we talked about preparing to use the phone and said that it is important to have available a list of in-house extensions next to the phone. This list can be maintained manually (for example, handwritten or typed) and regularly updated as required or maintained on the computer and be readily accessible to the telephonist. However it is maintained, it is important to be able to quickly locate the required extension number you need, know who can answer which type of enquiry at all times, and transfer calls to the right person the first time.

Example 1
'Good afternoon, The Crescent Hotel, this is Nicholas, how may I help you?'
'Can you give me some information about your rates please?'
'I'll transfer you to reservations, who will be able to help you.'

Example 2
'Good morning, Sanctuary Lodge, this is Frank, how may I help you?'
'Yes, Frank, my name is Suzanne, I'd like to talk to someone about my wedding reception, please.'
'Suzanne, I'll transfer you to Judy in our banqueting department who will be able to help you.'
'Thanks Frank.'

ACCEPTING INTERNAL INCOMING TELEPHONE CALLS

Calls from within the venue, from guests and colleagues, are also answered following a standard procedure. The call may be an external call transfer, such as when someone calls requesting accommodation, an in-house guest requesting a service, such as arranging to have their luggage collected, or a colleague requesting information or passing on information. Internal calls should also be answered within three rings.

When receiving internal calls:

1. greet the caller
2. identify the department
3. identify yourself
4. offer assistance.

'Good afternoon, reservations, this is Robyn, how may I help you.'

Again, it is important to be consistent in following the established procedure:

Example 1
'Good morning, reservations, this is Robyn, how may I help you?'
'Good morning, this is Mr Jones, can you tell me if you have availability for two nights from the 13th of October?'

Example 2
'Good evening, reception, this is Brendan, how may I help you?'
'Brendan, this is Margaret White in room 602, could I have my car brought around please?'

Example 3
'Good afternoon, housekeeping, this is Pam, how may I help you?'
'Hi Pam, this is Trisha in reception, can you tell me how long until rooms 602 and 603 are ready?'

TRANSFERRING CALLS

As you've seen, most external incoming calls and some internal calls are transferred—to another department, a guest or a colleague. The physical execution of this task will depend on the telephone system used in your workplace. What is important about transferring calls is that it is done following established procedure. This ensures the caller speaks to the person they asked for without delay and is not inadvertently disconnected.

Before transferring a call, let the caller know what you are doing.

Before transferring a call, let the caller know what you are doing. If the caller suddenly finds they are on hold, or transferred without knowing that this is what has happened, they may feel confused and disappointed with the service standard.

Example 1
'Good morning, Holiday Inn, this is Vincent, how may I help you?'
'I'd like to make a reservation please.'
'Certainly Madam, I'm transferring you to reservations now.'

PLACING A CALL ON HOLD

A call may be placed on hold for a number of reasons—either the extension requested is busy or you're busy, for example. Before placing a call on hold first *ask* the caller's permission. Where possible, give an explanation for having to place the caller on hold.

Example 1
'Good afternoon, the Park Hyatt, this is Soo Lin, how may I help you?'
'Could you put me through to Eliza in banquets please?'
'Unfortunately her extension is busy, would you mind holding?'

The guest will usually tell you if this is OK or not. If the guest replies that they don't want to hold:

▷ ask if there is anyone else they would like to speak with
▷ offer to connect them to someone else in the department
▷ ask if you can take a message for them.

If the guest replies that they don't mind holding:

▷ place the call on hold
▷ get back to the caller within 30 seconds and provide an update on the status of their call.
For example:
'The line is still busy, do you want to continue holding?' or 'The line is still busy, would you like me to take a message for you?'
Allow the caller to choose and wait for a response.

Example 2
'Good morning, Seaside Motor Inn, this is Jenny, would you mind holding please?'

In this instance, the caller hasn't even had a chance to say what they want, so it is very important that you give them the opportunity to accept or decline to be put on hold. In other words, wait for the reply, don't automatically put the caller on hold. So 'Good morning, Seaside Motor Inn, this is Jenny, would you mind holding please?'
'Certainly.'
or
'Good morning, Seaside Motor Inn, this is Jenny, would you mind holding please?'
'Actually, I'm in a hurry, I need to speak with the chef.'

If this happens put the caller through to the person they have asked for, if this is possible. Remember that it will only take a few seconds and will keep the caller satisfied.

Attending to phones calls on hold

Calls on hold should be monitored at short intervals, usually every 30 seconds, to ensure the caller wishes to continue waiting. Most switchboards have a facility that reverts the call automatically back to the telephonist if the call has been on hold for 30 seconds. By monitoring the call, the caller is reassured that they have not been forgotten.

Always thank the caller for holding. If the caller does not wish to continue holding, offer to take a message or have someone return the call.

Example 1
'Thank you for holding Mrs Gardner. Ian's line is still busy. Would you like to continue holding or can I take a message for you?'

When the line becomes available and you are able to connect the caller, thank the caller for waiting, tell them you are now transferring them and give the name of the person and the department to whom you are connecting the call. For example:
'Thank you for waiting, I'm putting you through to Eliza in banquets now.'

SCREENING CALLS

Due to the nature of the industry that we work in, it is necessary to screen some calls. Screening calls means that you ask the caller who they are and sometimes why they are calling before the call is transferred.

Example 1
'May I ask who is calling, please?'
'My name is Fred Palmer.'

By asking what the call is about, you are able to determine if the correct person is being asked for and if it is appropriate to put a call through.

Example 2
'Mr Palmer, may I ask what the call is about?'
'Yes. I'm from Micros Fidelio and I'm calling about the installation of your computer system.'
'Thanks Mr Palmer, I'll transfer you to Julie-Anne, the front office manager now.'

Once you know the caller's name (and possibly the reason for the call), and you know that the call can be transferred to the requested person, then transfer the call. Often, you may need to announce the caller first. Ask the caller if they mind being placed on hold and let the other person know who is calling and why. This person may then choose to accept the call or ask you to transfer it to someone else or even to take a message. If the person accepts the call, the caller is then transferred following the usual procedure.

Example 3
'Julie-Anne, I have Mr Palmer from Micros Fidelio on the line, shall I transfer him?'
'Yes. Thanks Tim.'

Alternatively, you may already know that the person being called is not accepting calls or only accepting calls from certain individuals. In this case, by asking the caller's name you can determine whether or not to transfer the call at all. Offer to take a message or ask if there is anyone else the caller would like to speak with.

Example 4

'Good afternoon, Shamrock Inn, this is Kerry, how may I help you?'

'Good afternoon Kerry, may I speak with the general manager please?'

'Certainly, may I ask who is calling?'

'My name is Andrea O'Hare.'

'Ms O'Hare, may I ask what the call is about?'

'Yes. I work for Hospitality Kitchen Components and I would like to discuss with the general manager a great new product we have available.'

'Ms O'Hare, would you mind holding?'

'Certainly.'

'Mrs Kilpatrick, this is Kerry, I have a Ms O'Hare on the line from Hospitality Kitchen Components wanting to speak to you about a new product.'

'Kerry, it sounds like she should be speaking with the chef. Can you transfer her to the kitchen?'

'Certainly Mrs Kilpatrick.'

'Ms O'Hare, Mrs Kilpatrick has asked me to transfer you to Greg Cornish, our chef. I'll transfer you now. Thank you.'

APPLY YOUR KNOWLEDGE

For the following situations how should the telephonist respond?

▷ *Screening a call* _____

▷ *Obtaining a caller's name* _____

▷ *Determining the nature of the call* _____

▷ *Standard greeting and identification* _____

▷ *Transferring a call* _____

▷ *Placing a call on hold* _____

TAKING A MESSAGE

When you take a message from a caller, be prepared: have a message pad and a pen available to record the caller's message, then:

▷ listen to the caller and write the message down, including:
   − time
   − date
   − caller's name and contact details
   − the guest's name and room number, or staff member's name and department
   − the actual message
   − your initials
▷ once the message is complete read the message back to the caller to confirm the details
▷ enter the message into the computer or write it down on a duplicate message pad
▷ have the message delivered promptly to the guest or staff member following the venue's procedures.

Example 1

'Good afternoon, The Herringbone Guest House, this is Melissa, how may I help you?'

'Hi Melissa, this is Mrs Andrews, I would like to speak with my husband, Phil Andrews in room 12, please.'

'Mrs Andrews, Mr Andrews is not in his room at the moment, would you like me to take a message?'

'Yes please. Could you tell him that I called and will meet him at the restaurant at 7 pm tonight.'

'Mrs Andrews, if I can just confirm the message, you will meet him at the restaurant at 7 pm tonight? Is this correct?'

'Yes.'

'Mrs Andrews, does he know which restaurant you mean?'

'Yes, it's your restaurant!'

'Thanks Mrs Andrews. I'll pass that on to him.'

'Thank you.'

'Goodbye.'

Figure 4.2 shows an example of a standard telephone pre-printed message pad. From the above example, write in the details of Mrs Andrews' message.

STD AND IDD ASSISTED CALLS

Most establishments provide a telephone system that allows the guest to dial direct national long distance calls (STD) and international calls (IDD) from their room. These calls are timed and charged according to the distance, time of day and day of the week. The cost of the call is greater than when made from a private telephone. The reason for this is the cost to the venue of maintaining its telephone system.

However, you may be required to place national and international calls for guests. These are referred to as **operator assisted calls**. There are several reasons why the guest may require an operator assisted call: the guest is unfamiliar with your telephone system, or is unsure how to place the call themselves, or wants to place a reverse-charge call, or wants to

Figure 4.2 ▷ **Telephone message pad**

Messages	
To: _____	
From: _____	
Message:	Date: _____
	Time: _____
	Tel.: _____
	☐ Telephoned
	☐ Will ring back
	☐ Please ring
	☐ Called in
	☐ Will call back

place a long distance person-to-person call. When guests require this service it is important for you to know how to quickly connect them to the telephone number they have requested.

You will need to find out:

▷ the name of the person or business to be called
▷ the telephone number to call (or you may need to find this out on behalf of the guest), and
▷ country and area code where applicable.

When you have this information, dial the number for the guest and then connect the caller. There are two ways this can be done (and this depends on the system in place):

1. keep the guest on hold while you dial the number then connect the guest; or
2. dial the requested number and when the connection is made call the guest and connect them to the call.

SKILLS FOCUS

There are a number of techniques you need to develop to effectively use the telephone—prepare yourself, speak distinctly, speak into the mouthpiece, don't be distracted and follow procedures.

Responding to incoming calls requires an ability to correctly use the venue's telephone system and follow standard procedures. Although similar, there are different procedures for receiving external and internal calls. Many calls received need to be transferred (to another department or a guest) or placed on hold. Calls placed on hold should be attended to at least every 30 seconds. If a call cannot be transferred to the requested extension, take a message. When taking messages, accurately record the details and promptly pass the message on.

Screening a call determines who the caller is and what the call is about before transferring it to the requested extension.

FOCUS REVIEW

▷ *The first telephone technique is preparing to use the telephone. What is involved in this technique?*
▷ *The next technique relates to how you use the telephone. What five things should you remember when using the telephone?*
▷ *What factors influence voice projection? Why is this important when using the telephone?*
▷ *Incoming calls are calls received by an extension from either external or internal sources. Explain how you would respond to calls from external sources and internal sources.*
▷ *What is the standard procedure for receiving calls?*
▷ *When connecting calls to guest extensions, why should you ask the caller for the guest's name as well as the room number?*
▷ *How might a caller feel if he or she is placed on hold without being told?*
▷ *Why might you need to place a call on hold?*
▷ *What should you do if the caller does not wish to be placed on hold?*
▷ *What information should you record when taking a message?*
▷ *What does 'screening calls' mean?*
▷ *Why might you need to screen a call?*
▷ *What is an operator assisted call? When might it be requested?*

Selling techniques on the telephone

As you learned in Chapter 2, the opportunity to promote the services and facilities in the workplace is taken when appropriate. It is part of your role no matter what area of accommodation services you work in. There are several techniques available to help you promote the venue. Most of the discussion focused on promoting the venue in face-to-face situations or using marketing tools such as brochures and advertising. However, many of these techniques used can be applied on the telephone.

Many of the people who call may not be familiar with the services available at most venues. It is an important opportunity, therefore, for you to promote your workplace to callers. It is also providing a service. There are several ways in which your venue can be promoted on the telephone. Most of these opportunities will arise when a potential guest calls enquiring about rates and room availability at the establishment.

The product knowledge you have can be used to suggest a choice for the guest: 'If you need a peaceful night's sleep may I suggest our courtyard rooms, which are away from the road' or 'You may prefer our deluxe double rooms which have an ocean view and spa in the room?' Describe the benefits and features (suggestive selling) of the establishment or the room and sell it to the guest: 'May I suggest an interconnecting room which would be perfect for a family.' Give more information about the room, packages or facilities to make it sound attractive: 'Our standard room rate is $140.00 per night. However we have a package for $160.00 which includes a fully cooked breakfast for two people.'

Upsell the room where possible by using the above three methods to upgrade the product sold in size, quality or price. For example, you could persuade the guest to extend their stay or suggest a suite at a higher price instead of a normal room: 'For only $45.00 more I can offer you one of our spa suites and the room has a lovely view of the ocean.'

You could also cross-sell by suggesting an additional product or service, which can be added to the original request, made by the caller. For example, offering to make a dinner reservation for the guest in addition to their accommodation booking. 'Mrs Sangster, as it's your wedding anniversary, would you like me to make a reservation in our restaurant for dinner on the Saturday night?'

To be able to effectively promote your venue over the telephone, you need to know and understand the venue's rates, packages, room types and venue features, so that you can confidently answer any of the caller's queries. Every telephone interaction is a moment of truth and your guests expect you to be able to provide information about things they have not even thought of yet!

SKILLS FOCUS

Telephone interactions provide many opportunities to promote the venue and its services. You can use a number of techniques to help you: upselling, suggestive selling and cross-selling are just a few using your broad product knowledge. To be successful when promoting your venue on the telephone, you need to know and understand the venue's rates, packages, room types and venue features.

FOCUS REVIEW

▷ What selling techniques can be used to promote your venue's products and services to callers?

▷ Why do you think it is important to recognise and take promotional opportunities?

▷ How is this helping the guest?

Carrying out emergency procedures

As the operator of the communication system the telephonist plays a vital role in any emergency. In most emergency situations, the telephonist is the first person to be called (either by a guest or colleague). However, almost any staff member may be in a situation where they need to respond to an emergency call.

The telephonist is responsible for calling emergency services—the fire brigade, ambulance and police—so these numbers must be displayed clearly near the switchboard.

Each establishment will develop its own system for managing emergency situations. In general terms, the following procedures are observed.

FIRE

If you receive a call telling you there is fire in the establishment:

▷ ask the caller the exact location of the fire

▷ ask the nature of the fire (what is burning?)

▷ ask the caller for their name (and department if a staff member) and location

▷ ask the caller what action, if any, they have taken.

When you have this information, *you* can then take action. For example, you may determine that the fire is under control or can be managed by staff or you may need to call the fire department. In all circumstances contact your supervisor.

In the event you need to call the fire brigade:

▷ give the exact location and name of the establishment

▷ explain the nature of the fire

▷ describe the location of the fire within the venue.

The fire department will usually tell you what to do. For example, they may ask if you have commenced evacuation and recommend that you do this if you have not done so already. Other action you may need to take includes:

▷ sound the fire alarm (if general evacuation is required and the alarm has not already been sounded)

▷ remain at the switchboard to convey instructions to all staff

▷ set in motion guest evacuation procedure

▷ seek assistance with evacuation from other members in the front office (advise guests of assembly area)

▷ make a general announcement over the public address system (that there is a fire in the building and guests should evacuate)

▷ receive calls from guests who are unsure what to do (and advise of evacuation procedures or reassure guests that assistance will be sent to their room)
▷ keep a list of all calls from guests
▷ keep other departments informed
▷ stay at the switchboard until:
  − fire alarm is declared false, or
  − advised to leave by manager or emergency services personnel, or
  − life is in danger.

BOMB THREAT

If you happen to be working on the switchboard when a bomb threat is received:

▷ keep calm
▷ don't hang up (even when or if the caller hangs up)
▷ take the call seriously (do not laugh or treat the call as a joke)
▷ try and question the caller:
  − where is the bomb?
  − when will the bomb go off?
  − how many bombs are there?
  − what type of bomb is it?
  − what is your name?
  − what is your location?
▷ record wording of the threat and any questions answered
▷ report call to management
▷ report the call to the police
▷ record the details of the call and caller, that is, identify any features, language, expressions, background noises, age if possible, sex of caller, date, time and duration of call.

While most bomb threats are pranks, it is necessary to take them seriously and put into effect both a search and potential evacuation of the building. Never laugh at the caller or call the person by offensive names.

ILLNESS OR ACCIDENT

When illness or an accident resulting in injury occurs, your role in receiving the call is to convey information and get assistance. You should:

▷ remain calm
▷ ascertain from the caller the nature of problem (illness or accident) and determine what action needs to be taken
▷ take caller's name and room number (or department)
▷ contact management and advise them of the situation
▷ contact ambulance, doctor or other service as required. You will need to advise them of the nature of the problem so will need quite specific details
▷ advise the guest (or other person taking charge) what action has been taken (for example, ambulance is on the way, the manager is on his way to see them, or an appointment has been made at the nearest doctor or hospital).

Whatever the nature of the emergency, all establishments need to practise emergency procedure drills on a regular basis. This helps to ensure staff are able to cope with a real situation.

These drills need to cover all emergency situations and no warning should be given to enable staff to put the procedures into practice, as one day they may save a life, possibly their own!

Guests and staff members' welfare is the main priority in a hospitality establishment. It should be part of your service ethic and attitude to your job to ensure that everything you do helps contribute to this. Your guests' and colleagues' welfare is the first priority in any emergency and your main aim is to assist and provide help in whatever way you can.

SKILLS FOCUS

The telephonist plays an important role in any emergency situation because it is often this person who is first called about the emergency. However, almost any staff member may be in a situation where they need to respond to an emergency call and must therefore have the skill and knowledge to deal with the situation. Whoever receives the emergency call is responsible for calling the appropriate emergency services department—fire brigade, ambulance or police.

Before calling emergency services, there are a number of details the telephonist should determine, especially specific details about the nature and location of the emergency.

Each establishment will develop its own strategy for managing emergency calls. Examples of emergency calls include a fire, bomb threat and illness or injury.

FOCUS REVIEW

▷ *What is the telephonist usually responsible for in the event of an emergency?*
▷ *What information do you need to get from a caller reporting a fire?*
▷ *How should you respond if you receive a bomb threat?*
▷ *What is your role when you receive a call about illness or an accident? What information do you need from the caller?*
▷ *What is the main priority of the establishment in the event of an emergency?*

Making telephone calls

While most of a telephonist's day is concerned with receiving calls, there will be frequent occasions when the telephonist makes calls. Having the ability to make an outgoing call is just as important as being able to accept an incoming call. The same rules as for accepting an incoming call apply—courtesy, preparation, concentrating, speaking clearly—when making calls because what you say is a reflection on your ability and the establishment's service standards. Calls are made to both external lines and internal extensions. When making a call, follow these guidelines:

▷ be familiar with the equipment you are using and follow the correct procedures at all times
▷ be prepared—have all the information you require to speak to the person you called
▷ have pen and paper available to record any information
▷ be pleasant and professional at all times
▷ concentrate on what the other person is saying
▷ avoid talking with others, eating, or anything else that may take your concentration away from your call.

MAKE THE CALL

Now that you are prepared to make the call, dial the required number, and when the call is answered:

▷ offer a salutation
▷ say who you are and where you are from
▷ ask to speak with the person you are calling
▷ when that person receives the call, clearly state the reason why you are calling.

Example 1

Calling a guest to confirm their reservation details:

'Good morning, my name is Frances and I'm from the Bayside Hotel, could I speak to Mrs Blake please.'

When Mrs Blake is on the line:

'Mrs Blake, this is Frances from the Bayside Hotel and I'm calling to confirm your reservation details for this weekend.'

Whether you are making a call to confirm a booking or making an enquiry, or even returning a call, it is usually appropriate to do so during normal working hours for external calls. When returning calls, do so in a timely manner. Don't make the caller wait anxiously to hear from you or make them call again because they have had to wait a long time for your call.

When calling another department within the venue you also need to be prepared and follow the accepted procedure. Calls to internal extensions can be made at any time appropriate to the situation.

Example 2

Reception calling housekeeping:

'Hi Bryony, this Gino at reception. Could you please arrange for a rollaway bed to be set up in room 2040 before 4 pm?'

APPLY YOUR KNOWLEDGE

Choose two large international hotels in the CBD (preferably of the same star rating). Call each hotel, and follow this suggested conversation:

▷ *As soon as the phone is answered—before it can be transferred—ask 'Do you have a room available for the night of . . .?'*
▷ *As soon as the call is transferred, advise the person you are speaking to that you are getting married and would like to book a room for the honeymoon night. Let the staff suggest a room type and try to sell it to you.*
▷ *Ask about dinner—what time? Prices?*
▷ *Ask about parking—is there a charge?*
▷ *Ask for directions to the hotel.*
▷ *Ask for brochures and tariff information to be sent to you while you are speaking to staff.*

Make notes about the following (you can record your observations on the form provided in Table 4.4):

a) The length of time taken to answer your call.

b) When the telephone was answered, was a standard procedure used?

c) How long it took to have the call transferred to the relevant department.

d) Were you placed on hold? Were you asked before this happened?

e) Whether the call is transferred without any problems.

f) The attitude of the staff, and their product knowledge.

g) After the call take a note of how long it takes for brochures to arrive.

Do not tell the hotel you are calling that this is a project for your studies. The call needs to appear to be as realistic as possible to get the information and telephone technique from the establishment you are dealing with. When you have called both venues, compare each and determine which venue is more likely to receive your custom if indeed you were planning to stay there.

Role-play practice is a good way to ensure that you are confident, and you are able to get the information from the establishment.

Table 4.4 ▷ **Hotel inquiry observation sheet**

HOTEL 1	HOTEL 2
Dinner:	Dinner:
Parking and directions:	Parking and directions:
Brochure and tariff information:	Brochure and tariff information:
Time taken to answer call:	Time taken to answer call:
Incoming call standard procedure:	Incoming call standard procedure:
Call transfer:	Call transfer:
Transfer problems:	Transfer problems:
Staff attitude—product knowledge:	Staff attitude—product knowledge:
Notes:	Notes:

Expressions to avoid

We finish this chapter with a few expressions to *avoid* on the telephone (they are useful also to avoid when dealing with guests face-to-face!) whether making or receiving calls. Why should you avoid these expressions? Because for most of your guests, use of these expressions does not reflect professionalism, they may be too casual (guests expect a certain level of formality) or they may not be understood (particularly for international guests). Next to each expression to avoid, write an appropriate alternative expression. Compare your alternatives with your colleagues and discuss the appropriateness of each.

▷ Yeah!

▷ G'day!

▷ He's out!

▷ What's your name?

▷ What did you say your name was?

▷ Can you speak up?
▷ What?
▷ Hang on!
▷ Transferring you.
▷ You wanna leave a message?
▷ What do you want?
▷ Thanks mate!
▷ Hang on a minnie!

SKILLS FOCUS

Telephone calls are made to both external lines and internal extensions. Before making any calls you need to be familiar with the equipment you are using and the procedure to follow. You need to prepare yourself for the call by first obtaining the phone number you are going to call, knowing the person's name and having all the information you need at hand.

Whether making or receiving calls, there are a number of expressions to avoid. The reason you should avoid these is because they do not reflect professionalism and may be too casual or even misunderstood by the guest.

FOCUS REVIEW

▷ *What are the rules to observe for making calls?*
▷ *How should you prepare for the calls you are making?*
▷ *What is the procedure for making a telephone call?*
▷ *What is the usual accepted time for making external calls?*

PUT YOUR KNOWLEDGE TO THE TEST

Robyn has moved into the telephonist area for her formal training and understands that she must demonstrate a high level of service, and be a competent and confident telephonist before moving onto the next stage of her traineeship. During her induction and training, Robyn was made aware of the role of a telephonist. She is to be trained for six days on the switchboard with another telephonist before being able to run a shift solo. When the day arrives for Robyn to work alone, she feels a little nervous. What if it gets busy? What if she transfers someone to the wrong extension?

As she sits down at the switchboard and attaches her headset, the phone rings. 'Er, good morning, this is Robyn, can I help you?' Before the guest has time to respond, the phone rings again. 'Ah, do you mind holding?' Again, before the guest has a chance to respond, she places the first call on hold. 'Good morning, Grand Central Hotel, this is Robyn.'

Robyn deals with both the calls in turn and successfully transfers them. She knows that these two calls didn't run exactly according to procedure so she pulls out her procedure book and reads through her notes.

The phone rings again and this caller wants some information about the venue's rates.

Robyn knows the reservations line is busy and besides, she knows her rates well and proceeds to help the guest with her inquiry. At the end of the call the guest wants to make a booking.

1. What did Robyn do well?

2. What did Robyn do wrong?

3. What are the standard procedures Robyn should use for answering a call? Placing a call on hold?

4. As a telephonist Robyn is expected to be able to know and sell the product. How will she do this?

5. Can you see any problems arising from Robyn dealing with room inquiries while working as the telephonist. Give examples. What should she do instead?

Receiving and Processing Reservations

LEARNING OUTCOMES

On completion of this chapter you will be able to:

▷ describe the roles and responsibilities of the reservations department;

▷ explain what rates are charged for a variety of room types and identify the factors that influence their determination;

▷ accurately process and maintain reservation requests;

▷ communicate reservation details to appropriate departments and colleagues.

Introduction

Why do people stay in accommodation venues? If we asked 20 different people why they were staying in a hotel or any other commercial hospitality establishment, we'd probably get 20 different answers. Not surprisingly, the most common reasons for staying in accommodation venues are for pleasure or for business. This would certainly simplify marketing the venue because guests would potentially represent only two target markets: pleasure and business.

However, within these two categories lie several other characteristics that further separate and distinguish each target market, and this makes marketing accommodation venues more complicated. For example, your guests could be enjoying a romantic weekend getaway, having a holiday, or could be in town to visit friends or family. All of these reasons for staying at your venue are pleasure-related. Your guests could be negotiating a business deal, attending a conference or just passing through. All of these reasons may be business-related. And each of these reasons represents a distinct target market, as you learned in Chapter 2.

Whatever the reason for their stay, most people who stay in accommodation venues first make a reservation. Being able to readily identify your target market assists in the reservation process. And being able to manage the reservation process efficiently is important for the on-going well-being of the venue and the guest's satisfaction with the experience.

Throughout this chapter we provide you with the skills and knowledge required to assist you in managing and maintaining reservations for a range of target markets.

The roles and responsibilities of the reservations department

The reservations department is an important part of the accommodation services team. It is where the guest's first impression of the venue is often formed and it is the first stage of the cycle of service—pre-arrival.

The role of the reservations department is to:

▷ manage and maintain guest room reservations
▷ maximise room yield
▷ sell rooms
▷ control travel agent commissions
▷ prepare sales forecasts
▷ plan promotional activities
▷ generate room occupancy related reports.

How the reservations department meets its responsibilities depends on how the department is structured. The reservations department may comprise a single person handling and processing all the bookings, or a number of staff headed by a reservations manager overseeing several reservations clerks. In large venues with many reservations clerks, each may be responsible for a specific type of reservation, for example individual bookings, inbound tourist groups, conference groups, leisure packages, travel agent bookings and corporate guests.

The reservations department in large venues usually operates between 7.30 am and 7.00 pm Monday to Friday. It may even be staffed on Saturdays. In smaller venues, the reservations department is more likely to operate between 8.00 am and 5.00 pm Monday to Friday only. Outside these hours it is usually the responsibility of reception staff to manage all reservations enquiries.

MANAGING AND MAINTAINING RESERVATIONS

The reservations department's primary role is to manage reservation enquiries and book guest rooms. When a potential guest or travel agent contacts the venue enquiring about room availability, the reservations clerk is responsible for handling these enquiries, and promoting the venue, which encourages the caller to make a reservation. The reservations clerk then records the details of the reservation.

Once the reservation has been made, the reservations clerk is responsible for maintaining the reservation. This means that confirmation of the reservation is processed and any subsequent changes to the original reservation are recorded. How reservations are managed and maintained is discussed in detail later in this chapter.

MAXIMISING ROOM YIELD

For the reservations department, **yield management** is a technique used to maximise the number of rooms sold, on a specific day, at the highest possible rate. Thus, the purpose of yield management is to obtain the maximum amount of revenue for the most number of rooms. This potentially means the difference between taking a one night booking at a high rate over a three night booking at a lower rate. The reservations clerk must decide which booking will contribute to the highest yield (revenue).

Yield management is not a tool used exclusively by accommodation venues; many other industries also practise yield management. For example, airlines maximise their flight capacity by offering advance booking rates and requiring a Saturday night stay-over to some destinations. Once a certain number of seats have been sold, the remaining seats are sold at a higher fare. Some cinemas offer half price tickets on a Tuesday to fill seats on a night that is normally quiet. Some hairdressers offer senior citizens a discount on, for example, a Wednesday, as this is not generally a popular day for other clients.

Room yield management—the technique used in an attempt to sell the maximum number of rooms possible on a given day, at the highest possible rate.

How to use yield management is demonstrated in the occupancy graph in Figure 5.1. From the chart it is easy to see that 7 October and 8 October are quiet days. To maximise yield, a venue may require all additional bookings taken for the 7th to include a stay on the 8th to boost occupancy.

SELLING ROOMS

Accommodation venues make the largest percentage of their revenue by selling rooms. And by *selling* rooms, rather than simply taking bookings for rooms, reservations are assisting the other departments in the venue because many guests use the facilities and services offered by the other departments (such as the bar, laundry, restaurant and room service).

Many people call to make enquiries about the venue's rooms and other facilities but not all these enquiries become bookings. To convert an enquiry into a booking, reservations must successfully promote the venue's products and services. There are a number of techniques that can be used to promote the venue—personal selling, upselling, down selling—and these were discussed in Chapter 2. In that chapter you learned also that the various sectors of the hospitality industry attempt to attract their various targeted markets through the way in which the venue packages and promotes its goods and services. Guests will only know the full

Figure 5.1 ▷ **Occupancy graph**

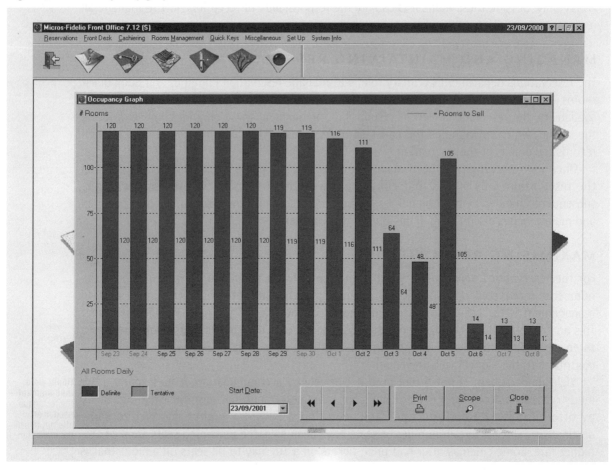

extent to which a venue can meet their needs and wants if the reservations clerk informs them of what is available.

Just as importantly, an understanding of your various target markets will help you decide which promotional techniques to use, and which goods and services to promote to which guests. So during the reservation process, it is important for you to determine the reason for the guest's stay (business, pleasure) so that the potential guest is advised of all the features of the rooms, room types available and room features, and facilities offered by the venue as they relate to the guest's reason for staying. For example, a couple booking a romantic weekend may appreciate being offered a reservation in the fine dining restaurant or may want champagne in their room on arrival and a late check-out (examples of cross-selling). On the other hand, a business person travelling alone is probably not interested in a package that includes theatre tickets but may want e-mail access in the room, business centre facilities and express check-out.

To find out the reason for the guest's visit, you can ask the caller during the reservation process. Most of the time your callers will tell you the reason for their stay and this will help you to help them. For example, a woman calls and explains she's in town on business next week and looking for a place to stay close to the Exhibition Centre. A man calls explaining he is looking for a weekend break for himself and his partner.

To be able to promote room features and the venue's facilities, you need to be familiar with all the products and services available in your venue and the layout and features of each room. It is often these features that attract particular market segments to specific room types. Table 5.1 lists some of the features that may be available in different room types that may attract your different market segments.

In addition to product knowledge and an understanding of your venue's target markets, the other important things for you to know about the rooms in the venue in which you work are:

▷ location of each room type on each floor
▷ number of smoking and non-smoking rooms
▷ number of disabled rooms (and facilities in these rooms)
▷ number of persons who can be accommodated in each room
▷ any other facilities provided in the room
▷ bedding materials (doona, blankets, feather pillows).

A final word on selling rooms—it is essential that you are honest and accurate in describing the features of each room type. You will remember from Chapter 2 that there are strict laws that regulate how accommodation venues can market their products. Promoting your venue to potential guests through the reservations process is a form of marketing. You are representing the venue and are therefore responsible for the information you communicate.

CONTROLLING TRAVEL AGENT COMMISSIONS

When travel agents make accommodation reservations on behalf of their clients, they receive a percentage of the room rate as a commission from the venue. A commission is an amount of money received as payment for making the booking. It is usually 10 per cent.

The travel agent's client, who becomes the venue's guest, does not pay extra for the room by booking the room through a travel agent. Indeed, travel agents who book many rooms with a particular venue or chain of venues are often in a position to negotiate better rates for their

Travel commissions—an amount of money, usually 10 per cent, received as payment for making the booking.

Table 5.1 ▷ **Examples of room features**

DOUBLE ROOM	DELUXE DOUBLE	JUNIOR SUITE	EXECUTIVE SUITE
Double bed	Queen size bed	Queen size bed	King size bed
Bath/shower	Bath/spa	Double spa	Double spa
Opening windows	Ocean views	Lounge room	Internet access
In-room video access	Balcony	Ocean/city view	Ocean view
Smoking/non-smoking	In-room video access	Balcony	Balcony
Air conditioning	Sofa bed	Kitchenette	Dining table and lounge room
Direct dial telephone	Direct dial telephone	Direct dial telephone	Direct dial telephone
In-room safe	Opening windows	Interconnecting room	Complimentary in-room video
View/balcony	Interconnecting rooms	Balcony	Computer modem
	Air conditioning	Air conditioning	Air conditioning
	In-room safe	In-room safe	In-room safe
			Television in bathroom
			Complimentary parking
			Facsimile machine
			Stereo system

clients. The commission is deducted from the normal room rate and it is the venue that pays the travel agent. After all, would the venue have this booking were it not for the travel agent recommending it?

Commissions are processed by reservations in one of two ways. First, if the guest pays for the room in advance, directly to the travel agent, the travel agent forwards payment to the venue, minus the commission. The travel agent issues the guest a voucher for the full amount paid (in other words, the voucher does not show the amount of commission the travel agent will receive), and the guest presents this voucher during the check-in process as their form of payment. For example, Mr Jenkins books one night's accommodation at the Bambra Hotel through his travel agency, Central Travel. The room is $250.00. Central Travel issues Mr Jenkins with an accommodation voucher to the value of $250.00 for the Bambra Hotel. Central Travel forwards a cheque to the Bambra Hotel to the value of $225.00—the cost of the room, minus their commission of $25.00.

Second, if a guest makes a reservation with their travel agent, but pays the venue directly, then the venue is responsible for paying the commission to the travel agent. Again, the guest pays the agreed amount, say $250.00, and the venue sends $25.00 to the travel agent.

When commissions are paid this way, the venue usually processes all travel agent commissions on a weekly or monthly basis. This helps the venue maintain better control over the accounting function. However, it is important for the venue to be consistent and prompt in making commission payments. If they are not, it is likely that the travel agent will reduce or even stop recommending the venue to their clients.

Quick payment of commissions is a good form of free marketing for the venue.

Impact of GST on commissions

Room rates are now inclusive of the Goods and Services Tax (GST), introduced nationally on 1 July 2000. The GST amount is usually 10 per cent and applies whether the guest books through a travel agent or directly with the venue. But the inclusion of the GST does not reduce the amount the travel agent receives as commission. For example, if the room rate was previously $250.00 and is now $275.00 (10 per cent of which is GST), the travel agent receives commission on the full amount; that is, for a room rate of $275.00, the travel agent's commission is $27.50 (10 per cent), not the rate before GST is included. The impact of GST on accommodation venues is discussed in greater detail in Chapter 8.

PREPARING SALES FORECASTS

Sales forecasts are estimates of the number of rooms the reservations department expects to sell on specific dates. The forecasts are based on:

▷ historical data (past occupancy levels)
▷ seasonal influences
▷ up coming special events (Grand Prix, international sporting events, visiting celebrities, AFL Grand Final)
▷ number of bookings at today's date (for the future dates)
▷ no-show estimates
▷ cancellation estimates
▷ economic climate.

The sales forecasts are then used to plan activities such as promotions, package deals, rate changes and staffing requirements. They are frequently prepared yearly or twice yearly for the coming six or twelve month period, or even longer, and are valuable because they assist the venue in measuring their overall success and that of their promotional activities. They also provide sales targets for the reservations department to achieve weekly.

Once a sales forecast is prepared, it is regularly reviewed and updated. It is also used to compare actual reservations (and revenues received) with what was forecasted. Each week, the reservations department reviews its progress in terms of how well the staff are meeting the sales target. The department can then plan and implement strategies for improving performance when needed. An example of a sales target and comparative actual results is shown in Table 5.2.

PLANNING PROMOTIONAL ACTIVITIES

The planning of promotional activities is usually undertaken in consultation with the sales and marketing department and management. Which promotional activities are undertaken will be influenced by the budget available (how much can be spent on the promotion), objectives of the activities (to increase occupancy, increase awareness of the venue, promote other departments in the venue etc), the sales forecast and resources required (such as the number of people involved and time commitment). Chapter 2 discusses types of promotional activities in detail.

Table 5.2 ▷ **Sales target**

Sales Targets—September

As at 23 September

	FORECAST	SOLD TO DATE	VARIANCE
No. of rooms	16,550	15,075	(1,475)
Average rate	$127.50	$126.45	($1.05)
Revenue	$2,110,125.00	$1,906,233.70	($204,891.30)

Goal to reach target 210 rooms per day!

SKILLS FOCUS

The reservations department is an important part of the accommodation services team as this is often where the guest's first impression of the venue is formed. The role of the reservations department is to manage reservations and maximise occupancy and revenue through yield management. Venues attempt to do this by selling the venue's products and services. To effectively sell the venue, you need an understanding of the target markets your venue attracts and you need to know the products and services available in the venue, and specific features of each room type. You must also be able to apply the principles of selling during the reservation process.

A reservations department may be managed by one person or several, and operates Monday to Friday, usually between 7.30 am and 7.00 pm in larger venues and between 8.00 am and 5.00 pm in smaller venues.

Travel agents earn commission on the rooms they book on behalf of their clients.

Commission is payment for these bookings and is usually 10 per cent. While the GST is now inclusive of room rates quoted, travel agent's commissions are based on the full amount of the room rate, not the rate less GST.

Preparing sales forecasts is an important role undertaken by reservations. It involves analysis of historical data, consideration of seasonal influences, no-show and cancellation estimates, up coming special events and other factors to estimate the total number of rooms the venue is likely to book. This information can then be used to plan promotional activities, set sales targets and compare actual results with forecasted results.

Promotional activities undertaken by the reservations department are usually in conjunction with the sales and marketing department and management according to the venue's objectives (increased occupancy, increased revenue, increased venue awareness).

FOCUS REVIEW

▷ What are the specific responsibilities of the reservations department?
▷ Explain in your own words what room yield management means.
▷ How does the knowledge of specific room features help the reservation process?
▷ How does an understanding of the venue's various target markets help you to sell rooms?
▷ In addition to product knowledge and an understanding of your various target markets, what else should you know about the venues in which you work?
▷ How do travel agents make money from booking rooms for their clients? Do you think they deserve this? Why or why not?
▷ How has the GST impacted travel agent's commissions?
▷ What value is there in forecasting sales? What factors are taken into consideration in forecasting sales?

The rates charged by venues

Each of the different target markets you learned about in Chapter 2 potentially pays different rates to stay in the same venue (and in the same room type). Why do venues do this? The answer to this question is simply that venues attempt to attract certain target markets by offering different rates, they want to reward frequent visitors for their loyalty, and because venues are attempting to maximise room yield.

Rack rate—a standard rate charged for a particular room type and determined by the cost structure of the venue and the venue's competition.

All venues first establish rack rates for their various room types. A **rack rate** is the standard rate charged for a particular room type. It is the maximum rate usually charged for any given room type and several factors influence its determination and subsequent adjustments to them.

Commonly, the rack rate is determined based on the cost structure of the establishment, that is, the cost to maintain the venue in terms of labour, operating expenses and maintenance among others. The rate is also influenced by competition, that is, what similarly structured venues in the same area are charging for their rooms. Although the rack rate is rarely charged, it is used for forecasting and budget determination.

The actual rate a guest may pay is rarely the rack rate. Many venues establish multiple rates to accommodate the various influences on the operation such as its:

▷ star rating
▷ location
▷ room types
▷ market segment
▷ room availability
▷ packages offered
▷ length of stay
▷ number of rooms booked
▷ meal plans.

STAR RATING

The venue's services and facilities and the quality of these services and facilities determine its star rating. The higher the star rating, the higher the rack rate and other rates are likely to be. For example, the rack rate for a double room in a five star city hotel may be $400.00 a night. A double room in a two star hotel in the same city may be $150.00 per night.

LOCATION

Not surprisingly, a city venue is likely to be more expensive than a country property or a suburban hotel. A four star resort next to the ocean in Surfers Paradise will be more expensive than a bed and breakfast venue five minutes drive from the beach. On the other hand, if there are very limited accommodation facilities in a particular location, this can increase the rate charged for a room. The location of the room itself in the venue may also influence the rate charged. For example, a room with a view may attract a higher rate than a room without a view (particularly if that view is in high demand).

ROOM TYPE

Many venues offer a range of room types, for example, double room, twin, suite, and family room, and this will influence the rate charged. The same rate is usually charged for a single and double room (whether one or two guests stay in the double room) but the rate increases for a triple share (an additional bed is likely to be required in the room). A suite, which is usually larger and more luxurious than a double room, is always more expensive.

Different room types are offered by most venues because of the different preferences of guests.

MARKET SEGMENT

Different market segments have different room requirements and may therefore be charged different rates for the same room type. For example, a government employee, with a very limited accommodation allowance, usually pays less than a corporate guest does (even though the corporate guest may stay more often). If a FIT is a walk in, then it is likely they will be charged the rack rate (although this depends on availability—if the venue has low occupancy, then a lower rate may be charged). Rooms booked for a group are usually charged a lower rate than a FIT would pay for the same room, because of the number of rooms required.

ROOM AVAILABILITY

The more in demand a venue is, the easier it is to maximise room yield and therefore charge rates closer to the rack rate. Seasonality can have a large influence on room availability and can play an important role in room rate determination. Seasonality refers to the time of year. For example, a beach resort will charge more during the summer months because room demand is high and room availability low. To attract business during the winter period, discounted rates are frequently offered, because rooms are in less demand and so the room availability is high.

Peak period—
time of high
occupancy.

Off peak—
time of low
occupancy.

Seasonality gives rise to **peak** and **off peak** periods. Peak periods are those times when room availability is low and off peak periods are those times when room availability is high.

So during times of low occupancy (off peak), rates are cheaper than when the establishment is experiencing high demand (peak). Even a FIT walk-in is likely to be offered a lower rate than the rack rate during off peak because the venue is trying to maximise revenue by selling the room. It is better to sell the room at a lower rate than to leave it empty and receive no revenue at all.

PACKAGES OFFERED

Many venues package their services and products to increase the volume of business at particular times of the year and to fill rooms during off peak periods. Each cost component of the package (room, breakfast, champagne on arrival and theatre tickets, for example) is not revealed to the guest; the guest is quoted one inclusive price. To capture a broader guest base, most venues offer a range of packages (at a range of prices).

Package rates and package inclusions vary, but can include any or all of the following:

▷ room
▷ food and beverages (for example, breakfast, dinner, champagne on arrival)
▷ picnic hamper
▷ car parking or limousine transfers
▷ flowers and chocolates
▷ theatre tickets or other event tickets
▷ late check-out/early check-in
▷ complimentary room upgrade
▷ free access to pool and gym.

LENGTH OF STAY

Some guests stay at an accommodation venue for several days, weeks or even months. An example of this is when a business person is transferred permanently interstate and, until suitable living arrangements are made in the new location, the business person stays at an accommodation venue.

Because of the length of stay, it is likely that the venue will negotiate a weekly or monthly rate rather than a nightly rate.

NUMBER OF ROOMS BOOKED

The room rate will be discounted if a large quantity of rooms is booked. For example, for groups or companies that book hundreds of room nights in one year, a lower room rate is offered than to guests, for example, who book only fifty room nights a year.

MEAL PLANS

Meal plans refer to the rate charged when a meal (or several) is offered with the room. There are three meal plans venues may offer: room and breakfast, half-board and full-board. Meal plans are most often arranged for groups, conference attendees and with package deals.

Meal plans refers to the meals that individual or group bookings may have booked as part of their room rate. A meal plan may include breakfast, half-board, or full-board.

Room and breakfast

As the name suggests, the room rate charged is inclusive of breakfast. The term 'bed and breakfast' is also frequently used. Venues are likely to offer this option to increase revenue. Even though the amount allocated as 'breakfast' in the package is less than might otherwise be realised if the guest ordered breakfast separately, if a room only rate is charged, there is no guarantee that the guest will actually buy breakfast at all.

Half-board

Half-board means that the rate includes the room, breakfast and one other meal (lunch or dinner). Again this is one way the venue is able to increase revenue. Instead of the guest going elsewhere to have dinner, they are likely to stay in the venue for this meal because they have already paid for it in the room rate.

Half-board— the rate includes the room, breakfast and one other meal.

Full-board

Full-board includes the room and three meals (breakfast, lunch and dinner). This revenue raising technique is frequently used by resorts where either external services are limited, or where the resort provides an inclusive holiday that encourages guests to remain on the premises at all times (thus the guest is not inclined to spend money elsewhere).

Full-board—the rate includes the room and three meals.

Impact of GST on room rates

As mentioned earlier, with the introduction of GST, room rates are now inclusive of a 10 per cent tax. While most guests are aware that the tax is included in the rate, the tax is not listed separately on the account presented to the guest (although the account is likely to say that the rate is GST inclusive and, if required, particularly by corporate guests, an account can be prepared that does show the GST component of the account).

Some venues have chosen not to add the GST to the already established rates, but will still be liable to pay the GST on the rooms sold. However, most venues have increased the room rates to reflect the 10 per cent GST. It is important to realise that accommodation venues are not now earning an additional 10 per cent. The GST portion of the room rate is payable to the Australian Taxation Office.

OTHER RATES

Several other rates are offered by many venues and a summary of the most common and a description of those rates are listed in Table 5.3.

What the rate includes

The rates listed in Table 5.3 include the charge for the room only, unless otherwise indicated. This is referred to as the **room only rate** (inclusive of GST). But this is misleading, as guests usually have free access to many of the facilities in the venue such as the gym and swimming pool. If meals or other items are included in the rate, then the rate becomes a package rate.

Table 5.3 ▷ **Common room rates**

RATE TYPE	DEFINITION
Rack rate	The regular rate for the room with no discounts, meals or other reductions.
Corporate rate	The standard rate charged for individuals travelling for business. This rate is usually available Monday to Thursday and may vary for different corporate guests (mainly because of the volume of business from individual companies).
Long stay rate	A discounted rate for leisure or corporate customers who are continuously staying in the hotel. This is usually for a minimum of one week or longer.
Children rate	Children who are 12 years and under usually stay free of charge as long as existing bedding in the room is used. If a rollaway bed or cot is required then there may be an additional charge.
Extra person rate	Most rates in Australia are the same for a single or double room but an extra charge is added for a third person.
Airline rate	Special rates available to customers who book an airline and hotel package.
Weekend rate	In large city venues a discounted rate is offered and usually includes breakfast on Saturday and Sunday. In country venues, packages may still be offered, but many country venues attract their greatest number of guests at this time, so may not heavily discount on the weekend.
Rate of the day	This rate can vary from day to day depending on the availability that day. In times of high occupancy the rate is high and on low occupancy days the rate is heavily discounted.
Day rate	This rate is charged for guests wanting to use a room usually between 9.00 am and 5.00 pm, if a room is available. The rate is usually less than the rack rate but may be the same during times of high occupancy.
Half day rate	Some guests require a room for a short period, for example two or three hours. This may be the case with guests in transit between flights. This rate may also apply if an overnight guest requests a late check-out.
Industry rate	The rate charged for people working in the hospitality industry including airline staff, travel agents and other hospitality staff and management. The rate is frequently 50 per cent of the standard rack rate.
FOC	Free of charge. This 'rate' is entered when the guest is not actually paying for the room. An FOC is often given to the organiser of a group/conference and at the general manager's discretion.

APPLY YOUR KNOWLEDGE

▷ *Design a leisure package for a romantic weekend away in a five star luxury hotel in a city location.*

▷ *Design a package that would appeal to a mid-week corporate guest staying in a four star suburban hotel.*

Indicate what is included in the packages, any conditions attached and the price you would charge. To get an idea of the sorts of things that are included in packages and the rates quoted, check local newspapers and magazines for advertisements or contact a venue in your area and make enquiries about the packages they offer.

Different target markets are likely to pay different room rates for similar room types because each venue is often trying to attract several different market categories, wants to reward frequent visitors and because they want to maximise room yield.

Room rates charged are influenced by a number of factors including the venue's star rating, location, the time of year, the guest's length of stay, room availability and market segment among others.

The rack rate for each room type is the maximum or standard rate charged for a room and is determined by the cost structure of the venue and the venue's competition.

There are a number of room rates used depending on the target market and the required use of the room. The rate may vary also if a meal plan is required and during peak and off peak periods.

Unless a package is quoted, rates are classified as a room only rate, but this does include GST, and usually use of some of the venue's facilities such as the swimming pool.

FOCUS REVIEW

▷ *What is the rack rate? What is it used for? What is it based on?*
▷ *Explain how the location of a venue can influence the room rate.*
▷ *Why do you think venues have available different room types?*
▷ *What is meant by 'seasonality'?*
▷ *How is room availability affected during peak and off peak times?*
▷ *How might the number of rooms booked affect the rate charged for a room?*
▷ *What is included in half-board? Full-board? Why would venues offer these options?*
▷ *Why would a venue offer a 'package'?*
▷ *What does 'rate of the day' mean? Why would a venue offer this type of rate?*
▷ *What is meant by 'room only' rate?*

The reservation process

The reservation process, or managing the reservation, involves that important first contact with the guest that we talked about at the beginning of this chapter. It is an important moment of truth that influences the success of the venue and the guest's satisfaction. To effectively manage the reservation process, all venues follow a step-by-step procedure that ensures accuracy and consistency, and that all necessary information is recorded.

Whether a reservation request is from a FIT, corporate guest, group, travel agent, airline or other source, the reservation procedure remains essentially the same:

1. receiving a reservation request
2. checking availability
3. recording the reservation details
4. confirming the reservation details
5. maintaining the reservation details.

First we look at how you process reservations from individuals and then we look at how you manage reservations for groups and from travel agents and airlines.

1. RECEIVING A RESERVATION REQUEST

Reservations
are made:
• by telephone
• via the
  Internet and
  e-mail
• through a CRS
• by facsimile
• in person
• by a walk in
• through same
  chain referrals
• through other
  venue
  referrals
• by mail.

Walk in—a
guest who
arrives at the
venue seeking
accommodation
for that night
without first
making a
reservation.

**Same chain
referrals**—
reservations
received for
guests from
venues that
belong to the
same group or
chain.

**Central
reservation
system**—a CRS
is a reservation
system capable
of controlling
and maintaining
the reservations
for several
venues (within a
chain) in one
location and
automatically
redirecting the
reservation to
the required
venue
accordingly.

Most reservations are received by telephone. But as modern technology continues to change the way in which we transact business, more and more reservations are received by other means such as via the Internet, e-mail and facsimile and through a **central reservation system** (CRS). And of course there are the more conventional means of making a reservation such as in person at the venue, **same chain referrals**, other venue referrals, and **walk in** trade.

2. CHECKING AVAILABILITY

However the request for accommodation is received, before it can be accepted you need to determine:

1. which dates are required
2. the number of people to be accommodated
3. the number of rooms required
4. room type(s) required.

Example

Step 1: 'What date would you like to stay and how long will you be staying with us, Madam?'
Step 2: 'How many people is the booking for?'
Step 3: 'How many rooms do you require?'
Step 4: 'What type of room would you like?'

Some of these steps may be omitted. For example, if the guest tells you that the number of people staying is one, obviously only one room is required.

When you have this information you then need to check availability. Figure 5.2 shows a room rack and the rooms available for 1 January 2002 to 10 January 2002.

Whether a fully automated or manual system, room availability information is stored on a room rack (or room availability screen) or reservations book. The room rack or reservations book contains all the necessary information to determine the occupancy level and current room status, and therefore room availability (according to type).

At step 4, when you ask which room type the guest requires, this is usually your opportunity to promote the various room types available using the selling techniques you learned in Chapter 2. Many guests will already know what type of room they require (such as a double room, twin, etc), while others may ask about room types specific to your venue, packages available and prices. When you have confirmed availability, room type required and room rate, the guest is able to confirm their acceptance.

APPLY YOUR KNOWLEDGE

Using the example of the availability screen in Figure 5.2, determine the number of rooms available for:

▷ *queen room (QEN), 24 September, three nights*
▷ *twin (TWN), 30 September, two nights*
▷ *double room (DBL), 1 October, one night.*

Could these requests for accommodation be accepted?

Figure 5.2 ▷ **Room rack and availability screen**

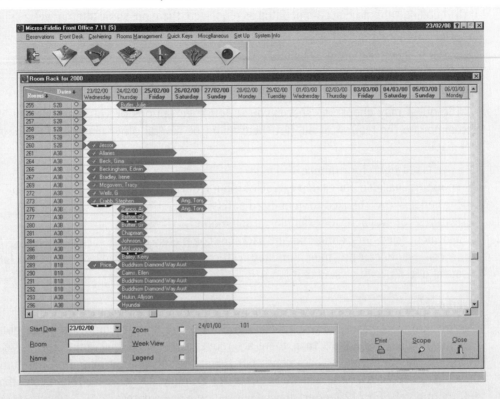

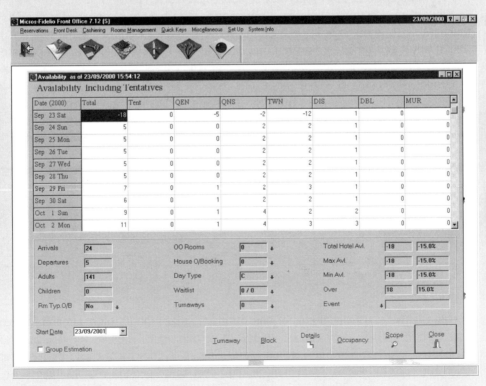

What if the date or room type is not available?

If the booking cannot be accommodated as requested, there are some alternatives available:

▷ offer another date
▷ upsell to a better room if available
▷ offer to waitlist the booking in case of cancellation, or
▷ book the guest into another hotel within the same chain.

The guest may choose to accept your alternative options or you may find you cannot accommodate the request at all. But there might be several other reasons why a booking is not made:

▷ price is not right, for example, too high
▷ no rooms available, for example, type of room requested or no rooms available at all
▷ the venue is over-booked for requested date(s)
▷ features not available, for example, no spa rooms
▷ allotment filled, for example, airline packages completely booked
▷ special events can put minimum stay restriction requirements over that period (and the guest doesn't want to stay that long).

Overbooking

Overbooking occurs in many establishments. It is the practice (and often the policy) of accepting more reservations than there are rooms available in the venue. The overbooking policy will vary between establishments, but there is usually a limit placed on the number of bookings accepted over the available rooms, for example 20 per cent. This means that in a 100-room hotel, up to 120 rooms may be booked on a given date.

While it may seem strange (even unreasonable) to maintain a policy for overbooking, its foundations are quite logical. Because the venue is trying to maximise the number of rooms sold at any given time, it can often only achieve this by overbooking to compensate for the **no-shows** (a reservation that does not arrive or who cancels their booking), late cancellations and **under-stays** (guests who depart earlier than the booked dates).

Of course, the venue runs the risk of having to 'walk' a guest who has a confirmed reservation. To walk a guest means to make alternative arrangements for the guest at a similar or higher rated venue. The procedure for 'walking' a guest is explained in Chapter 6.

APPLY YOUR KNOWLEDGE

If your venue has a 20 per cent overbooking policy in place, would all dates on the room rack in Figure 5.2 now be available? Explain.

Special events

Special events are usually annual or one-off events that produce high demand for occupancy over certain periods. They can be unique to certain areas, such as the AFL Grand Final in Melbourne and the Gay and Lesbian Mardi Gras in Sydney, or it could be New Year's Eve celebrations or Christmas. As demand is high over these periods, establishments attempt to maximise revenue by selling rooms at higher rates and imposing minimum stay periods.

APPLY YOUR KNOWLEDGE

Make a list of all the special events for your state or region that increases demand for accommodation during that time. What stay restrictions, if any, would you implement? Why?

3. RECORDING THE RESERVATION DETAILS

The next step in the reservation process, if you are able to accommodate the guest, is to ask for and record the guest's details. The details can be recorded directly into a computer system or recorded manually first and entered into the PMS later. This is often a preferred procedure by venues because it provides support documentation of the reservation. We have taken the manual approach as shown in Figure 5.3.

Figure 5.3 ▷ **A manual reservation form**

GRAND CENTRAL HOTEL
505 The Boulevard, Sydney
HOTELS OF DISTINCTION

Reservation Form

Confirmation Number: _____

Date: _____

Res. Clerk: _____

Arrival Date	ETA	Departure Date	ETD	No. of nights	Room Type	No.	Adults	Child	Rate Code/$Rate/Pkg Name

Surname		First name		Title	Company/Travel Agent	

Home Address	Company/Travel Address

Business Phone	Home Phone	Mobile	E-mail Address

Booked By:	Method of Payment	Guarantee ☐ Yes ☐ No	Credit Card No./Deposit/Account No.:
			Exp Date ....

Special Requests/Comments

Each section of the reservation form is discussed below. It is important to record the details accurately and legibly.

1. **Name.** Surname and first name (or initial) and title. Be sure to spell the guest's name correctly. Don't assume you know how people spell their names. An incorrect spelling may cause problems during the check-in process. Ask the guest to spell their name for you.
2. **Date of arrival.** In Australia the procedure for recording dates is day, month, year, for example 10/11/2002, or 10 November 2002.
3. **Date of departure.** This is the day the guest is checking out, not the last night they are staying. For example, if the guest is arriving on 10 November for three nights, the date of departure is 13 November.
4. **Number of nights.** This is usually recorded as a cross-reference with the departure date, for example '3'.
5. **Estimated time of arrival (ETA).** This is used to help reception establish peak times during the business day, and to remind the guest of check-in time (most venues allow check in from 2.00 pm, although arrangements can be made for an earlier check-in if required).
6. **Room type.** This is the room type that has been requested by the guest. Many venues use codes to identify room type and features. For example 'OK' or 'King' for ocean view king room or 'QD' or 'Queen' for a queen deluxe room.
7. **Number of rooms.** For example, one double or three triples. If more than one room type is requested or the rooms booked are in several names, complete a separate reservation form for each booking.
8. **Number of adults/children.** This is important as it may affect the room rate charged and, to ensure the correct room type is booked to correspond with the number of sleeping spaces in the room.
9. **Rate quoted.** Quoted during the availability request negotiations and what the rate includes. This is entered at this stage, and later reconfirmed to avoid possible misunderstandings.
10. **Home address** and/or business address or travel agency address or billing address, if different.
11. **Company name/travel agency name.** For corporate guests and travel agent bookings, the name of the travel agency or the company the guest works for, and who is often paying the account, is entered here.
12. **Telephone number.** Contact number of the person who booked the reservation.
13. **Booker/booked by.** This is the person who made the booking if that person is someone other than the guest. This could be, for example, corporate guests whose secretaries book the accommodation on their behalf, or when travel agents make the booking on behalf of their clients.
14. **Method of payment.** This records the details about the guest's preferred method of payment, for example, credit card details or voucher numbers.
15. **Account number.** If this is a booking for a corporate account holder or travel agent, then the venue will have issued the company with an account number. Record the number here.
16. **Guaranteed or non-guaranteed booking.** A method of ensuring the venue receives money for the room whether or not the guest arrives.
17. **Confirmation number.** This is the number generated from the computer when the booking is entered into the PMS.

18. **Date.** Date that the booking was made.
19. **Taken by.** This is the person from the venue who took the booking.
20. **Special requests/comments.** In this space any special requests can be recorded, such as requests for a cot, late arrival, room with a view or non-smoking room.

While there is a lot of information to be recorded, it is not necessary for you to remember every aspect. Reservation forms are pre-printed with all the section headings. If you follow the reservation form, you will not forget to ask for any particular information.

Payment methods

Determining the guest's method of payment during the reservation process is important because you often need to advise the guest about the venue's policy for accepting certain payment methods and you need to record specific details about certain payment methods.

The most common methods of payment in Australian accommodation venues are cash, travellers' cheques, credit and charge cards (American Express, Diners Card, Bankcard, Visa and MasterCard) and company charge.

Cash

If the guest wants to pay by cash, you may need to ask the guest to send a deposit to secure their booking (cheque or bank cheque or pay cash in person). You will also need to advise the guest of the venue's cash policy. For example, cash paying guests are usually asked to pay for their room in advance, to pay a bond (the equivalent of one room night) and provide personal identification at check-in. Once the cash deposit is received, the money is held in the deposit ledger and transferred to the guest's account at check-in. The venue sends a receipt to the guest as confirmation of having received the deposit.

Credit and charge cards

If the guest wishes to use a credit or charge card, you need to record:

▷ credit card type
▷ credit card number
▷ name on the credit card
▷ expiry date.

Company charge

Many venues allow companies to arrange a **charge back** facility. This means that when a guest who works for a particular company stays at the venue, the guest's account is settled by the company at a later stage. Before this can happen, the company must apply to the venue for a credit facility. Each time a staff member of that company stays at the venue, a written authority is sent to the venue, stating which charges incurred by this guest it will pay for.

If a guest is paying some or all of their account with a company charge back authority you will need to record:

▷ company name
▷ company account number
▷ person authorising the charge back
▷ services the charge back applies to (for example, room and breakfast)
▷ name of person using the charge back (that is, the name the reservation is held in).

Charge back facility—the ability to charge some or all of the account back to a company.

You will also need to advise the person making the booking that a company charge back authority needs to be forwarded to the venue in advance, or advise that the guest needs to bring one with him to be able to register. An example of a company charge back authority is shown in Figure 5.4.

Figure 5.4 ▷ **Example of a charge back authority**

ABC Consulting Pty Ltd
771 Hollywood Drive
Beverley Hills
Sydney NSW 2123

Facsimile:

TO:	**Robyn**
FACSIMILE No:	9347 8129
FROM:	Bryony Ghino Accounts Payable
No of PAGES:	1 (including this page)
SUBJECT:	Charge back authority for Mr Coxhill
DATE:	Wednesday, October 22, 2001
	Should you have any difficulty receiving this facsimile please contact the sender on 9555 1234.

Dear Robyn,

As per our conversation today, please accept this fax as authority to charge back to ABC Consulting, Mr Coxhill's accommodation and breakfast charges.

Arrival: 15 Nov.
Departure: 17 Nov.

1 standard double room.
Rate: $150.00 per night.

All other charges are the responsibility of Mr Coxhill.

Please forward this account to:

Attn: Bryony
Accounts Payable
ABC Consulting
771 Hollywood Drive
Beverley Hills
SYDNEY NSW 2123

Kind regards

Bryony Ghino

Blanket authority

Sometimes referred to as 'permanent charge back', a blanket authority is an agreement between the venue and certain companies that allows that company's staff to charge back to the company some or all charges without written authority every time the guest stays at the venue. You will need to obtain the same information required when accepting a company charge back authority.

Blanket authority—a charge back arrangement that allows the guest to charge some or all of the account without written authority each visit.

Guaranteed or non-guaranteed bookings

When a guest makes a booking they can choose to guarantee the requested accommodation. A **guaranteed booking** means that the guest has agreed to pay for the room whether they arrive or not, and the venue agrees to keep available the room until the check-out time the day following the day of arrival. A room can be guaranteed in a number of ways:

Guaranteed booking—a reservation held all night and charged whether or not the guest arrives.

▷ by leaving a credit card number (and faxing authorisation to charge the room to the credit card)
▷ sending a deposit or full payment
▷ by arranging charge back facilities (including a blanket authority).

If the guest doesn't arrive or cancel the booking, the venue can then charge (the guest or company) for the reserved accommodation (one night's accommodation).

A **non-guaranteed booking** means that the guest decides to pay by cash or cheque but does not send a deposit or leave credit card details during the reservation process. A guest who wants to pay his or her account with cash can still guarantee the reservation using a credit card. The credit card details are recorded, but the guest informs reception during check-in that the account will be settled with cash. The card details are then disregarded.

Non-guaranteed booking—a reservation held until 6.00 pm or an otherwise agreed time.

A non-guaranteed booking allows the venue to **release** the room if the guest has not arrived by 6.00 pm (or has made alternative arrangements for a late arrival). Most venues set 6.00 pm as the release time and the guest should be advised of this during the reservation process.

4. CONFIRMING THE RESERVATION DETAILS

When you have recorded all the reservation details, you need to confirm the information with the guest. This simply means that you read back to the guest all the information you have just recorded to ensure accuracy. It is particularly important to accurately record and confirm the following:

▷ spelling of guest's name
▷ contact details
▷ dates of arrival and departure
▷ room type and number requested
▷ rate quoted
▷ method of payment details for guaranteed bookings
▷ special requests if any.

Many establishments send also a written confirmation of the reservation, particularly once a deposit has been received. The following is an example of the complete procedure for checking availability for a room request through to confirming the details for the guest.

Example

Samitta: 'Good morning, reservations. This is Samitta, how may I help you?'

Mrs Foo: 'Good morning Samitta. I'm looking for a room for my husband and I for a few days next week.'

Samitta: 'What date is that for, Madam?'

Mrs Foo: 'Thursday, 16 November.'

Samitta: 'Certainly. I'm just checking our availability for next Thursday, 16 November. How many nights would you like to stay with us?'

Mrs Foo: 'Three nights please.'

Samitta: 'So you would be arriving on Thursday 16 November and departing on Sunday 19 November. Is this correct?'

Mrs Foo: 'Yes, that's right.'

Samitta: 'How many rooms do you require?'

Mrs Foo: 'Just the one room, thanks.'

Samitta: 'OK. I have those dates available. Do you know which type of room you would like?'

Mrs Foo: 'I'm not familiar with your rooms, could you tell me what is available?'

Samitta: 'Certainly. We have a deluxe double room with an ocean view and a king size bed available.'

Mrs Foo: 'That sounds nice. How much is that?'

Samitta: 'Including a bottle of champagne on arrival and a full buffet breakfast in the Sea Shell Restaurant each morning, that room is only $175.00 per night, per person.'

Mrs Foo: 'Do you have anything cheaper?'

Samitta: 'We have a standard double room on the same package without the champagne for $140.00 per person per night.'

Mrs Foo: 'Well . . . The champagne does sound like a nice touch . . . OK. I'll take the first option thanks.'

Samitta: 'Great. I'll just need to take a few details from you. May I have your name please?'

Mrs Foo: 'Mrs Foo.'

Samitta: 'Mrs Foo, I have booked an ocean view deluxe double room for you arriving next Thursday, 16 November for three nights, departing on Sunday 19 November. Mrs Foo, do you know what time you will be arriving?'

Mrs Foo: 'Around lunchtime.'

Samitta: 'Mrs Foo, our usual check in time is 2.00 pm. However, if you arrive earlier, we can store your luggage for you.'

Mrs Foo: 'Thanks Samitta. That will be fine.'

Samitta: 'Mrs Foo, do you have a preference for smoking or non-smoking?'

Mrs Foo: 'Non-smoking please and a room away from the lift as I prefer a quiet room.'

Samitta: 'That's fine. Mrs Foo, I just need a few more details. Could I please have your address and contact phone number?'

Mrs Foo: '239A Brighton Road, Ripponlea, 3185, Victoria. My phone number is 9347 2555.'

Samitta: 'How will you be paying your account, Mrs Foo?'

Mrs Foo: 'Visa card.'

Samitta: 'And would you like to use your credit card to guarantee your booking?'

Mrs Foo: 'Can you tell me what that means?'

Samitta: 'Certainly. By guaranteeing your reservation it means a room will be available for you no matter what time you arrive on the 16th. To guarantee your reservation I need your credit card details.'

Mrs Foo:	'OK. Yes I have a Visa card and the number is 4128 0031 4829 5531. The expiry date is October next year.'
Samitta:	'Thanks Mrs Foo, I would like to confirm the details of your reservation now. The booking is for Mr and Mrs Foo, spelt F-O-O, arriving on Thursday 16 November, for three nights. We have booked you into a deluxe double room with ocean view, away from the lift. The rate of $175.00 per person per night includes champagne on arrival and buffet breakfast each morning. I have also noted your request for a room away from the lift and a non-smoking room. Your address is 239A Brighton Road, Ripponlea, 3185, Victoria and the contact phone number is 9347 2555. Is this correct Ms Foo?'
Mrs Foo:	'Yes, thank you.'
Samitta:	'Is there anything else we can do for you Mrs Foo?'
Mrs Foo:	'No. That's everything, thank you.'
Samitta:	'Thanks Mrs Foo. We look forward to seeing you next week.'
Mrs Foo:	'Goodbye.'

APPLY YOUR KNOWLEDGE

Using the blank reservations pad below, record the details of the reservation taken by Samitta.

Reservation Form

Confirmation Number: _____

Date: _____

Res. Clerk: _____

Arrival Date	ETA	Departure Date	ETD	No. of nights	Room Type	No.	Adults	Child	Rate Code/$Rate/Pkg Name

Surname		First name		Title	Company/Travel Agent

Home Address	Company/Travel Address

Business Phone	Home Phone	Mobile	E-mail Address

Booked By:	Method of Payment	Guarantee ☐ Yes ☐ No	Credit Card No./Deposit/Account No.:
			Exp Date ....

Special Requests/Comments

5. MAINTAINING THE RESERVATION

When the reservation is first recorded manually, as in the example with Mrs Foo, and the details are confirmed with the guest, the data is then entered into the computer. The computer reservation is shown in Figure 5.5. Sometimes the reservation details are entered immediately after the reservation is taken; at other times, reservations are entered later that day. At whatever stage it is done, the information must be transferred accurately. This is the first stage of maintaining the reservation.

Transferring the reservation to the computer

From the manual reservations slip all the information is carefully entered into the computer. The computer allocates a reservation number, which is then recorded on the handwritten reservation slip along with the name of the person who took the booking and the person who entered the information into the computer. (The person entering the information into the computer is not necessarily the person who took the booking.)

The reservations screen is made up of many different *fields* where the information is entered. Some of these fields are compulsory, which means that you must enter information in this field before you can move onto the next field or complete the reservation. Examples of compulsory fields include the guest's name, room type, date of arrival and length of stay.

Figure 5.5 ▷ **Maintaining the reservation on the computer**

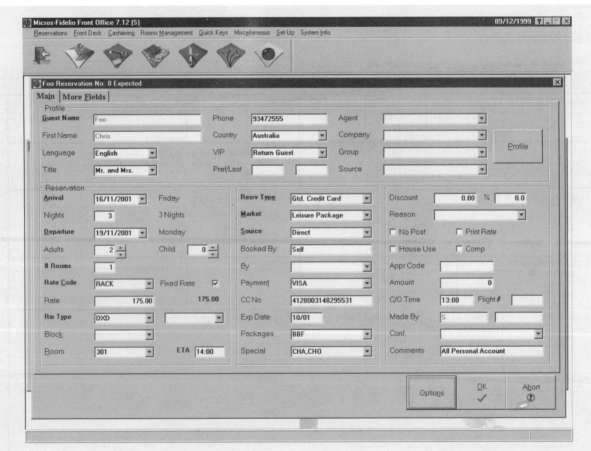

Once the reservation details are recorded in the PMS, the manual record of the reservation is then filed manually according to the date of arrival.

Guest profile

When entered into the computerised PMS, the reservation can be linked to the guest history profile if the guest has stayed at the venue before. If it is the guest's first visit, many computerised systems automatically create a guest history profile either when the reservation details are entered or at check-out. An example is shown in Figure 5.6.

The guest profile is a record of personal details of each guest who has stayed at the venue. It can be maintained manually or electronically and be retrieved every time a guest makes a booking. The information on the guest profile includes not only the guest's personal details but also information about their preferences:

▷ name and preferred title
▷ address and phone number
▷ company details (if a corporate guest)
▷ company charge back authority details, if applicable
▷ travel agency details, if applicable
▷ room type and features preferred
▷ preferred method of payment
▷ rate charged
▷ special requests
▷ preferred newspaper

Figure 5.6 ▷ **Example of a guest profile**

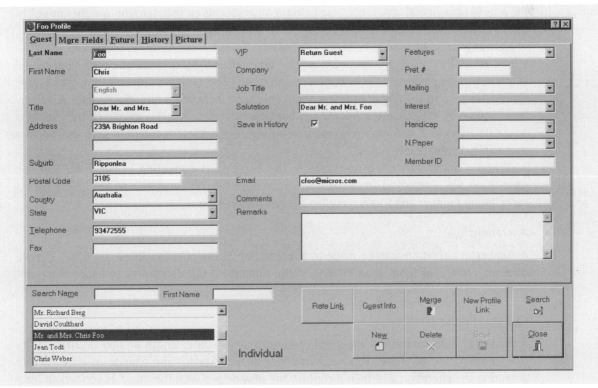

▷ interests

▷ past stays and revenue spent.

By maintaining this information, all these details can be linked to the guest's new booking each time they stay and the guest does not need to repeat every detail or make the same requests. It is also an important tool for making your guests feel important and valued.

When guests make a reservation, it is sometimes part of the procedure to ask if they have stayed at the venue before. This enables you to check their personal details and special requests, if any, in their profile. It is also a useful way to track the number of room nights booked by individuals, particularly if this information is linked to the venue's loyalty program.

Some accommodation venue chains maintain a central database that allows each venue in the chain to access guest profiles. For example, if Mrs Foo requests a non-smoking room at a venue in Canberra, when she stays at a venue in the same chain in Darwin, they will know to allocate her a non-smoking room.

Cancellations and alterations

Maintaining the reservation refers also to a number of other activities that require you to make changes to the original booking, such as cancellations and alterations. When a reservation is altered in any way, this information must be recorded.

Cancellations

Cancellations occur when a guest advises the venue that they no longer require the reservation. Most establishments ask the guest the reason for the cancellation and this information is recorded on the reservation when it is cancelled. It helps the venue keep track of the reasons for the cancellation and in turn can influence policies and procedures within the reservations operations. It can also help the reservations clerk determine whether or not to offer an alternative date to the guest in order to avoid a cancellation altogether.

Cancellation policies vary between establishments, but most cancellation policies establish a **lead time**. This is the minimum amount of time allowed for a cancellation to be accepted without incurring a penalty. For example, a corporate hotel with a short lead time may accept cancellations up to the day of arrival without the guest incurring a financial penalty. A holiday resort, however, may charge a fee for any booking cancelled within a month of the expected arrival date (because it is less likely that a resort venue can resell its rooms at such short notice than can a corporate city venue).

When a guest cancels a reservation, the booking is cancelled in the PMS and the reservation slip is removed from the reservation date file. All cancellations are issued with a cancellation number and this is recorded against the booking.

Alterations

A number of alterations can be made to a reservation at the guest's request, such as a change of dates, change of room type, change in the number of guests staying and special request changes.

Change of dates

A change of dates can affect the guest's intended arrival date, length of stay, departure date or a combination of these. You need to check availability for the change of dates before accepting the alteration and then reconfirm the new details with the guest as you would for a new reservation. It is important to note and advise the guest of different room rates that may now apply to the new dates.

Change of room type

This does not occur often, but occasionally guests may change their mind about the type of room they want, or the location of the room or the number of rooms. You need to check availability of the new room type for the requested dates before making the change. A different room rate may apply, or there may be other conditions, such as a minimum stay requirement, which must be confirmed with the guest.

Special requests

Guests sometimes want to make special requests they had not thought to ask for earlier. Special requests differ from room features in that they are provided in addition to the standard features and guests are sometimes required to pay for them. Table 5.4 lists common special requests according to whether or not the guest is required to pay for it.

Table 5.4 ▷ **Special requests**

FEE CHARGED	FREE OF CHARGE
Rollaway bed	Room with view (but the room rate may be higher)
Third person in the room	Newspaper delivered
Cot	Non-smoking room
Champagne/fruit on arrival/flowers (unless included in the package)	Early check-in
	Power adapter
Late departure	Feather pillows (instead of foam or cotton)
Birthday cake	Blankets (instead of doona)
Luggage storage	Change booking to a guaranteed reservation
Car parking	

MANAGING GROUP RESERVATIONS

Managing group reservations requires time and attention to detail as negotiations may take several weeks, or even months, before a reservation for the group is actually made. Groups also frequently create other challenges not common to other types of bookings. The group is comprised of a number of individuals all of whom may have different dietary requirements, sleeping requirements and special requests (non-smoking, ground floor room etc), and each of these individual needs must be accommodated. Group reservations are usually made well in advance of the required accommodation date—in some instances, up to five years in advance.

For GITs and SITs, the booking (and negotiations) is usually conducted entirely with the group organiser. This person will make all the necessary arrangements with the venue and the first contact you are likely to have with any member of the group is when they arrive to check-in.

Conference groups on the other hand, are administered in one of two ways. The first option is for the conference organiser to book the rooms for the delegates and supply the venue with a **rooming list** (a rooming list is supplied also by GIT and SIT group organisers). The rooming list details:

> arrival date and time
> departure date and time
> payment details
> all guests' names (and who will be sharing a room with whom).

The second option is for the venue to block an allotment for the conference group. Delegates are then required to contact the venue directly to book their room. The individual guest's reservation is processed in the same way as a FIT but a room will be allocated within the allotment given to the conference group.

All groups are likely to need some or all of the following:

> accommodation (frequently twin share)
> meals (breakfast only or half- or full-board)
> morning and afternoon tea
> conference rooms (various layouts, sizes and quantity)
> presentation facilities (overhead projectors, slide projector, screen and so on)
> business centre back up services
> bus/car parking facilities
> wake up calls.

Processing a group booking

Negotiations mainly centre on the price of the accommodation, meals and use of venue facilities. Once these details have been agreed upon, and the venue has confirmed it can accommodate the groups' requirements (number and type of rooms, for the required length of stay), this information is entered onto the group inquiry/reservation form. An example is shown in Figure 5.7. The other information you need to record is:

> group name
> company name and address
> contact details
> purpose of stay (for example, conference, tour etc)
> name of tour/conference organiser or leader
> total number of people (adults, children, babies)
> account details (what the company or group organisers will be paying for)
> arrival and departure dates
> estimated times of arrival and departure
> mode of transport (for example, coach or own arrangements)
> meal requirements each day
> special requests (wake up calls, special meals, cots, rollaway beds)
> prices (for room, meals and extras)
> conference room hire
> equipment required (overhead projector etc).

The group reservation form will also have room for comments, the date the reservation was taken and the name of the person who took the reservation.

When you have manually recorded this information, you then need to enter it onto the computer. You also need to block the required rooms for the group's stay. When the rooming list arrives, the details (guests' names) are entered into the PMS and a copy placed on file with the manual record of the reservation.

Figure 5.7 ▷ **Example of a group reservation form**

GRAND CENTRAL HOTEL
505 The Boulevard, Sydney
HOTELS OF DISTINCTION

Group Reservation Form

Enquiry Date: _____

Res. Clerk: _____

Conference/Group Name		Arrival Date	Departure Date	Adults	Child

Arrival Details:

ETA	Mode of transport	Special transport requirements

Room requirements

Total No of rooms:	Total No of People	Disabled rooms		

Room Type	No of rooms	Rate code	No of nights	Total
Standard single				
Standard double				
Twin				
Suite				
Deluxe suite				
Total				

Meal Plans (enter dates required)	Breakfast (enter No required)	Lunch	Dinner
Day 1			
Day 2			
Day 3			

Billing requirements (what to charge to which account)

Master Account charges:		Billing address:
Rooms	$	
Breakfast	$	
Lunch	$	
Dinner	$	
Total	$	

Extras Accounts details

Comments/Special requests _____

_____

_____

_____

AIRLINE ALLOTMENTS

The reservations received from airlines are for guests who have booked a package holiday with that airline. The airline has already negotiated an allotment with your venue, so when the airline takes flight bookings for its customers who require accommodation, it reserves rooms in its allotment. If the allotment is not filled seven days before the due date of arrival (or other agreed date), the airline releases the rooms back to the venue so that the venue can attempt to sell the rooms itself.

If the airline requires more rooms than its allotment for a given date, it can request these with the venue which is likely to provide additional rooms if they are available.

When you process airline reservations where allotments are held, you need to record the reservation against the allotment in the PMS, and not block a room that is available for general sale. Recording of all other reservation details follows the same steps as processing a reservation for an individual. The airline will send the venue a rooming list for each night, usually one week before arrival.

SKILLS FOCUS

The reservation process involves a number of steps. It begins with a request for accommodation and includes checking availability, recording the details, confirming the details and maintaining the reservation.

Before a request for accommodation can be confirmed, availability must be checked. It is first necessary to determine the date, number of nights, number of people and the number of rooms required. Once you can confirm requested dates are available, it is necessary to find out the room type required and explain rates and features of the room to the guest.

If the requested dates are unavailable, it is important to identify and offer alternative dates. It is also useful to offer an alternative room type, place the guest on a waitlist or refer the guest to another venue in the same chain.

Requested reservation details and the guest's personal details must be accurately recorded. The information can be entered directly into a computerised system or recorded manually first. A manual and computerised record is preferred to a computerised only system because it provides a backup of the reservation information.

Many venues overbook. The reasons for this are so that the venue can attempt to maximise occupancy by compensating for the no-shows, cancellations and under-stays.

While recording the reservation you need to obtain details about the guest and their method of payment. Payment methods are recorded and can be used to guarantee the booking. A guaranteed booking is one that is held all night and charged for whether or not the guest arrives. A non-guaranteed booking is one whereby the venue is not likely to receive revenue for a room if the guest becomes a no-show. Non-guaranteed bookings are released at 6.00 pm so the venue can attempt to resell the room.

Accurately recording the reservation details onto the reservation form and repeating the information back to the guest helps ensure that no detail is overlooked.

Maintaining reservations requires you to accurately record the reservation details into the computerised PMS and record cancellations and alterations. When the reservation is entered into the PMS, the details can be linked to the guest's history profile, which contains personal details relating to that guest and details about their preferences and past stays with the venue.

Cancellations occur when the guest no longer wants or needs the reservation held with your venue. Alterations to a reservation may result from changes to the date, room type, number of rooms, or special requests and are noted in the original reservation.

Group reservations are usually made well in advance of the arrival date and require time and attention to detail. Negotiations for group reservations are usually conducted with the group or conference organiser.

Conference groups are administered in one of two ways: either the conference organiser makes all the arrangements and supplies the venue with a rooming list, or the organiser blocks an allotment with the venue and the delegates make their own reservations directly with the venue.

Processing group bookings is similar to individual reservations but requires some additional information such as group members' special needs or requests.

Airline allotment bookings are managed in a similar manner as that of individuals, but the room booked must be allocated from the airline's allotment. Airlines release any remaining rooms in their allotment seven days before the due date of arrival back to the venue so that the venue can attempt to resell these rooms.

FOCUS REVIEW

▷ What is involved in the reservation process?
▷ Why is it important to follow a step-by-step procedure when processing reservations?
▷ Before accepting a request for accommodation what information do you need?
▷ What is a room rack? What information does it contain?
▷ Why do think accuracy is so important in recording reservations? How may an incorrect name spelling affect the check-in process?
▷ What should you do if requested dates of room types are not available?
▷ Why do you think accommodation venues overbook? Do you think this is an ethical practice? Why? Why not? Do you know of any other industry that maintains a policy of overbooking? What is the policy?
▷ How do no-shows and under-stays affect the overbooking policy of a venue?
▷ Explain the difference between a guaranteed and non-guaranteed booking.
▷ How may a guest guarantee their reservation?
▷ If a guest wishes to guarantee their booking, what methods of payment are usually accepted?
▷ What does a 'blanket authority' mean?
▷ Why is it important to confirm the reservation details with the caller?
▷ What is involved in maintaining guest reservations?
▷ What benefits are there in maintaining a guest profile? How is this information used?
▷ Why would a venue maintain a manual and computerised record of a reservation?
▷ What is a lead time? Why do you think a venue would implement a lead time policy?
▷ How is managing group reservations different from managing individual bookings?
▷ Explain the two ways conference groups can arrange their accommodation booking. Which do you think is preferred by accommodation venues? Why?
▷ What is a rooming list?
▷ What happens if an airline that has an allotment with your venue does not use all rooms in its allotment? What happens if they want more rooms?

Communicating reservation details to other departments and colleagues

Reservation information is communicated to other departments and your colleagues in accommodation services so that they can ascertain the impact on their departments of the number of guests booked into the venue. For example, occupancy levels and expected arrivals can affect other department's staffing requirements, operating hours and supply needs.

HOW IS THE INFORMATION COMMUNICATED?

Communicating reservation information is crucial to the success of the venue in meeting guests' expectations. It can be achieved in a number of ways. It must be timely and accurate because it affects not only each department, but also ultimately the guest's satisfaction.

The arrivals report

The arrivals report is a computer-generated report detailing the reservations for a specified date or number of days such as for the coming week or month. The report is compiled and distributed daily to each department and to management. The report lets everyone know how well the venue is performing (in terms of number of rooms sold); it also provides the relevant information that each department needs (number of rooms sold, number of guests expected in-house, length of stay).

Traces

In addition to the reservation report, many computer systems allow **traces** for special requests. Traces are computer messages sent electronically to the various departments on the arrival date of the guest indicating what is to be done by that department for the guest. For example, if a guest requires a bed board, then a message is sent to maintenance to put it in the room before the guest arrives. A request for extra blankets would be handled by housekeeping and room service would place champagne in the appropriate room.

Verbal communication

Of course, departments talk to each other either face-to-face or by telephone. Arguably the biggest problem with relying on verbal communication, however, is that the information may be communicated or interpreted incorrectly or forgotten altogether. There is also no way of confirming the accuracy of the message if it is only passed on verbally. However, particularly for a same day booking, it is important to call all departments that may be affected by the bookings and make sure that everything is ready for the guest's arrival.

WHO DO YOU INFORM ABOUT RESERVATIONS?

All departments (and outlets) and management should be informed about reservations on a daily basis, even if the department isn't affected that particular day. This way, it is not likely that any department will be omitted from important communication about reservations.

Housekeeping

Housekeeping is informed of the number of rooms booked and due to arrive not only that day, but frequently, weeks in advance. This enables planning of staff schedules and productivity levels, as well as associated budgets, supplies purchasing and cleaning scheduling among other activities.

Housekeeping is also advised of any VIPs due to arrive and any special requests a guest may have that is the housekeeping department's responsibility, such as the set up of a rollaway bed or cot. From expected arrival information, housekeeping determines which rooms to prepare, and in which order, to meet demand.

Food and beverage

The food and beverage outlets are advised of the number of guests due to arrive and particularly those booked with a meal plan or participating in a conference. The department needs to schedule staff (according to the level of occupancy), purchase food and beverage supplies and prepare special requests that are the department's responsibility such as fruit platters, chocolates and other food items. The food and beverage department (room service) is also often responsible for delivering food and beverage items to meet special requests and package inclusion items.

Maintenance

The maintenance department needs to be aware of the expected occupancy to ensure all required rooms are available to meet demand. This may mean that rooms currently on out-of-order status are brought back on line and other maintenance requirements on the property are attended to.

Front office

Your front office colleagues need to be kept up to date with reservations not only because they may have joint responsibility for managing reservations but also because it can influence how the department is staffed and structured. Front office needs to undertake a number of pre-arrival activities, such as prepare registration forms for expected arrivals, and can only efficiently perform their duties if kept informed.

Concierge

Similarly, the concierge department needs to plan for staff and to make arrangements for services such as luggage storage and parking facilities (particularly for groups arriving by coach).

Potential reservations problems

We conclude this chapter with a brief look at some of the potential problems you may encounter managing and maintaining reservations. By being aware of the most common problems that can arise, it is easier to avoid the problems in the first place. Problems can arise at any stage of the reservation process but the most common problems are:

▷ inaccurate recording of the reservation information, for example, incorrect spelling of a guest name or recording of dates
▷ poor communication within the venue, such as failing to provide updated same day reservation information
▷ inaccurate transfer of reservation information to the computer

▷ computer failure (another good reason for keeping a manual record)
▷ misunderstanding due to use of industry jargon.

Simply put, to eliminate potential problems:

▷ always reconfirm details with the guest at the time of the reservation
▷ check the spelling of names
▷ maintain a manual record of all reservations
▷ check for accuracy of all data transferred to the computer
▷ avoid use of industry jargon when communicating with guests
▷ give the guest accurate information about the venue
▷ communicate with your colleagues and other departments in a timely and effective way.

SKILLS FOCUS

Reservation information is communicated to other departments and your colleagues because the number of rooms booked can affect other areas in the venue in a number of ways. For example, occupancy and arrivals can affect other departments' staffing requirements, operating hours and supply needs.

Communication with other departments must be accurate and timely if it is to be of use to the other departments. Communication channels include reservation reports, traces and verbal communication. Maintaining an open and efficient line of communication and following all procedures for managing and maintaining reservations will help minimise reservation problems.

FOCUS REVIEW

▷ *With which departments must reservations communicate and why?*
▷ *What are the three primary means of communicating reservation information to other departments and colleagues?*
▷ *Why is verbal communication potentially unreliable?*
▷ *Potential reservations problems can be eliminated in a number of ways. What are they?*

PUT YOUR KNOWLEDGE TO THE TEST

After working at Grand Central Hotel for a few months, Robyn felt confident with all the new skills she had learnt working in different departments. That was until her first day in reservations. She was a little overwhelmed with the volume of knowledge she needed to be an effective reservations clerk. Grant, the reservations manager, had spent the morning explaining the reservation department's role within the hotel. In the afternoon Jane, the reservations supervisor, explained the reservations procedures to Robyn and where to get information if she needed it.

The whole time this was happening, the phone had been ringing constantly and everyone was very busy. Jack, one of the reservations clerks, smiled at Robyn and said 'You'll get used to it'. Robyn just shook her head and wondered how she'd ever remember everything.

Her first reservation was from a travel agency. Fortunately, the travel agent seemed to know more about the venue than Robyn did. The next reservation was a little more complicated. The caller wanted to know all about the packages available and the layout of each room type. Even though Robyn had all this information to hand, she was sure the caller realised that she didn't really know what she was doing.

The next day was better. By the afternoon of the second day, Robyn felt more confident. That morning she had arrived early and asked the executive housekeeper if she minded Robyn tagging along with the housekeeping supervisor so she could gain a better appreciation of the facilities and layout of each room.

1. Pretend you are Grant, the reservations manager, and explain the role of the reservations department.

2. Now pretend you are Jane, the reservations supervisor, and explain to Robyn the five steps in the reservation procedure.

3. Working in a group of three, role play processing reservations using the details below (make up whatever information you need to complete the reservation) and the reservation form on page 147. One person is to be the guest, the other the reservations clerk. The third person is to observe the process and provide feedback on the success of the role play. The roles are then rotated until everyone in the group has gained experienced in taking a reservation.

At the end of the role play, enter the data on the reservation forms into the PMS used.

Reservation 1
Mr Paul and Mrs Jane Tombleson
1 × child
234 Heathmont Road
London UK SW1 098
Arriving: 6 June
Departing: 12 June
Double room with view, non-smoking, late check-out, cot required.
Visa card

Reservation 2
Mr C Hughes-Smith
Managing Director, Scoonie Industries
PO Box 11111
Werribee VIC 3030
Arriving: 14 October, three nights
Double room, late arrival, room and breakfast (company charge back), VIP guest, fruit platter in room.

Reservation 3
Ms S Dwyer and Mr C Charming
44 Beechworth Drive
City Beach WA 6015
Arriving: 12 December, two nights

Suite, non-smoking, champagne on arrival.
Paying cash, deposit requested.

4. Write confirmation letters for each of the three reservations.

5. Explain what the different departments in the hotel should be informed of for each of the above reservations. How should they be informed?

6. What value might Robyn have gained by visiting rooms with the housekeeping supervisor? Do you think this was a good tactic? Why or why not?

7. How else do you think Robyn might learn about the venue's products, rates, services and facilities?

Providing Accommodation Reception

LEARNING OUTCOMES

On completion of this chapter you will be able to:

▷ accurately describe the role and responsibilities of reception;

▷ describe and accurately perform guest pre-arrival activities;

▷ correctly demonstrate how to welcome and register a guest;

▷ identify why a guest may be refused accommodation;

▷ explain release times and why venues have them;

▷ identify and explain the procedure for performing other services offered to guests by reception during the guest's stay;

▷ explain the procedure for organising a guest's departure and correctly follow the departure procedure;

▷ accurately identify and compile reports and records to be distributed.

Introduction

The front office or reception area of an accommodation venue has a very important role in the arrival, occupancy and departure stages of the cycle of service. Every encounter presents a moment of truth on which guests judge their experiences of the venue.

The arrival stage of the cycle of service sets the scene for the guest's satisfaction with their entire stay. To create a good first impression on arrival, the guest's welcome needs to be warm and friendly and the check-in process proficient.

At the time of arrival most guests have made a reservation. They have had contact with the venue over the telephone or via facsimile or e-mail. They have already begun to form expectations of the venue and its staff. Sometimes a guest may not have made a reservation and gains his or her first impression of the venue by how face-to-face requests for accommodation are handled.

During their stay, guests may have many encounters with the front office—requests for information, requests for services, account enquiries and so on.

At the time of departure, the guest is looking for a fast and efficient settlement of their account. It is important that the guest leaves with a positive final impression created by the departure process.

Throughout this chapter we aim to provide you with the skills and knowledge required to work in the front office of an accommodation venue and which are necessary to make a positive impression on every guest every time they have contact with reception. We consider not only the arrival stage, but also reception's role during occupancy and the departure stage of the cycle of service.

The roles and responsibilities of reception

The role of reception is one of service throughout the guest's stay. From arrival to departure, all guests at some point must pass through reception. The venue must be able to meet guests' needs and expectations in a timely and professional manner. Reception is open 24-hours a day, every day of the year and usually consists of two day shifts: 'A' shift is from 7.00 am to 3.30 pm. 'B' shift is from 3.00 pm to 11.30 pm. The 'D' shift, usually commencing at 11.00 pm and finishing at 7.30 am, is the night audit shift. You will notice that the start and finish times of each shift overlap by half an hour. This is to allow for a 'handover' (communication about what is happening in the venue) from one shift to the next, and to give you time to prepare for guest arrivals.

Shift A—
7.00 am–
3.30 pm

Shift B—
3.00 pm–
11.30 pm

Shift D—
11.00 pm–
7.30 am

Swing shift—
11.00 am–
7.30 pm

In larger, busy venues, a swing shift may be rostered from 11.00 am to 7.30 pm. This shift is used to cover meal breaks (lunch for the morning shift and dinner for the afternoon shift) and the peak check-in period. Reception usually has two peak periods in the day: 7.30 am to 9.30 am for departing guests and 3.00 pm to 7.00 pm for arriving guests. On the weekend, guests tend to check-in earlier (from 2.00 pm) and check-out later (up to 2.00 pm).

Whichever shift you are rostered, most of the tasks you need to be able to do are similar:

▷ check guests in and out
▷ post charges and balance the shift
▷ arrange transport, luggage collection and tours
▷ exchange currency

▷ allocate rooms and issue keys
▷ take messages and forward mail
▷ meet guest requests for services and local area information
▷ provide secretarial support and wake up calls
▷ communicate with other departments
▷ generate reports
▷ handle complaints.

You must be able to perform these tasks, often simultaneously, following established procedures. The procedures help you to perform your job by following a step-by-step approach to the task to ensure that nothing gets overlooked. A procedure exists for everything.

SKILLS FOCUS

As a 24-hour operation, the front desk of a hospitality establishment needs to be manned all day, every day. To achieve this, four shifts operate—A, B, D and a swing shift. The role of reception is to assist guests with a range of activities related to their stay, for example, check guests in and out of the venue, arrange transport, special requests and secretarial services, allocate rooms and issue keys.

Reception tasks are completed following the procedures in place that have been established by the venue. This ensures that nothing gets overlooked.

FOCUS REVIEW

▷ *What is a 'swing shift' and why is it used?*
▷ *Why do shifts overlap?*
▷ *Why is it important to follow procedures when completing reception tasks?*

Preparing for guest arrival

On arrival at work there are a number of tasks that must be completed before you have contact with any guests. These tasks prepare you for the guests' arrival and require you to familiarise yourself with what has happened earlier that day, as well as what is likely to take place during your shift (shift hand over). This preparation time also requires you to collect and count your **float**, log on to the computer system and check your supplies and equipment; they are sometimes referred to as pre-arrival activities. Finally, you will print a range of reports that help you to quickly identify the activities taking place in the venue, allocate rooms to guests with reservations and then print expected arrivals registration cards. The order in which these tasks are completed may vary but in general, follow a systematic approach:

Pre-arrival activities:
• shift hand over
• collect the float
• log on
• check equipment and supplies
• generate reports
• allocate guest rooms
• print registration cards.

1. shift hand over
2. collect the float
3. log on
4. check equipment and supplies
5. generate reports

6. allocate guest rooms
7. print registration cards.

1. SHIFT HAND OVER

The shift hand over takes place at the end of every shift and at the commencement of each new shift. An effective shift hand over reduces the likelihood of unpleasant surprises during your shift. It is a time when you are able to find out what has happened during the previous shift, what is likely to happen on your shift, and any other important information that you need to be aware of.

The information is passed on from your colleagues about to finish their shift, verbally, through written messages, the front office diary and reports.

The front office diary

As you learned in Chapter 3, the front office diary is a valuable tool for keeping track of what is happening. Issues that may affect your shift are detailed here. If you have had a couple of days off, it is also useful to read what has happened in the venue during that time.

2. COLLECT THE FLOAT

Float—the starting 'bank' to enable financial transactions.

The float is the starting 'bank' for you to be able to conduct financial transactions. The float is collected from the duty manager or supervisor, counted for accuracy and placed in the cash or till drawer. Your float is signed out at the beginning of your shift and signed in at the end of your shift. This helps the venue keep track of where all floats are (thereby reducing the likelihood of loss).

3. LOG ON

Most computerised front office systems (PMS) require each user to log on at the commencement of their shift (and log off at the end). This means that you enter a password or your name, which registers you in the computer and allows the computer to keep track of all entries made by you during your shift. This is important for performing balancing procedures, which are discussed in Chapter 7. It is also important for keeping a track of your different work, for example any changes you have made to a guest record or reservations you may make during your shift.

4. CHECK EQUIPMENT AND SUPPLIES

Before starting your shift, it is important to check that your equipment is in good working order and that you have sufficient supplies of stationery. This takes just a short time and potentially saves time later. You need to check:

▷ front desk printer—check it has sufficient invoice paper
▷ fax machine—check that the paper tray is full
▷ registration cards—check that there are sufficient blanks to print today's arrivals
▷ stationery—check supplies of envelopes (for guest messages and facsimiles), guest message pads, reservation pads (if reservations are taken after hours on the desk), venue marketing materials, pens and other commonly used stationery
▷ credit card machine (EFTPOS)—check if sufficient dockets are in place and a spare supply available
▷ promotional material—check that the display units are filled and tidy; stock up as required.

If any equipment is faulty or supplies are running short, report to your supervisor immediately so that the problem can be fixed.

5. GENERATE REPORTS

Once you are logged onto the computer system, you need to generate a few reports that also help you identify what activities are likely to take place that day, such as expected departures and arrivals and special requests requiring your attention.

The night auditor prints most activity reports near the end of their shift. It is common, however, for reception staff to print a more up to date version at the commencement of their shift to account for changes that have taken place in the venue since the reports were last printed. The main reports required are:

▷ house status report
▷ arrivals list
▷ departure list
▷ specials
▷ flags
▷ group arrivals.

House status report

The house status report provides details of the status of all rooms in the venue. Status refers to the state of each room. In other words, whether a room is occupied, vacant, clean or dirty. Table 6.1 explains the room status codes most commonly used.

From this information, you are able to determine the number of rooms available to sell for the day.

As you can see, house status is divided into four major areas: room summary, movement, housekeeping, and end of day projection. Figure 6.1 shows an example of a typical computer generated house status report.

Room summary

The room summary indicates the total number of rooms to sell and the total number of **out of order** rooms (OOO). Rooms listed as out of order are not available for sale for a period ranging from a couple days to long term (such as for maintenance or refurbishment). Out of order

Room summary— indicates the total number of rooms to sell and the total number of out of order rooms.

Table 6.1 ▷ **Room status codes**

STATUS	DESCRIPTION
V = Vacant	
O = Occupied	
VD = Vacant Dirty	Guest has vacated room but it is still to be cleaned.
VC = Vacant Clean	Room is ready for the guest to check-in.
OD = Occupied Dirty	Guest still in the room (usually a stay over, but may be a late departure) and housekeeping hasn't cleaned the room yet.
OC = Occupied Clean	Guest is in the room and it doesn't need to be serviced today as they may have just arrived or room has already been serviced today.
TU = Touch Up	A guest has been in the room and then quickly been moved to another room. For example, smoker moved from a non-smoking room. Housekeeping just needs to check the room.

Figure 6.1 ▷ **House status report**

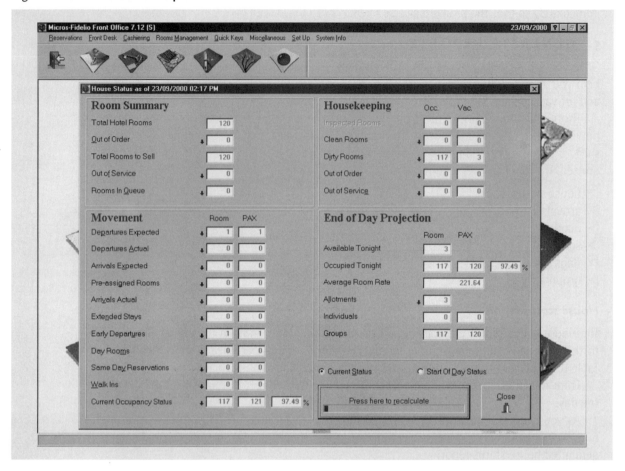

rooms reduce the number of rooms an establishment has to sell for that day. For example, if a hotel has 150 rooms and two rooms are OOO, then only 148 rooms are available to sell.

Out of service rooms (OOS) are rooms that cannot be used for a brief time during the day. For example, the bedspread is being laundered and will be returned by 6.00 pm. Another example of a room being listed as OOS is when the sales department has requested a room to show potential guests and the room needs to be kept available for the appointed showing time.

OOO—Out of order.

OOS—Out of service.

Movement

Movement shows the number of rooms and people that are coming and going today.

▷ expected departures list the rooms due to leave today
▷ actual departures list the rooms that have already checked out
▷ expected arrivals list the rooms due to check-in
▷ actual arrivals lists the rooms already checked-in
▷ pre-assigned rooms are the rooms already blocked for a guest as per their request, for example high floor rooms, quiet rooms, fold out sofa bed, or a room near the lift
▷ extended stays are guests who were meant to depart today but decided to stay longer
▷ early departures are guests who were meant to stay longer but checked out today instead

▷ day rooms lists the number of day use rooms being used. A day use room is usually used from 9.00 am–5.00 pm. These rooms are then cleaned and can be resold that night.
▷ same day reservations are guests who book their room the same day they are arriving
▷ walk ins are guests who arrive at the venue seeking accommodation without a reservation.

Housekeeping

The housekeeping section is further broken down into two columns: vacant rooms and occupied. A vacant room is a room that doesn't have a guest while an occupied room has a guest registered in that room.

If reception does not have a computerised system then it is very important that front office and housekeeping regularly communicate room status. The reason is that as guests arrive, reception needs to know which rooms are ready for guest arrival and housekeeping needs to know which rooms to clean and when.

End of day projection

The final box is end of day projection. This is the total number of rooms in the venue minus expected occupied rooms and OOO rooms. The remaining rooms on the list are available for sale. Occupied tonight are all rooms that are sold tonight including stay overs and arrivals but not OOO rooms.

Allotments indicate any rooms still held for groups or airlines that have not been booked. Allotment rooms should be released (made available for sale) by reservations at this stage.

Expected arrivals report

As well as checking today's house status, it is important to be familiar with the establishment's expected occupancy for the next few days. Frequently, guests request an extension of their stay while others make late minute bookings. By being familiar with the availability of rooms, you are able to quickly respond to a guest's request for accommodation or extension of their stay.

The expected arrivals report (see Figure 6.2) lists all guests alphabetically with reservations for that day. As a guest checks-in, the name is marked off the list and the guest is now classified as an actual arrival. Read the list at the beginning of the shift and:

▷ look for regular guests
▷ allocate room preferences (smoking/non-smoking, bath, high floor, away from lift etc)
▷ check status of bookings (guaranteed/non-guaranteed)
▷ check arrival times if listed
▷ look for pre-registered guests.

Expected departures report

This report lists all rooms by room number expected to check-out today. Look for:

▷ day use rooms (these rooms can be allocated to late arrivals)
▷ late check-outs (allocate these late check-out rooms to late arrivals).

Specials report

A specials report will list all requests by guests such as a particular room, rollaway bed, fruit and champagne, and anything else that makes this reservation special. You need to check:

Figure 6.2 ▷ **Expected arrivals report**

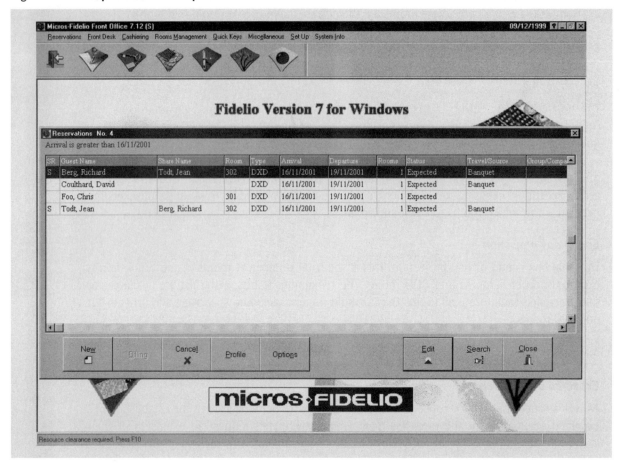

▷ that special request rooms have been allocated, and

▷ special request details are forwarded to the correct department, for example, cot requests to housekeeping, champagne requests to room service.

Flag reports

Flag reports are a list of activities to be completed during the shift. For example, when Mr Lade's secretary made the booking, she wasn't sure if he wanted breakfast included in the rate. A flag is sent to reception (indicated on the guest's reservation in the computer) asking reception to check with Mr Lade when he checks-in if he wants breakfast included in the rate.

Flags may also include a need to check a guest's rate, collect an authority to charge services to the guest's company or any number of things. Whatever is 'flagged' needs to be followed up on your shift (or handed over to the next shift).

Group arrivals report

Group arrivals are a busy time at reception. Being well prepared is important to minimise the disruption to other guests. The group arrivals report lists the number of guests due to arrive, expected time of arrival, individuals' names and who is sharing with whom, and who belongs to a group. It also lists the group leader, with whom most contact is made. Check that:

▷ the groups rooms are blocked

▷ room keys are set aside to give to the group leader at check-in

▷ breakfast vouchers and any other information is prepared for their arrival

▷ housekeeping has been informed of arrival time so rooms can be cleaned.

6. ALLOCATE ROOMS

A guest's room is sometimes allocated prior to arrival. This task is completed by reception. However, most computer systems will automatically allocate a room according to the details entered (from the reservation information) during the check-in process. Rooms are allocated according to guest's preferences, such as a suite, double or twin, and the guest's needs, such as an **interconnecting room** (two rooms next to each other with a door providing access between them) or a non-smoking room.

Pre-register guests

To pre-register a guest means that you 'register' a guest in the PMS and assign them a room before they arrive. Pre-registering is convenient both for the venue and the guest. For example, Ms O'Leary is arriving from Dublin on a 2.00 am flight on Tuesday and wishes to be pre-registered. When she arrives at the venue, she wants to be issued immediately with a key and go straight to her room.

Inbound groups are frequently pre-registered. This ensures that all rooms are cleaned and allocated before expected time of arrival. On arrival, the group is issued with their keys, thus minimising the check-in time and disruption to the other guests.

Both examples of pre-registration are for guaranteed bookings only. Non-guaranteed bookings are not usually pre-registered because of the risk of the guest not arriving. If the booking results in a no-show, then it becomes necessary to reverse the check-in and reverse the room revenue posted, and this affects all the internal statistics.

7. PRINT REGISTRATION CARDS

Once rooms have been allocated, the next step is to print and alphabetically file, in the expected arrivals file, all expected arrivals registration cards. This task may, however, be performed by the night audit shift. The registration card lists the guest's reservation details and any special requests. At check-in, the guest signs the card as confirmation of their stay and confirms the payment method before being issued with a room key.

SKILLS FOCUS

At the beginning of a shift, a number of tasks must be completed in readiness to receive guests. The tasks include a shift hand over, collecting the float, logging onto the PMS, checking your equipment and stationery supplies, printing reports, allocating special request rooms and printing registration cards for guests with a reservation.

Checking equipment and supplies ensures that everything is in working order and sufficiently stocked, minimising disruption to your reception duties.

Reports accurately identify the expected activities in the venue that day.

Allocating rooms considers the guests' needs according to the information provided on the reservation. It may also save time during the registration process.

Pre-registering the guest, particularly groups, facilitates the registration process for the group and reduces the likelihood of disturbing other guests.

FOCUS REVIEW

▷ What happens during the first half hour of your shift? Do you think this is important? Why? Why not?

▷ What are the tasks to be completed as part of the preparation for guests' arrival? Do you think it matters in what order they are completed? Why? Why not?

▷ Why is the float signed out? Why do you think you need to count it?

▷ Briefly explain the information contained in the 'house status report'. How does this information help you do your job?

▷ Explain the difference between OOO and OOS.

▷ What is meant by the term 'room status'?

▷ What do the following room status codes stand for—VD, OC, OD and VC?

▷ When might a room need a 'touch up'?

▷ When does a guest change from being an expected arrival to an actual arrival?

Guest registration

Having completed all the pre-arrival tasks, you are now ready to welcome guests and complete the guest registration process in a professional, organised and efficient manner. Guest registration, while following an established procedure, does not happen in isolation. By this we mean that guest registration will occur at various times of the day and it is likely you will be completing several other tasks simultaneously. For example, not only might you be checking a guest in but also answering the telephone, organising photocopying, arranging tours for another guest, sending a newspaper up to a room and confirming champagne for a honeymoon.

Being able to cope with a variety of jobs simultaneously requires good interpersonal skills, time management skills, and organisational skills.

PURPOSE OF GUEST REGISTRATION

Purpose of registration—to formalise the relationship between the guest and the establishment.

The purpose of guest registration is to formalise the relationship between the guest and the establishment. By signing the registration card, the guest is entering into a formal contract with the establishment. In simple terms, the contract is for the provision of a room in return for a fee. The venue agrees to provide the room and the guest agrees to pay. There is a legal requirement for the venue to maintain registration records for five years. There are several other legal implications of the registration process to be aware of. These are mentioned below.

Fire

In the event of a fire, the registration process enables accountability of all in-house guests. If an evacuation takes place, reception is responsible for having with them an up to date list of all in-house guests.

Insurance claim

An insurance claim may arise as a result of any number of incidents involving the guest such as an accident, negligence, property damage and theft.

Locating an individual

From time to time it may be necessary to locate a guest after departure. The registration form provides details of the guest's address. The most common reason for wanting to locate the guest after departure is for account settlement. However, it may also be because of civil or criminal action taken by the venue.

Theft

Theft from guests' rooms is quite common. For small losses (ashtrays, mini-bar up to $20) most venues wear the cost unless they catch the guest in the act. For larger losses (fixtures and fittings, towels, bathrobes, mini bar over $20) the venue is likely to follow up with requests for payment.

Property liability

Most damage caused by guests is accidental. However, where the damage is substantial and deliberate, the venue needs to make an insurance claim, may call in the police and may need to commence legal proceedings against the guest.

By understanding the importance of the registration process it is easier to understand why the steps in the registration process must be followed. Skipping any one of the steps may expose the venue to unnecessary costs and liability.

REGISTRATION STEPS

The registration process should be fast and efficient. You can only achieve a fast and efficient registration process if you follow the step-by-step procedures in place and know how to manage any problems that sometimes arise during check-in. The steps of the registration process are:

Legal implications of registration:
• legally binding contract
• fire
• insurance claim
• locating an individual
• theft
• property liability.

1. greet the guest
2. confirm the reservation details and register the guest
3. confirm method of payment
4. offer additional services
5. room the guest.

1. Greeting the guest

When the guest approaches the desk, greet the guest warmly and courteously then offer assistance. For example: 'Good morning. How may I help you?'

On arrival at the establishment, your guests have several expectations about the way they are greeted. They expect to be greeted in a warm and friendly manner that makes them feel welcome. They do not expect to be left standing at the desk while you take telephone calls, chat to a colleague, complain you are short-staffed or make other excuses. The guest expects you to be able to do your job no matter what problems may arise, and the guest expects you to be sufficiently capable to manage the things that do sometimes create problems.

Warm welcome

No matter what has just happened in the lead up to the guest's arrival, guests are acknowledged the *moment* they arrive. If you are busy with another guest, all it takes is a smile to tell the guest you have seen them and won't be long. It is frustrating for a guest to feel ignored (negative 'moment of truth') and if they have already had a bad experience or are tired, this is often the last straw.

Body language

Even behind a large desk your guests are able to read your body language. When you greet your guests stop the other activities you may be completing and concentrate on the person in front of you. Your guests deserve your full attention, open and friendly body language (a smile, eye contact) and a professional attitude.

Use the guest's name

After the greeting, the guest will tell you how you can help them. For example, they may say, 'Good morning, I have a reservation in the name of Ms O'Leahy'.

Now you know the guest's name, you can begin to use it. Recognition is something that everyone likes. Many people dislike being referred to as 'sir' or 'madam' so it is a sign of good service when you use every opportunity to refer to the guest by name. If you can't remember the guest's name after they say it or you have difficulty pronouncing it, ask the guest to spell the name for you (you need the correct spelling to locate their reservation). For example, the name 'O'Leahy' may be pronounced as 'OLay' or 'OLay-he'.

Regular guests like to be recognised and can feel snubbed or unimportant to the organisation if you don't use their name. In addition, take the time to learn how to pronounce regular guests' names properly.

APPLY YOUR KNOWLEDGE

How would you pronounce the following names? Write the name phonetically next to each.

▷ *Ng*
▷ *Van Denderen*
▷ *Zvervgandski*
▷ *Smyth*
▷ *Thunsapooknal*
▷ *Soulillou*

For more examples, use the experiences of your colleagues and try pronouncing each other's names.

2. Confirm reservation details and register the guest

Once the guest has been welcomed, and the spelling of the name confirmed, it is time to confirm the reservation details and register the guest. There are several steps in this part of the procedure.

1. Locate the registration card (remember, you printed these earlier and filed them alphabetically in the arrivals file).
2. Hand the registration card to the guest (with a pen) and ask them to check their personal details. Indicate where the guest is to sign.
   'Mrs Goldberg, would you please check the details on the registration form and then sign down the bottom.'
3. While the guest is completing the registration card, find the booking in the computer and proceed to check the guest into the system (how you do this will depend on the computer

system you use). If a room has not been allocated, the venue's computer will automatically allocate a room and guest account number.

4. Confirm departure details with the guest and any special requests.

'Mrs Goldberg, we have you departing on Thursday the 14th, is this correct?'

'And a non-smoking room away from the lift has been allocated for you. Is this suitable Mrs. Goldberg?'

After checking and signing the registration card, the guest will then hand it back to you. An example of a registration card is shown in Figure 6.3 on page 180.

Signing of the registration card

The registration card lists all the reservation details of the guest:

▷ name and address
▷ room type requested
▷ length of stay
▷ arrival and departure details
▷ special requests
▷ payment method.

Additional information printed on the reservation card often includes:

▷ reservation confirmation number
▷ motor vehicle registration
▷ credit card number
▷ registration disclaimer.

The guest should be asked to check all these details. If the information is inaccurate or incomplete, the guest is then able to make the necessary alterations and the venue records can be adjusted accordingly.

Registration card disclaimer

At the bottom of the registration card there is a **disclaimer**. The disclaimer limits the liability amount payable by the venue in the event of theft, loss or damage to the guest's personal belongings while on the premises. The guest accepts this limited liability by signing the registration card.

What to do if you can't find a booking

Occasionally, when attempting to register a guest, you may not be able to find the reservation (either on a registration card or in the computer). If this happens, you need to be tactful and helpful to prevent undue worry or inconvenience for the guest. Do not argue with the guest about the situation and do not blame anyone for the missing reservation. Helping a guest who may be tired and confused is part of your job.

When you realise you cannot find the guest's reservation:

▷ check for similar sounding names. Mr Smyth could be filed under Mr Blythe or spelt incorrectly and entered as Mr Smith. Just check the first one or two letters of the family name
▷ check under the guest's first name. Mr Trevor Nathan could be reserved as Mr Nathan Trevor

Figure 6.3 ▷ **Example of a registration card**

GRAND CENTRAL HOTEL
505 The Boulevard, Sydney
HOTELS OF DISTINCTION

Guest Registration Card

Room Number:	
Account Number:	
Room type:	

Check-out time 11.00 am

Arrival Date	Arrival Time	Departure Date	Daily Rate	No. of Guests

I will depart on: _____

Title	Surname		Other
Home Address			
Business Address			
Group Name			
Vehicle Reg No.	Vehicle Type		Preferred Newspaper

Method of Payment (please tick one)

☐ Visa ☐ MasterCard ☐ American Express ☐ Diners Club ☐ Bankcard
☐ Cash ☐ Voucher ☐ Company Charge (by prior arrangement)

Guest signature: _____

Every person signing this document and/or actually occupying any accommodation or utilising any services shall be personally liable for all accommodation, restaurant and other charges in addition to the customers named above notwithstanding that an account is sent in the first instance to that customer.

Innkeepers Act
(Act No 24, 1988 Section 7)
Loss or damage to guests' property

Under the Innkeepers Act, 1988, an Innkeeper may in certain circumstances be liable to make good any loss or damage to a guest's property even though it was not due to any fault of the Innkeeper or any servant in his employ. This liability however:

a. extends only to the property of guests who have engaged sleeping accommodation at the Inn;
b. is limited to one hundred dollars to any one guest except in the case of property which has been deposited, or offered for deposit, for safe custody;
c. does not cover motor vehicles or other vehicles of any kind or any property left in them, or horses or other live animals.

This notice does not constitute an admission either that the Act applies to these premises or that liability thereunder attaches in any particular case.

▷ ask the guest if they have a confirmation number from the venue. If they do, you can use this number to search for their reservation

▷ check the arrival date. The date of arrival may have been incorrectly entered or, if the guest was due yesterday his booking may have been cancelled, as he didn't turn up yesterday

▷ if another person made the booking, check under that person's name

▷ enquire if the guest could have made a booking at another venue. For example, the guest is booked for the Rydges Carlton and your venue is the Carlton Crest. If this is the case, and you have a room available offer to accommodate them at your venue and cancel their other reservation

▷ if the guest wants to go to the other venue then assist with arranging transport for them.

If, after checking everything, you are still unable to locate a reservation but you have a room available, apologise to the guest for the inconvenience, pass the guest a blank registration form and continue with the registration procedure.

If you cannot find a reservation and you are unable to accommodate the guest, apologise for the inconvenience and politely explain that you do not have a reservation for them nor do you have a room available. Offer to arrange a room at a nearby establishment, with the same star rating if possible, then arrange transport for the guest to take him there.

It is important to remember that this is still potentially a guest of your establishment and you want that person to return. Handling a missing reservation efficiently and effectively will help maintain good relations with this guest.

3. Confirm the payment details

An equally important component of the reservation process is confirming the payment method. How you process the guest's preferred method of payment will depend on whether the booking is guaranteed or not.

Processing guaranteed bookings

A guaranteed booking is one that is secured with a method of payment that ensures the venue receives payment for the room (whether the guest arrives or not), such as a credit card or company charge back. This information is shown on the registration card. When the guest checks in, ask if payment will be by the method indicated on the registration card. For example: 'Mr Frame, will you be settling your account with American Express?'

This gives the guest the opportunity to confirm the payment method or make alternative arrangements.

Credit cards

In our example, Mr Frame tells you he would prefer to pay by Visa card. Once the method of payment is confirmed, ask the guest for the credit card so you can take an imprint of it, or 'swipe' the card and then return it to the guest. For example: 'Mr Frame, may I please have your Visa card so I can take an imprint?'

The imprint voucher is kept on file (with the registration card) until the guest settles his account. The guest does not sign the voucher at check-in. By holding a credit card voucher imprint the guest is then able to charge the venue's services to their room during their stay. The credit card also acts as confirmation of the guest's identity.

Gaining authorisation

There are two ways authorisation can be obtained. If the venue operates a manual credit card system (imprint vouchers), then a call must be placed to the credit card company to gain authorisation. If the venue has a point of sale terminal, which is linked to a financial institution (bank), then a **pre-authorised amount** can be requested at check-in. This means that the card is 'swiped' and a specified amount of credit is arranged and held by the venue until check-out time.

The pre-authorised amount is held for the establishment for seven days. If after this time, the guest changes their mind and pays cash or by another card on check-out, it is important to call and cancel the pre-authority and make the funds available to the guest again.

Company charge

In Chapter 5 you learned that a company charge back is a method of payment whereby an authority to charge a service back to a company is obtained by the venue. An authority to charge back may be held permanently by the venue (blanket authority) or a new one required each time a guest from that company stays at the venue.

Whatever system is arranged, a copy of the charge authority is collected at check-in, or, if received in advance, attached to the registration card for reception stating what can be charged back to the company. For example 'all charges' means the guest doesn't have to pay anything at the time of check-out. 'Room and breakfast only' means the company will pay for room and breakfast but that the guest must pay any 'extras' such as mini-bar, laundry or room service dinner.

Depending on the organisation's policy, a guarantee for the extras is taken from the guest: either as a cash deposit or credit card. Sometimes a guarantee isn't asked for because if the guest skips, they can be traced through the company if necessary.

Vouchers

A voucher is issued in exchange for money and is used when the guest prepays for accommodation through their travel agent. When the guest checks in, the vouchers are paid to reception in the same way cash would be. A voucher is usually only valid for the room charge, but may include breakfast or another meal offered at the venue.

For example, Mrs Zevo is travelling to Perth on business. She paid her travel agent for the flights and accommodation and in exchange the travel agent issued her with a flight ticket and accommodation voucher. When Mrs Zevo arrives at her hotel, she will hand the voucher over to the receptionist during the check-in process. If, during her stay, Mrs Zevo uses other services in the venue, she will either need to pay cash for these or leave an imprint of her credit card with reception at check-in so that she can charge these services to her room.

Prepayment or advance deposit

A prepayment or advance deposit is money paid by the guest to the venue before the guest arrives (a receipt is issued to the guest). A prepayment or advance deposit guarantees the guest's booking and is handled in the same way as a guest with a voucher. When the guest checks in, their deposit is transferred to their account from the deposit ledger, and shown as a credit.

Processing non-guaranteed bookings

Non-guaranteed bookings are those that are not secured, that is, the venue has no way of guaranteeing it will be paid for its services. Non-guaranteed bookings are those that have indicated they will be paying with cash (or EFTPOS—Electronic Funds Transfer at Point of Sale) or cheque (personal or traveller's). Again it is necessary to confirm the method of payment. For example: 'Mr Finn, how will you be settling your account?'

Mr Finn can then confirm he is paying by cash or offer an alternative method of payment.

When guests choose to pay by cash or cheque, it is common practice to then ask for:

▷ proof of identity—usually a driver's licence as this confirms the guest's name and home address (record the identity details on the registration card)

▷ deposit for the room—this may vary but the first night's accommodation rate is standard

▷ security deposit—again this may vary, but frequently the equivalent of one night's room rate is charged. If a security deposit is collected, some venues will allow the guest to charge services to their room up to this amount. The security deposit is returned to the guest on departure (minus any services, such as mini-bar, consumed during their stay).

Cash and cheque paying guests are not permitted to charge services to their room account. If the guest dines in the restaurant or orders room service or uses any other service, such as mini-bar, the telephone or in-room pay-for-service videos, they must pay cash. This is because of the lack of guarantee the venue has that the guest will pay their account. Some venues may even remove the mini-bar, in-room movies and access to outside telephone calls.

The cash policy (that guests must pay for services as they use them) is explained at this point in the registration process, to the guest.

Cash

Cash may be paid in local or foreign currency. When you receive cash payments, count the money in front of the guest. If a deposit is taken, a receipt must be issued. Foreign currency needs to be converted to local currency first. If change is required, it is given in local currency. If a cash guest wishes to extend their stay, they must pay for this in advance.

Personal cheques

Personal cheques are rarely accepted, except for advance deposits or when the guest is well known to the venue. Guests approved to pay by cheque are frequently asked to sign a blank cheque at check-in, payable to the venue. The amount is left blank until departure. Depending on the venue's policy and procedure, a phone call may be made to check the validity of the cheque and the ability to pay the account.

Traveller's cheques

Traveller's cheques are always signed in front of you and proof of identification (passport, driver's licence) recorded on the cheque. If the traveller's cheques are in foreign currency, the equivalent local currency value must first be calculated. Change is then issued in local currency cash.

Extras accounts

When a guest is checking in and paying different services by two (or more) different means, then separate accounts are set up for the guest. For example, Mr Appleby is staying for two nights. His company will pay for his room and breakfast. Mr Appleby will pay for everything else. During his stay, you will post the relevant charges to the appropriate account as agreed. At check-out, Mr Appleby will be presented with two accounts. One is for his room and breakfast, which he signs and which is then sent back to his company for payment. The other account is paid by Mr Appleby by whatever means is arranged at check-in.

The account paid for by the guest's company (room and breakfast) is referred to as the **master account**. The second account is referred to as the **extras account** and includes all other charges. The different types of accounts used in the front office are discussed in detail in Chapter 7.

4. *Offering other services*

Once the reservation details are confirmed, the registration card signed and the method of payment organised you are then able to offer additional services to the guest. For example, you may:

▷ arrange a newspaper to be delivered to their room in the morning
▷ explain the restaurant opening times
▷ offer to make a booking in the restaurant
▷ offer a local area map or tourist guide
▷ mention the fully equipped gym and 25-metre pool on the first floor
▷ explain the safety deposit box facility or in-room safe for their valuables
▷ advise the guest of the best place to park
▷ explain the services available through the business centre
▷ provide local area information or mention sites of particular interest nearby.

Guest on a package

If the guest is on a package, explain what is included in that package (breakfast, champagne in the room) and how to use the features of the package. For example, explain that breakfast may be served in their room or is available in the restaurant between 7.00 am and 10.00 am.

Complimentary upgrade

If the guest has received a complimentary upgrade for some reason—reservations may have overbooked standard rooms and this guest has been given a suite for this stay—it is important to explain this. If the guest receives an upgrade without knowing why, when they re-book next month they will be disappointed at paying the same money for a standard room!

Most of this part of the procedure (offering services) takes place while you are taking an imprint of the credit card voucher, entering the guest's details into the computer or while rooming the guest. It only takes a few moments. Not only is it helpful to the guest, it is an opportunity to 'sell' other services of the venue.

5. *Rooming the guest*

The term '**rooming the guest**' means issuing the guest with a key, instructing the guest on how to find their room, and, in many venues, arranging a porter to escort the guest to their room.

Issuing the key

Before giving the guest a key always double check the computer to confirm the name, room number and room status (make sure it is a vacant clean room). A guest is never amused to be given a key to someone else's room or a dirty room! Locate the key for the room in which the guest is staying. Pass the key to the guest and tell them which floor their room is on. For example: 'Mrs Jansen, your room is on the 12th floor.'

Along with issuing the key, hand the guest any messages, faxes or parcels that have been held at reception for them. If an electronic key is used, you need to explain how to use it.

Electronic keys (or key cards) have been introduced to reduce the cost of replacing lost keys and to minimise the risk of security breaches in accommodation venues. It is more difficult to access a room (illegally) with a key card lock than a room with a traditional lock. The key card is programmed for the allocated room but does not show a room number. If a guest loses their key card, a new one can be issued automatically at reception. No security risk is caused because the room number is not printed on the card.

If a traditional key is lost, this poses more of a problem to the venue, particularly if the room number is printed on the key. Because of the potential to misuse the key by whoever finds it, the locks on that room door will need to be changed.

Show the guest where the room number is written, for example, on the key itself or on an information booklet, if one is used. An information booklet is a mini-guide to the venue services and the guest's name, as well as their room number, is usually written on this information booklet.

It is recommended that the guest's room number not be mentioned at the reception desk. The reason for this is the guest's security. Because the reception desk is in a public area, anyone could be hanging around, overhear the room number and attempt to gain access.

Rooming the guest—issuing the guest with a key, instructing the guest how to find their room and, if applicable, escorting the guest to their room.

Giving directions to the room

Particularly in larger venues, it is useful to explain to the guest how to find their room. Begin by specifying where the lift is, repeat the floor their room is on and then say which way they should turn when they exit the lift. For example: 'Mrs Jansen, the lift is directly behind you. Take the lift to the 12th floor, turn left out of the lift and your room is down the end of the corridor on the right.'

Escorting to their room

Guests may or may not be escorted to their room. If the guest is escorted, a porter is summoned who will carry the guest's bags. At other times, luggage may be delivered to the guest's room later. For example, when the guest arrives, the porter may collect the bags from the guest and take them to the room after the guest has already checked in.

There are several advantages to escorting the guest to their room. The first is the additional service and attention that the guest receives. Next, on the way up to the room, the porter is able to highlight, or 'sell' the services and features of the venue to the guest. It also allows time for the guest to ask questions about the venue and the surrounding area. And finally, once the guest is in their room, the porter is able to point out the features of the room and even how to operate some of the equipment.

A pleasant stay

When the formalities of the registration process are finished, it is common practice to ask the guest if there is anything further you can do for them, then wish your guest a pleasant stay. For example: 'Ms Tombleson, is there anything else we can do for you?'

This gives the guest an opportunity to ask questions or request something. Once the guest has responded, wish them a pleasant stay and explain how they can contact reception if they require anything. For example: 'Ms Tombleson, I'm sure you will enjoy your stay with us and if you need anything else, please call "9" for reception. Goodbye'.

The entire check-in procedure should take only a few minutes. Remember that there may be other people waiting to check-in so the amount of personal interaction may need to be kept short. This means that the amount of information passed on to a guest needs to be monitored so others guest are not inconvenienced while waiting their turn to check-in.

WHAT IF A ROOM IS NOT READY FOR THE GUEST?

Most venues allow check-in to commence after 2.00 pm. This allows housekeeping time to clean the necessary rooms required for expected arrivals. However, some guests arrive before this time and before their room is available.

If the room is not available for the guest to check into when they arrive, there are a few things you can do. What you actually do will depend on the individual venue and your level of authority. Register the guest up to the point of rooming the guest, then:

(a) Allocate another clean room to the guest that meets the guest's requirements and room them following the standard procedure. If this is not possible, then

(b) Advise the guest that their room is not yet ready (indicate how long it may be until it is), offer to store their luggage and then offer the guest coffee in the lounge/foyer (some venues offer a complimentary breakfast or light lunch depending on their policy).

(c) If the guest is not satisfied with this, and wants to freshen up, you may have the option of a courtesy room for guest use.

Immediately call housekeeping to request the assigned room be cleaned as soon as possible and to determine how long until the required room is ready. Convey this information to the guest at intervals so that they don't feel they have been left stranded. When relaying the time to the guest, add an extra 15 minutes to the time in case of a further delay. It is better to have the room earlier than expected than later.

If option (b) or (c) was all that was available, once the room is ready, apologise for the delay, advise the guest that the room is now available, and complete the rooming the guest procedure.

If the room is going to be longer than an hour or the guest needs to freshen up, offer the guest use of the facilities in the gymnasium or, if they need to work, offer them the use of the business centre.

REGISTERING A WALK IN

A guest who arrives seeking accommodation but who does not have a reservation is referred to as a walk in. The type and location of the venue influences how much walk in trade it is likely to attract. The procedure for registering a walk in is similar to that of a guest with a reservation with a few elements of the reservation process attached. Because of the preparation completed by reception at the start of the day, it should be easy to determine quickly and efficiently whether or not the walk in can be accommodated.

▷ greet the guest. The guest will tell you that they would like a room
▷ ask the guest what sort of room is required and how many people it is for
▷ ask the guest how long they would like the room for
▷ check availability
▷ advise the guest what room types you have available (that match as closely as possible to their request), and the price (depending on the occupancy level, length of stay, room night and time of day, the rate may be rack rate or another, lesser rate). During this step, use your selling skills to assist the guest in making their decision, particularly if you do not have the preferred room type available

▷ if the guest accepts the offer, pass the guest a blank registration form and ask them to complete it. Confirm and process method of payment, and then room the guest.

There is a higher risk of skippers with walk in trade than with guests who hold a reservation. For this reason, many venues ask for identification when registering a walk in and will often also ask for the registration number of the guest's car (if they drove to the venue). Ensure that the payment procedure is strictly followed to reduce the likelihood of financial loss.

If you are unable to accommodate the walk in, explain why (such as, no rooms available). You may even like to suggest an alternative venue they could try.

WHEN THE GUEST HAS LEFT RECEPTION

Whether the guest is one with a reservation or a walk in, once they have gone to their room, there are a number of tasks you must complete to ensure the accuracy and security of the registration process:

1. Complete the registration process in the computer if it was not finished while the guest was at the desk. This may include updating the guest's address and other personal details.
2. Set up charging and if there is more than one method of payment, then billing needs to be split correctly (extras account).
3. If a credit card is being used it must be pre-authorised according to the venue's policy.
4. Check that all relevant details are attached to the registration card, for example, a copy of a charge back authority, voucher or credit card details. File these in room number order in the registration file (often referred to as the registration 'pit').
5. Post cash payments to the guest's account and place the money in the till drawer.

It may not be possible to complete all these tasks as soon as the guest leaves the desk, but all of the above tasks must be completed at some time during your shift.

Before finishing with the registration process, let's look at a complete registration procedure for a guest with a guaranteed booking. Keep in mind that the following is completed in approximately three minutes.

Reception:	'Good afternoon sir. How may I help you?'
Mr Abacus:	'Good afternoon. My name's John Abacus. I have a reservation.'
Reception:	'Mr Abacus, is your name spelt A B A C U S?'
Mr Abacus:	'That's right.'
Reception:	'Mr Abacus, would you please confirm the details on the registration card, then sign down the bottom. You're staying with us two nights, leaving on the 22nd. Is that right?'
Mr Abacus:	'Yes. That's correct.'
Reception:	'And how would you like to settle your account, Mr Abacus?'
Mr Abacus:	'With Visa card.'
Reception:	'May I have the Visa card so I can take an imprint please?'
Reception:	'Mr Abacus, our restaurant serves breakfast between 6.30 am and 10.00 am. You won't need a booking for breakfast. Dinner is available from 6.00 pm. Would you like me to make a dinner booking for you?'
Mr Abacus:	'No thank you, I'll be having dinner in my room tonight.'
Reception:	'The restaurant menu is available in your room also Mr Abacus. Would you like a newspaper delivered in the morning? We can arrange for *The Age*, *The Financial Review*, the *Sydney Morning Herald* or the *Herald-Sun*.'

Mr Abacus:	'Could I have the *Sydney Morning Herald* please.'
Reception:	'Certainly. I'll arrange that for you now. Mr Abacus, this is your key and your room is located on the 14th floor. The lift is straight down this passageway to your left. When you get to the 14th floor, turn left out of the lift and your room is the first room on the right. Would you like a porter to help with your luggage?'
Mr Abacus:	'No thanks. I haven't got much with me.'
Reception:	'Is there anything else I can do for you?'
Mr Abacus:	'Yes. I need a hire car. Can you arrange that for me?'
Reception:	'I'll let the concierge know and he will take care of that for you, Mr Abacus. Is there anything else?'
Mr Abacus:	'No thanks.'
Reception:	'Mr Abacus, I hope you enjoy your stay with us and if there is anything else you need you can call reception on "9". Goodbye.'
Mr Abacus:	'Thanks. Goodbye.'

SKILLS FOCUS

The guest registration process follows an established procedure that ensures the guest is quickly and efficiently checked into their room. This means that the guest checks and signs the registration card (which is a legally binding contract) and confirms their method of payment before being roomed. The purpose of registration is to formalise the relationship between the venue and the guests and there are several legal implications of the registration process.

The registration procedure follows several steps: welcome the guest, confirm the guest reservation details and register the guest in the PMS, confirm and process the guest method of payment, offer the guest additional services and room the guest.

If the guest's reservation cannot be located during the check-in procedure, there are several steps to follow before proceeding with the registration process. Ensure the guest is caused minimal inconvenience and do not blame anyone if you are unable to locate the guest's details.

If the guest's room is not yet ready to be occupied you may be able to register the guest to another room, offer to store their luggage, offer refreshments while they wait or offer the guest the use of a courtesy room.

Registering a walk in follows the same procedure as for a guest with a reservation. However, some of the steps include part of the reservation process and there is greater risk of financial loss.

Once the guest has left the desk, finalise the registration process in the PMS and file their details in the registration 'pit.'

FOCUS REVIEW

▷ *What is the purpose of the guest registration?*
▷ *What are the other legal implications of the registration process?*

- ▷ What are the five steps to the guest registration process? Do you think it is important to follow these steps in order? Why? Why not?
- ▷ What difference do you think it makes to the guest's experience of the venue if you use their name?
- ▷ When registering a guest, why are the reservation details confirmed?
- ▷ A disclaimer is printed at the bottom of the registration card. What is a disclaimer and what does it mean for the venue?
- ▷ What steps should you take if you cannot find a guest's reservation details?
- ▷ Why is processing guaranteed and non-guaranteed bookings different?
- ▷ If a guest wants to charge services used in the venue to their room, what must they do at check-in?
- ▷ As a cash paying guest, what arrangements can I make to charge services to my room?
- ▷ For a cash paying guest, it is common practice to ask for three additional things not asked of a guest paying by other means. What are these three things?
- ▷ Why is it valuable to advise the guest of additional services available in the venue?
- ▷ Why should you advise a guest they have received a complimentary upgrade?
- ▷ What does 'rooming the guest' mean?
- ▷ Why is the guest's room number not mentioned at the reception desk?
- ▷ What procedure should you follow if a guest's allocated room is not ready when they arrive at the venue?
- ▷ What are the differences between registering a walk in and registering a guest with a reservation?
- ▷ What do you need to do once the guest has left reception?

APPLY YOUR KNOWLEDGE

This activity gives you the opportunity to put into practice the skills and knowledge required to register guests. Working with two other colleagues, take it in turn to register guests. One person is the receptionist, another the guest, and the third person the observer. At the end of each role play, the observer is to give feedback on how well the procedure was followed. Roles are then rotated until everyone has had a turn at registering a guest with a reservation and a walk in.

Use the reservations you created in Chapter 5 and follow the five steps of the registration procedure. Repeat the exercise for a walk in.

During your role play, check-in a guest paying by cash, another by credit card and another by company charge back. Then register a booking where you can't find the reservation.

Refusing accommodation to a guest

There are times you will find yourself in the position of having to refuse a guest accommodation. There are a number of reasons why this may occur. When refusing a guest accommodation be professional at all times. Be sympathetic, courteous, polite and empathetic. Explain politely why accommodation is being refused without accusing the guest of any

Reasons for refusing a guest accommodation:
• venue full
• venue overbooked
• guest intoxicated
• guest on the black list
• insufficient funds.

wrongdoing. Apologise for refusing them a room but never argue the point. Never offer a second-class level of service to any guest.

VENUE FULL

If the establishment is full, it is not possible to accommodate a guest. If the guest is a walk in, simply apologise and say you are unable to accommodate them. You may even recommend another venue for them to try. If it is a regular guest of the venue, try to find an alternative venue for them.

The guest may also be refused if the establishment does not have any of the room types requested available. However, if you have alternative room types available, offer these to the guest.

OVERBOOKED

You learned in Chapter 5 that many venues take more bookings than they have rooms available. The reasons for this are the percentage of no-shows, under-stays and late cancellations the venue frequently experiences. In trying to maximise occupancy (ensure as many rooms as possible are booked), the venue will overbook (for example, by 20 per cent) knowing they can still achieve 100 per cent occupancy even if a few guests don't show or cancel late in the day.

If the venue is overbooked, then at 6.00 pm all non-guaranteed bookings still not checked in may be released (cancelled) for re-sale if necessary. This means that the venue may not be able to accommodate the guests with non-guaranteed reservations if they arrive after this time.

If guests with reservations turn up and find the venue is full, the venue will 'walk' or 'bump' these guests to another venue. To walk a guest means to accommodate them at another venue. If you need to walk a guest:

Walk or bump—to arrange to transfer the guest to another venue (because of overbooking at your venue).

▷ apologise for the inconvenience
▷ make arrangements for the guest to stay at another venue of the same or better standard than your venue. There is no additional cost to the guest. Explain this to the guest and explain that you will be covering all associated costs in transferring them to the other establishment
▷ make arrangements to transport the guest to the other venue. This may mean transferring the guest in the venue's limousine or booking a taxi
▷ invite the guest to stay another time.

An important component of walking a guest is getting them to return to your venue next time. If the experience is well managed, the guest will understand and return. A poorly managed walk may result in the loss of that guest forever.

INTOXICATION

A guest may be refused accommodation for being drunk. Apart from there being laws in most states and territories that forbids the presence of intoxicated persons on (liquor) licensed premises, a drunk person cannot be held legally liable if they sign a contract (registration form) and may in fact be unable to sign the registration form at all.

People who are rowdy, quarrelsome, violent or disorderly may also be refused accommodation. If a guest appears to be out of control, it may be necessary to call for management or security intervention.

BLACK LIST

A black list is a list of guests who have stayed previously at the venue but are now banned from doing so. The decision to place a guest (or company) on the black list is entirely at management's discretion. The reason for black listing is usually a past experience with the guest, such as intoxication, offensive behaviour, poor payment record, and damage to the property.

Another reason why a guest or company may be black listed is prior warning about the guest from other establishments, for example, this guest has 'skipped' before, or caused problems in other venues.

INSUFFICIENT FUNDS

A guest may attempt to check-in without any money or credit available on their credit cards. Reception has a responsibility to protect the venue's financial interests by following the correct procedure for verifying the guest's ability to pay (during the check-in procedure).

Releasing of bookings

Non-guaranteed reservations are assigned a 'release' time. This means that if the guest has not checked in by a predetermined time (usually 6.00 pm), then the room is released so that it can be sold to another person. This helps the venue maximise its occupancy. If a room is booked, but the guest doesn't turn up (no-show), releasing the room allows the possibility of selling the room to a walk in, thus reducing the likelihood of lost revenue.

The release time varies but non-guaranteed bookings are usually held until 6.00 pm. If the guest arrives after this time and the room they reserved has been released you can check the guest into another room meeting the guest's criteria, if one is available, upgrade this guest or, if a room is not available, walk the guest.

A guest can make arrangements in advance to have their room held for longer. For example, Mr and Mrs Wallace know their flight doesn't arrive into Sydney until 9.30 pm. By the time they get to the hotel it will be after 10.00 pm. On the day of arrival, they can arrange with the venue to have their room held until 10.00 pm.

NO-SHOW

A guest is classified as a no-show if a reservation has been made and the guest fails to arrive without cancelling the booking. Both guaranteed and non-guaranteed bookings can result in a no-show. If the booking is guaranteed, the establishment can charge the guest for one night's accommodation. However, this may not happen if the room is released *and* resold or the guest is a regular or from a company that gives the venue numerous room nights each year.

If the booking is a non-guaranteed one, then it will be released at 6.00 pm and there is no charge. This is part of the risk a venue takes when booking non-guaranteed reservations.

SKILLS FOCUS

Refusing a guest accommodation must be handled politely and courteously. There are a number of reasons why accommodation may be refused: the venue is full, overbooked, the guest is intoxicated, black listed or has insufficient funds available. The reason should be explained to the guest.

Non-guaranteed bookings may be released at 6.00 pm particularly when the venue is full or overbooked. The reason venues sometimes do this is to maximise their potential to achieve a high occupancy. If a room is released and the guest with the reservation later turns up, the venue may need to allocate another room to the guest if one is available, upgrade to a better room or walk this guest to another venue.

A no-show is a person who makes a reservation but fails to arrive without cancelling the reservation. Both guaranteed and non-guaranteed bookings may result in a no-show. The venue is able to charge a guaranteed booking if it results in a no-show, but cannot receive any revenue if a non-guaranteed booking results in a no-show.

FOCUS REVIEW

▷ *What is meant by the term 'bump'?*
▷ *If you have to 'walk' someone, why should you take responsibility for locating alternative accommodation?*
▷ *Explain four reasons why a venue may 'walk' a guest.*
▷ *What is meant by 'released'?*
▷ *Why do venues 'release' rooms? Do you think this is a fair practice? Why? Why not?*
▷ *How might you handle a guest who has a reservation but whose room has been released and sold?*
▷ *What is a no-show and what are the financial implications of a non-guaranteed and guaranteed no-show?*

Other reception duties and services

So far we have considered the role of reception in registering a guest. But there are numerous other tasks front office staff are responsible for and perform on a regular basis. Here we consider the most common tasks undertaken by reception.

INFORMATION

Passing on information is one of the most common tasks you will undertake. You will pass on information to guests and colleagues and you therefore require excellent communication skills. You will also need considerable knowledge about the venue (services and facilities offered) and local area knowledge (attractions, entertainment, directions). On a daily basis, guests will ask you for information about both the venue and the local area. You must be able to respond to these requests efficiently and knowledgeably.

POSTING CHARGES

When guests charge services to their room, the charge is added to their account. The process of recording a charge (or a payment) on a guest account is referred to as **posting**. Posting of charges means recording the details of the financial transaction on the account of the guest who used the specified service.

Most of the information you need to record charges to be posted comes from the various departments in the venue. However, there are other transactions that you process and post such as foreign exchange. Posting charges and payments to guest accounts is discussed in detail in Chapter 7.

FOREIGN CURRENCY EXCHANGE

The exchange of foreign currency is a service offered by many venues. Knowing how to perform this task is important because guests may also choose to settle their account with foreign currency.

In most cases, the venue places a mark-up on the bank quoted currency exchange rate, or charges a fee for the service. This helps to increase the venue's revenue. Most guests accept this because of the inability to get to a bank or because of the convenience. Exchange rates are displayed at reception to encourage guests to use the venue's exchange facility. How to exchange foreign currency is explained in Chapter 7.

ROOM MOVES

Once a guest has their key and goes to the room, they may request a **room move**. This means that the guest is moved from the room they were allocated to a new room. There could be a variety of reasons for this:

▷ a smoker in a non-smoking room
▷ they require a bath as well as a shower
▷ the room is too noisy
▷ the window doesn't open
▷ the in-room facilities are faulty
▷ the room doesn't suit their needs.

Assuming the venue has another room to move the guest to, a room move is a straightforward procedure.

1. Find out why the guest wants to be moved. This helps you determine which room type to move the guest to and makes you aware of any problem that may need to be addressed.
2. Quickly find another room meeting the guest's criteria and then offer to bring the new key up. When the room is moved in the PMS, the old room will come up with a TU status so housekeeping know they must straighten the room. If the establishment is using a manual system, housekeeping needs to be paged and informed of the move.
3. Take the key to the guest and escort them to their new room. Allow the guest time to check the room to confirm that it is suitable.

If the guest requests to move the next day then ask the guest to have their bags packed and ready, make a note in the front office diary and inform housekeeping of the move. In the morning arrange to have the guest's bags moved to a new room when one becomes available.

Room moves need to be recorded in case anything is misplaced, and also to let other departments know of the move. A room move slip is usually completed. An example of a room move slip is shown in Figure 6.4.

If the room move was due to a maintenance or cleaning problem, report the complaint to the relevant department so that it can be fixed.

Figure 6.4 ▷ **Room move slip**

Room Move Slip	
Date: **23 Jan**	Time: **3.35 pm**
Name: **Oldham**	
Old Room No: **1062**	New Room No. **940**
Old Room Rate: **$275**	New Room Rate: **$275**
Airconditioning out of order	
Departure Date: **25 Jan**	
Receptionist: **Robyn**	

SAFETY DEPOSIT BOXES

Whether guests are on business or holidays they tend to carry some valuables with them. Valuables may include money, documents, jewellery, a passport or any number of other items. Hospitality establishments have an obligation to provide an area for the safekeeping of the guests' valuables.

Most venues offer some form of security arrangements for personal valuables. Many venues have an in-room safe while others offer a safety-box option located at or near reception. Alternatively, guests' items are sealed in an envelope and stored in the venue's main safe.

For the safety box or envelope option, reception is responsible for receiving and controlling the procedure to ensure the security of the guests' valuables. In most venues the safety box procedure is:

1. Ask the guest to complete the safety box form. The form contains the following information: name, room number, and signature (some venues will ask that the valuables be listed, and checked). An example of this form is shown in Figure 6.5.
2. Place the items in an A4 envelope and seal it. Tape is then placed over the seal and the guest signs over this seal, so if the envelope is opened the guest can tell right away.
3. Record the details in the safety box log.
4. Place the envelope in the safe until the guest requires it when it is logged out and signed for by the guest. Alternatively,
5. Issue the safety box key to the guest who places the items in the box themselves.

Safety deposit boxes are usually in a secure area of reception and require two keys to access. These boxes can only be opened with both keys being turned simultaneously. One key is kept at reception and the other is given to the guest. The guest is required to sign in and out every time the safety deposit box is used in acknowledgement of their access to the box.

Figure 6.5 ▷ **Safety box record slip**

GRAND CENTRAL HOTEL
505 The Boulevard, Sydney
HOTELS OF DISTINCTION

Safety Deposit Box

Date		Safety Box No.	
Guest Name		Room No.	
Address			
Guest signature		Receptionist	

Loss of key will incur a charge of $200.00			
For security reasons, you are asked to sign the safety deposit box register each time you access your valuables.			
Date	Time	Signature	Venue Representative

WAKE UP CALLS

Reception is often responsible for both booking and executing guest wake up calls. However, the telephonist, porter or night auditor may also take on this responsibility, or, depending on the switchboard capabilities, wake up calls may be programmed directly into the system. The call is then placed electronically (pre-recorded wake up call is placed to the guest's room at the specified time).

When a guest requests a wake up call, you need to record the following information:

▷ guest's name
▷ room number
▷ wake up call time
▷ if second reminder call required (and what time).

SECRETARIAL SERVICES FOR GUESTS

Most city venues catering to the business market will offer a range of secretarial services to their guests, including:

▷ photocopying
▷ typing
▷ printing and collating files
▷ sending and receiving facsimiles
▷ sending guest mail.

Alternatively, many venues have a business centre where guests can perform most of these tasks themselves.

OTHER SERVICES

Depending on the venue, reception may perform a range of other services such as:

▷ tour bookings
▷ car hire
▷ theatre and sporting event tickets
▷ airport transfers
▷ airline reservation confirmation.

If the venue has a concierge department, the concierge frequently provides these services. Porter services are discussed in detail in Chapter 9.

SKILLS FOCUS

A room move takes place when the guest requests an alternative room to the one they have been allocated. The reasons for the room move vary and must be completed quickly and with minimal disruption to the guest.

Reception provides a range of services including safety deposit facilities, wake up calls and secretarial services. Depending on the venue, reception may also arrange tour bookings, transport and theatre tickets.

FOCUS REVIEW

▷ *What is the procedure for moving a guest to another room? List two reasons why a guest may request a room move.*
▷ *Who should reception inform when a guest is moved to another room? Why?*
▷ *Why do safety deposit boxes require two keys to open them?*
▷ *If Mr Hughes had signed the safety deposit card and his wife wanted to retrieve the items from his box, would you let her do it? Why? Why not?*
▷ *Apart from those listed here, what other services do you think guests may reasonably expect reception to provide?*

Processing guest departure

Like the check-in process, the efficient and smooth guest departure procedure is achieved through prior preparation and organisation. All information relating to the guest's stay must be accurately recorded so that at check-out, the guest is presented with an accurate account and is able to finalise payment quickly.

Also, like the check-in procedure, the check-out procedure serves several purposes. It:

▷ settles the guest's account balance
▷ allows you to update the room status

▷ creates (or updates) the guest's profile

▷ allows you to receive guest feedback.

ACCOUNT SETTLEMENT

A departure report is printed at the beginning of the shift. This is an accurate indication of who and how many guests are due to depart today. An example is shown in Figure 6.6.

Before guests come to reception to check-out, you need to complete any postings that have not yet been entered and you need to:

▷ call the restaurant—check for breakfast charges for guests due to check-out

▷ call room service—check for late breakfast orders for guests due to check-out

▷ call housekeeping—check for mini-bar charges and overnight laundry charges

▷ check reception—a guest may have used the secretarial service for example, and the charge may not yet be posted.

If any of these departments has charges for guests due to check-out, the source documents (documentation detailing the charges made by the guest) need to be collected and the charge posted to the guest's account. Even if the guest has requested a late check-out, post all of these charges now so they aren't forgotten later.

Figure 6.6 ▷ **Expected departure report**

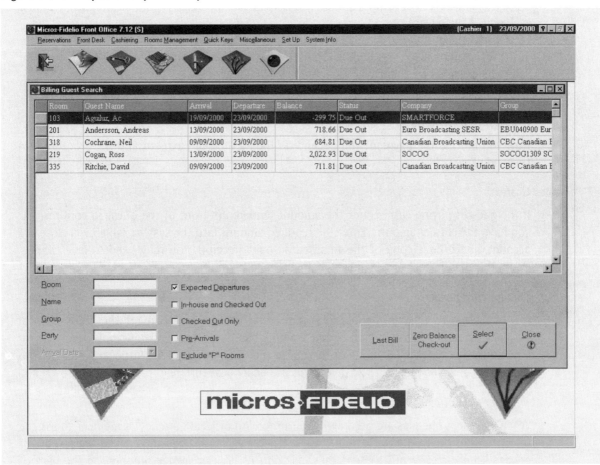

CHECK-OUT PROCEDURE

When you have checked for additional charges and posted these, the guest's account should be up to date and accurate when the guest wants to check-out.

The procedure for checking a guest out is:

1. Greet the guest. 'Good morning sir, how may I help you?'
2. Request the room number (retrieve the account on the screen). Check that the name matches the room number in the system. Collect the registration card, which was filed in the pit.
3. Request the room key. If the guest does not have the room key on them ask if it has been left in the room. It is important to get the room key from the guest so that the locks do not have to be changed.
4. Ask the guest if there are any further charges, such as breakfast, mini-bar, laundry.
5. If the guest tells you that they have had breakfast, for example, and this has not been posted, you will need to call the restaurant to find out the amount to charge, then post this amount to the account.
6. Print the account.
7. Present the account to the guest and ask them to check the details.
8. Ask the guest how they will be settling their account. When they confirm the payment method, request payment and process it according to the establishment's procedures. (Enter the details onto the computer. This will close the account and automatically print a copy of the receipt.)
9. Present the guest with a copy of the account (receipt).
10. Offer additional services, such as transport arrangements, luggage storage or for their car to be collected for them.
11. Farewell the guest.

Processing payments

How you process the payment will depend on the method of payment and the procedures in the workplace.

Cash

If the guest is paying cash, count the amount tendered in front of the guest to confirm that you have the correct amount. Enter the required amount into the system, which will close the account, and print a copy of the finalised account (receipt). You may need to give change. Count the change back to the guest when you hand them their receipt.

Foreign currency

If a guest wishes to pay in foreign currency, you will need to convert the required local currency amount into the foreign currency amount so that the guest knows how much to give you. Count the currency in front of the guest and enter the amount (in local currency) into the system. If change needs to be given, this will be in local currency.

Traveller's cheques

When traveller's cheques are used, (whether in foreign or local currency) remember to ask the guest to sign them in front of you. Ask for proof of identification, such as a passport or driver's licence and record these details (passport or driver's licence number) on the back of each cheque. If the traveller's cheque is in foreign currency, you will need to follow the same procedure for conversion as handling foreign currency cash.

Company charge/Blanket authority

If the account is a company charge, check if there is an extras account as well as a master account. The master account is the one being paid by the company. Ask the guest to sign the bottom of the master account when they have finished checking it. Then ask the guest to check the extras account and process payment according to the standard procedure (for cash, credit card etc).

Credit cards

The credit card is 're-swiped' and the correct amount of the account entered. Ask the guest to sign the credit card voucher, check the signature, and enter the amount in the system. Return the credit card, a copy of the voucher, and a copy of the account to the guest.

Vouchers

For guests who paid their accommodation using a prepaid voucher, it is important to check for an extras account for those services not covered by the voucher. Process their payment for extras according to the agreed method of payment.

Skippers

A **skipper** is not strictly an account settlement method, but the account balance must be processed. A skipper is someone who has departed without settling their account. When reception realises that a guest has departed without settling their account, the account is transferred to a **city ledger** account. This allows the account to be finalised but still leaves the problem of an amount which is unaccounted for. City ledgers are discussed in Chapter 7.

> **Skipper**—a person who departs without settling their account.

If the account is a company account, it can be forwarded to the appropriate company for settlement. If a credit card voucher is held (pre-authorisation), the account can be paid using this credit card. If the account is an extras account, again it can be settled by credit card if a voucher is held, or, if being settled by cash, then a letter requesting payment is sent to the guest.

Items in dispute

On occasion, you will find guests dispute items on their account. How this is managed depends on the venue. Some venues will automatically deduct the item (known as a **correction**) while other venues will first track the disputed item to determine if the guest or the venue is in error.

> **Correction**—the total charge for an item removed from the account.

Tracking items in dispute requires a search for and checking of the source documents for the disputed charge. This can be time-consuming as the relevant documents may have been processed days earlier and be filed away with the accounts department (although most venues keep an open file on all in-house guests with a copy of all charges placed in that file).

> **Adjustment**—the total charge for an item altered (reduced).

If the item in dispute is about the total charged for a service, for example, the guest indicates that dinner was $45.00 not $65.00, then the charge is not corrected but adjusted. An **adjustment** means that the total is changed but the item remains on the account. Make the adjustment then represent the account to the guest.

It is important that you do not argue with the guest, that you do apologise for the inconvenience and correct the account quickly before representing the adjusted account. It may be necessary to call a supervisor to authorise an adjustment or a correction.

Late charges

Not all charges reach reception before the guest checks out. A **late charge** is a service used by the guest, the details of which arrive at reception after the guest has departed. And because most establishments rely on the 'honour system' for guests to declare at time of check-out what they have used, it is not uncommon to find unpaid services after check-out.

Some guests forget to tell reception about a service or think it is included in the room charge. This is why credit cards are a preferred method of payment as establishments can then **delay charge** (charge later) any items not claimed.

Delay charged items frequently include:

▷ undeclared mini-bar
▷ hotel limousine to the airport
▷ bathrobes or hotel towels removed from the room
▷ breakfast charges posted after the guest has checked out
▷ postage (the guest may ask reception to mail items and charge it to their credit card when the cost is known).

When a delay charge is processed, a letter is forwarded to the guest together with a copy of the credit card voucher. If the guest paid by any means other than a credit card a letter requesting payment for the item or service is sent.

EXPRESS CHECK-OUTS

The majority of corporate guests will check-out between 7.00 am and 9.00 am, which is a peak period for reception. Many corporate guests are in a hurry and do not like to wait in queues so venues offer an express check-out service relieving the pressure at reception and offering the guest a speedy departure. The express check-out procedure is as follows:

1. Night audit finalise the accounts of those guests due to check-out the next morning and any guest who is paying by credit card or company charge has their account attached to an express check-out form, which is then placed in an envelope and slipped under the guest's door.
2. The guest fills in the form, checks the account and fills in a mini-bar form (if necessary) and then leaves the account, with the room key, in the room or at the express check-out box at reception.
3. Reception then posts any additional charges to the account, processes the credit card or company charge, and mails the finalised account to the guest.

GROUP DEPARTURES

Inbound groups that have all their accommodation and meals charged back to the tour company could all be checked out at once (for computerised systems). This is referred to as a **bulk check-out**. A computerised PMS will only allow a bulk check-out if all guests in the group have a zero balance in their account (that is, if individual guests do not have extras accounts to pay). Print out the individual guests' extras accounts and give them to the tour leader who will arrange for the members of their group to pay before departure. A bulk check-out saves time and congestion at reception. Once the group has left and all extras paid the check-out can be processed.

Conference groups usually need to check-out individually as they have to settle their own extras accounts. If using a credit card they may be able to use the express check-out service.

AFTER THE GUEST HAS DEPARTED

During the departure process, it may not be possible for you to process the guest's departure entirely. So there are a number of tasks you may need to complete after the guest has departed. For example, you will need to collate all the documentation that relates to each individual guest and file it in readiness for your end of shift balance. The end of shift balance is a procedure that requires you to check the accuracy of all the transactions undertaken during your shift. How you do this is explained in Chapter 7.

After the guest has departed you may also need to update the guest profile and room status and follow through on any comments made by the guest.

UPDATING ROOM STATUS

When the guest's account is settled (payment posted or transferred to a city ledger account), the account balance shows zero. The guest's account is closed in the computer and the PMS automatically records the room as a departure and updates the room status to vacant dirty (VD).

This information is important for reception and reservations because you need to know the status of each room to enable you to resell the room or register new guests in that room. This information is important for housekeeping because they need to know which rooms to clean and the order in which to clean them. Housekeeping then reports to reception that the room has been cleaned. Housekeeping duties are discussed in Chapter 10.

When the room has been cleaned and front office advised of its change of status to vacant clean, then the room is again available to sell.

UPDATING GUEST PROFILES

Most computerised systems automatically create or update the guest's profile on departure. In Chapter 5 you learned that the guest profile records the personal and company details of each guest and maintains a record of each guest's contact with the venue: when they stayed, how long they stayed, room preferences, room rate and method of payment. When the guest checks-out, the details relating to that stay are automatically transferred to their profile, thereby updating their specific information.

Loyalty programs

Many accommodation venues have in place loyalty programs of their own which recognise and reward frequent user guests. The rewards are usually linked to the number of nights a guest stays in a one-year period. The rewards awarded a guest for their loyalty may include free accommodation, free meals or gifts. The venue is able to keep track of the accumulated award points through the guest profile.

Many establishments also enter into loyalty program reward systems with airlines. Membership of the airline loyalty program may entitle the guest to cheaper rates or help the guest accumulate points on the reward system by staying at specified venues.

Many venues that have these arrangements in place can link the issue of reward points to the guest's loyalty program in their PMS. The link is usually maintained in the guest profile, which can interface with the airline's loyalty program. The points awarded are automatically generated if the guest's information has been entered correctly into their profile.

The guest profile and marketing

The guest profile is used also by the sales and marketing team. They use the details to keep track of the guest's preferences and requirements and to match these to the services provided (or that could be provided) by the venue. For example, if 75 per cent of all guest profiles listed a non-smoking room as a preference and only 50 per cent of the venue's rooms are allocated as non-smoking, then potentially the venue is not catering to most of their guests' needs and an adjustment may need to be made.

GUEST FEEDBACK

In Chapter 2 we discussed at length the value of guest feedback for identifying guest preferences and needs. It is frequently at check-out time that the guest is likely to offer an opinion or make a comment about services and facilities. Guests' comments enable you to identify opportunities for improving services and facilities and creating a positive final impression.

It is not uncommon at check-out for guests also to raise any problems they have experienced during their stay. The guest may or may not be making a formal complaint but their comments must be handled according to the standard complaint handling procedure in place. We discuss complaint handling in Chapter 13.

Before finishing this section, we review a complete check-out procedure for a guest paying her account by credit card.

Reception:	'Good morning. How may I help you?'
Ms Dwyer:	'Good morning. I'd like to check-out please.'
Reception:	'Certainly. May I have your name please?'
Ms Dwyer:	'Yes. My name is Dwyer.'
Reception:	'Thanks Ms Dwyer. May I have your room number please?'
Ms Dwyer:	'Room 1414.'
Reception:	'Ms Dwyer, do you have your key with you? Thank you. Do you have any other charges this morning, such as breakfast or anything from the mini-bar last night?'
Ms Dwyer:	'Yes, I had a diet coke from the mini-bar last night.'
Reception:	(posts the diet coke) 'Thanks Ms Dwyer. This is your account. Would you mind checking it for me please?'
Ms Dwyer:	'Yes, that's correct.'
Reception:	'How will you be settling your account today?'
Ms Dwyer:	'With my American Express.'
Reception:	'May I have your card please?' (Swipes card and enters payment into computer.) 'Ms Dwyer, would you please sign here?' (Presents voucher for signing.) 'Thank you. This is your receipt and card. Ms Dwyer is there anything else we can do for you? Do you need a hand with your luggage or can I call you a taxi?'
Ms Dwyer:	'Yes thanks. I need a taxi going to the airport. And if someone could please collect my bags I would be grateful.'
Reception:	'Certainly. I'll arrange that now. If you take a seat in the foyer, a porter will let you know when your taxi arrives. Thank you for staying with us. I hope we see you again soon, Ms Dwyer. Bye.'

The guest departure process is the last stage of the cycle of service. The departure procedure serves four purposes: account settlement, room status update, guest profile creation or update and guest feedback.

There are a number of activities you must perform before the guest checks-out. These include checking for additional charges and posting these charges to the guest's account.

At check-out, guests are presented with their account to check for accuracy and payment is made so that the balance of the account can be reduced to zero. Payment can be made in a number of ways (cash, credit card, charge back, traveller's cheques) and must be processed according to the venue's procedures.

Skippers are guests who leave without settling their account. Their account balances are transferred to a city ledger account and later forwarded to the guest for settlement.

If items on the account are in dispute, they may be corrected off or adjusted according to the venue's policies.

Late charges are those charges that arrive at reception after the guest has departed.

Express check-out is used mainly for corporate guests to facilitate the check-out process and reduce congestion at reception during peak periods. Groups may be checked out in bulk after extras accounts have been settled.

Most computer systems update the room status after departure and also automatically update the guest profile.

Guest feedback is often received during the check-out process and must be acted upon immediately.

FOCUS REVIEW

▷ What are the four purposes of the guest departure procedure?
▷ Why should you contact other departments as part of the preparation for guest departure?
▷ What is the procedure for processing foreign and local currency traveller's cheques (as a method of payment)?
▷ What is the difference between a 'correction' and an 'adjustment'?
▷ How would you manage a disputed item on the guest's account?
▷ In what circumstances would we delay charge a guest?
▷ Why do venues offer an express check-out service?
▷ What is the difference between checking out an inbound group and a conference group?
▷ Why is the room status update important to housekeeping?
▷ What value is there in maintaining a guest profile?

APPLY YOUR KNOWLEDGE

Using the guests you registered for Apply your Knowledge on page 189, post a room rate as per their booking, and now check these guests out, following the procedure you have just learned. You may want to work in the same group. One guest wishes to settle their account with cash and another guest wishes to settle their account with a Visa card. A third guest, paying by company charge back (all services) disputes one item on the account. Handle this situation and then complete the check-out procedure.

Remember, the observer is to give feedback on the success of your check-out.

Preparing records and reports

A number of departments in your venue require timely and accurate details of guests. One of your responsibilities is to ensure that your colleagues receive this information. This information is compiled and distributed by you either on a daily, weekly or per shift basis, and takes the form of records and reports. Earlier in this chapter we discussed a number of these reports; here we look at several others that you may need to complete and distribute:

▷ in-house guest lists
▷ back up lists
▷ key check reports
▷ no-show reports
▷ over-stays and under-stays.

IN-HOUSES GUEST LISTS

In-house guest lists are frequently updated and distributed among the various departments in the venue such as the bar, restaurant and room service. This list identifies which guests are in what room and which guests are able to charge services to their room. You will remember earlier we discussed that cash paying guests are regularly flagged as not being able to charge services to their room as there is no guarantee that they will pay their bill.

An up to date guest list is also left next to the key rack to confirm the guest is issued with the correct key. A list is also posted next to the switchboard for easy reference when incoming calls are received for in-house guests. The list is usually updated before meal service times so the outlets have a current list at all times.

BACK UP LISTS

Reception prints certain reports regularly so that they have a back up of the information held on the computer in the event the computer crashes or in the event of an emergency that may require an evacuation. These reports include:

▷ in-house guest list—numerical by room number
▷ in-house guest list—alphabetical by guest name
▷ room status
▷ expected arrivals
▷ expected departures (including account balances).

Often printed at the start of each shift, they are also updated after peak check-out and check-in periods.

KEY CHECK REPORT

Venues using traditional key locks need to maintain strict control over key security. Replacing room keys on a regular basis can be a large expense for an establishment and indicates a breach of security or a failure to follow correct check-out procedures.

At the end of each morning shift you are required to take an inventory of the keys for all rooms to ensure the departing guests have returned all keys. Any keys not returned should be reported to management and followed up using the correct procedure of the establishment.

Electronic keys are coded each time a guest checks in and this eliminates the security problem. It is cheaper to replace an electronic key than to replace a traditional key.

NO-SHOW REPORT

At the end of the day, a no-show report is printed so that reception can determine which rooms may be resold and so that reservations can follow up on the reasons for the no-show, for example:

▷ is the booking for today's date?
▷ did the guest call and cancel?
▷ was the cancellation properly recorded?
▷ if the guest is due to stay for several days, have they possibly been delayed (for example, plane delayed) or did they not mention to reservations they would be arriving late?

UNDER-STAYS AND OVER-STAYS

Many guests, especially corporate guests, frequently change their travel plans depending on how their business progresses. If a guest has originally booked for five days and leaves after three, that guest is referred to as an **under-stay** as they didn't stay for the whole of the booked period. If a guest extends their booking then that person is referred to as an **over-stay**.

Under-stay—a guest who checks-out of the hotel at a time prior to the original departure date.

Because over-stays and under-stays can affect both the number of rooms available to sell and the occupancy levels, venues need to keep track of these guests. A report is usually generated daily and a copy given to reservations.

Over-stay—a guest who stays beyond the original date of departure.

SKILLS FOCUS

Reception is responsible for regularly updating and distributing information to other departments about the activities of guests. This information is in the form of reports.

An in-house guest list assists other departments in controlling activities by guests using their services, such as whether or not a particular guest can charge that department's services to their room.

Back up reports of up to date guest lists, room status and expected arrivals and departures are regularly generated in the event the computer crashes.

Other reports and records generated by reception include no-shows, over- and under-stays and the key check report.

FOCUS REVIEW

▷ Why do the organisation's outlets need to have regular copies of the in-house guest list?

▷ Name three reports required for back up in case of emergency. Why else might you need these reports?

▷ Why might a guest be a no-show? Why would a venue follow up to determine why a guest is a no-show?

▷ When would an accommodation venue waive a guaranteed no-show charge?

▷ What is the difference between an under-stay and an over-stay?

▷ Explain the importance of the key check report.

PUT YOUR KNOWLEDGE TO THE TEST

Robyn has been working in reception for six weeks now and after some intensive training and being 'shadowed' by her supervisor for the first two weeks, she was finally ready to work a shift as a receptionist. Robyn knew her training had prepared her for dealing with many issues and to complete a variety of tasks at the same time, but she was still nervous. Robyn arrived early and after completing the hand over, counting her float and logging on to her computer, she was ready to go. Several guests arrived at once to register. As she was registering these guests, a guest called to complain about the leaking tap in the bathroom. Another guest impatiently stood by tapping his fingers.

When things quietened down, Robyn completed the usual tasks required after a guest registers and goes to their room. She then has several charges to post.

1. Prepare a checklist of tasks for Robyn to complete if she is on shift A. Now prepare a checklist for the B shift.

2. Imagine you have a large international conference arriving at Grand Central Hotel. Write a welcome letter to the delegates outlining the services offered at Grand Central Hotel (make up what information you think you need).

3. As well as the large conference there is an inbound group arriving. Make a list of instructions to tell the tour leader on arrival.

4. The hotel is overbooked by five rooms at 6.00 pm and Mr Joe Burns, a regular guest, calls looking for a room. What can Robyn do to accommodate Mr Burns? What can she look for to make sure the hotel is really booked?

5. Howard Adams arrives at 9.30 pm. He is very intoxicated and rude and is demanding the room that was booked through his company's travel agent. Robyn is unable to locate his reservation. How should Robyn handle this situation?

6. Ms Holly Greig in Room 1607 calls Robyn to tell her that she requested a non-smoking room and after just going to her room at 10.00 pm, she discovers her room is a smoking room and she wants to move. What should Robyn do if the hotel is full? If the hotel is only 65 per cent occupied what could Robyn do differently?

7. When Robyn is posting the mini-bar charges for the day she discovers unclaimed mini-bar charges. Mr Munroe in room 1511 forgot to declare $8.95 of mini-bar charges and

Ms Hunt in room 1413 didn't declare her $35.00 mini-bar bill. Also, housekeeping reported that the bathrobes in room 1612 where Mr and Mrs Saunders were staying are missing. Robyn reports these amounts to her supervisor. As her supervisor, how would you handle this? If appropriate write a letter to the guests you would chase up.

8. What should Robyn do with the complaint about a leaking tap?

9. What tasks is Robyn likely to be completing after a guest has registered and gone to their room?

10. How should Robyn deal with the man tapping his finger?

11. Robyn has many things to hand over to D Shift at the end of her first shift. Prepare a hand over report and diary entries from Robyn's shift.

Processing and Maintaining Financial Transactions

LEARNING OUTCOMES

On completion of this chapter, you will be able to:

▷ define a financial transaction and identify the objectives of a guest accounting system;

▷ identify the three stages of the guest account cycle and describe its characteristics;

▷ explain the purpose of the different types of accounts maintained by the front office;

▷ explain the use and purpose of the various ledgers used by front office;

▷ describe the impact of the Goods and Services Tax on the accounting process;

▷ accurately process and maintain financial transactions;

▷ describe the role of the cashier;

▷ explain what a source document is and what it is used for;

▷ perform balancing procedures;

▷ conduct all transactions and transporting of cash and non-cash documentation in a manner that meets security procedures and customer service standards.

Introduction

All accommodation venues provide a range of services and facilities for which the guest must pay. These services and facilities are the means by which the venue generates revenue and makes money. However, unlike a lot of other goods and services, those provided by accommodation venues are not always consumed and paid for simultaneously. In other words, some guests may charge services and facilities to an account while staying in the venue and pay their account at departure or even at a later stage. This means that it is necessary to maintain strict control over who owes money, how much and for what.

To be able to provide services and facilities to its guests, the venue must also incur expenses. Expenses include staff wages, the provision of food and beverages, furnishing the venue, marketing and office equipment. There are many other areas for which 'supplies' that are required to carry out the business of managing an accommodation venue must be purchased.

Generating revenue and incurring expenses are both examples of financial transactions. In this chapter we focus on the types of financial transactions that take place in the front office, how they are processed and how to balance them.

Financial transactions and the guest accounting system

Financial transactions— the exchange of something of value, usually money, in return for a service or product.

A **financial transaction** is the exchange of something of value, usually money, in return for a service or product. For example, a guest who stays overnight in a hotel pays for the use of the room. Processing financial transactions involves recording and maintaining the records of each financial transaction. Balancing financial transactions involves checking that the financial transactions were *accurately* recorded and that all money received is accounted for.

As with almost every other activity undertaken in the front office, the processing of financial transactions follows a step-by-step procedure that records the details of each exchange between the guest and the venue. To keep track of every exchange, procedures are established in the form of a **guest accounting system** that is usually built into the venue's PMS. This control is necessary so that all transactions can be accounted for and so that the venue does not lose money through theft or poor control.

The guest accounting system

The guest accounting system allows control of the financial transactions that take place by following the guest accounting cycle. Its main objectives are to:

1. Monitor and maintain accurate financial transactions between the guest and the establishment throughout the guest accounting cycle.
2. Create and maintain an accurate financial system for guest accounts, and provide management information on departmental revenue.
3. Achieve effective means of internal control within the financial system of a front office, by monitoring credit given to guests, and preventing fraudulent staff practice.

4. Have the ability to post charges and balance charges on guest accounts.
5. Have the ability to collect and process payment for all guest transactions.
6. Balance cash posted, cash received and all departmental charges.
7. Produce trial balances and prepare reports.

CHARACTERISTICS OF THE GUEST ACCOUNTING CYCLE

The system and procedures used for achieving these objectives will vary between establishments. The system used may be computer-based or maintained manually. These systems are considered later in this chapter. Whichever system is used, there are two characteristics they have in common:

▷ the processing of financial transactions throughout the cycle of service resulting in the three stages of the guest accounting cycle—creation, maintenance and settlement (shown in Figure 7.1).
▷ all accounts must balance.

The guest accounting cycle:

Creation—arrival stage

Maintenance—occupancy stage

Settlement—departure stage.

How the guest account cycle works can be demonstrated with an example.

Mrs Monro makes a reservation with the Grand Central Hotel. She later sends a deposit to the hotel, which guarantees her booking *(pre-arrival)*. When Mrs Monro checks-in, she decides that her method of payment will be credit card, so the cashier takes an imprint and registers the guest *(account creation)*. This allows Mrs Monro to charge services and products consumed during her stay to her room *(account maintenance)*. When she is ready to depart, the credit card imprint taken on arrival will be used to settle the balance on Mrs Monro's account. She will sign the credit card voucher and is now ready to leave *(account settlement)*.

The guest account cycle has run its course. Each and every other guest who chooses to stay at any accommodation venue will follow this same course.

Figure 7.1 ▷ **Guest accounting cycle**

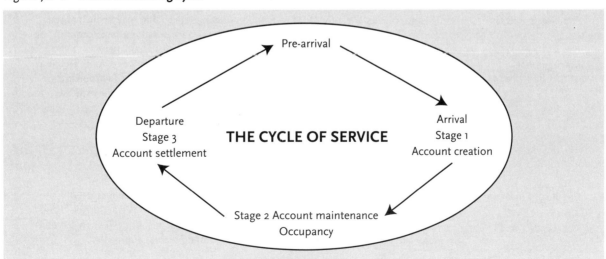

Pre-arrival

Departure
Stage 3
Account settlement

THE CYCLE OF SERVICE

Arrival
Stage 1
Account creation

Stage 2 Account maintenance
Occupancy

Different types of accounts

As we have seen, all venues need to keep track of every financial transaction that takes place. The venue keeps track not only of what expenses the guest incurs and method of payments, but also of which department earned the revenue and how much of each type of payment is received. To do this several 'accounts' are maintained by the front office to allow for accurate and timely control over the accounting process. Every charge incurred and every payment made is recorded on the guest's account *and* on the corresponding department account. The types of accounts most venues are likely to maintain are explained in Table 7.1.

Table 7.1 ▷ **Types of accounts**

TYPE OF ACCOUNT	USE OR PURPOSE
Individual	These accounts are set up when a guest checks into the venue. They are used for posting charges for goods and services used by the guest during their stay and usually settled on departure.
Master accounts	These accounts are set up to accept charges for goods or services not chargeable to an individual guest account. They are closed off when payment is received or when they are moved into the **city ledger**. For example, a group booking may establish a master account. All charges relating to the group's stay (such as breakfast and room charge) are not payable by the individual but are charged to the group master account.
Split or extras accounts	An extras account refers to dividing the account into two or more separate accounts because different types of charges or different methods of payment require separate accounts.
Group extras accounts	Groups often ask for extras accounts. A master account is set up to accept certain charges specified by the travel agent or company, such as accommodation and breakfast charges. Additional charges, such as mini-bar and laundry, are charged to the individual's guest (extras) account. So individual accounts are usually set up for each of the individuals who belong to the group.
Individual extras accounts	An individual guest may request an extras account, for example, when the company they work for is paying for part of the account, such as accommodation and breakfast, and the individual is paying the balance such as dinner and laundry.
Function/conference	These accounts are set up for any function or conferences that may be held at the venue. Charges and payments are posted in the same way as for guest accounts but the revenue generated is credited to the food and beverage department.
Management	These accounts are set up to accept charges for all management activities. This may include entertaining guests and clients and can also be used for any complaints or deductions made to guest accounts to keep track of revenue and some expenses incurred by front office. Other examples of management accounts include: ▷ staff meals ▷ laundry ▷ marketing ▷ telephone
Credit card masters	Credit card masters are set up to accept charges for goods and services used in the hotel and paid for by an American Express or Diners Club card (Visa, Bankcard and MasterCard are placed in a different category). The guest account will show a credit entry and a debit entry is posted to the corresponding credit card master.

Table 7.1 ▷ **(continued)**

TYPE OF ACCOUNT	USE OR PURPOSE
Point of sale (POS)	A POS system allows food and beverage and other revenue-generating outlets to post guest charges directly to the guest's account and to record non-guest transactions. Any American Express and Diners Club payments are posted directly to the American Express and Diners Club master account. If the venue does not have POS technology the front desk cashier will post the charges.
Skippers	These accounts are set up to keep track of unresolved accounts, for example, guests who have left the hotel without paying their account, or accounts that are awaiting authorisation for payment from a company or travel agent. If allowed to go unchecked for a period of time they may accumulate and payment may be harder to collect, which may result in loss of revenue for the hotel.
Department accounts	Each revenue-generating department in the venue has its own account. As charges are posted to a guest's account it is necessary to show where the charge originated. Each payment method has its own account. As guests settle their accounts, it is necessary to know what form of payment was used (Visa, MasterCard, Bankcard, cash, cheques).

There are several other types of accounts that require further explanation: the **cash folio**, **city ledger**, **deposits ledger** and **in-house guest ledger**.

CASH FOLIO

The **cash folio** is used for posting all cash transactions *not* linked to a guest room. Unlike a guest account where a charge is posted but not a payment (until a later stage, usually at check-out), the cash account records both a debit and credit entry at the same time. This is because the service or goods are paid for at the time of consumption, thus the cash account remains at a zero balance at all times. For example, a guest dines in the restaurant but decides to pay cash instead of charging the amount to his room. The food and beverages consumed are posted to the cash folio, as is the cash payment, because the venue has received payment at the same time. No charge is recorded on the guest's room account.

Cash folio— used for posting all cash transactions not linked to a guest room. Must always have a zero balance.

The cash folio is also used for the processing of cash from other departments. For example, a couple not staying in the hotel dines in the restaurant and settles the bill with cash. The restaurant transfers the cash to front office, which records the food and beverage charge and then posts the cash payment on the cash folio leaving a zero balance. Figure 7.2 shows a cash folio with both the charge and payment posted, indicating that the service has been consumed *and* paid for. Note the zero balance.

CITY LEDGER

The city ledger is a collection of **accounts receivable** held for non-in-house guests. For example, local businesses may open an account with the venue that allows them to charge services such as food and beverages for which they pay at a later date. In addition, the city ledger is used for any unpaid accounts or accounts checked out with balances still owing, such as skipper accounts. Other accounts in the city ledger include those not settled by guests on departure such as company charge backs or travel agent guests. The Diners International and

Figure 7.2 ▷ **Cash folio**

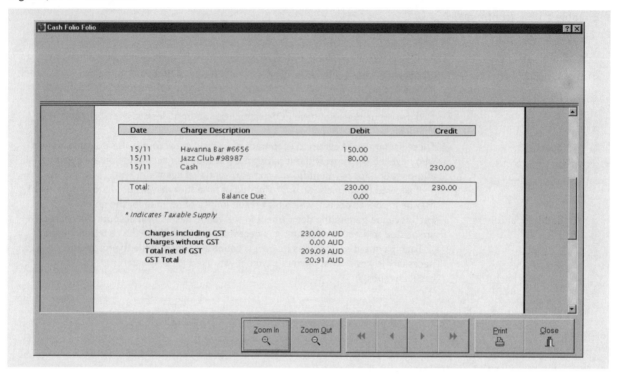

City ledger—
a ledger that contains a collection of accounts receivable for non-in-house guests and the accounts with balances not finalised on departure.

American Express credit card charges are also held in the city ledger until such time as the respective card company pays for them.

Normally accounts in this ledger require a credit facility set up prior to arrival at the venue, so payment is guaranteed and bad debts don't occur.

The outstanding accounts are printed and sent to the company or agent in the form of an invoice, usually monthly, with payment usually expected within 30 days of receipt.

All guest accounts (which should be signed by guests on check-out to indicate their agreement and approval for payment) are required to contain the following information before being transferred from the city ledger to accounts receivable:

▷ name of guest(s)
▷ address where the account is to be sent
▷ dates of stay
▷ room number
▷ account number (assigned by the venue to the business using the venue's services)
▷ room rate
▷ full listing of all charges incurred, each with:
   — date, type of charge, amount, docket number
   — telephone calls with the date, time of call, duration of call, number called, the amount, and
▷ written authorisation from the company detailing:
   — where account is to be sent
   — which charges will be accepted
   — contact name and the person responsible for authorising the payment.

THE DEPOSIT LEDGER

When a pre-payment or deposit is received from a guest, the payment must be recorded and a receipt sent to the person/company/travel agent who sent the deposit. This payment is placed on an account with a credit balance, and the amounts are held in the **deposit ledger** until required. The deposit is then transferred to the relevant guest account at check-in when their individual account is created.

Deposit ledger—this holds payments received in advance from guests.

IN-HOUSE GUEST LEDGER

To be able to keep track of the total amount owed by all in-house guests, an **in-house ledger** is maintained. The amounts on the accounts are held in the in-house guest ledger until they are paid for or moved to the city ledger.

In-house guest ledger—this holds the amounts of all guest accounts staying at the venue at present.

APPLY YOUR KNOWLEDGE

In the left column is a list of transactions. In the right column state which type of account and/or ledger is required for processing the transactions.

Transaction type	Account required	Ledger required
A guest pays cash in the restaurant.		
A guest charges room service to their room.		
A group has all their accommodation charged to one account and the individual group members pay for other services consumed.		
A guest checks-out. Her company is paying for the bill.		
A guest sends a deposit to secure the booking.		
A guest complains about the food in the restaurant and management deducts the amount from the bill.		
A guest wishes to pay for accommodation on one account and everything else on another account.		

COMPUTERISED ACCOUNTS

When a venue maintains a computerised accounts system financial transactions are processed by a cashier or receptionist directly into the computer which records the transactions in essentially the same way as manual record keeping, only the entry needs to be made just once; the computer records the entry in the appropriate accounts and automatically updates those accounts. The computer recognises the type of transaction, whether a charge or payment, and through the use of codes corresponding to each of the venue's departments, knows where to record the information. Codes may be either numerical or alphabetical but whichever is used is usually easily recognisable as the department they represent. Table 7.2 lists examples of the types of codes that may be used for the various transactions and the corresponding department or transaction type.

When a charge is posted to a guest's account, the computer records the details of the charge on the account and automatically maintains a tally of all charges incurred at the point of origin. For example, if Mr and Mrs Yerondais have dinner in the restaurant, and it costs $85.00, the charge is posted as $85.00 (restaurant food) on their room account. The computer will automatically add the $85.00 to the restaurant food account.

When Mr and Mrs Yerondais check-out of the venue they will settle their account. Assume they are paying by Visa card. The balance on their account is $385.00. $300.00 for the room and $85.00 for dinner. When the payment for $385.00 is recorded on their account it will also record on the Visa account. Figure 7.3 shows each of the entries made.

MANUAL RECORD KEEPING

For venues that maintain a manual system for recording financial transactions, the most common system used is the **tabular ledger**. Similar to a computerised system, a tabular ledger maintains two records: one for the guest's account in columns, the other to keep track

---

Table 7.2 ▷ **Venue departments and codes**

CODE	DEPARTMENT CHARGES	CODE	PAYMENT METHOD
BF	Breakfast food	VI	Visa
LF	Lunch food	MC	Master Card
LB	Lunch beverages	AE	American Express
DF	Dinner food	CA	Cash
DB	Dinner beverages	PC	Personal Cheque
TE	Telephone	CC	Company Cheque
FX	Facsimile	CD	Company Charge
BC	Business Centre Services	VO	Voucher
PO	Paid out		
LS	Laundry services		
RF	Room service food		
RB	Room service beverages		
FE	Foreign exchange		
MB	Mini-bar		
VP	Valet parking		
IM	In-room movies		
GY	Gymnasium, sauna, spa, masseur services		
MC	Miscellaneous		
GST	Goods and Services Tax		

Figure 7.3 ▷ **Computer transactions for the Yerondais account**

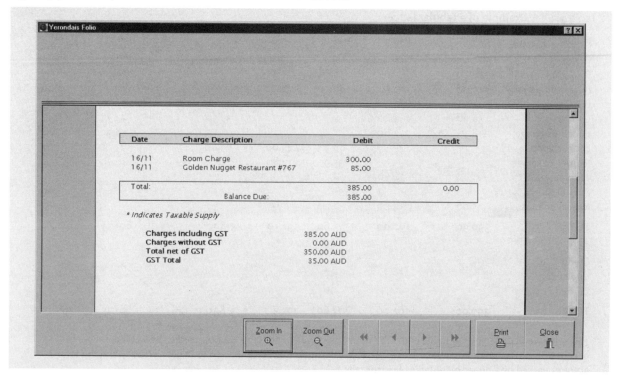

Date	Charge Description	Debit	Credit
16/11	Room Charge	300.00	
16/11	Golden Nugget Restaurant #767	85.00	
Total:		385.00	0.00
	Balance Due:	385.00	

* *Indicates Taxable Supply*

Charges including GST	385.00 AUD
Charges without GST	0.00 AUD
Total net of GST	350.00 AUD
GST Total	35.00 AUD

of and summarise all the charges incurred by guests during the day, according to the department, in rows. All the details are recorded manually. An example is shown in Table 7.3.

The top half of the ledger records charges incurred that day. The bottom half of the ledger records payments and deposits received that day. The totals across the bottom of the ledger are the totals owed by the guest in that column. Payments and deposits recorded are deducted from the charges incurred to arrive at the total. The totals across the rows of the ledger are the total revenues received for each corresponding department.

The amount in the 'Brought Forward' row represents the total of the charges incurred by the guest the previous day(s). The 'Carried Forward' amount refers to any payments received from that guest the previous day(s).

APPLY YOUR KNOWLEDGE

For this activity, all the answers can be found in Table 7.3.
   What is the current balance of the following accounts?

▷ *Van Denderen*
▷ *Howard*
▷ *Jones.*

How much revenue did the following departments make?

▷ *accommodation*
▷ *breakfast*
▷ *dinner beverage.*

Table 7.3 ▷ **Example of a tabular ledger**

ROOM	1101	1102	1103	1104	1105	1106	1107	TOTAL
GUEST NAME	Van Denderen	Howard	Leahy	Sangster	Singh		Jones	
Brought Forward	176.00		249.50				222.00	647.5
Accommodation	120.00	120.00	180.00	120.00	180.00		120.00	840.00
Breakfast	14.50		14.50	14.50	29.00			72.50
Lunch Food	56.90	34.80			37.50		72.75	201.95
Lunch Beverage	18.50	12.60					38.90	70.00
Dinner Food			86.50	45.00	35.60		73.00	240.10
Dinner Beverage			35.90	12.80	24.00		46.70	119.40
Telephone		12.60						12.60
Paid Outs					12.00		28.00	40.00
Miscellaneous	5.00	12.00	7.20					24.20
TOTAL	**390.90**	**192.00**	**573.60**	**192.30**	**318.10**		**601.35**	**2268.25**
Cash								
Credit Card								
City Ledger								
Carried Forward								
TOTAL	**390.90**	**192.00**	**573.60**	**192.3**	**318.10**		**601.35**	**2268.25**

You will note that the vertical totals equal the horizontal totals. The totals do not need to be written in twice because of the design of the tabular ledger—the guest amount owed to the venue tallies vertically and the total amount earned by a department tallies horizontally.

SKILLS FOCUS

Financial transactions are the exchange of something of value, usually money, in return for a service or product. To maintain the integrity of the transactions, a guest accounting system is maintained and usually forms part of the venue's property management system (PMS). The guest accounting system provides control of all financial transactions that take place within the venue following the guest account cycle. The guest accounting cycle has two characteristics—the processing of financial transactions and the balancing of all accounts.

There are three stages to the guest accounting cycle: creation, maintenance and settlement. Each stage is directly linked to the guest's cycle of service from the point of arrival, through occupancy and finally departure.

Whichever accounting system is used—computerised or manual—various accounts and ledgers are used to keep track of the financial transactions. For every entry made to an account a second entry must take place to keep track of where the charge originated or what type of payment was received.

The ledger system is used to maintain accurate and timely information about the totals of all guest accounts. A computerised system automatically assigns guest accounts to a pre-determined ledger according to the nature of the account. There are three types of ledger: the deposit ledger, the in-house guest ledger and the city ledger.

▷ What is a financial transaction?
▷ What is involved in processing financial transactions?
▷ Why do you think it is necessary for venues to maintain strict control over the accounting procedures?
▷ What is the relationship between the cycle of service and the guest accounting cycle?
▷ What are the two characteristics common to all types of accounting systems?
▷ Explain the difference between a master account and an extras account.
▷ What are management accounts used for?
▷ Distinguish between a city ledger and an in-house ledger.
▷ What is the cash folio used for? Why must it always show a zero balance?
▷ Why are codes used for recording charges and payments in computerised accounting systems?
▷ What is the difference between 'brought forward' and 'carried forward' in a tabular ledger?

Impact of the GST on the accounting process

On 1 July 2000, the Australian government introduced a new tax system of which a goods and services tax (GST) is a major element. The GST is a broad-based tax of 10 per cent on the supply of most goods and services. It replaced the wholesale sales tax, which was applied at varying rates to a range of products.

Most accommodation venues need to apply the GST to the goods and services (rooms, food, beverages) they provide their guests. This means that a previous room rate of $200.00 will now be at most $220.00—$20, or 10 per cent, being the GST component. It is important to note that other parts of the GST scheme mean that the price rise due to GST isn't necessarily the full 10 per cent; the price rise depends on the wholesale tax, if any, that applied previously.

Businesses from whom the venue purchases supplies (some food products, most beverages, linen, stationery and the like) add GST to the price of the goods they sell to the venue. For example, a venue needs to purchase 100 tablecloths, and the price it pays is $1100. There is a 10 per cent GST component included in this price. In other words, the price of the tablecloths was $1000 plus $100 GST.

ACCOUNTING FOR THE GST

The GST a venue collects from its guests for the goods and services they buy is payable to the Australian Taxation Office (ATO); *it is not additional revenue*. The GST paid by the venue to purchase supplies can offset the amount the venue owes the ATO; *it is not an additional expense*. In other words, the amount the venue has to pay the ATO is the difference between:

▷ the GST included in the price of goods and services sold, and
▷ the GST paid for the purchase of supplies used by the venue.

Table 7.4 shows a simple version of how this works.

All venues are required to maintain accurate records of the GST collected and paid. How it does this will depend on the accounting system in place. For most venues, the computerised PMS is programmed to account for the GST.

Table 7.4 ▷ **Calculating GST payable to the ATO**

DESCRIPTION OF SUPPLY	TOTAL RECEIVED (INCLUSIVE OF GST)	GST RECEIVED (PAYABLE TO ATO)	TOTAL GST RECEIVED
Rooms	11,000	1,000	
Food	3,300	300	
Beverage	3,300	300	
			$1,600

DESCRIPTION OF PURCHASES	TOTAL PAID (INCLUSIVE OF GST)	GST PAID	TOTAL GST PAID
Food	1,100	100	
Beverages	1,100	100	
Stationery	550	50	
Linen	1,100	100	
			$350
Total received less total paid (and payable to ATO)			$1,250

HOW IT WORKS

When guests stay at an accommodation venue or dine in a restaurant, the price they pay includes a GST amount. The GST component is not usually listed separately on the guest's account for each good or service. The account total will state that the total is **GST inclusive**. An example is shown in Figure 7.4.

Figure 7.4 ▷ **Guest account showing the total inclusive of GST**

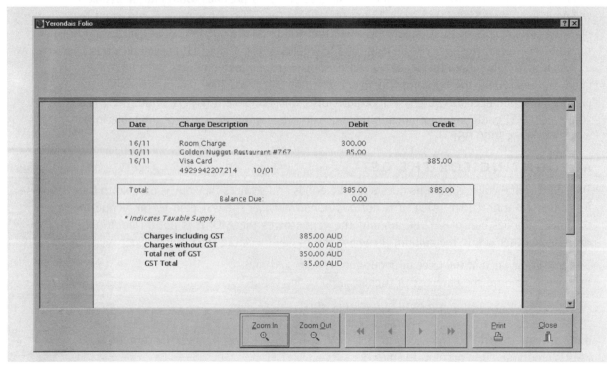

However, if a guest requests an account (tax invoice) that separately shows the GST portion, this can either be generated through the PMS, or, if not, a separate account can be written up for the guest. A guest may request a tax invoice when the purchase of hospitality services is to be claimed against their business expenditure (in the same way they would claim other GST paid for goods and services as part of their operating expenses). The total shown on the account is **GST exclusive** and therefore the GST component is listed separately.

INCLUSIVE OR EXCLUSIVE?

Under the new tax system, guest rooms and restaurants, take-away and prepared food is subject to GST. This includes all food and drink supplied for consumption in the venue's restaurant or in the guest's room, or food prepared for the guest to consume away from the venue, such as a picnic hamper.

In accommodation venues, GST is not listed separately. In other words, the new room rates quoted and menu prices are GST inclusive. For example, assume that your venue now charges $220.00 per night per double room. This rate includes the GST amount of $20.00. If you wanted to calculate the amount of GST applicable on a GST inclusive price, divide the amount ($220) by 11, which is the GST portion, for example, $220/11 = $20.

Prices quoted may show GST separately, that is, the price is GST exclusive and the GST is shown as a separate amount. To determine if the GST amount shown is correct, multiply the GST exclusive price by 10 per cent. For example, $200 × 10% = $20.00.

TAX INVOICES

A tax invoice is essentially the same as a receipt and is issued by the business supplying the goods or services on request. For purchases made, the venue must receive a tax invoice to be able to claim the difference between GST collected and GST payable.

Typically, a tax invoice will show:

▷ the Australian Business Number (ABN) of the supplier
▷ the GST inclusive price of what was supplied
▷ the words 'tax invoice'
▷ date of issue of the tax invoice
▷ name of the supplier
▷ brief description of what was supplied; and
▷ whether the amount is 'inclusive of GST', or 'exclusive of GST'.

An example of a tax invoice is shown in Figure 7.5.

To operate under the tax system, businesses are required to hold an **Australian Business Number (ABN)** and be registered for GST. The ABN replaces the previously used Australian Company Number (ACN). The ABN is an exclusive identification code that enables businesses to deal not only with the ATO but also with a range of other government departments and agencies, using just one number.

If a business does not hold an ABN, the business to which they supply goods and services can withhold 48.5 per cent of the amount due to be paid, and that business must forward this amount to the ATO.

Tips and the GST

If a tip is given voluntarily, it is not subject to GST. If, on the other hand, the tip is included in the price charged, say for a restaurant meal, then it is subject to GST.

Figure 7.5 ▷ **Example of a tax invoice**

Green Fields Linen Supply
Lot 65, Maddison Court
Murrumbeena Vic
03 9876 9876

Tax Invoice/Receipt
Date: _____

ABN: 4380000000

Customer Details
Name: _____
Address: _____
_____
Phone: _____
Order Number: _____

Description of Goods Supplied

Qty	Description	Unit price	Total

Sub Total: _____
Transport Cost: _____
GST: _____
Total Inc GST: _____

Terms:

Balance Due: _____

Promotions and the GST

If the venue undertakes a promotion that includes the supply of something free of charge (for example, a free beverage) and without conditions, the GST is not payable. It, however, the free of charge item is supplied in conjunction with a service or good that the guest must pay for (for example, a free cocktail for guests who stay a Saturday night), the cocktail is GST free but the room is still subject to GST).

SKILLS FOCUS

The GST is a broad-based tax of 10 per cent on the supply of goods and services. Most accommodation venues are required to apply the GST to the goods and services it supplies—rooms, food, and beverages.

Businesses from whom the venue purchases supplies add GST to their goods and services.

The GST collected from guests is payable to the ATO. This amount can be reduced by the amount of GST paid by the venue to purchase goods and services required to operate the business.

GST inclusive means that the total on the tax invoice includes a GST component. GST exclusive means that the GST component is not included in the total but shown separately.

To operate under the new tax system, businesses are required to hold an Australian Business Number (ABN), an exclusive identification code, and be registered for GST.

FOCUS REVIEW

▷ What is the GST?
▷ What is the difference between GST inclusive and GST exclusive?
▷ How has the GST impacted an accommodation venues?
▷ When is GST payable on tips? Promotions?
▷ What is a tax invoice? What information must be included on a tax invoice?
▷ How does a venue determine what it owes the ATO?
▷ Why is it important for a business to have an ABN?

Processing financial transactions

The processing of financial transactions requires first that the account be created. Earlier we looked at the types of accounts that a venue may have. Now we look at how to create the guest account; then we'll look at the other stages of the guest accounting cycle: maintaining the account and account settlement.

CREATING THE GUEST ACCOUNT

A guest account (also referred to as the **guest folio**) is created by the front office at the arrival stage of the cycle of service. On arrival, the guest registers and their personal and payment details are entered into the PMS (Chapter 6 explains how to register a guest). An account is automatically created and an account number assigned. The creation of this account for each new guest is important because it is the record of all financial transactions between the venue and the guest during the guest's stay. Thus, the purpose of account creation is to allow accurate recording of all financial transactions between the venue and that guest.

Different guests have different billing requirements and to help meet these differences more than one type of account may be set up for the guest at check-in. Each account will have its own account number. For example, Ms Dooley checks in at the Grand Central Hotel. Her company is paying for her accommodation and breakfast. Ms Dooley must pay for any other expenses incurred during her stay. A master account is set up for the accommodation and breakfast charges and an extras account is set up for any other charges.

At check-out, Ms Dooley will sign the master account and its balance will be transferred to the city ledger. She will pay for the extras amount by whichever means was agreed at check-in.

CREATING OTHER TYPES OF ACCOUNTS

All the other types of accounts maintained by front office (departmental accounts for charges and payments) are programmed into the PMS and therefore do not need to be created every time they are used. This means that they exist permanently. However, these accounts are 'opened' at the beginning of each shift and 'closed' at the end of each shift. The reason for this is that for the information recorded on departmental accounts to be useful, the venue needs to know how much was posted to each department on a daily or shift basis and, at the end of each shift a shift 'balance' is performed. Shift balancing procedures are discussed later in the chapter.

The role of the cashier

The cashier works alongside the reception staff and often performs the same or similar duties, such as guest registration and departure procedures. Their principal role however, is managing the financial transactions that take place at the front office:

▷ process payments and non-cash transactions
▷ maintain accurate financial records for in-house guests
▷ perform balancing procedures
▷ control cash and other money.

A front office cashier must handle cash when:

▷ payment is received from a guest
▷ change is to be given to a guest
▷ foreign currency needs to be exchanged
▷ deposits are received
▷ paid outs are posted to a guest account
▷ petty cash is managed
▷ refunds are given
▷ the float is counted.

Table 7.5 ▷ **Cashier float record**

DENOMINATION	ACTUAL AMOUNT	OPENING BALANCE	CLOSING BALANCE
$100.00	$100.00	✔	$100.00
$50.00	$100.00	✔	$150.00
$20.00	$100.00	✔	$60.00
$10.00	$90.00	✔	$80.00
$5.00	$60.00	✔	$90.00
$2.00	$60.00	✔	$42.00
$1.00	$50.00	✔	$37.00
.50	$10.00	✔	$13.50
.20	$14.60	✔	$9.40
.10	$13.10	✔	$12.70
.05	$2.30	✔	$5.40
Total	**$600.00**	**$600.00**	**$600.00**

The front office float

Before the cashier (or other front office staff member) is able to undertake any cash-handling duties it is necessary to have cash with which to trade. You will remember from Chapter 6 that a float is a starting bank, for example, $600.00, to enable cash transactions. The float is comprised of different denominations of money at a set limit, for the cashier to work with and for which they are responsible at all times.

When the float is collected it is counted (to determine accuracy) before being placed in the cash or till drawer. Table 7.5 shows an example of a cashier float record. The cashier counts each denomination and must confirm that the actual amounts recorded on the cashier's float record match the amounts that are in the float bag. They do this by placing a tick or writing the amount in the opening balance column.

At the end of the shift the cashier will perform the balancing procedure, which will involve banking. As part of the balancing process, the cashier counts the float again, confirms the amounts of each denomination and completes the cashier float record with the actual amounts in the float. The 'closing balance' column is completed with the actual amounts entered. Coins are counted first and the balance of the float is made up with notes.

Maintaining the guests' accounts

The front office is responsible for maintaining the guest accounts. Maintaining means timely recording of financial transactions to the relevant account. Having checked into the establishment, the guest can now be charged for the room they occupy and, if the guest has guaranteed payment for services they use with a credit card or company charge authority, or other means, they can now charge services to their room account.

HOW DOES FRONT OFFICE KNOW WHAT TO CHARGE?

The front office knows what to charge to each guest account because the various departments in the venue provide the information. Let's return to our example with Mr and Mrs Yerondais. When they checked in, an imprint of their credit card was taken which allows them to charge services to their account. They then have dinner in the restaurant and when they finish their meal, the restaurant presents them with a bill, which they sign. They then leave the restaurant. No money is exchanged, but a financial transaction has taken place. By signing the bill, Mr and Mrs Yerondais know that the amount of their dinner will be added to the room account.

At the end of the night, the restaurant sends a copy of the Yerondais restaurant bill to the front office, as well as all other in-house guests' bills and any financial transactions for non-in-house guests. Front office posts the details of each financial transaction.

WHAT IS A SOURCE DOCUMENT?

Source document— a document providing evidence of the charges to be posted to a guest's account.

The restaurant bill that Mr and Mrs Yerondais signed is referred to as a source document. Indeed, any document that provides details of a charge to be added to a guest's account is referred to as a source document. A source document provides evidence of the charges incurred by the guest and contains the following information:

▷ guest's name and room number
▷ date service provided
▷ details of the service provided (for example, food and beverage)
▷ amount to be charged
▷ the guest's signature.

An example of a source document from the restaurant is shown in Figure 7.6.

Source documents are also used for the expenses incurred by the venue, for example, when the venue pays for services or supplies, such as food and beverage. In these instances the source document must include the following information:

▷ company name and ABN
▷ cost of services or goods provided
▷ date of service
▷ signature of authorised venue staff member (to acknowledge receipt of goods or authority to purchase)
▷ the document must state 'tax invoice' and show a precise breakdown of the services and goods provided, respective prices and GST applicable.

All source documents must be checked to ensure they record the correct information.

Front office staff do not usually process source documents for expenses. Instead, these are sent directly to the accounts department.

Figure 7.6 ▷ **Restaurant source document**

GRAND CENTRAL HOTEL
505 The Boulevard, Sydney
HOTELS OF DISTINCTION
ABN 220 006 005 004

Tax Invoice
No. 67034

The Bistro at Grand Central

Food Docket

Date	Time	Table/Room No.	Room Service	No. of Covers	Waiter

Qty	Food Item		$	c
	Food Total			

Qty	Beverages		$	c
	Beverage Total			
	Total			

Room Number _____
Name _____
Guest signature _____

Types of source documents

The types of source documents (charges and expenses) used by a venue will depend on the services it offers and the expenses it occurs. They will correspond to the departments used in the venue. Table 7.6 lists a variety of source documents you may use.

POSTING CHARGES AND PAYMENTS

In Chapter 6 you learned that the posting of charges and payments means recording the details of a financial transaction on the guest's account. When charges and payments are

Table 7.6 ▷ **Types of source documents**

CHARGES	EXPENSES
Bar	Invoices
Telephone, facsimile, e-mail	Receipts
Business centre	Cheques
Laundry services	Purchase orders
Valet services	Requisitions
Mini-bar	Transfer notes
Gymnasium services and facilities	Staff time sheets
Restaurant Food	
▷ breakfast	
▷ lunch	
▷ dinner	
Restaurant beverages	
▷ lunch	
▷ dinner	
Room services	
▷ food	
▷ beverages	
Miscellaneous	
Bar services	
Paid Outs	
Foreign Exchange	

posted to a guest's account they are recorded twice: to the guest's account *and* to the department where the charge originated or the method of payment account.

Charges are posted to guest accounts by the:

Financial transactions—charges and payments—are referred to as debits and credits and each has a different effect on the guest's account.

▷ cashier or receptionist—each department in the venue maintains its own system for recording **financial transactions** and when these are balanced at the end of the shift, they are transferred to front office to be processed, that is, charged to those guests who used the service in that department;

▷ department cashiers if they have point of sale (POS) technology as soon as the charge is incurred;

▷ night auditor if charges are collected and posted at the end of the day; and

▷ venue's computer—for example, the computer posts all accommodation charges simultaneously, on direction from the night auditor. Telephone charges are posted directly to the computer (individual guest accounts) by the PABX interface as soon as the call is completed.

Debits

Debit charge—an amount that *increases* the balance owed by a guest to a venue.

Charges posted to the guest's account for services they have used are classified as **debits**. A debit charge to a guest's account *increases* the amount the guest owes the venue.

Credits

Payments made by the guest to the venue for services they have used are classified as **credits** and *decrease* the balance of their account. There are several types of transactions that reduce the guest's account balance.

Payments

Payments to guest accounts can be recorded as cash, cheque, credit card, advance deposits and travel agent commissions. For example, if the guest makes a payment on their account any time during their stay, this is posted to their account and recorded as a credit.

Credit charge— an amount that *decreases* the balance owed by a guest.

Corrections

Another entry that can reduce a guest's balance is a correction. Corrections occur when a charge (debit) is removed from a guest's account. This could happen if the charge was incorrectly posted to the account or the venue decides not to charge the guest for a particular service. If corrections are necessary, a correction form must be completed and usually authorised by the manager on duty before the procedure is performed. The correction slip becomes the source document. An example is shown in Figure 7.7.

Because the venue still needs to account for the charge, it is posted to another account, usually a marketing account, a complaints account or some other account.

Adjustments

An adjustment is necessary if a debit entry is to be reduced, for example, if an incorrect amount was charged. The total amount is deducted and then the correct amount reposted. This prevents any confusion for the guest and helps the cashier with balancing procedures at the end of the shift. For example, at the time of departure, a guest disputes the $3.50 orange juice charge from the mini-bar on their account. The charge should be $3.00. The entire charge of $3.50 is first deducted from the account and then reposted correctly as $3.00.

Figure 7.7 ▷ **Example of a correction form**

GRAND CENTRAL HOTEL
505 The Boulevard, Sydney
HOTELS OF DISTINCTION

Correction/Adjustment

Account/Room No:		
Date:	Cashier:	
Reason for correction/adjustment	Amount	
	$	c
Authorised by:		
Guest Signature:		

Let's look at how this works. Assume Mr Hughes-Smith bought his wife a gift in the gift shop. Mr Hughes-Smith decides to charge the purchase to his room. He signs a docket (source document) that records the transaction and takes the gift with him. In the gift shop the attendant records the details of the transaction according to the venue's financial transaction processing procedure and later sends the details to front office so that the charge can be posted to Mr Hughes-Smith's account. Figure 7.8 shows how the posting process works.

How is this transaction recorded to Mr Hughes-Smith's account? How you record the transaction will depend on the type of accounting system used, but in general terms:

1. open Mr Hughes-Smith's account
2. select the option to post charges and record the department (gift shop or miscellaneous) then enter the amount
3. close the account.

The gift shop account that corresponds to the charge recorded on Mr Hughes-Smith's account increases.

NON-INCOME TRANSACTIONS

Non-income transactions are transactions posted to guest accounts that display a credit or debit that will be a direct substitute for services rendered. There are two types—advance deposits and contra accounts.

Advance deposits

Advance deposits are prepayments made by the guest usually to secure a reservation for a room. Advance deposits are held in the deposits ledger until the guest checks in and an account is created for them. The deposit is then transferred to the guest's account.

Contra accounts

Contra transactions are transactions involving the exchange of a service for a service. For example, the local print shop may provide services to the venue to the value of $300.00.

Figure 7.8 ▷ **Posting process**

Mr Hughes-Smith purchases a gift in the gift shop.

↓

He signs the record of purchase docket (source document) and the gift shop attendant records the details in a financial transactions record book.

↓

The charge details are sent to the front office at the end of trading (when the gift shop closes for the day).

↓

The transaction is recorded on Mr Hughes-Smith's room account as a debit (and automatically registers in the gift shop departmental account). The balance of his account increases.

When Mr Hughes-Smith checks out, the settlement of his account is recorded as a credit (payment). The balance of his account decreases.

Instead of paying the $300.00, the venue agrees to provide services to the print shop to the value of $300.00 in return. This may be in the form of accommodation or food and beverage or other services offered by the venue.

WHAT IS A PAID OUT?

Earlier we said that the front office knows what to post to each guest's account because the various departments in the venue supply the information in the form of a source document. There are two transactions for which front office will create the source documents: a **paid out** and **foreign exchange**.

Most source documents are self-explanatory: a restaurant food document means the guest has consumed food in the restaurant; a mini-bar document means the guest has consumed goods from the mini-bar. But what has a guest consumed if you have a 'paid out'? A paid out refers to a charge incurred by the guest that has been paid for by the venue on behalf of the guest. For example, Mr Yerondais would like two tickets to the theatre tonight. The porter purchases the ticket for Mr Yerondais and adds the charge to his room account.

A paid out may also arise if a guest leaves a tip either on the account to be charged to their room or on their credit card voucher. For example, Ms Monro dined in the restaurant tonight and paid using her American Express Card. She left a tip for the waiter. Her account was as follows:

Food:	$28.50
Beverages:	$12.50
GST:	$ 4.10
Tip:	$ 5.00
Total	$50.10

There is no GST payable on tips if the guest gives the tip voluntarily. If the tip is earned as a result of a service charge imposed by the venue, then GST is payable.

How do we process each of the charges on this account? Remember, the GST is revenue-neutral so is not included with revenue received from the restaurant, but it is accounted for separately because it will be paid to the tax department. The tip is also not classified as revenue and usually passed onto the staff member who earned the tip that night, or when the guest checks out, or at a pre-determined day specified by the venue. When you process this transaction each of the items are posted once but recorded twice.

Remember also that because the service has been paid for at the time of consumption, the transaction is not posted to a guest's account. In this case it is posted to the method of payment (American Express master account).

The first thing to be completed is a paid out slip. The paid out slip is completed because the amount of the tip is removed from the cash drawer and given to the waiter. In place of the cash will be the paid out slip. Figure 7.9 shows an example of a paid out slip. If the cash is handed over to the waiter without a record of where the cash went, it would not be possible to balance the cash till at the end of the shift (it would be $5.00 short).

Next, all the items are posted to the American Express master account because this is the method of payment and it will show that payment has been received for the services. By posting to the American Express master account the other departments will be automatically updated. The American Express master account is opened and:

Figure 7.9 ▷ **Example of a paid out slip**

GRAND CENTRAL HOTEL
505 The Boulevard, Sydney
HOTELS OF DISTINCTION

Paid out slip

Account/Room No:		
Guest Name:		
Date:	Cashier:	
Details of transaction:		Amount
		$ c
Authorised by:		
Guest Signature:		

▷ $28.50 posted as RF (restaurant food)
▷ $12.50 posted as RB (restaurant beverages)
▷ $4.10 posted as GST (Goods and Services Tax)
▷ $5.00 posted as PO (paid out tips).

The American Express master account now shows $50.10 and where the charges originated. Each department is automatically updated with the amounts posted. Because you have received payment (American Express), you need to also post this.

The paid out slip (which is the source document) and the credit card voucher are placed in the till drawer. The restaurant source documents are filed with the other source documents processed on your shift.

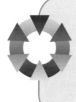

APPLY YOUR KNOWLEDGE

How would you process the following transactions? Where applicable, state whether the transaction is a credit or a debit. For example, a charge posted to a guest's account also registers on the corresponding department account. The charge is a debit and will increase the guest's account and increase the department account (revenue earned).

TRANSACTION TYPE	SOURCE DOCUMENT REQUIRED?	PROCESS METHOD/ EFFECT ON ACCOUNTS	DEBIT/ CREDIT
Mr and Mrs Yerondais incurred the following charges: ▷ laundry $14.40 ▷ mini-bar $26.50 ▷ room charge $125.00			
Staff meals $240.00			
The porter purchases theatre tickets valued at $75.00 for Mr Jones.			
Mr Hughes-Smith wants to pay $400.00 on his account with Visa.			
A party of five dines in the restaurant and pays with cash. ▷ food $389.00 ▷ beverages $205.00 ▷ they leave a tip of $50.00 ▷ GST equals $54.00			
A group has checked in. The group master will pay for accommodation only.			
Mrs Monro has left a $10 tip on her American Express card.			
Mr Sangster incurred the following charges: ▷ telephone $12.50 ▷ valet parking $30.00 ▷ accommodation $290.00			

FOREIGN EXCHANGE

Foreign currency cannot be recorded in the accounting system; only Australian dollars. So during the exchange process, whether paying an account or providing an exchange service, it is necessary to complete a foreign exchange voucher. This voucher represents the Australian dollar equivalent and is placed in the cash drawer along with the foreign currency. The voucher provides details about the amount of currency exchange and the rate used and frequently, the guest's name and room number and the date of the exchange. This is important because the rate may change daily.

The voucher is used in completing balancing procedures at the end of the shift. Without the voucher it would not be possible to determine the Australian dollar equivalent you now have. It is important to note that foreign currency coins are not accepted. An example of a foreign exchange voucher is shown in Figure 7.10.

Figure 7.10 ▷ **Example of a foreign exchange voucher**

GRAND CENTRAL HOTEL
505 The Boulevard, Sydney
HOTELS OF DISTINCTION

Foreign Exchange Voucher

Guest Name/Room No:	
Date:	
Cashier:	
Currency:	Amount:
Exchange rate:	
$AUD value:	
Change issued:	

Exchanging foreign currency

The starting point for foreign exchange is familiarity with a number of different currencies and the abbreviations used for each country and its currency. Currencies can and do change daily. This is important because each day you need to obtain the current exchange rate to ensure the venue does not lose money by using an incorrect rate. The current rate is available from the bank or the newspaper.

Table 7.7 is a copy of an exchange rate listing. The first column lists the country and the unit of currency. The next column lists the rate at which the bank will buy cash of that currency and the next column shows the rate at which they are selling cash of that currency. Accommodation venues buy foreign currency from their guests; they do not sell foreign currency. They do, however, sell the currency they have exchanged for their guests to the bank.

Table 7.7 ▷ **Exchange rate listing**

CURRENCY	BUY	SELL
Austria, schilling	8.4400	8.2300
Belgium, franc	24.7500	24.185
Canada, dollar	0.8296	0.79353
Denmark, krone	4.5679	4.4059
EU, Euro dollar	0.6521	0.62307
France, franc	4.0256	3.9844
Germany, mark	1.2500	1.1564
Hong Kong, dollar	4.0712	3.9512

Table 7.7 ▷ *(continued)*

CURRENCY	BUY	SELL
Indonesia, rupiah	5216.0000	4059.0000
Ireland, punt	0.4832	0.4795
Italy, lira	1288.0000	1158.0000
Japan, yen	57.0700	55.9862
New Zealand, dollar	1.3050	1.2235
Singapore, dollar	0.9075	0.8765
South Africa, rand	4.0580	3.9585
Switzerland, franc	0.9341	0.9200
Thailand, baht	23.0800	21.3695
US, dollar	0.5890	0.5780
UK, sterling	0.3956	0.3895

APPLY YOUR KNOWLEDGE

This activity is to help familiarise you with some common currencies used.

Using the exchange rate listings in Table 7.7, and the listing from today's newspaper, enter the unit of currency for each of the following countries and the exchange rates from the two listings.

COUNTRY	UNIT OF CURRENCY	TABLE 7.7 RATE	TODAY'S RATE
France			
United States			
England			
Germany			
New Zealand			
Canada			

The manager on duty or the accounts department calculates the enterprise's exchange rate on a daily basis. Once these rates have been calculated they are either updated in the computer system, or the cashier will use the rates to calculate how much to give a guest in exchange for the foreign currency they have presented.

How to calculate foreign exchange

A standard formula is used to calculate foreign exchange. The formula includes a service charge and is often 5 per cent of the value of the amount being exchanged. This is generally a higher rate than is charged by a bank. Most of the time you will be converting foreign currency into the Australian dollar equivalent. You use the buy rate because you are buying that foreign currency. To convert foreign currency into the Australian dollar equivalent, and assuming a 5 per cent mark up is used, the formula is:

1 divided by the *bank rate* (supplied on the bank exchange rate) multiplied by the *venue's mark up (5%), minus the result.*

For example, if you are exchanging US dollars and the current exchange rate is .65c, the formula would be:

$$1/.65 \times 5\% - .769 = 1.4615.$$

This means that for every US$100.00 you would exchange $AUD146.15. Because the Australian currency does not have coinage lower than .05c, the amount is rounded up to the nearest .05c.

Sometimes you will need to calculate how much foreign currency a guest needs to give you to settle their account. For example, assume a guest's account is $AUD500.00. The guest wants to pay using English pounds. How much should the guest give you?

First you calculate the exchange rate. Assume the exchange rate is .40 and the mark up is 5 per cent:

$$1/.40 \times 5\% - .125 = 2.375.$$

This means that UK£1 is equal to $AUD2.375.

You now need to convert the Australian dollar amount to a pound sterling equivalent. To do this you divide the $500 by the exchange rate. Thus:

$$\$500.00/2.375 = £210.53.$$

Because you cannot accept foreign coins, this amount will be rounded up to £215.00 for example. This means that you need to give change to the guest. Change is given in local currency only. Thus, if the guest gave you £215.00 for his account, you need to convert the balance back into Australian dollars to give change. The amount of the change due is £4.47. To convert this back to Australian dollars:

$$4.47 \times 2.375 = \$10.62.$$

This would be rounded down to $10.60.

APPLY YOUR KNOWLEDGE

For the following activity calculate the exchange rates using the above formula and the rates listed in Table 7.7.

EXCHANGE RATES
NOTES

COUNTRY	BANK RATE	HOTEL RATE
United States		
England		
Germany		
New Zealand		
Canada		
Japan		
France		

Once the exchange rate has been calculated the cashier is able to work out how much the exchange is for each currency. There are a couple of rules you need to remember when exchanging foreign currency:

1. When you convert foreign currency to Australian currency the sum must be *multiplied* by the venue's exchange rate. For example, Mr Collins wants to exchange $US100.00 traveller's cheques into Australian currency. How much would we give him? $100.00 × 1.46 = $AUD146.00. so for every $US100.00 traveller's cheques Mr Collins will receive $AUD146.00.

2. When a guest presents foreign currency to settle an account, the balance owed by the guest is first converted to the foreign currency equivalent so that you know how much in that currency the guest must give you. You then need to convert it back to Australian currency to know how much change to give (as foreign currency change is never given). For example, Mr Collins's account balance is $AUD500.00. He wishes to pay in American dollars. The American dollar equivalent is $341.25 (500 × .65 × 1.05 = $US341.25) and he gives you $US400.00. You need to give Mr Collins the equivalent of $US58.75 in change, so convert this back into Australian dollars. 1/.65 × .5% − 0.769 = 1.4615 × $US58.75 = $AUD85.86 (rounded down to $AUD85.85).

When converting foreign currency to Australian currency MULTIPLY by the exchange rate.

When converting Australian currency to foreign currency DIVIDE by the exchange rate.

The following activity is useful for manual foreign currency exchange.

APPLY YOUR KNOWLEDGE

Using the hotel exchange rate that you calculated in the activity on page 236 work out the following by using the above exchange methods shown in points 1 and 2 above.

HOW MUCH AUSTRALIAN CURRENCY WOULD BE EXCHANGED FOR EACH OF THE FOLLOWING FOREIGN CURRENCY AMOUNTS?	ANSWERS	HOW MUCH FOREIGN CURRENCY WOULD BE NEEDED TO PAY EACH IN AUSTRALIAN CURRENCY?	ANSWERS
a) **NZ** $150.00 Notes		a) $435.00	
b) **US** $1200.00 Notes		b) $120.00	
c) **EURO** $75.00 Notes		c) $175.00	
d) **CAN** $300.00 T/C		d) $320.00	
e) **DM** 150.00 Notes		e) $240.00	
f) **YEN** 10,000 T/C		f) $95.00	
g) **EURO** $600.00 T/C		g) $400.00	
h) **GBP** £400.00 Notes		h) $195.00	
i) **NZ** $500.00 T/C		i) $620.00	
j) **US** $275.00 T/C		j) $585.00	
k) **GBP** £1000.00 T/C		k) $640.00	
l) **YEN** 1500 Notes		l) $140.00	

SKILLS FOCUS

Guest accounts are maintained by the front office. Maintaining accounts refers to the accurate recording of financial transactions. The front office knows what to record on the guest's account because the various departments in the venue provide this information when the guest uses a service. The information is provided in the form of a source document. A source document provides the details relating to each charge incurred by the guest.

Charges recorded to a guest's account are debits and these increase what the guest owes the venue. A payment recorded on a guest's account is a credit and reduces what the guest owes the venue. A guest account may also be reduced by a correction, adjustment or deposit.

Charges and payments are posted by either the cashier or receptionist at front office, department cashiers if POS technology is used or the night auditor.

> *A paid out refers to any transaction that requires the venue to pay for a service or good on behalf of the guest. The transaction is recorded as a debit on the guest's account.*
>
> *A foreign exchange voucher is completed when a foreign exchange transaction takes place to enable accurate recording of the equivalent Australian dollar value. To convert foreign currency to Australian dollars, divide the amount of currency by the exchange rate to arrive at the Australian dollar equivalent. To convert Australian dollars to a foreign currency, multiply the amount by the exchange rate for that currency.*

FOCUS REVIEW

▷ *When are charges posted to a guest's account?*
▷ *What effect does a debit have on a guest's account?*
▷ *What effect does a credit have on a guest's account?*
▷ *Apart from a payment, how else may a guest account balance be reduced?*
▷ *What are the two types of source documents front office is likely to create?*
▷ *Why is the paid out slip placed in the till drawer?*
▷ *If you post a debit (charge) to a guest's account what effect does it have on the corresponding department account?*
▷ *What are non-income transactions?*
▷ *What are contra accounts? Why do you think a venue may operate a contra account?*

Settling the guests' accounts

Account settlement is the final stage of the guest accounting cycle. The primary objective of account settlement is to zero balance accounts by posting the payment due. This means that the account balance must be at zero and this is achieved by recording payment. Settlement of an account reduces the ledger to which the account belongs (for example, the in-house guest ledger or city ledger).

Most in-house guests settle their account at check-out. However, as we have seen, the guest may transfer the account to the city ledger. A guest's account that has been settled is shown in Figure 7.11.

Settlement can be processed in a number of ways:

▷ cash
  — local currency
  — foreign currency
▷ credit cards
  — American Express
  — Diners Club International
  — Visa card
  — MasterCard
  — Bankcard
  — JCB (Japanese Credit Bureau)

Figure 7.11 ▷ **Example of a settled guest account**

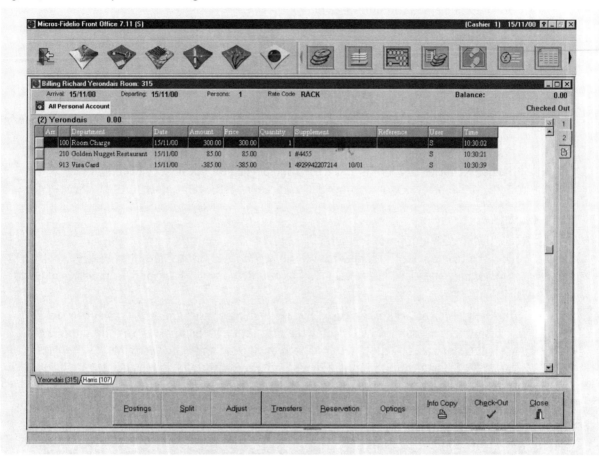

▷ cheques
- traveller's cheques
- personal cheques (at the discretion of individual establishments)
- company cheques
- bank cheques

▷ city ledger (by transferring to the city ledger the guest account is zero balanced and the in-house ledger is decreased, but note that the city ledger will increase)

▷ EFTPOS—this directly debits money from the account holders chosen bank account.

The processing procedure for accepting payment is determined by the individual venue and is discussed at length in Chapter 6.

ISSUING RECEIPTS

Every transaction that involves the exchange of money requires the issue of a receipt. A receipt is a detailed record of the transaction indicating what the transaction was, the amount paid and the method of payment. When a guest account is settled, the payment is posted to the account, which will zero balance the account. A copy of the account is then presented to the guest as a form of receipt.

If the venue operates a manual accounting system, a handwritten receipt is created. It will contain the same information as a computer printed receipt but in summary form. Figure 7.12 shows an example of a computer receipt.

To demonstrate how an account is settled we will use an example. Mr Sangster is checking out of the venue. He has two accounts: a master account and an extras account. The venue holds a company charge back authority for Mr Sangster for accommodation only. The extras account is Mr Sangster's responsibility and he will pay with cash.

1. Open Mr Sangster's master account. Follow account settlement procedures for check-out.
2. Present Mr Sangster with a copy of the account (which he checks) and ask him to sign the account.
3. Post the payment method. In this case, transfer the balance to the city ledger. Mr Sangster's master account is now closed and a receipt is automatically printed.
4. Open Mr Sangster's extras account. Follow account settlement procedures for check-out.
5. Present Mr Sangster with a copy of the account (which he checks) and ask him for the cash.
6. Count the cash in front of the guest.
7. Post the cash amount (balance due on the account) to the account. This will zero balance the account and close it. A receipt will print automatically. Hand this with any change to Mr Sangster.

The city ledger balance is increased by the amount of Mr Sangster's master account. The cash department account is increased by the amount of Mr Sangster's extras account. The in-house ledger decreases by the amount of both the master and extras accounts.

The cash department account is different from the cash folio. Remember, the cash folio is only used for those transactions *not* linked to an in-house guest.

Figure 7.12 ▷ **Example of a computer receipt**

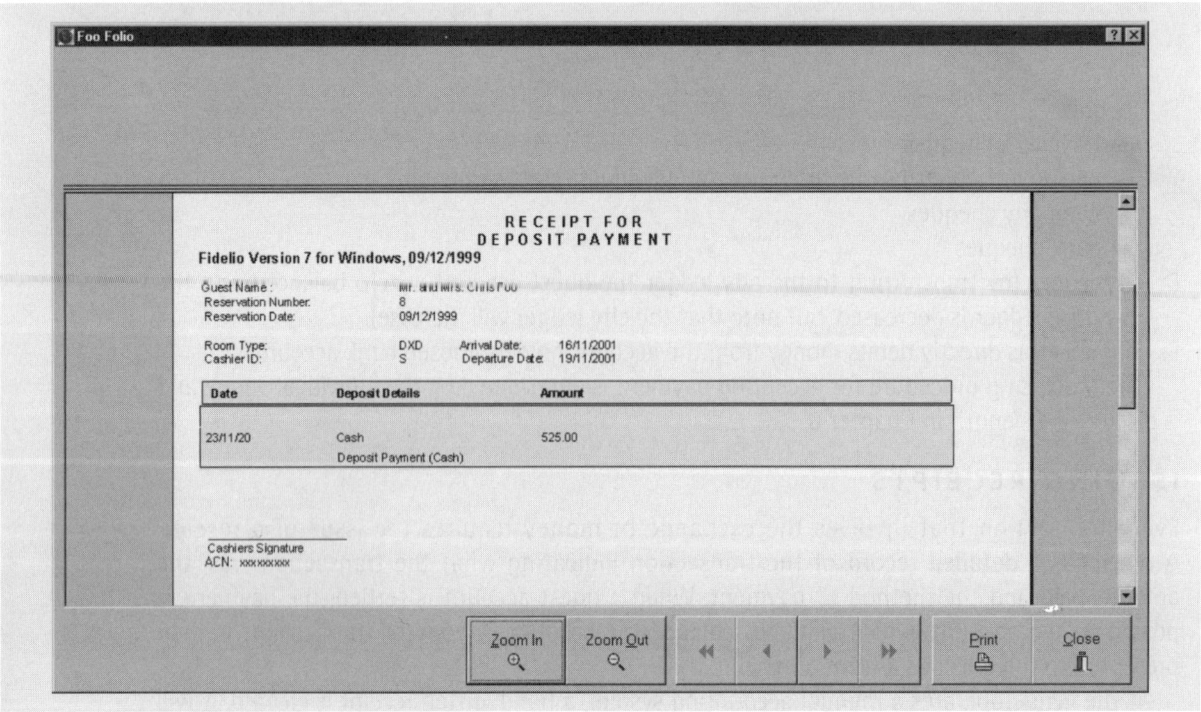

Account settlement is the final stage of the guest accounting cycle. Its main objective is to settle the account by recording the method of payment. By recording the method of payment, the balance of the account is then zero.

Account settlement can be with: cash, cheques, credit card, transfer to city ledger, EFTPOS. A receipt is issued to acknowledge payment has been received.

Settlement of guest accounts results in a decrease in the in-house ledger and an increase in the balance of the method of payment account.

FOCUS REVIEW

▷ *What is the primary objective of the guest account settlement procedure? How is this achieved?*
▷ *What does EFTPOS stand for? How does this method of payment work?*
▷ *Why is it necessary to count the cash received from the guest?*
▷ *Why is a receipt issued?*
▷ *What effect does account settlement have on the in-house ledger?*

Balancing the accounts

To make accounts balance, every transaction is recorded twice, that is, every charge incurred by a guest is recorded on the guest's account *and* on the department's account where the charge originated. Each charge posted to the guest's account increases the amount owed to the venue and increases the total revenue earned by the department where the charge originated.

Every payment made by the guest is recorded on the guest's account *and* on the method of payment account. Each payment posted to the guest's account reduces the amount owed to the venue but increases the method of payment account total.

If any of these transactions are incorrectly posted, then the accounts won't balance. At the end of every shift, you need to check that every transaction you recorded is accurate and that every account balances. You do this by performing the end of shift balance.

PERFORMING BALANCING PROCEDURES

To perform the balancing procedures you must check that source documents and physical money equals what was posted as debits and credits to the accounts. The main objectives of the balancing procedure are to close the shift and balance all the transactions.

Each department that has transactions recorded against it are 'closed'. This means that you account for only those transactions that occurred during your shift. Guest accounts are not closed until the time of check-out. Instead they are carried over to the next day's trading, or until check-out.

The procedure to follow may vary between venues. Most computerised PMSs are programmed with an end of day or end of shift balancing function. If this is the case, by selecting this option, you will be guided through the necessary steps to balance all the debits and credits posted that day and then to close the shift. A procedure is followed because in balancing financial transactions, certain steps must be performed before you can move onto the next step. In general terms the procedure to follow is:

1. Print a copy of each department account in which charges have been recorded (for example, laundry, mini-bar, paid outs and restaurant).
2. Tally all source documents per department posted during the shift. Attach an add strip to each batch. For example, tally all the restaurant food documents, bar documents, room service documents, etc.
3. Compare the source documents tallies (totals arrived at in step 2) with the computer printout for each department. If these balance, continue to the next step. If not, find the error and fix it.
4. Print a copy of the banking report. This report lists all the payments received that day according to type (Visa, American Express etc).
5. Remove the till drawer. Before counting any money, remove the till drawer to a secure area, usually the back office.
6. Count out the float and complete a float sheet.
7. Count the remaining money and record the totals of each type (for example, cash, Visa card, traveller's cheques) on a banking envelope.
8. Compare the banking report totals with the banking envelope totals.
9. If these match, enter the amounts in the PMS to show that you balance. If they do not balance, find the error and fix it.
10. Close the shift. This will close all department accounts (but not in-house guest accounts).
11. Sign in the float to the duty manager or supervisor.
12. Place all the department printouts, source documents and money in the banking envelope and put them in the safe.

We demonstrate how the balancing procedure works with a simple example. Let's assume that during your shift you posted the following total charges to various guests' rooms:

Restaurant food	$ 500.00
Mini-bar	$ 68.50
Laundry	$ 87.90
Cocktail bar	$ 786.00
Total	$1452.40

The computer arrives at these totals from the charges you posted. Print out a copy of each department's transactions (step 1). Tally your source documents for each department (step 2). Compare your manual tallies with the computer reading for each department. Each of the totals should match. So you should have restaurant food dockets to the value of $500.00, laundry dockets to the value of $87.90 and so on (step 3).

You also posted the following payments:

Room 106	$100.00 (Visa card)
Cash	$250.00

Print a copy of the banking report (step 4). Remove the till drawer to a secure area (step 5). In your till drawer you have your float, plus $250.00 in cash and a Visa card voucher to the value of $100.00. Count out your float (step 6) and count your takings (step 7). If what is in your drawer matches what the PMS says you should have then you have balanced (step 8). Enter the amounts in the computer to show you have balanced (step 9).

Close the shift (step 10) and sign in the float to the duty manager or supervisor (step 11). Place all the department printouts, source documents and money in the banking envelope and place in the safe (step 12).

Figure 7.13 shows an example of a cashier's report at the close of shift indicating the amounts posted and the moneys the cashier should have.

Figure 7.13 ▷ **Cashier's end of shift balance**

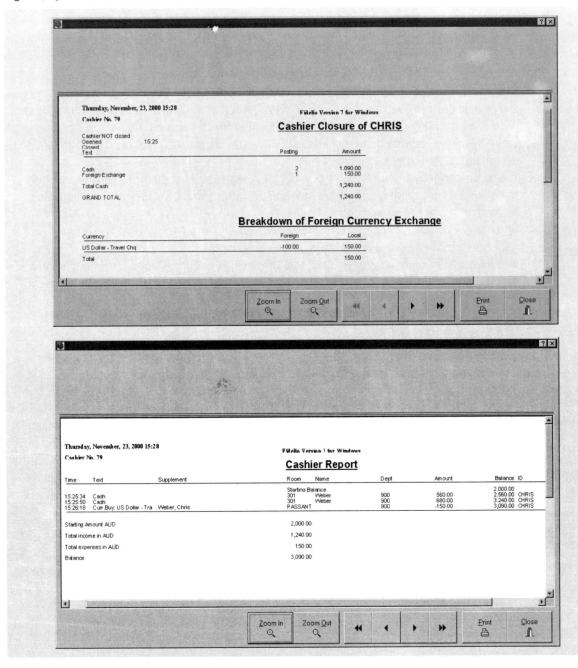

This simple example makes the balancing procedure appear quite straightforward. And often it is. Problems begin to arise when the physical money you have or the source documents you have don't match what the PMS says you should have. Here we consider some of the problems that may arise and what to do about them.

TRACKING ERRORS

You can't close your shift until everything balances. If the shift does not balance, it is necessary to track and correct the error. Errors may be in either debit or credit postings. To **track** an error means to find where the error exists by checking and recalculating entries made during the shift until the error is located and then making the necessary adjustment to fix the problem. This doesn't mean you have to check every guest account to which you posted entries. It does mean that you first determine in which department the error is. The following step-by-step tracking procedure should help you find your errors.

1. Check which of your manual totals match the computer totals. Obviously these are correct and you don't need to check here for the errors. When you identify the department(s) that doesn't match then you know where to start looking for the error.
2. When you have identified the department where the error exists, recalculate your source document totals. If these are correct then:
3. The computer department account printouts will list each of the entries you made. Check these against the individual source documents. This should show you in which guest account the error has been made.
4. When you have identified where the error is, you will need to make a correction or an adjustment to the relevant account.
5. When you have made the necessary adjustment or correction, reprint the department balance and again compare your totals. You may need to follow this procedure several times until every department balances.

OVERS AND UNDERS

The cashier, not the computer, is usually responsible for errors. And one of the most common errors is to find that you have more (overs) or less (unders) money than the computer says you should have. Unfortunately, it is not a simple case of putting in some yourself or taking out the excess. The mistake must be found and fixed.

If you find that the physical money doesn't match the computer printout, follow the same procedure for tracking departmental errors. Begin by recounting your float and money again. If you still don't balance, you will need to determine which department has the error (Visa, American Express, cash, etc) and then you will need to locate the actual entry error and make the necessary corrections or adjustments, reprint the computer totals and check again if you now balance.

BANKING PROCEDURES

A **banking report** contains the summarised amounts for the cash, credit cards, cheques, foreign currency and EFTPOS taken for the day. Once this has been checked and overs and unders accounted for, a banking envelope needs to be completed. The amounts of the credit cards, foreign currency and cheques are written on the envelope and the cash takings for the day are taken from the float. The amount of cash required is determined by how much foreign currency was exchanged, how many paid outs were processed, and how much EFTPOS was used. These amounts are subtracted from the total banking amount. The difference is how much cash comes out of the float.

This is written on the banking envelope in separate denominations and the figures for cash, cheque, foreign currency and EFTPOS transactions are added up and should match the banking figure printed with the balancing report.

The banking report is placed inside the envelope with the currency and then sealed and signed by the cashier and given to the manager on duty or placed in a drop safe. The manager on duty will retrieve it, check it and sign it to acknowledge that the amounts and figures are correct.

The float is also returned to the duty manager once the cashier has confirmed that the amount is the same as that when the shift started.

All documentation is completed and the float bag is sealed with a numbered tag and also dropped into the safe. The cashier's shift is completed.

SECURITY PROCEDURES FOR CASH HANDLING

Because of the large quantities of money and non-financial transactions that take place on a daily basis, accommodation venues need to be very aware of security issues. The main concern is the security of cash and other legal tender.

Balancing procedures are performed away from the front desk either in a back office or a safe, locked room. Not only is this for security reasons, but also for customer service standards. While standing at the front desk counting money, it is highly probable that a guest might arrive needing your attention. You cannot ignore the guest, nor can you leave the money exposed and unattended.

If you are seen handling large amounts of money at the front desk, the establishment might be seen as a prime target for hold-ups and robbery. Both you and the money are at risk.

SKILLS FOCUS

To balance the accounts, every transaction—debits and credits—is recorded twice. The balancing procedure requires you to close the shift by checking that what should have been done has been done. This is achieved by following a step-by-step procedure that ensures all transactions are accounted for.

If errors are discovered, these must be tracked and adjusted. Tracking errors requires rechecking entries made until the error is located.

The balancing procedure is completed away from the front desk for security reasons and to ensure customer service standards are met. Because of the large quantities of money handled by many enterprises, it is neither safe nor appropriate to balance the shift in the public view.

FOCUS REVIEW

▷ *What is the main objective of the balancing procedure?*
▷ *Why is it necessary to follow a procedure when balancing financial procedures?*
▷ *What is meant be 'tracking'? What should you check first?*

> *What is an 'over'? What is an 'under'?*
> *Why must the shift balance?*
> *Why is it important to balance the shift away from public view?*

PUT YOUR KNOWLEDGE TO THE TEST

Robyn was looking forward to completing her first cashiering shift and took extra time to recheck all her calculations to make sure they were correct. To help Robyn with the process of managing financial transactions, she has been trained to record all transactions manually and in the computerised PMS. Table A represents all the transactions performed on Robyn's shift. Table B is where the transactions are to be recorded. Using the figures from Table A, manually enter the transactions onto the posting sheet provided in Table B. When you have completed the tabular ledger, use the information to balance your shift. Table C is a blank cashier's report that will allow you to enter your departmental totals. You can then perform the balance in the computerised PMS if you have access to one.

Table A

Accommodation Charges	Single		$150.00			
	Double		$165.00			
Brought Forward Balances	Room	1101	Mr/s Jones	$170.50		
		1103	Mr/s Gawron	$236.50		
		1105	Mr Tante	$320.00		
Breakfast Charges		1101	$32.00			
		1105	$16.00			
		1103	$24.00			
Telephone Charges		1105	$12.60			
		1103	$23.70			

Mr Lewis checks into Room 1104, pays $250.00 on account.

Luncheon Charges	1101	Food $46.00	Beverage $12.00
	1103	Food $29.50	Beverage $22.50
	1104	Food $22.00	

Ms Elliot checks into Room 1102, pays $300.00 on account.

Telephone Charges	1101	$12.30
	1104	$8.50
	1105	$11.00
	1102	$3.20

Mr and Mrs Jones receive a delivery of flowers, charged at $25.00.
Mr Lewis requires $5.60 to purchase some cigarettes from the foyer cigarette machine.
Mr Elliot purchases goods to the value of $12.50 from the foyer gift shop.

Dinner Charges	1101	Food $52.00	Beverage $26.00	Tip $8.00
	1104	Food $26.50	Beverage $6.00	
	1105	Food $16.00	Beverage $3.50	Tip $5.50
	1103	Food $ 86.00	Beverage $ 56.00	Tip $ 12.00
	1102	Food $ 39.00	Beverage $14.50	

Room 1103 check-out after dinner; they are to be charged a day use fee of $ 80.00 they pay their account with a Bankcard.
Mrs Jones pays $ 200.00 on her account using an American Express.

Table B ▷ **Manual posting sheet**

ROOM	1101	1102	1103	1104	1105	1106	1107	TOTAL
GUEST NAME								
Brought Forward								
Accommodation								
Breakfast								
Lunch Food								
Lunch Beverage								
Dinner Food								
Dinner Beverage								
Telephone								
Paid Outs								
Sundries								
TOTAL								
Cash								
Credit Card								
City Ledger								
Carried Forward								
TOTAL								

Table C ▷ **Cashier's report/banking envelope**

GRAND CENTRAL HOTEL
505 The Boulevard, Sydney
HOTELS OF DISTINCTION

Cashier's Banking Envelope

Date: _____   Cashier Name: _____

Department/Shift: _____

Signature: _____

Float Count			Contents of Banking Envelope		
Notes			Notes		
$100.00			$100.00		
$50.00			$50.00		
$20.00			$20.00		
$10.00			$10.00		
$5.00			$5.00		
Coins			Coins		
$2.00			$2.00		
$1.00			$1.00		
.50			.50		
.20			.20		
.10			.10		
.05			.05		
			Cheques		
			Traveller's Cheques		
			Vouchers		
			Foreign Currency		
			EFTPOS		
Float Total					
			Total Enclosed		
			Amount Due (Till Reading)		
			Difference		

248   ACCOMMODATION SERVICES

Conducting Night Audit

LEARNING OUTCOMES

On completion of this chapter, you will be able to:

▷ describe the role of the night auditor;

▷ process late arrivals and no-shows;

▷ process outstanding charges and payments;

▷ audit and balance all financial transactions of the establishment;

▷ implement procedures to ensure the accuracy of financial systems within an establishment;

▷ produce accurate reports for establishment management in a timely manner.

Introduction

The third shift of the 24-hour day in accommodation venues is the night audit. Often referred to as D shift, the hours worked are normally 11.00 pm to 7.30 am and, depending on the size of the venue, may require only one person to be on duty, or several including a night manager, assistant night manager and night auditor(s). The main function of the night audit role, irrespective of the number of people who undertake to complete the tasks, is to audit the financial transactions that took place that day.

Auditing—the process of checking and reviewing financial and non-financial transactions to determine their accuracy.

__Auditing__ is the process of checking and reviewing all financial and non-financial transactions to determine their accuracy. Auditing ensures that guests staying in the establishment receive their correct account on departure, that all revenues are accounted for, that errors are found and corrected and that control is maintained over the guest accounting system in place.

Although based in reception, the night auditor undertakes his or her auditing duties, while also completing a number of other duties that, during the day, are usually undertaken by their colleagues. In this chapter you will learn how to perform the auditing duties performed by D shift, irrespective of the title of the person who may carry out the tasks.

The role of the night auditor

As we said in the introduction, the night audit function is to audit the financial and non-financial transactions that take place that day. But in addition to this the night audit shift may be responsible for:

▷ General reception and cashiering duties. During the night, guests arrive and depart, exchange currency and request other services, as they do during the day. The night auditor operates a shift, separate from the auditing duties, and is required to manage these guests' services, as well as account for his or her own financial transactions while on duty.

▷ Porter duties. This may include storing or retrieving luggage, placing wake up calls, delivering newspapers or booking transport.

▷ Telephonist duties. Rarely is a telephonist on duty at night so it is up to D shift to manage the switchboard.

▷ Reservations. Similarly to the telephonist, it is unlikely that a reservations clerk is on duty during the night, so the night auditor must manage reservation enquiries. Most of the reservation enquiries received during the night originate from overseas because of the time difference.

▷ Room service duties. In some venues, D shift may be responsible for managing a limited 24-hour room service menu including taking the order, preparing the food and beverages and delivering the items to the guest's room.

▷ Security. All venues are potentially vulnerable at night so a number of security duties are performed by D shift. Security is discussed later in the chapter.

Even if the night auditor does not undertake any of the tasks listed above, that person needs to be conversant with these duties, particularly reception and cashiering duties, as it is the work of these departments that is being audited.

Upon arrival, the D shift must:

▷ undertake a shift handover
▷ log on to the computer
▷ collect a float
▷ check for late arrivals, no-shows and rooms to sell
▷ process any late charges
▷ register any late arrivals.

The next primary concern of the night auditor is to perform the first of several security checks for the night. This first check is usually completed before C shift departs. Remember, there is always a shift overlap which allows for these types of duties.

Next, the night auditor is able to begin the audit process. This requires the night auditor to be on hand at the front desk for the next couple of hours before another security check is undertaken. The night auditor then:

▷ collects room service orders from room door knobs, collates these for the chef and posts the orders to the room accounts
▷ checks function sheets for the next day and updates the foyer function board
▷ prepares express check-out envelopes and accounts and delivers these to the rooms that requested express check-outs (an example is shown in Figure 8.1)
▷ determines the venue's newspaper requirements and orders these (according to occupancy level).

Later, a third security check is undertaken, newspapers and even early breakfast orders are delivered, early wake up calls are placed, and all night audit reports are generated.

Finally, at the end of the night audit shift, the night auditor will:

▷ process any early departures
▷ process early room service breakfast charges
▷ distribute reports generated
▷ distribute floats where required
▷ handover to the next shift.

WHAT IS INVOLVED WITH SECURITY CHECKS?

Security is concerned with the conservation and preservation of the venue's and the guests' assets (property, valuables, money) and the safety and well-being of staff and guests. Security checks therefore play an important part in the night auditor's role. Often, there is no other security system in place, so the 'presence' of someone patrolling the public areas of the venue, both internally and externally, is important. Patrols are usually conducted at least three times a night but not following any obvious set pattern. When conducting a security check, the night auditor will patrol:

▷ venue car parks
▷ venue perimeter
▷ external and internal entertainment areas, such as the pool and bars
▷ external and internal walkways, gardens and corridors
▷ all back of house areas.

During patrol the night auditor is:

▷ checking that gates, doors and windows are securely locked

Figure 8.1 ▷ **Example of an express check-out**

GRAND CENTRAL HOTEL
505 The Boulevard, Sydney
HOTELS OF DISTINCTION

Express Check-out

Dear Guest,

At Grand Central, we understand that *your time* is valuable. To help save you time, we have introduced this simple and effective express check-out system.

1. Enclosed you will find a copy of your account. Please check the details.
2. If your account details are correct, please complete the express check-out form at the bottom.
3. Drop the form in the Express Check-out box, along with your key, at reception on your way out.

Any late minute charges, such as breakfast and telephone calls will be added to your account for you after departure.

If there is an error on the account, please contact reception any time, day or night.

We hope that you have enjoyed your stay with us and we look forward to welcoming you back soon.

With thanks

Grand Central

Name: _____

Room No: _____ Departure date: _____

Please settle my account with (please tick)

☐ Company   ☐ MC   ☐ AX   ☐ DC   ☐ BC   ☐ VC

    Charge (please enter details below)

Card Number _____

Expiry ___ / ___

Signature _____

Please forward my account to:

_____

▷ looking out for suspicious behaviour or packages, damage to the venue or vehicles
▷ ascertaining maintenance requirements.

To ensure no area is overlooked and that all areas are in fact secured, a security checklist can be used. An example is shown in Table 8.1. As you can see from the list a number of things must be checked when on patrol, such as that doors and gates are locked and secure, that there are no signs of damage or break in, no suspicious people, cars or packages, and that all lighting is in good repair. It is important to record the time of the security patrol because if a security breach does occur (such as a break in or property damage), the time of the incident can be more easily ascertained.

Table 8.1 ▷ **Security checklist**

GRAND CENTRAL SECURITY CHECKLIST

Date: _____

Patrol One: Time _____	Initials _____
Patrol Two: Time_____	Initials _____
Patrol Three: Time _____	Initials _____

- ☐ Exterior of the hotel checked—all doors leading outside are securely locked
- ☐ Loading dock all closed up and bolted
- ☐ Car park—all lighting is on and security entrance working
- ☐ Swimming pool gate is locked and all outside equipment correctly stored
- ☐ All function rooms are locked and lights turned out
- ☐ Corridor lighting in order
- ☐ All kitchen appliances switched off
- ☐ Fire doors closed
- ☐ Guest laundry area secured
- ☐ Foyer correctly lit

Notes: _____
_____
_____

SKILLS FOCUS

The third shift of the 24-hour day in accommodation venues is the night audit, which usually operates from 11.00 pm to 7.30 am. The primary role of this shift is to manage the auditing of the financial and non-financial transactions that have occurred in the last 24 hours. It is likely that auditing staff will perform a range of other duties usually undertaken by other staff during the day such as general reception, telephony and porter duties.

Auditing is the process of checking and reviewing all financial and non-financial transactions to determine their accuracy. This is an important task as it ensures that guests receive timely and correct accounts, that all revenues are accounted for, and that any errors that have occurred are corrected.

The night auditor is also often responsible for managing the security of the venue during the night. This entails security patrols of the venue's internal and external public areas and checking that everything is safe and in good order.

FOCUS REVIEW

▷ *What is the main function of the night audit role?*
▷ *What is auditing?*
▷ *Why is it important for the night auditor to be able to perform other roles within the front office as well as the auditing role?*
▷ *What is involved in the security of the venue?*
▷ *Why would security checks not follow any obvious set pattern?*

Before commencing the audit process

Once you have completed a shift handover with your colleagues, logged on to the computer, and collected and counted your float, the next thing you do is check for late arrivals and no-shows. **Late arrivals** are those guests with reservations who have made arrangements for a late check-in. No-shows are those reservations the venue expected earlier in the day but who have not arrived.

You also need to check which rooms, if any, are available to sell. Depending on the venue's location and depending on the night (day of the week), many venues will have walk ins throughout the night; travellers looking for a short rest, airline passengers whose flights have been cancelled or delayed, late night revellers not wanting to drive home. It is just as important for night audit to try to maximise occupancy as it is for other roles in the front and back office.

PROCESSING LATE ARRIVALS AND NO-SHOWS

How late arrivals and no-shows are managed is likely to vary between venues and will depend on the policies and procedures in place, but in most instances:

▷ guaranteed late arrivals are registered in the PMS (and if they do arrive, processed as usual)
▷ no-show reservations are cancelled
▷ guaranteed no-show reservations are charged for one night's accommodation.

No-show reservations are then passed on to the reservations department to follow up the next day. This may entail the reservations clerk calling the guest to determine why they failed to arrive (for example, the expected date was incorrect), or simply filing the information in the guest's profile.

PROCESSING OUTSTANDING CHARGES AND PAYMENTS

At the start of your shift you collected a float and logged onto the PMS. You need the float to manage your own shift, and you must process outstanding charges and payments. The most likely transactions to be processed are from the various outlets in the venue such as the bar and restaurant, which usually close around midnight, and room service charges from the evening shift. There may also be front office transactions that also need processing, such as late check-ins and paid outs.

Processing floats

At this time you will also receive the floats from the various departments and outlets that are now closed (restaurant, bar, room service). Each department is responsible for checking that its float is accurate, but you are responsible for re-checking its accuracy. When you receive floats from the various outlets:

▷ recount the float
▷ ask the department cashier to sign the float 'in', then
▷ drop the float in the safe.

If the float has insufficient coinage for the next day's trading, exchange notes for coins accordingly.

When the float is deposited at the front office (signed 'in') it may be placed directly into the venue's safe or **drop box**—a drop chute situated in a safe for the depositing of floats and takings received from other departments. The same float is issued to the same outlet for the next day's trading. A staff member from the department will collect the float, check it again for accuracy, and sign it 'out'. The signing in and out of floats allows an accurate record of where a float is at any time and who collected or deposited it.

BALANCE YOUR SHIFT

Because the transactions you have processed need to be included in the audit, before commencing the audit you need to perform your own shift balance. The difference for night audit is that you need to balance your shift twice; first after you have posted all the night work and before you rollover to the next trading day, and again after you have changed the trading day in the computer (finished the audit process). At this time you need to log on again and process all the work for the morning such as posting room service breakfast and early departures. Your second balance is completed near the end of your shift.

The reason why you need to balance twice is so that all transactions are recorded in the correct day. For example, dinner eaten in the restaurant on Wednesday night needs to be recorded in Wednesday's revenue, and room service breakfast to be consumed on Thursday morning needs to be recorded in Thursday's revenue, for correct account keeping procedures.

Both shift balances are performed exactly as a shift balance for any other front office role (refer to Chapter 6).

SKILLS FOCUS

Late arrivals are guests with reservations who have made arrangements for a late check-in. Guaranteed late arrivals are registered in the PMS and processed as any other guest registration when they do arrive. These reservations are cancelled and, for guaranteed reservations, charged one night's accommodation. No-shows are passed onto the reservation department to follow up.

Depending on the venue's locations, and the night of the week, many venues will have walk ins during the night. It is important to know which rooms, if any, are available to sell so that walk ins can be accommodated.

Any outstanding transactions such as payments and charges are processed at this time. The most likely source of these charges is the food and beverage outlets (restaurant, bar and room service).

The night auditor processes floats from the various departments which involves checking them for accuracy, and, when necessary, changing notes for coins, then dropping them in the safe.

The first of two shift balances is then performed.

FOCUS REVIEW

▷ *How are late arrivals processed?*
▷ *How are no-shows processed?*
▷ *What responsibility does night audit have for the floats from other departments?*
▷ *Why does the night auditor complete two shift balances? When are these balances performed?*

Conducting the night audit

Now that you have processed late arrivals and no-shows, posted outstanding charges and payments and performed your first shift balance, you can commence the actual audit. During the audit process, the front office does not close. This means that any time during the night, while conducting the audit process you may receive telephone enquiries or walk ins or need to respond to any number of guest requests.

Most businesses conduct an audit on a monthly, quarterly or half-yearly basis. Most accommodation venues conduct an audit on a nightly basis. One reason for this is that most other businesses do not undertake as many financial and non-financial transactions as do accommodation venues in a single day; and there are many different outlets. Another reason is that it is far simpler to track errors on a daily basis than on a weekly or monthly basis. Finally, another important reason the audit must be completed nightly is because errors relating to guest accounts need to be found and corrected before the guest departs.

The auditing process not only finds errors and corrects them but is intended also to:

▷ accurately identify and allocate revenues according to departments
▷ monitor and control the extent of credit (outstanding guest accounts)
▷ accurately monitor the venue's financial performance
▷ balance all cash and credit card payments
▷ balance all other transactions
▷ prove accounting integrity (by verifying that account postings match source documents).

These days most of the auditing functions are enabled by computerised PMSs. Not only does this greatly reduce the time it takes to complete the procedure but it is also more accurate. A computerised PMS can organise and compile relevant financial data far more efficiently than a manual system.

STEPS TO THE AUDIT

The audit follows a logical sequence of events resulting in the commencement of a new trading day.

1. Prepare documentation
2. Balance all departments
3. Verify room rates
4. Post room rates
5. Perform close of day procedures:
   (a) close accounts
   (b) deposit banking
   (c) back up the system
   (d) rollover to new trading day
6. Generate and distribute audit reports.

Once the night audit procedure is commenced, no other transactions can be entered into the computer until the entire process is complete. This is why it is important beforehand to register any expected late arrivals. Keep a separate list of available rooms in the event walk ins arrive and, during the auditing process, manually process any financial transactions. When the audit is complete, the walk ins and manual transactions can then be entered in the new trading day.

1. PREPARE DOCUMENTATION

All departments will have 'deposited' their source documents, balance sheets and takings (money) with the front office at the end of each shift (such as after breakfast, lunch and dinner in the restaurant or at the end A and B shift in front office). All of this 'paper work' and money is held in the venue's safe.

So at this stage you:

▷ gather together all receipts and separate them into each type of charge or credit card
▷ print a journal copy for each posting code
▷ reconcile each voucher (or receipt) to each posting.

Batching departmental charges

To verify that all the necessary paperwork is in order, remove the shift and departmental balances from the safe and physically check it. For example, you know that the venue operates three restaurant shifts, so you should have three restaurant balances and associated source documents and money. You should also have all balances from any other shift operated in the venue (such as room service, laundry and the bar). When you have checked that these have all been deposited, verify that they are correct (that they do in fact balance). You can then move on to the next stage—batching.

To **batch** means to put all the same charges (source documents) together.

All documents relating to the same source (department), such as all telephone charges, beverages, food and laundry, from each shift are batched and tallied. **Batching** means to put all the same charges (source documents) together. For example, put together and tally all the telephone charges from shift A and B, put together and tally all the laundry charges from shift A and B, etc.

The reason everything is batched and tallied is so that when the time comes for you to verify that what has been done (the totals on the source documents) is what should have been done (the totals in the computer), all the department transactions are tallied and easy to follow.

Batching credit card postings

Batch all Bankcard, MasterCard and Visa Card transactions in the same way as you batched the source documents. American Express and Diners Club Card receipts are stapled to the account that they settled. For example, a Diners Club card may have been used to settle a restaurant food account, while another guest may have used American Express to pay for their accommodation. This verifies that they have been processed correctly.

If operating on a manual system, Bankcard, MasterCard and Visa receipts are banked similarly to cash and cheques and included in your total banking for the night. American Express and Diners Card receipts are forwarded to the respective company for payment at a later date.

If the venue has a **fast track machine**, then payment for Visa Cards, MasterCards, Bankcards, American Express and Diners Cards can be processed electronically and immediately. These card transactions can be batched and you can arrange for the money to be deposited directly into the venue's bank account. A fast track machine is linked to the EFTPOS machine.

The total of the credit card batch must equal the total of each credit card posting for the day. When accounts staff perform the bank reconciliation the batching figures are displayed on the establishment's bank statement. If any items have been posted under an incorrect code (for example, a Visa Card posted as a Bankcard) this will be discovered, as will any mistakes in completion of the credit card voucher. Any errors must be corrected before the credit cards are batched. Fix the error by removing it from the relevant account and re-posting the transaction.

Batching occurs daily when credit card payments for the day are totalled and sent to the bank (or Amex and Diners to their respective companies) for payment. Batching should occur as soon as possible to the close of day in order to minimise differences between daily postings and batch totals.

Next, you need to count all physical money (cash) and complete a cashier's report/banking envelope. An example of a night auditor's banking envelope is shown in Figure 8.2.

Once you have completed batching all charges and payments you are then ready to balance all departments.

Figure 8.2 ▷ **Cashier's report/banking envelope**

GRAND CENTRAL HOTEL
505 The Boulevard, Sydney
HOTELS OF DISTINCTION

Cashier's Banking Envelope

Date: _____   Cashier Name: _____
Department/Shift: _____
Signature: _____

Float Count			Contents of Banking Envelope		
Notes			Notes		
$100.00			$100.00		
$50.00			$50.00		
$20.00			$20.00		
$10.00			$10.00		
$5.00			$5.00		
Coins			Coins		
$2.00			$2.00		
$1.00			$1.00		
.50			.50		
.20			.20		
.10			.10		
.05			.05		
			Cheques		
			Traveller's Cheques		
			Vouchers		
			Foreign Currency		
			EFTPOS		
Float Total					
		Total Enclosed			
		Amount Due (Till Reading)			
		Difference			

In preparation for the balancing step of the night audit, you have the following balance sheets information:

Front office charges

CHARGE	SHIFT A	SHIFT B	TOTAL
Telephones	$672.80	$786.50	
Paid outs	$ 72.00	$18.90	
Laundry	$145.65	$256.90	
Room service beverages	$976.45	$1089.50	
Room service food	$1245.05	$890.35	
Gift shop	$789.30	$678.00	
Mini-bar	$450.70	$23.90	

Front office payments

PAYMENT	SHIFT A	SHIFT B	TOTAL
Visa	$8,900.75	$2,450.50	
MasterCard	$700.90	$3,900.00	
American Express	$4,096.00	$3,007.10	
Cash	$2,867.90	$1,987.40	

Restaurant revenue

CHARGE	BREAKFAST	LUNCH	DINNER	TOTAL
Food	$345.90	$1,567.95	$2,890.00	
Beverages		$650.80	$1, 095.90	

Restaurant payments

PAYMENT	BREAKFAST	LUNCH	DINNER	TOTAL
Visa		$105.85	$785.30	
MasterCard			$456.35	
American Express		$456.25	$1,080.75	
Cash	$89.60	$236.10	$890.00	

Batch and tally each department (charges and payments).

2. BALANCE ALL DEPARTMENTS

This procedure is not unlike balancing a reception or cashier shift. The main difference is that you are balancing the totals of *all* shifts' entries, for *all* departments. The main objective of the night audit balancing procedure, therefore, is to verify that the balancing procedures were correctly performed by the previous shifts that day.

▷ Print a copy of all the charges posted that day according to department, for example, telephones, laundry, restaurant food, restaurant beverages etc. This printout provides you not only with the balance of all charges to the specified department, but lists the charges individually also (an example is shown in Figure 8.3).

▷ Print a copy of the banking report. This report lists all the payments received that day according to type (cash, Visa, American Express etc) and each cashier's banking figures. You need to verify that the contents of each cashier's banking envelope and the totals are correct to arrive at a total banking figure for the venue (an example is shown in Figure 8.4).

▷ Compare the departmental (posting codes) totals with the batched tallies you completed at step 1.
▷ Compare the banking report totals with the batched tallies you completed at step 1.

Figure 8.3 ▷ **Example of a department computer printout**

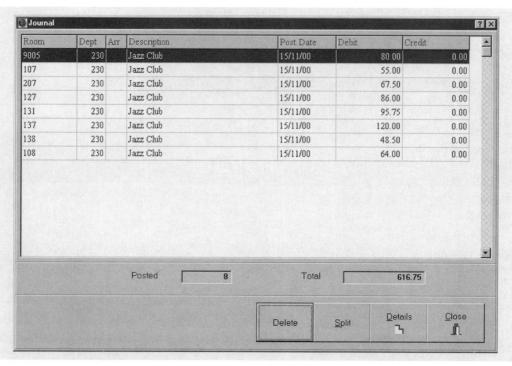

Figure 8.4 ▷ **Night auditor's banking report**

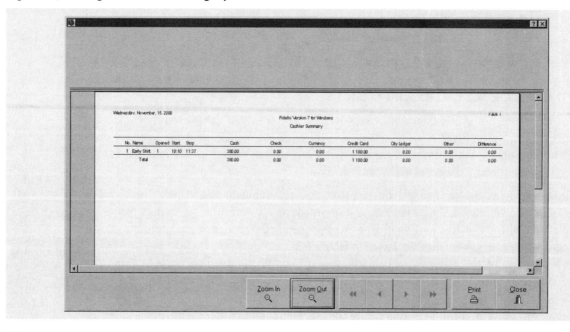

If computer totals and manual totals balance, then most of the time you will move directly on to the next step in the night audit process. If the manual tallies and the computer tallies do not match, then you will need to track the variance and correct it before moving on to the next step.

To track errors:

▷ check that each cashier's banking sheet has been correctly totalled. If this is correct:
▷ recalculate your batch total for the department (charge or payment) that does not balance. If you arrive at the same tally:
▷ work out the difference between the two totals and look for a source document with the same amount
▷ check that all dockets are accounted for. If they are then:
▷ compare the source documents with the department printout.

For example, the manual tally for restaurant food charges is $2,908.50. The computer departmental tally for restaurant food is $2,996.75. Recheck the cashier's banking sheet. If this is correct, recalculate your manual total. If this is still $2,908.50, then calculate the difference between this total and the computer total (which is $88.25). Look for a source document that matches this amount. If you still have not found where the error lies, check each source document against the computer printout of charges posted under the restaurant food code.

When you find the error, correct it by deleting the whole amount of the incorrect posting and re-posting the correct charge. Don't adjust by just posting the difference.

You will need to repeat this for each department that is not in balance. Most errors are found after recalculating your batch tallies. Often, if one department does not balance, there is a corresponding error amount in another department. This often points to where the error lies. For example, if the restaurant food tally is out of balance for $88.25 and the restaurant beverage tally is out of balance for $88.25, then it is likely that one only charge has been incorrectly posted—food posted as beverage or beverage posted as food. You will need to correct this on the respective guests' account.

However, a balance does not necessarily mean that in fact all charges and payments were processed correctly. For example, if a charge was incorrectly posted to a guest's room but the amount and department was correct, then you will still balance. What will be incorrect is the recording of a charge to a guest room that should not be there and the failure to record a charge to another guest room that should be there. In reality, it is not likely that this error will be picked up until the guest with the incorrect charge recorded to their account points it out at the time of departure. The guest who should have received the charge may or may not let the cashier know at the time of their departure that there is a charge missing.

Of course, it is the night auditor's responsibility to verify that *every* transaction is correct, but, because of time constraints, this would be almost impossible. So if the batched tallies match the computer printouts, then it is assumed that the transactions balance. It may, however, be a venue policy that the night auditor randomly checks a number of postings nightly even if the transactions balance.

What you have done so far

▷ removed all shift balances from the safe to check that they have been deposited
▷ verified that all balances balance
▷ batched departmental charges
▷ batched and processed credit and charge card payments

▷ counted the cash and completed a cashier's banking envelope
▷ printed a copy of each department's balance
▷ printed a copy of each payment method balance
▷ compared the manual batched tallies with the computer printout
▷ verified all departments' (charges and payments) balances, or identified errors and corrected them.

APPLY YOUR KNOWLEDGE

When you batched and tallied each department for which there were transactions posted, you then printed a copy of the computer totals for each department. The results were as follows:

DEPARTMENT	TOTAL
Telephone	$1459.30
Paid outs	$90.90
Laundry	$402.55
Room service beverages	$2205.95
Room service food	$2135.40
Gift shop	$1267.60
Mini-bar	$474.90
Restaurant food	$4803.85
Restaurant beverages	$1546.65
Visa	$12242.40
MasterCard	$5057.25
American Express	$8964.20
Cash	$6071.00

Compare these totals with the totals you arrived at for Apply your Knowledge at page 259.

1. Do all departments balance?

2. If not, which ones are out of balance? By how much?

3. How might you track where an error lies?

3. VERIFY ROOM RATES

Room rate variance report—this provides a listing of all occupied rooms sorted by room rate code.

The rate to be charged for each room is shown on the individual guest folios in the computer. Before posting accommodation, you must verify that all registered rooms contain the correct rate. To do this, print a **room rate variance report**. This report provides a listing of all occupied rooms sorted by room rate code. Under each rate code there is a list of those room numbers to which the rate applies, guest name, dates of stay and remarks relevant to the rate charged. Figure 8.5 shows an example of a room rate variance report.

If a variance to a room rate exists, you must investigate why. Check the remarks section, which should indicate why a variance exists. If it doesn't, then check the original copy of the reservation (held in the pit), which may indicate why. If you are unable to determine a reason for a variance to a correct room rate, then the rate is changed to reflect the correct rate. If you do change a rate, you will need to note this in the front office diary so that the next shift can follow up the variation.

A comprehensive knowledge of all rates charged by the establishment is necessary, as in some establishments significant rate variations exist to cater to the venue's various market

Figure 8.5 ▷ **Room rate variance report**

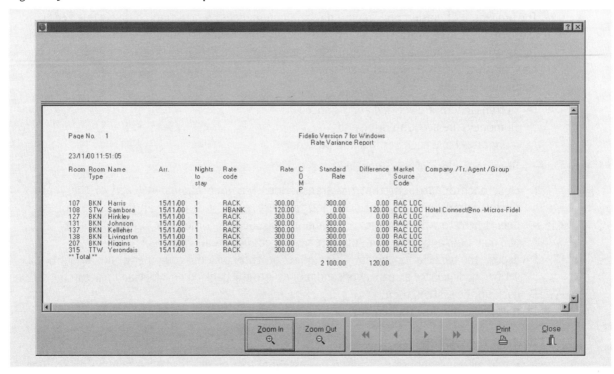

Page No. 1   Fidelio Version 7 for Windows
                                                     Rate Variance Report

23/11/00 11:51:05

Room	Room Type	Name	Arr.	Nights to stay	Rate code	Rate	C O M P	Standard Rate	Difference	Market Source Code	Company /Tr. Agent /Group
107	BKN	Harris	15/11/00	1	RACK	300.00		300.00	0.00	RAC LOC	
108	STW	Sambora	15/11/00	1	HBANK	120.00		0.00	120.00	CCO LOC	Hotel Connect@no -Micros-Fidel
127	BKN	Hinkley	15/11/00	1	RACK	300.00		300.00	0.00	RAC LOC	
131	BKN	Johnson	15/11/00	1	RACK	300.00		300.00	0.00	RAC LOC	
137	BKN	Kelleher	15/11/00	1	RACK	300.00		300.00	0.00	RAC LOC	
138	BKN	Livingston	15/11/00	1	RACK	300.00		300.00	0.00	RAC LOC	
207	BKN	Higgins	15/11/00	1	RACK	300.00		300.00	0.00	RAC LOC	
315	TTW	Yerondais	15/11/00	3	RACK	300.00		300.00	0.00	RAC LOC	
** Total **								2 100.00	120.00		

Zoom In   Zoom Out   ◀◀ ◀ ▶ ▶▶   Print   Close

segments. Varying corporate rates, inbound rates, different travel agent rates, specials and packages must all be known or easily accessed.

4. POST ROOM RATES

Once the room rates are verified (and confirmed as accurate or changed accordingly) the room charge can be posted to each room. Because GST is inclusive in the room rate, a separate rate for the tax does not have to be posted. A computerised PMS allows the posting of room charges to be performed simultaneously. A manual system however, requires you to post the room charge to each guest account individually, as you would all other postings.

Even though the room rate is automatically registered on the guest's account at time of check-in, the room charge will not be recorded on the guest's account until you process room rates in the computer. Room charges are not posted earlier in the day because of:

▷ room changes
▷ room rate changes
▷ unexpected departures.

If a walk in is registered after this stage in audit, then the room rate can be posted manually, similarly to posting any other charge to a guest account. This rate will then be recorded against the next day's revenue.

5. PERFORM CLOSE OF DAY PROCEDURES

As you learned earlier, most accommodation venues reconcile their accounts on a nightly basis. After balancing all charges and payments and posting the room rate charge, the trading day is 'closed' and a new trading day commenced (this is also referred to as rollover).

Close accounts

The procedure of closing one trading day and commencing a new trading day is referred to as 'close of day'. **Close of day** procedures are usually commenced around 2.00 am; because this is frequently the quietest time, when few transactions are likely to take place and when you have finished the other duties necessary before this step. So close of day procedures can only commence once:

▷ all transactions are verified and balanced
▷ all moneys are accounted for, and
▷ room rates have been verified and posted.

To perform close of day procedures:

▷ close each department that has transactions recorded against it (each of the venue's outlets, management accounts, ledgers, etc). This will print another copy of each department to which charges or payments have been recorded (for example, laundry, mini-bar, paid outs and restaurant, management accounts, credit cards etc)
▷ deposit the banking for the day. This requires an entry into the computer of the amounts you verified earlier. Place all paperwork and money into the banking envelope and place in the safe
▷ back up the system, then
▷ rollover to the new trading day.

Back up the system

Now that all transactions are finalised it is essential that all records be backed up. This requires you to save all the information recorded in the computer to disk(s). The disks are then secured in the safe or a cupboard under lock and key.

The back up is an important and crucial step in the night audit process. If for some reason the computer breaks down ('crashes'), all transactions and records can be retrieved from the disk version. Once the system is running again, all information from this disk can be restored and the venue can post information from this point.

The back up step is completed systematically; each day of the week has its own disk and then once a week, a weekly back up is also completed. A weekly back up is necessary because if the computer breaks down on a Saturday, for example, and the information cannot be restored from Friday's disk then the Thursday disk is used and so forth until the information can be retrieved.

Rollover to new day

The PMS in an accommodation venue doesn't just rollover to a new day at midnight each night. Although it keeps track of the time, the system cannot acknowledge a new accounting day until you complete each step in the audit process and then 'run' the night audit function in the PMS. The system goes through a list of items it needs to prepare and then it can roll onto another day. Figure 8.6 lists the steps involved (processed in the computer) before changing day. This step can be as easy as hitting the start button on the PMS and just watching that the correct information is generated and that no errors come up on screen.

What you have done so far

Before looking at the final step in the night audit process, this is what you have completed since step 2 (the balance):

Figure 8.6 ▷ **Night audit screen**

▷ printed a copy of the room rate variance report
▷ verified room rates are correct or changed them accordingly
▷ posted room charges
▷ closed each department with a balance recorded against it
▷ deposited your banking and paperwork
▷ backed up the system
▷ rolled over to a new day.

6. GENERATE AND DISTRIBUTE AUDIT REPORTS

As a consequence of the auditing process, reports relating to the venue's activities are generated nightly. The reports relate to both financial and non-financial activities and are used by management for operational control and decision-making. The types of reports generated by the night audit process, and their uses are discussed later in the chapter.

Once these reports are printed, you are able to log back into the system and process any transactions that you dealt with during the audit. These transactions will become part of the next night's audit.

Procedures to ensure accuracy and security of financial systems

Not surprisingly, the amount of revenue that passes through an accommodation venue on a daily basis is substantial. Also not surprisingly, venues establish procedures for managing financial system accuracy and security to help reduce the likelihood of theft or loss. And while not every system discussed below may be in place, each is useful for maintaining the integrity of financial transactions.

It is often the case that a venue will not establish financial control procedures until after an incident such as theft. And although the venue may be able to identify how the incident occurred and even who was involved, it is only then that implementing procedures that ensures that it cannot happen again are considered.

If all staff follow the procedures in place for maintaining the financial system's accuracy and security, then it is unlikely that losses will occur. If they do occur, they are readily detected and action can be taken.

CASH SECURITY

All cash received by the establishment that day, whether received directly by front office from guests, or from outlets in the venue, is forwarded to and checked by the night auditors. Each outlet's balance is transferred immediately after the shift closes (for example, immediately after lunch or dinner). Takings are not held in the various outlets until the end of the day. All floats are also retained and secured at the front office. However, one float only for each outlet, may be issued for a day's trading, or need to be accounted for, for each shift. In this way, all cash is secured in a central location.

Another important feature of cash security is the counting of cash out of the guests' or public's view. Cash counting and balancing procedures are best undertaken in a secure environment, such as a locked room.

DOCKET CONTROL

Many venues maintain a docket numbering system to ensure that all dockets are accounted for, even those that are subsequently cancelled. In those venues where this occurs, it is not uncommon to find that the night auditor is responsible for accurately recording the numerical sequence of the dockets issued to each department each day. That department then becomes responsible for the dockets issued to them on a daily basis.

Each docket must be used to record charges incurred by guests. Spare dockets are returned to the night auditor at the end of the trading day along with any cancelled dockets.

Each of the venue's outlets completes a control sheet, issued with the actual dockets, on which all docket numbers are listed. As a docket is used, the cashier in that outlet records the transaction details on the control sheet, similarly to the information contained on any other source document.

While docket control procedures seem tedious, it does help reduce the opportunity for theft or fraud on behalf of establishment employees.

DEBTOR CONTROL

A debtor is any business or individual who owes the venue money for services rendered; in other words, any company or individual to whom credit has been extended. This means that the company or individual can charge services and goods to their account and pay at a later stage.

Debtor—any business or individual who owes the venue money for services rendered.

City ledger debtors

Most debtors are companies or travel agents who have made prior arrangements for their employees or clients, who use the venue's facilities and services, to charge all or part of their account to the company for payment. Other accounts in the city ledger are skipper accounts or individuals who paid their account on departure but have incurred late charges. These accounts are held in the city ledger until they are transferred to the accounts receivable.

To allow guests to charge expenses to the company's account, the venue must first take steps to ensure that the company is able to pay its account. A venue does this by establishing a credit limit (maximum amount a company can charge to its account at a venue) and seeking security from the company or individual in the form of a guarantee.

Credit limit—the maximum amount that a company can charge to its account at a venue.

Security for credit

The accounts department needs the following information from companies before a credit facility can be established:

▷ reference from the company's bank
▷ references from other entities with whom they trade (companies already extending credit)
▷ company director's authority—company directors must sign the credit application form stating that if the company becomes insolvent the directors will be personally liable for any charges not paid.

This information is then passed on to a credit agency that specialises in this type of work. When approved, it is set up in the establishment's debtors section and given an account code. The company will then be added to the establishment's list of approved companies, which is distributed to the reservations department.

In-house guest debtors

Most guests who stay in the venue and secure their booking with a charge or credit card, or company charge back (where the company has arranged a credit facility) are also debtors until account settlement (usually on departure for credit and charge cards but at a later date for those accounts transferred to the city ledger). Until departure, these accounts are held in the in-house guest ledger. On departure, payment is settled with the guest's credit card or, for company accounts, the account transferred to the city ledger.

CREDIT LIMITS

A **credit limit** is the maximum amount which a guest's account can total before some form of payment is required. Venues tend to monitor the credit limits extended to guests closely and it is usually the night auditor's responsibility for monitoring credit limits. There are two types of credit limits—those set by the venue called a **house limit** and those set by the credit or charge company called a **floor limit**.

Floor limit— the maximum amount a guest may charge to a credit card before the venue must seek authorisation from the respective card company.

A house limit, set by the venue, is the amount a guest or company can charge to their account before some form of payment must be made. For example, the house limit may be $1000.00. Once an account reaches this amount, the guest is asked to pay all or some of the account. The house limit may be the same as a credit card floor limit or it may be a different amount set by the venue. If it is more, the venue is responsible for ensuring that credit card transactions are authorised when they reach the floor limit.

House limit— the maximum amount a guest can charge to their account before the venue seeks payment. The house limit is set by the venue.

Credit card companies set limits on how much a venue can allow a guest to charge to their credit card before authorisation by the credit card company must be sought. This is referred to as a floor limit. For example, Visa may allow the Hilltop Hotel a floor limit of $500.00. This means that when a guest's account reaches this amount the venue must obtain authorisation for the transaction from Visa before the guest can make further charges to that credit card. If the venue fails to obtain the authorisation, Visa can decline to pay the hotel what is due.

Credit limits between companies

A different credit limit may be extended to different companies. Often, the extent of credit is determined by the extent of business a company is likely to transact with the venue. The payment history of a company will also affect the amount of credit it is extended. For example, companies that have established a proven track record for timely payment are likely to receive a higher credit limit than those that are known to be delinquent in payment of their accounts.

A **credit check report** is produced each night. This report lists all the accounts whose totals are near to or in excess of their limit. Those guests or companies whose credit limit is reached or who are in excess are asked to make a payment (all or some of the outstanding balance) on their account, thereby ensuring credit is maintained and the establishment does not expose itself to losses.

If guests cannot be contacted in person, a letter is forwarded to their room, or for city ledger accounts, to the business, requesting that they pay their account. In extreme cases guests may have their door 'double locked'. This means that the guest has to contact the duty manager and make a payment on their account, before being let back into their room or receiving any further credit.

City ledger account holders are not usually permitted to make further charges on their accounts until they make a payment to reduce its balance.

City ledger to accounts receivable

The city ledger is closed off daily (during the close of day procedures) and outstanding accounts are transferred to accounts receivable. Accounts receivable refers to all moneys owed to the venue by entities other than in-house guests. Maintenance of accounts receivable is the responsibility of the financial controller.

CREDIT CONTROL AFTER DEPARTURE

At the end of each month a statement for company accounts (city ledgers) is sent to each company with an outstanding account balance. Credit terms (that is, when companies are expected to settle) are usually seven, 14 or 30 days. The statement will list all charges incurred during the past 30 days, any payments received, and any outstanding balance from previous accounting periods.

If a company has not forwarded payment to the establishment within the required time, the venue is likely to:

▷ telephone the company as a reminder
▷ after 45 days write officially to the company requesting immediate payment
▷ after 60 days, send a strongly worded letter, possibly threatening legal action, then:
▷ if still no payment is received after 90 days, most venues will proceed with legal action.

While night audit is often responsible for identifying and reporting to management those accounts that have reached or exceeded their credit limit, it is not usually their responsibility for the follow up of unpaid accounts. This is normally the responsibility of the accounts department.

Late charges

Venues set limits for which they will not seek payment for non-declared or late charges (charges to be posted after the guest has departed) for certain services, such as the mini-bar. For example, if a guest departs and the venue then learns that an outstanding mini-bar charge is owed, if it is less than $10.00 for a local guest or $50.00 for an overseas guest, then the venue will not seek restitution. Instead, the venue will 'write off' the lost revenue. This is usually cheaper than trying to retrieve payment. Also, the effect of sending an incorrect account to a guest may not be worth the money the establishment may receive. The venue needs to be certain that the most recent guest was the one who in fact consumed the 'missing' or undeclared items from the mini-bar, and this at times is difficult to prove.

DOCUMENTATION

All transactions of the day must be supported by written documentation. This documentation includes vouchers, receipts, guest folios, dockets, adjustment or correction slips, printed reports, registration cards, control sheets and auditing documents and any other source documents.

It is a legal requirement that all source documents are kept by the venue for a minimum of five years. They are stored so that they are easy to access and retrieve. Source documents are usually kept in a bag (referred to as a 'day bag') or box identified by date, and stored in the back office on a monthly basis. Cashiers and accounts staff may have to refer to these documents to answer guest queries. Each month's documents are later placed in long-term storage.

SKILLS FOCUS

Most venues put in place procedures to help minimise their losses. If all procedures are followed, then the result should be minimal loss. All cash received by the venue is deposited at the front office at the end of each shift. The night auditor verifies the cash takings as part of the balancing procedures. All floats are also deposited at the front office. They are signed out and in by each department as they are required.

Docket control is a system of numbering all dockets used in the venue for verifying financial transactions. All dockets issued to departments must be returned to the front office as part of the department's balancing procedures, whether used or not, or cancelled. Transactions are recorded on a control sheet that corresponds with the numerical sequence of the dockets issued that day.

Debtor control involves minimising the likelihood of loss that may result from non-payment by in-house guests and city ledger account holders. A debtor is any company or individual who owes the venue money for services rendered.

Before credit is extended, companies that apply for city ledger accounts are reference checked. In-house guests use their credit card as a form of security.

Credit limits are set by the venue (house limit) and credit and charge card companies (floor limits). The house limit may vary for different guests, depending on the extent of the business they transact with the venue and their payment record.

A credit check report is produced each night to keep track of those accounts that are near to or in excess of their limits. Individuals and companies are asked to settle all or part of the account before further credit is extended.

All transactions in the venue must be supported by written documentation. This is usually in the form of source documents. Source documents are then held by the venue for a minimum of five years.

Producing and distributing accurate reports

Earlier you learned that as part of the audit process a number of reports are generated. These reports help management and staff to do their job. Some of the reports you have already encountered. Others are specific to the night audit role. Table 8.2 lists the types of reports most commonly generated by the night audit process, the information contained in each and what the information is likely to be used for.

There are other reports that are produced during the night audit, but their relevance to front office operations is minimal. For example, food and beverage outlets' reports include average spend per customer and number of covers per dining session—useful information for food and beverage management. Other night audit reports, such as expected arrivals and departures, are discussed in Chapter 5.

END OF MONTH REPORTS

Several other reports are generated at the end of the month and others at the end of the year or other accounting period. They are designed to analyse the performance of the venue. The sort of information these reports generate includes a monthly analysis of where the venue's guests originated, what rates they paid, how much was spent in outlets (and what for) and a comparison of performance against budget. This information is also used to set the new budgets, review rates, renegotiate corporate agreements and for comparison of the venue's performance against its competitors.

Reports generated at the end of the month and end of year include:

▷ revenue reports
▷ competitor analysis
▷ productivity reports
▷ rate code reports
▷ occupancy and average rate reports.

Table 8.2 ▷ **Night audit reports**

REPORT NAME	INFORMATION CONTAINED IN REPORT	USE
Departmental revenue: ▷ rooms ▷ restaurant ▷ bar ▷ laundry ▷ gym/pool ▷ room service ▷ valet	A report is generated for each department or outlet to show the amount of revenue earned for that day. Can also be generated weekly, monthly, quarterly or for other periods. It is important to allocate revenues according to the department that earned the revenue.	▷ To determine how well the department is performing (meeting its budgeted and forecast revenue) ▷ To help plan promotional activities
In-house guest ledger	Shows the balance of moneys owed to the venue by in-house guests.	Used by the accounts department for a daily reconciliation.
Occupancy level	Number of occupied rooms that night. Calculated by dividing the number of rooms occupied by the total number of rooms available in the venue.	Used to determine how well the venue is meeting forecasts.
Average room rate	Calculated by dividing the total rooms' revenue for the night by the number of rooms occupied.	This is compared to budget figures and to the average rate of competitors.
Room status	Shows the status of all rooms.	
Credit check	Shows all in-house guest and city ledger balances that are near to or have exceeded their credit limit.	Action taken according to venue policy on controlling credit extended. It is used in preparation of express check-outs, and to determine: ▷ if paying by credit card, whether additional pre-authorisations are required ▷ if paying by cash, whether the guest is required to make a payment to the hotel, or ▷ if the guest's account is being settled by a company or travel agent (that is, a city ledger account), whether or not the company should be sent an interim bill.
Source of business breakdown	Tracks where in-house guest bookings originated.	Used by the sales department.
Market segment analysis	Tracks the market segment of each in-house guest.	Reviewed by the sales department.
Forecasted occupancy	Forecasted occupancy for the next day, week or other period.	Used to determine number of rooms booked and the number available to sell.
Complimentary rooms	A listing of all FOC rooms and the names of the guests.	The general manager and other management review FOCs to ensure that not too many FOCs are given away. FOCs affect the average room rate.
Guest in-house with balance	An alphabetical listing of all guests in house and their account balance.	This can be used by reception if a guest wants to check-out and the computer is down.

DISTRIBUTION OF REPORTS

For most of the reports listed in Table 8.2, we provided a guide as to who may use which reports and why. Reports are only useful if they are distributed in a timely manner and read! Department heads and some front-line supervisors (and staff) use the reports on a daily basis to help them perform their jobs. The night auditor must distribute the appropriate reports to the right person consistently and on time. All reports are filed for future reference.

Examples of who gets which reports is shown in Table 8.3.

The general manager requires, on a daily basis, reports which indicate the level of activity within the hotel, such as the manager's report, forecast report and the complimentary rooms report.

Food and beverage outlets require in-house guest lists to allow verification of guest room numbers when charging services to the guest's room.

Sales and marketing require productivity reports to assess the success of their advertising or other marketing activities, and VIP reports to determine whether a personal welcome is required.

Housekeeping needs reports such as forecasted occupancy and room status to plan their daily activities.

Table 8.3 ▷ **Report distribution**

STAFF MEMBER	REPORT
General manager	▷ occupancy levels
	▷ total revenue
	▷ occupancy forecasts
	▷ manager's report
	▷ credit control report
	▷ average room rate
	▷ departmental revenues
	▷ forecast report
	▷ complimentary rooms report
Department heads	▷ expected arrivals and departures
	▷ departmental revenues
	▷ occupancy forecasts
	▷ room status report
	▷ manager's report
Supervisors	▷ expected arrivals and departures
	▷ in-house guest lists
Sales and marketing	▷ occupancy levels
	▷ occupancy forecasts
	▷ VIP reports
	▷ source of business
	▷ market segment breakdown
Front-line staff	▷ expected arrivals and departures
	▷ in-house guest lists

APPLY YOUR KNOWLEDGE

Although it is likely a venue's PMS will calculate occupancy figures and average spends, it is always useful to know how to calculate these manually. From the information given in the chart, calculate:

▷ *the average spend per cover per day*
▷ *occupancy levels per night*
▷ *average room rate per night.*

Front office statistics

DAY	ROOMS AVAILABLE	OCCUPANCY	OCCUPANCY AS A %	TOTAL ROOMS REVENUE	AVERAGE ROOM RATE
Wednesday	500	430		$91,160	
Thursday	500	289		$54,621	
Friday	500	378		$84,672	
Saturday	500	498		$99,102	
Sunday	500	404		$79,184	

1. What is the highest occupancy percentage?
2. Which day had the highest average room rate?

SKILLS FOCUS

The generation of reports is an important part of the night audit process. Reports help the venue to identify the activities that take place on a daily basis. Reports also help in the planning and decision-making processes necessary for a successful operation. For example, departmental reports let the venue know on a daily basis how much revenue each department received.

Several other reports also help the venue determine how well it is performing, including average room rate, occupancy level, in-house guest ledger, source of business breakdown, expected arrivals, variances to budgets, group business reports and daily banking summary.

Reports are only useful if they are distributed in a timely manner to those who most need the information.

FOCUS REVIEW

▷ *What value is there in a departmental report?*
▷ *How might this information be used?*
▷ *Why might the average room rate be useful? How is it calculated?*
▷ *What use is a source of business breakdown report?*
▷ *Why must reports be distributed in a timely manner?*

PUT YOUR KNOWLEDGE TO THE TEST

Robyn had spent a couple of weeks on the night audit shift learning all the different tasks to be completed at night. She quite enjoyed the quiet of the night and enjoyed seeing where all her reception work ended up. Robyn also learnt why it was so important to balance properly during the day shift and not leave it for the night auditor to sort out—it's not fun cleaning up everyone else's balances. It also slows down the night-time procedures. Damien, the night manager, felt Robyn was making good progress and asked her to complete a few tasks.

1. Damien asked Robyn to calculate the average room rate for the Grand Central Hotel. Using the figures below, calculate the average rate with and without breakfast. Which figure do you think is more useful when comparing average room rate against your competitors' average room rate? Why?

ROOM NUMBERS	NO OF GUESTS	RATE	BREAKFAST INC ($10.00 per person)
1201	2	$135.00	Yes
1202	1	$125.00	Yes
1203	2	$150.00	No
1204	1	$150.00	No
1205	2	$110.00	Yes
1206	1	$150.00	No
2201	3	$175.00	Yes
2202	2	$150.00	No
2203	1	$150.00	No
2204	1	$150.00	No
2205	2	$180.00	Yes
2206	1	$150.00	No
2207	1	$145.00	Yes
2208	1	$145.00	Yes
2209	2	$195.00	Yes

ADVANCE BOOKING CHART—Grand Central Hotel

MONTH OF JUNE 2001

ROOM NUMBER	ROOM TYPE	DATE 11	12	13	14	15	16	17
1201	DOUBLE	Booked	Booked	Booked	Booked		Booked	Booked
1202	DOUBLE			Booked	Booked	Booked	Booked	Booked
1203	DOUBLE		Booked	Booked			Booked	Booked
1204	DOUBLE	Booked	Booked	Booked	Booked	Booked		Booked
1205	TWIN	Booked	Booked			Booked	Booked	
1206	TWIN	Booked	Booked	Booked	Booked	Booked		Booked
2201	FAMILY	Booked					Booked	Booked
2202	DELUXE		Booked	Booked		Booked	Booked	Booked
2203	SUITE	Booked						Booked
2204	DOUBLE		Booked	Booked	Booked			
2205	DOUBLE	Booked						Booked
2206	DOUBLE		Booked					Booked
2207	DOUBLE							
2208	TWIN	Booked	Booked	Booked	Booked			
2209	TWIN		Booked	Booked	Booked	Booked	Booked	Booked

2. Using the advance booking charts for the Grand Central, calculate the occupancy for the next seven days. The occupancy budget for the next week is projected to be 85 per cent. How many rooms per day (if any) do the staff at Grand Central need to sell to make budget?

3. While Robyn was calculating occupancy, Mr G. W. Bush from the USA called looking for a double room for 13, 14 and 15 June and again on 17 June. Is there a room available at the Grand Central Hotel? If there is, how does this affect the occupancy level for next week?

4. While the night audit was in progress, Jenny Thomson, a no-show from the night before arrived. Because Robyn can't access the computer, what reports does she need to determine if Ms Thomson can be accommodated? How is the check-in procedure different during this time? What should Robyn do about payment for the room? What must Robyn remember to do when the night audit process is completed?

5. While Robyn was batching the daily credit card totals she noticed that Visa was $365.25 over compared with the fast track machine and that American Express was $365.25 under. How should Robyn fix this? As the problem occurred on the A shift, should Robyn be fixing the problem? If not, what procedure do you think could be put in place to prevent this from reaching night audit?

6. When Damien returned from the security patrol he asked Robyn to back up the system and rollover to a new day. How would Robyn go about doing this?

Providing Porter Services

LEARNING OUTCOMES

On completion of this chapter you will be able to:

▷ accurately describe the role and responsibilities of the porter;

▷ demonstrate the correct procedure for handling guest arrivals;

▷ correctly manage the collection, storage and transportation of guests' luggage;

▷ correctly manage a range of guest services;

▷ describe the porter's role for security.

Introduction

In Chapter 6, we said that the first face-to-face contact many guests have with an accommodation venue is often with reception staff. This is particularly true in smaller accommodation venues where the organisational structure does not clearly distinguish all front office roles. In many smaller venues, it is not uncommon to find that reception staff also provide porter services and must therefore be able to perform duties in both roles. In larger establishments, where roles are more clearly defined, it is more common to find reception staff and porters or rather, a concierge department.

For many people wanting to build a career in accommodation services, their first opportunity will be as a porter. It is a front-line position and for the guest, the porter represents the link between establishment and non-establishment facilities, services, activities, attractions and events.

The role and responsibilities of the porter

The concierge department is responsible for providing the porter services, and may answer directly to the front office manager or operate independently (while remaining integral to front office operations). Whatever the structure, the concierge department fulfils a very important guest services role.

Porters:
- greet guests on arrival
- manage guests' luggage
- provide general information services.

Porters are the people who greet guests as they arrive at the venue, manage guests' luggage and provide general information services to guests as part of their role in the concierge department. Not unlike reception, in large venues porters may be rostered 24-hours a day, every day of the year. In smaller venues, reception staff are likely to undertake portering duties during the night shift.

The porter's role is to provide a range of services to guests that may not be available through other departments. It is a non-revenue generating department, however, on a porter's recommendation, a guest may use facilities and services offered by the venue and these do earn revenue.

In simple terms, **concierge** means 'door keeper'. But as you will learn in this chapter, to receive the title of concierge requires considerable skill, knowledge and experience; not just the ability to mind the door, carry luggage, provide information and park cars.

Where the department operates independently, the concierge is likely to hire, fire and roster their own staff. The concierge is head of the department; under the concierge is the head porter or captain, and under this person are the porters, valets (car park attendants) and bellhops.

WHAT THE PORTER DOES FOR THE GUEST

Later in this chapter we will look at the porter's role as it relates to the guest cycle of service. However, in general terms a porter:

▷ greets guests on arrival
▷ parks and picks up the guest's car
▷ manages guests' luggage
▷ makes recommendations and provides information about:
  — the establishment

- local area attractions
- things to do and see
▷ arranges transport (car hire, coach parking)
▷ books and picks up tickets for tours, sporting events and the theatre
▷ passes on messages and mail
▷ confirms forward accommodation bookings
▷ confirms flight arrangements
▷ attends to guests' personal needs (personal shopping)
▷ coordinates group arrivals and departures
▷ acts as the central point of contact for groups.

The status of porter is often not highly regarded, yet the porter's role is invaluable. Guests are frequently on a first name basis with the porter, and come to depend on him or her for information and services that most other staff in the venue aren't able to provide. In fact, guests frequently cite the skill of the porter as the reason for their return. This makes the porter a relatively influential individual!

DESIRABLE QUALITIES OF A PORTER

The porter maintains constant contact with guests and must therefore possess certain qualities that are representative of the individual and the venue. The porter must:

▷ have a high regard for personal grooming and hygiene
▷ be attentive and courteous
▷ be organised
▷ be discreet, tactful and sympathetic
▷ be resourceful (know where to get things that others probably can't get)
▷ have a high level of product knowledge
▷ have excellent interpersonal skills (good social and communication skills)
▷ have highly developed selling skills
▷ understand the various needs of the venue's target markets.

BECOMING A CONCIERGE

To officially receive the title of concierge and receive the honour of membership into the world-renowned *Les Clefs D'Or* ('The Golden Keys'), a porter must be able to demonstrate all the qualities listed above and also possess a sound background in the hospitality industry (usually a minimum of five years' experience in the concierge department and two years in charge).

Les Clefs D'Or

Les Clefs D'Or originated in France in 1952 when a small group formed the association for porters with an emphasis on quality and 'service through friendship'. Members are recognised by the cross of golden keys worn on the lapel of their uniform. The aims of the association include:

▷ wider recognition of the concierge
▷ image and professionalism
▷ integrity and leadership
▷ continuous concierge service
▷ pride and respect in the position
▷ training of future concierges.

Handling guest arrivals and departures

The porter's place of work is located next to or is part of the reception desk. Alternatively, it may be located next to the front door of the venue. Whatever its position, it is situated for ease of access and the guest's convenience. The porter's desk (also referred to as the concierge desk or bell desk) is usually constantly manned, but this does not mean that the porters are confined to the foyer area. Because of the nature of their work, the porter is constantly on the move.

GUEST PRE-ARRIVAL

Not surprisingly, the porter's role can be defined in terms of the cycle of service (see Chapter 1).

When the shift commences, the porter will check the front office diary and the porter's diary. Similar to reception, the porter's diary is a communication tool that helps keep everyone in the department up to date with what has happened and is going to happen that day. The porters will receive constant updates in the form of reports from reception about the daily activities in the venue and guest movements. So before guests arrive, porters check and plan for:

▷ expected arrivals and departure
  — number of guests expected and departing
  — groups arriving and departing
  — early and late arrivals and departures
  — VIPs

▷ special requests for arrivals
▷ delivery of special requests
▷ tickets to be booked and collected
▷ parking arrangements to be made
▷ luggage arrangements
▷ tourist information booklet displays arrangement
▷ the cleanliness of the foyer area.

GUEST ARRIVAL

The guest may arrive in a number of ways:

▷ by private car
▷ taxi or hire car
▷ coach (groups)
▷ on foot.

However guests arrive, they must be welcomed promptly and service offered immediately. For example, a guest arriving by car (private or taxi) will have the door opened for them and their luggage collected from the car. In the case of the elderly or disabled, the guest may be assisted out of the car. The guest is then directed to the reception desk (the front door to the establishment held open for the guest) to register, and their luggage 'tagged' (for identification) if it is not automatically transferred to the guest's room.

If the guest has arrived by private car, the porter will then arrange for the car to be parked, the car keys secured and the charge for parking (if there is one) added to the guest's account. If the guest arrived by taxi, the porter may even arrange payment for the taxi on behalf of the guest. This is an example of a paid out. The taxi fare is added to the guest's account. The porter may then direct the taxi to the venue's taxi rank (if there is one) ensuring both a constant flow of traffic and nothing to block the next arrival.

When groups arrive, the porter must ensure that the coach is able to park easily, and that there is sufficient space in the foyer for the guests and their luggage. The porter is likely to guide the coach to the correct disembarkation point and give directions to the group about the check-in process.

Even if a bulk check-in takes place on the bus for a group, there needs to be sufficient staff on hand to manage the group's luggage, which may be transported to each of the guest's rooms after check-in.

Rooming the guest

Once the guest is registered, the porter in many venues is called upon to escort the guest to their room. This gives the porter an opportunity to:

▷ build rapport with the guest
▷ answer any questions the guest may have
▷ highlight facilities and services available in the venue
▷ discuss upcoming events in the town
▷ point out room features
▷ advise the guest of the venue's emergency evacuation procedure.

Remember that every interaction with the guest is a moment of truth, and the porter is responsible for ensuring that the guest's moment of truth at arrival is positive.

OCCUPANCY

The occupancy stage of the cycle of service provides porters with the opportunity to demonstrate their skill and knowledge. The services provided by the porter will vary between establishments and will be influenced by the market segment the venue caters for. There are several things a good porter will always know and be able to provide information about, such as:

▷ emergency procedures (for the venue)
▷ all facilities and services available in the venue
▷ places of worship and service times (for various religions)
▷ business trading hours (such as banks, post offices, retail outlets)
▷ major tourist attractions such as the zoo, parks and gardens, beaches, museums, art galleries, geographical landmarks, as well as how to get there, cost, opening hours, etc
▷ location of theatres and cinemas (what's on will vary but its useful to keep up to date— keep a schedule on hand)
▷ local event information, particularly sports (a good porter will either have tickets or be able to get them quickly)
▷ good restaurants (variety of cuisines and suitability to dietary requirements, budgets and special occasions)
▷ transportation details (public, hire car and limousine, timetables)
▷ shopping facilities and their locations
▷ baby sitting services
▷ local recreation facilities (gym, sports clubs, sauna, massage).

And if that isn't enough, more specific requests may include:

▷ personal shopping (flowers, toiletries, gifts, clothing)
▷ shoe shine
▷ laundry
▷ forward mail
▷ running errands.

Keeping track of information

The porter's directory may contain:
• attractions
• costs
• transport information
• directions
• contacts.

It is not hard to realise that a porter needs to know a lot of information. While much of it may be kept in the porter's head, this isn't very useful for new staff, nor is it reliable. Most porter's desks maintain a **directory**. And if there isn't one, it is a good idea to start one. Usually maintained alphabetically, the directory gives the porter the information needed quickly and efficiently. It isn't always convenient to ask a colleague the answer to a question or to rely on memory.

The directory contains information relating to all of the above (places, costs, directions, service providers) and a list of contacts and telephone numbers for those harder to get items. An example of a directory and the sort of information you might want to put in yours, is shown in Figure 9.1.

Responding to requests from guests

Guest requests to the porter can come at any time and may or may not be the porter's responsibility. But this does not mean the porter doesn't *take* responsibility for ensuring the request is met. For example, a guest requesting their room be serviced is the responsibility of housekeeping. However, if it is the porter the guest asked to clean the room, it is the porter's

Figure 9.1 ▷ **Example of a porter's directory**

P

- **Parliament House**—Spring St, Melb. Tue 2–11 pm, Wed 10 am–11 pm & Thur 10 am–5.30 pm. Tel: 9651 8568
- **Phillip Island**
- Seal Rocks Sea Life Centre—Tel: 61 3 9793 6767
- Phillip Island Nature Park—Tel: 61 3 5956 8300
- Fairy penguin parade, Phillip Island. AATKings offer half-day trips departing daily, from 123 Swanston Street, at 3.00 pm, returning at 10.30 pm. Cost $65 per person.
- **Planet Hollywood**—Crown Entertainment Complex, Southbank. Open 7 days a week from 11.30 am.
- **Public Holidays**—New Year's Day—Jan 1, Australia Day—Jan 26, Labour Day—1st or 2nd Mon in March, Easter—Good Fri through to Monday, Anzac Day—April 25, Queen's Birthday—2nd Mon in June, Melbourne Cup—1st Tuesday in November, Christmas Day—December 25, Boxing Day—December 26.
- **Police**—Flinders Street, Swanston Street.
- **Polly Woodside**—Lorimer St, East Southbank. Daily 10 am–4 pm. Tel: 9669760.
- **Post Office**—GPO, Corner of Burke St. Mall and Elizabeth St. Open Mon to Fri 8.15 am to 5.30 pm and Sat 10.00 am to 1.00 pm. Also 246 Flinders Lane. Open 8.45 am to 5.00 pm.
- **Princess Theatre**—Spring Street.
- **Puffing Billy**—Open every day of the year except Christmas Day. Tel: 9754 6800.

responsibility for ensuring the request is completed. In this instance housekeeping is contacted and the request is passed on.

For porter related requests, guests expect you to respond in a timely manner. The guest expects the porter to be able to respond appropriately and accurately. The request may be received face-to-face or over the telephone. Requests for porter services are also received through other departments. For example, a guest ready to check-out may call reception and ask for her luggage to be collected and her car brought round to the front of the venue. Reception passes this information on to the porter's desk.

GUEST DEPARTURE

At the time of departure, a guest may request several services from the porter:

▷ luggage collection and/or storage
▷ transport arrangements (private car, taxi)
▷ forward mail
▷ directions.

For groups, the porter again needs to arrange coach parking facilities (ensuring that the arrival and departure of other vehicles is not hindered), guest embarkation and coordination of the guest's luggage. The porter is likely to assist with ensuring that all luggage is stored safely onto the coach, that guests have not left personal items behind and that guests are left with a positive final impression of the venue.

SKILLS FOCUS

The porter's work station is located in the foyer of the venue. This is for ease of access and convenience for the guest. The porter's role can be defined in terms of the cycle of service. During pre-arrival, the porter is preparing the work area for the day, checking expected

arrivals and departures, delivering special requests to rooms and booking and collecting tickets for special events, among others. At arrival time, the porter is responsible for welcoming the guest, collecting their luggage and directing the guest to the registration desk. The porter is also likely to escort guests to their rooms. During occupancy, the porter offers services to guests such as recommendations for places to eat, sights to see and things to do, and may perform a number of personal services. At departure, again the porter is arranging luggage collection, coordinating transport and providing directions for guests.

FOCUS REVIEW

▷ *What is the porter's directory? What purpose does it serve?*
▷ *What does the guest expect of the porter in response to requests?*
▷ *Explain the role of the porter in terms of the cycle of service. Give an example of a service the porter may provide at each stage.*
▷ *What information is the porter likely to give while rooming the guest?*
▷ *What is the porter's role in coordinating groups?*
▷ *If the porter receives a request for a service that is the responsibility of another department, how should this be handled?*
▷ *How might porter services be requested?*

APPLY YOUR KNOWLEDGE

In your town, research and record details on the following:

▷ *four major tourist attractions including opening hours, entry cost and directions to get there*
▷ *opening hours and location of the post office and major banks*
▷ *location and directions to the major shopping complexes*
▷ *local places of worship (as many denominations as are available) and service times.*

To make this a useful tool that you can use and add to, use an alphabetised notebook. The entries can be cross-referenced to assist in remembering specific details. For example, under 'A' for attractions, you may want to list all attractions in your area, such as the zoo, and then enter the details again under their alphabetical heading, in this case 'Z' for the zoo.

Handling guest luggage

One of the most frequently performed tasks a porter undertakes is handling luggage. Guest luggage is collected from their car, delivered to and collected from their room, and often stored.

CORRECT MANUAL HANDLING

The manual handling aspects of dealing with guest luggage represents potential manual handling injuries. Most of these injuries are back related and result from poor lifting, pushing, pulling and stretching. To lift luggage (and other items) safely, there are a few guidelines to follow:

▷ Think about what you are going to lift. Assess the shape of the object to determine whether you can comfortably lift it; if the object is too heavy, get help.
▷ Stand close to the object and slightly part your legs.
▷ Bend your knees and hold the object close to your body.
▷ Raise your head and pull in your chin to keep your back straight.
▷ Use your legs to lift (not your back) and move the load to your waist slowly by straightening your legs.
▷ To put down the load, bend your knees and keep your back straight.

Many venues use a trolley to transport luggage but it is still necessary to lift the luggage onto and off the trolley. When stocking the trolley, place large, heavy items on the bottom and place first those pieces of luggage that are to be delivered last. Most trolleys have a number of 'hooks', which allows the porter to hang garment bags, handbags and other light items with handles.

TAGGING LUGGAGE

It is not always possible to immediately transfer a guest's luggage to their room. And in the case of groups, there is a lot of luggage that needs to be correctly identified and later transferred to the appropriate room. In some cases, luggage may be delivered to a guest's room before the guest arrives there. For these reasons, luggage is often **tagged**. This means an identification label is attached to the handle of every piece of luggage. The bottom portion of the tag is detached and given to the guest. To claim their luggage, the guest presents their portion of the label to a porter. The identification label will contain:

▷ the guest's full name
▷ their room number, when known.

When tagging bags, always write the number of items belonging to that guest on the tag. For example, if the guest has four pieces of luggage, the first tag will have written on it '1 of 4', the second will have written on it '2 of 4' and so on. In this way you are able to ensure that the guest is returned the correct luggage and the correct number of pieces.

The full name is important because it is possible that you are storing luggage for guests with the same surname. If Mr Smith in room 115 asks for his luggage and you have another Mr Smith's luggage stored, the full name helps identify the correct owner. Another reason why writing the guest name and number of pieces on the label is that a different porter may collect the luggage from the one who stored it. And while you may remember Mr Smith and his luggage, your colleague may not. An example of a luggage label is shown in Figure 9.2.

Luggage is then stored according to the floors and delivered as soon as possible.

For groups, 'as soon as possible' may mean guests do not receive their luggage for some time. If the group is going straight out after checking in, then this may be acceptable. However, most individual guests prefer to get their luggage as soon as they have checked into their room. Luggage should be delivered within 15 minutes after arrival when possible.

COLLECTING LUGGAGE

Many guests request their luggage to be collected from their room when they are due to depart. The guest will either call the porter's desk directly or call reception who will advise the

Figure 9.2 ▷ **Luggage label**

178609

GRAND CENTRAL HOTEL
505 The Boulevard, Sydney
HOTELS OF DISTINCTION

Luggage Storage

Guest Name: _____

Room No: _____

Date Received: _____

Pick up date: _____

☐ Coat   ☐ Shopping Bag

☐ Suitcase   ☐ Garment Bag

☐ Briefcase   ☐ Handbag

☐ Umbrella   ☐ Rain Coat

☐ Parcel

☐ Other _____

Accepted by: _____

Luggage Claim

Your luggage can be claimed from the porter's desk.

It is agreed by the holder of this luggage claim check that the hotel shall not be liable for loss or damage to the property being held caused by the negligence of the hotel or its employees, or by water, fire, theft or other cause. If property covered by this check is not claimed within six months the hotel may sell the same without notice by public or private sale.

The hotel is authorised to deliver to any person presenting this check without identification.

178609

porter that luggage needs to be collected. The guest will usually indicate the time for luggage collection and the porter must collect it at the guest's convenience.

TIMELINESS

As already mentioned, luggage should be delivered and collected in a timely manner. Guests do not expect to be kept waiting for their personal belongings and may fret if they do not receive them in a reasonable amount of time. Reasonable for most guests will be within 15 minutes of arrival.

STORING LUGGAGE

Luggage may need to be stored at the time of arrival or departure. At the time of arrival, a guest's room may not be ready. To give the guest the freedom to leave the venue without the inconvenience of holding onto their luggage, the venue will store it for them. Conversely, at the time of departure, the guest may be required to vacate the room by 11.00 am but is not due to leave the town until that evening. Again, the venue will store the guest's luggage for them until required. Luggage is usually stored in a safe and convenient location. Access is restricted to the porters. Stored luggage is tagged and sorted by guest name.

Some venues may allow the guest to retrieve their own luggage from the storage facility; however this compromises the security and safety of other guests' luggage.

Porterage

It is not uncommon to find that in some venues, a small service fee is charged to the guest when storage and/or delivery of luggage are required. This is referred to as **porterage**. While rates may vary, $3.00 per piece of luggage is usual.

SKILLS FOCUS

Handling luggage is one of the most frequently performed tasks undertaken by a porter. When handling luggage, it is important for the porter to practise appropriate manual handling techniques. Luggage is frequently tagged, which means an identifying label is attached to each piece of the guest's luggage. The reason for this is because luggage cannot always be delivered to the room at the same time as the guest and must be identified for delivery later.

Luggage should be delivered and collected in a timely manner. Luggage is often stored for the guest because on arrival, the guest's room may not yet be ready for the guest to occupy, and on departure the guest may not yet be ready to leave the town.

FOCUS REVIEW
▷ *Why is correct manual handling an important consideration of the porter's job?*
▷ *What is 'tagging'? Why is correct tagging important?*
▷ *How should luggage be stored on the porter's trolley?*
▷ *Why might luggage need to be stored for a guest?*
▷ *What is porterage?*

The porter's role in security

The porter plays a significant role in minimising the possibility of a security breach. Porters spend most of their time in the public areas of the venue, (those areas to which the public has access) which means they are in an excellent position to observe the comings and goings of guests and other people. Because any person can access these areas, not just guests, there is considerable potential for security breaches, such as theft and disturbances to occur. A porter needs to be constantly alert to people who seem 'out of place', uncomfortable or suspicious.

THEFT

Hospitality establishments have a legal obligation to protect against the loss of guests' personal belongings. They also need to be vigilant to theft of their own property. During the course of the day, the porter is able to watch the activities that go on and be alert to people who act in a suspicious manner.

People who may thoughtlessly leave their belongings unattended can be warned by the porter about the risk of theft.

SUSPICIOUS BEHAVIOUR

Suspicious person—any person who is behaving in a way that seems unusual.

A **suspicious person** is any person (guest, staff, other) who is behaving in a way that seems unusual. For example, the person seems to be constantly looking around as though checking for something, refusing to make eye contact, acting nervously or fidgeting. Suspicious people are also those people who attempt to or actually do gain access to restricted places, such as staff only areas and restricted guest floors.

Of course it is possible that the person may just be lost or confused but such a person should never be ignored. If you notice someone behaving suspiciously:

▷ note down details about the person (how they look, what they were doing and where they appear to be going)

▷ alert your supervisor or security department

▷ offer assistance to the suspicious person if you feel comfortable doing so

▷ continue to observe them (if they realise they are being watched, this often encourages them to leave if, in fact, their intentions are suspicious).

It is often very difficult to tell the difference between guests and unauthorised visitors. The best thing you can do is to keep an eye open for people acting suspiciously. Look out for people who are aimlessly floating around without any real purpose or acting in a nervous or anxious manner.

DISTURBANCES

Disturbance—any event or occurrence that interrupts the normal activities of the venue.

A **disturbance** is any event or occurrence that interrupts the normal activities of the venue. For example, it may be a group of over-enthusiastic sports fans, a drunken person, two people having an argument or a person attempting to steal or damage the venue's property. People causing a disturbance pose a potential threat to security and safety.

Many disturbances are not foreseeable and may be beyond the initial control of the porter. However, many disturbances can be averted when the porter is alert to what is going on in the public areas. If you notice a disturbance, it is important to involve security and your supervisor immediately. It is not usually appropriate to attempt to manage disturbances alone. Unless you are a registered crowd controller (security person) then it is likely that you do not have the authority or legal right to physically remove a person from the premises.

KEY CONTROL

Of major concern to all hospitality establishments is key control. There are two types of keys the porter may be responsible for: car keys and room keys.

Guests often leave their room key with the porter who must immediately secure it in the appropriate place behind the reception desk. Porters do not keep spare guest room keys at the porter's desk and do not issue keys to guests on their return to the venue. The guest must be directed to reception for key collection.

Porters are not allowed to give guest room numbers to anyone. Indeed in many venues, if an enquiry is made as to whether a particular guest is staying at the venue, the venue declines to confirm this information.

Because porters are responsible for parking and retrieving guests' cars, they are also responsible for securing the guests' car keys. Not unlike the procedure for tagging luggage, car keys are tagged identifying the guest's name, room number and car licence plate. In many cases, it is also useful for the make of the car to be recorded. The keys are then kept in a locked key rack, accessible only by the porters. The guest must produce their half of the tag to retrieve their car.

SKILLS FOCUS

The porter plays an important role in minimising the possibility of a security breach in the venue because most of their time is spent in the public areas where theft, suspicious behaviour and disturbances can occur.

A porter has a responsibility to be constantly alert to people who seem 'out of place', uncomfortable or suspicious or who are acting nervously.

Key control is important and porters are not permitted to hand guests their room key, rather they must direct the guest to reception. Porters do not provide information about guests staying in the venue. The porters maintain car key security.

FOCUS REVIEW

▷ *What role does the porter play in minimising security breaches?*
▷ *What should the porter do if he or she believes someone is acting suspiciously?*
▷ *What is a disturbance? How should the porter handle a disturbance?*
▷ *What security measures must the porter take to secure guests' room and car keys?*

PUT YOUR KNOWLEDGE TO THE TEST

It is Robyn's last week as porter. She has enjoyed her experience in this department and feels she is better equipped to handle guest enquiries. Bryce, the concierge, has asked Robyn if she would show Willem, the new porter, 'the ropes'.

Robyn begins by explaining to Willem the process of preparing for guests' arrival. Today, there are two tour groups arriving and the venue is expected to be full tonight. While this discussion takes place a guest rushes over to Bryce and shakes his hand vigorously. 'Bryce, how fantastic to see you. Do you think you can get me tickets to the play at the Regent tonight? I promised my wife I'd take her.' 'Certainly Mr Blake. Would you like me to book the limousine for you as well?' 'Ah, Bryce, you think of everything. Have to run. Can you leave the tickets in my room for me? Bye.' This interaction took only a few moments and Willem just looked on in surprise. Robyn smiled and said 'That's all right, Willem, in a few years you'll be able to do the seemingly impossible too.'

The next guest came up to the desk and asked Willem what activities he could arrange for the kids during their stay. The Gardner family was visiting for four days and was tired of watching videos. Willem looked at Robyn with a pleading expression and Robyn stepped in to help the guest.

After these brief exchanges, Robyn then showed Willem how the luggage storage area was arranged and explained the importance of correctly tagging the bags.

Willem later accompanied Robyn when she was collecting the luggage from the guest rooms of the group due to depart. Robyn took this opportunity to show Willem how to correctly load the luggage onto the trolley and correctly manually handle heavy items. Finally, near the end of the shift, Robyn explained to Willem his role in security.

1. What pre-arrival activities do you think Robyn explained to Willem?

2. What resource (apart from Robyn) would Willem have at his disposal to help guests with their needs?

3. What activities might Robyn have recommended to the Gardner family? Plan a four-day itinerary for the family. Assume the children are young teenagers.

4. How do you think it is possible for Bryce to 'seemingly do the impossible'?

5. What systems are available for managing luggage storage?

6. What do you think Robyn explained to Willem in terms of his role in security?

Providing Housekeeping Services to Guests

LEARNING OUTCOMES

On completion of this chapter, you will be able to:

▷ describe the housekeeping department's areas of responsibility;

▷ describe the positions available in housekeeping;

▷ manage housekeeping requests in a polite and friendly manner;

▷ advise guests on the correct usage of in-room equipment;

▷ manage malfunctions of in-room equipment according to enterprise standards and procedures.

Introduction

The housekeeping department plays an important role in accommodation services. It is responsible for cleaning guest rooms and the public areas of the venue and managing a range of guest services, such as laundry. It must meet its responsibilities according to the standards of the establishment and in a way that helps meet the guests' overall expectations.

Housekeeping functions are performed throughout the entire cycle of service and to be able to successfully achieve the required cleaning and services standard, the housekeeping department must liaise closely with most other departments in the venue—front and back office operations, porters, maintenance and food and beverage outlets. Indeed, many venues today require their front and back office staff to gain experience in the housekeeping department because of the important relationship between the two. This experience provides front and back office staff with an opportunity to gain a better appreciation of the standard of rooms offered, the quality of the fixtures and fittings of each guest room, as well as a clear picture of the room layout and other features relating to the rooms. This in turn assists staff in promoting the rooms to guests.

In this chapter you will learn about the role of housekeeping in accommodation venues and develop the skills and knowledge required to provide a range of general housekeeping services to guests.

Housekeeping's areas of responsibility

Housekeeping primary functions— cleaning rooms and public areas.

The housekeeping department's primary responsibility is for maintaining the venue's standard of cleaning in guest rooms and public areas. Guest rooms are where guests sleep. Public areas are those areas accessible to the public, such as the restaurant, bar and foyer.

The secondary functions performed by housekeeping vary between establishments, but in general terms include some or all of the following:

▷ meeting guest requests (room supplies and amenities, local information inquiries)
▷ managing venue and guest laundry
▷ maintaining linen stock control (for rooms and other departments such as food and beverage outlets)
▷ managing lost and found (guest personal property)
▷ managing staff uniforms (issue, laundering, alterations)
▷ controlling mini-bar
▷ providing butler services
▷ providing turn-down service
▷ undertaking sewing services
▷ managing floral arrangements.

The standard of cleaning and the services offered are determined by several factors, including the establishment's star rating, the skills of the staff and the policies and procedures in place. The venue's target market can also influence what services and facilities are provided. For example, a venue seeking to attract corporate guests is likely to offer both laundry services and a turn down service, while a two star country motel seeking to attract holiday-makers travelling by car, will offer basic room cleaning services but not a turn-down service or laundry service (although the venue may have an on-site self-service guest laundry).

CLEANING ROOMS

Guest rooms are cleaned during the guest's stay, after guest departure and sometimes again before a guest is due to arrive. The front office advises housekeeping of the rooms that require cleaning, and, once the rooms are cleaned, housekeeping advises front office of the change of room status. Because of the frequency of use of guest rooms and the variety of guests who use them, maintaining a high level of hygiene in the cleaning process is important. Room cleaning is discussed in Chapter 12.

CLEANING PUBLIC AREAS

Most public areas are cleaned daily. Many of these areas are cleaned more frequently, such as after service periods, as in the restaurant; or when the need arises, such as after a spill in the foyer; or according to schedule, such as a daily cleaning schedule. Because public areas often provide the first visual evaluation of the venue by the guest, cleaning public areas to a high standard is very important. Cleaning public areas is discussed in Chapter 11.

Public areas:
• foyers
• restaurant
• bar
• public toilets
• lifts
• stairwells.

GUEST REQUESTS

Meeting guests' requests is a major function of the housekeeping department. The requests are met usually by whoever is available from housekeeping at the time or, by a person designated by the team leader, often the houseperson.

Requests are made in a number of ways. For example, requests may be made directly by the guest to the room attendant while the room is being cleaned, or by telephone to the housekeeping department, or sometimes through another department. For example, a guest requesting a laundry service may call the porter. The porter in turn lets housekeeping know there is laundry to be collected from a guest's room. No matter where the request comes from, what is important is that the guest expects the request to be met quickly and efficiently. Requests are discussed in detail later in the chapter.

Guest requests:
• directly to room attendants or public area cleaners
• over the telephone to housekeeping
• through another department.

LAUNDRY SERVICES

Many venues launder their own linen and may offer a full laundry service to their guests including washing, ironing and dry cleaning. Other venues do not have the facilities to launder their own linen or their guests', so they use the services of a commercial laundry operation.

If a laundry is maintained by the venue, a range of specialist skills is required, depending on the extent of the operation. For example, laundry staff need to be able to safely and correctly operate a range of laundry equipment, understand the laundering requirements of a range of fabrics, safely and correctly use a range of chemicals, and manage the flow of linen and guest laundry into and out of the laundry area.

LINEN STOCK CONTROL

Linen represents a large expense to the venue, whether or not it is laundered on the premises or sent to a commercial laundry, so considerable care should be taken in handling and controlling it. Theft of linen is a major concern for all establishments and it is not difficult to imagine a venue running out of linen supplies if a tight control on linen stocks is not maintained. Most venues therefore have in place a stock control system to reduce the likelihood of theft and meet the linen needs of all departments for whom they launder linen.

There are several methods of controlling linen stock. The one that is used will depend on the size of the operation. For most venues, linen is only accessible by those who work in the laundry or other areas of housekeeping. When the venue's outlets require linen, they must request it from the laundry. One system used is a clean for dirty exchange. A clean for dirty exchange means that if a department, such as the restaurant, requires clean linen (table cloths, napkins, service cloths) someone from that department exchanges their dirty supply for a clean supply—thus, 50 dirty napkins will get you 50 clean napkins.

Of course, this is only one stock control system. And whichever is used, it is likely that a regular stocktake of linen is also undertaken to assist control.

LOST AND FOUND

It is not unusual for a room attendant or public area cleaner to find guests' personal belongings, in guest rooms or public areas, after guests have departed. Whether it is a pyjama top or a diamond ring, the item must be secured and held for the guest to collect. Housekeeping maintains records of lost and found items. Procedures for managing lost and found are discussed in Chapter 11.

STAFF UNIFORMS

The responsibility for the care and laundering of the staff uniform is frequently left to the individual. However, in large venues, to maintain a consistently high standard in personal grooming, a uniform is provided and the responsibility for the care of the uniform becomes a dual responsibility: the individual staff member and housekeeping.

A clean for dirty exchange system ensures all staff members have a clean uniform when required. It helps keep track of uniforms and meet the venue's standards for staff grooming and presentation. Housekeeping launders the uniforms, makes alterations as required and mends damaged uniforms.

MINI-BAR

Even though the mini-bar contains food and beverage items, more and more venues have made control of the mini-bar the responsibility of housekeeping. A room attendant may check the mini-bar as part of their room cleaning duties and replenish stock as required, or a staff member may have sole responsibility for checking and replenishing mini-bar stocks daily. Guests pay for the items consumed from the mini-bar.

Traditional butler services:
- unpacking and packing luggage
- laundering and dry cleaning clothing
- ironing the newspaper
- shining shoes
- maintaining the guest room in an orderly manner
- running the bath
- personal shopping for the guest.

BUTLER SERVICES

Butler services were once the domain of only international five star hotels. Today, many hotels offer butler services without necessarily calling it a butler service. The butler traditionally provided a very personalised service to certain guests. Duties performed include unpacking and packing guests' luggage, laundering and dry cleaning clothing, ironing the newspaper (to remove the creases and reduce the ink), shining shoes, maintaining the guest room in an orderly manner, running the bath, personal shopping for the guest, and a range of other services.

Today, the service is not so personalised but many of the services are still standard in large, international standard venues. For example, laundry services are available in most accommodation venues, a shoe shine service is available, tours and transport can be booked for the guest and of course, housekeeping maintains the cleanliness of the guest's room.

TURN-DOWN SERVICE

A turn-down service is provided in the early evening by mainly large city venues. This is the turning down of the blankets on the bed in readiness for the guest to go to sleep. The service is also a room tidying service. The guest's room is not completely re-serviced in the evening but it is likely that the room attendant will remake the bed if required, then turn down the blankets, tidy the bathroom and replace towels, draw the curtains and dim the lights. Some venues also place a chocolate or similar treat by the bed. The guest does not pay extra for this service.

Turn-down service—turning down the blankets of the bed in readiness for the guest to go to sleep. The room and bathroom is tidied and towels are replaced if required.

SEWING SERVICE

Laundry staff usually undertakes sewing tasks. The seamstress is likely to be responsible for mending tears and other damage in linen and soft furnishings, staff uniforms and even guests' clothing.

FLORAL ARRANGEMENTS

Housekeeping may be responsible for placing the floral arrangements in strategic locations in public areas and guest rooms. Usually, however, a florist provides the arrangements. In some establishments, this service is contracted out and the florist will not only create the arrangements but also put them in place in the public areas of the venue.

Positions available in housekeeping

Now that you know what the main functions of housekeeping are, it is important to link each task with the person who usually performs it. While housekeeping has traditionally been viewed as a female domain, more and more males now work in the housekeeping department. For many, housekeeping represents an entry point into the hospitality industry. Many of the roles can be trained on the job and entry level positions do not require formal qualifications.

ROOM ATTENDANT

Room attendants, as the name suggests, attend to the cleaning of guest rooms. This is an entry level position and requires skills in the use of a range of equipment and room cleaning techniques, knowledge of the venue's facilities and standards, the department's services and procedures, and occupational health and safety related issues.

Room attendants are in frequent contact with the guest so excellent interpersonal skills are necessary as well as an eye for detail, local area knowledge and the ability to meet guest requests.

PUBLIC AREA CLEANERS

Public area cleaners are responsible for cleaning all the public areas of the venue. It is not unusual to find that public area cleaners also have room cleaning skills or are able to undertake other housekeeping roles, such as houseperson duties.

HOUSEPERSON

The houseperson is also called a houseman. Today both males and females undertake this role. The houseperson is responsible for a range of support duties to the room attendants.

For example, the houseperson will collect all dirty linen from the floors and transfer it to the laundry. The houseperson will also restock clean linen in the storage facilities on each floor, assist with the set up of equipment such as a rollaway beds and cots, and may use heavy industrial cleaning equipment. The houseperson may also assist in the laundry when required and often clean rooms and public areas. Because the houseperson is constantly moving around the establishment, he or she is likely to wear a pager so that contact may be easily made; it is often the houseperson's responsibility to meet guest requests of the housekeeping department. This is an entry level position.

LAUNDRY ATTENDANT

Laundry attendants work in the laundry and require skills in the operation of the various pieces of equipment required to meet the venue's laundry needs. This is an entry level position and does not require formal qualifications. However, the laundry attendant must be familiar with all job related health and safety issues, must have knowledge of correct laundry procedures and must have the ability to manage the flow of linen.

TEAM LEADER

It is not uncommon for housekeeping staff to gain experience in all the above roles before moving onto a team leader or supervisory role. The team leader has many names: supervisor, shift leader, assistant manager. Whatever the title, the team leader is responsible for checking that the cleaning standards of the venue have been met. For example, after the room attendants have cleaned the guest rooms, the team leader will check that each room is cleaned to the required standard. Team leaders are also often required to allocate tasks to be performed, train new employees and assist with cleaning when needed.

While many team leaders do not have formal qualifications, this is becoming a desirable attribute and is certainly a distinct advantage for this career move.

ASSISTANT EXECUTIVE HOUSEKEEPER

This role is one of support to the executive housekeeper. The assistant helps the executive housekeeper manage the housekeeping department. Not all venues require an assistant executive housekeeper, relying instead on the support of the team leaders.

EXECUTIVE HOUSEKEEPER

Also referred to as the housekeeping manager, this is a senior management role in the venue hierarchy answering directly to the general manager. Formal qualifications are usually required and the role is usually attained by a progression through the ranks in housekeeping (room attendant, team leader, assistant manager). It is not uncommon to find that the executive housekeeper has experience in other departments of the establishment, such as front office. The executive housekeeper is responsible for the daily management of the department including:

▷ rostering
▷ budgeting and department expenses
▷ laundry management
▷ development of standards and procedures
▷ quality control of the cleaning functions

▷ ordering and stock control of chemicals, cleaning cloths and cleaning equipment

▷ decision making about fabrics and furnishings used.

The organisational chart in Figure 10.1 represents a typical career path in housekeeping.

HOURS

In a large, five star venue, it is likely that housekeeping will be manned from 8.00 am to 11.30 pm. The first shift is rostered from 8.00 am and will work through to 4.30 pm. A second shift may commence at 3.00 pm and work through until 11.30 pm.

The first shift will comprise a greater number of staff than the second and is responsible for cleaning guest rooms and public areas, taking care of laundry services, and providing a range of other guest services. In the evening, housekeeping staff provide the turn-down service, meet guest requests and when required clean some public areas and guest rooms (for example, there may have been a day-use room and the guest departed at 5.00 pm. The room is needed for a late check-in that night and so needs to be serviced). Most venues do not operate the laundry in the evening.

In smaller venues, only one shift may operate, from 8.00 am until 4.30 pm (or similar hours). A turn-down service is not likely to be offered and if it is, only one person may be rostered to perform this role. In the absence of housekeeping staff in the evening, either a porter or front office staff member will fulfil guest requests that are usually the housekeeping department's responsibility.

CONTRACT CLEANING

More and more venues contract the services of commercial cleaners to fulfil their cleaning requirements. For the venue, this can be a more cost effective way of managing the cleaning functions. Contractors are responsible for employing, and therefore paying, cleaning

Figure 10.1 ▷ **Typical housekeeping career path**

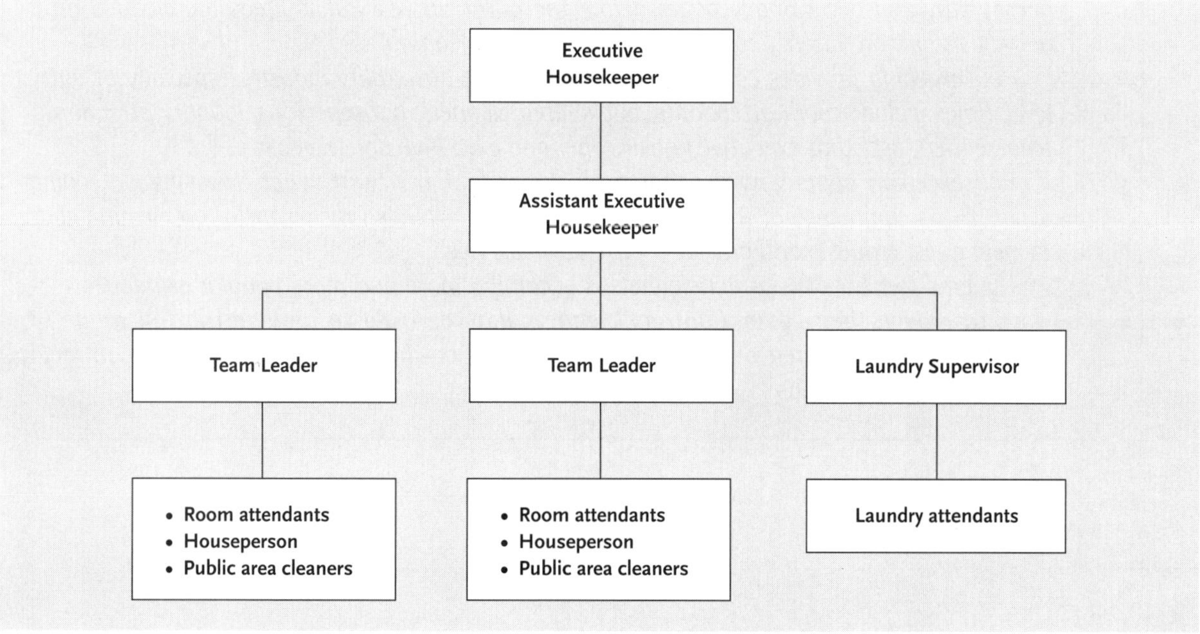

staff and the contractor is paid per room cleaned. The contractor may also be responsible for supplying all the cleaning equipment and chemicals, cleaning staff uniforms and most other costs associated with cleaning rooms and public areas. Venues that employ the services of contract cleaners are not likely to have an on-premises laundry. All venue linen and guest laundry is sent to a commercial laundry service for processing.

While this type of cleaning arrangement is becoming more and more popular, it has the potential to reduce the housekeeping services available to in-house guests (for example, it is unlikely that butler services or a turn-down service is provided). Front office staff or porters in these venues now fulfil many of the guest requests that are still available in a venue previously managed by housekeeping.

Another way that housekeeping fulfils its functions using contract cleaners is to maintain a full service housekeeping department itself, but contract commercial cleaners to undertake much of the more difficult and more thorough cleaning duties. For example, for a venue that has expansive function, foyer and other public areas, housekeeping can clean these areas during the day but at night (usually between 11.00 pm and 7.00 am) commercial cleaners provide a more thorough cleaning service.

Commercial cleaners are also frequently used when an area to be cleaned is particularly soiled, for example, for steam cleaning carpets in function rooms and grease build-up in the kitchen (such as the flues).

SKILLS FOCUS

The primary responsibilities of the housekeeping department are to clean guest rooms and public areas. Secondary responsibilities of housekeeping include laundry services, fulfilling a range of guest requests, managing lost and found and mini-bar, providing butler and turn-down services and linen stock control, among others.

The cleaning of guest rooms is undertaken after guest departure, sometimes during the guest's stay and occasionally again before the guest arrives. Public areas are cleaned on a daily basis or more often, depending on the need for cleaning.

Housekeeping provides career opportunities in the hospitality industry especially at entry level. Roles include room attendants, public area cleaners, housepersons, laundry attendants, team leaders, assistant executive housekeeper and executive housekeeper.

Housekeeping hours vary depending on the style and size of venue. Most housekeeping departments commence at 8.00 am and some venues will also roster on for an evening shift to meet guest requests and provide a turn-down service.

The employment of contract cleaners is becoming more and more popular as venues seek ways to reduce their costs. Contract cleaners may be used to provide the full range of cleaning services required or retained in addition to the housekeeping department to meet additional cleaning needs.

Managing housekeeping requests

Guest requests to housekeeping are made in a number of ways. For example, requests are made face-to-face directly to the room attendant while a guest room is being cleaned; or to a public area cleaner while cleaning the foyer; through another department such as the porter's desk or front office; or by telephone directly to the housekeeping department or another department. However requests are received, they must always be handled in a polite and friendly manner and in accordance with the guest service standards in place.

Earlier you learned that housekeeping fulfils its many duties throughout the entire cycle of service. Table 10.1 lists some of the most common requests guests make at each stage of the cycle of service.

Several housekeeping requests may need to be met at once, particularly when the venue has high occupancy. It becomes necessary to prioritise requests in order both to meet demand and to meet it within a reasonable time frame. As a general rule:

▷ complete simple requests first
▷ complete requests for the same floor at the same time
▷ seek help if you can't meet requests in a timely manner.

PROVIDING GUEST SERVICES

However you receive a guest request and irrespective of what that request is, there are a few rules that are important to remember:

▷ never say 'no' to a request
▷ use the guest's name
▷ always be courteous and polite
▷ confirm request details with the guest when necessary
▷ promptly locate and deliver requests within the agreed timeframe
▷ collect items within an agreed time frame
▷ set up requested equipment for the guest.

Table 10.1 ▷ **The cycle of service and guest requests**

CYCLE OF SERVICE	TYPES OF REQUESTS
Pre-arrival	▷ cot
	▷ rollaway bed
Arrival	▷ cot
	▷ rollaway bed
	▷ additional room supplies
Occupancy	▷ fresh towels
	▷ additional room supplies and amenities
	▷ room to be serviced
	▷ cot
	▷ rollaway bed
	▷ local area information
	▷ venue facilities and services information
	▷ additional pillows or blankets
	▷ laundry services
	▷ shoe shine
	▷ iron and ironing board
	▷ turn-down
	▷ how to use equipment
Departure	▷ lost and found

Never say no!

Perhaps the most important thing to remember when guests make a request is never to say no, even if you know that the request cannot be met. An example of a request that cannot be met is for something that is illegal, such as drugs. Another example is something that is not realistic, such as a request for front row seats at the Australian Tennis Open final, one hour before play starts!

When requests cannot realistically be met, it is important not to say no. Why? Because sometimes it is surprising to find out that what you think can't be accomplished can be (it's just possible your concierge knows how to get those tickets for the tennis final). And even if it can't be, the guest must believe that every effort was made on their behalf to accommodate that request. In other words, if you don't think a request can be met, let the guest know you will find out. Then ask your supervisor.

Here are a few more examples of what guests do not want to hear when they make a request:

▷ 'That's not my responsibility.'
▷ 'You'll have to call reception/porter/room service.'
▷ 'I don't have time right now.'
▷ 'I don't know.'

If a request made of you is not usually provided by housekeeping, record the details of the request anyway and let the guest know you will pass their request to the appropriate department. For example, if a guest requests their luggage be collected, let the porter know. If the guest wants to order breakfast in their room, let room service know.

Use the guest's name

Using the guest's name is one of the most important things you can do. Not only is it courteous but it is expected of all hospitality professionals. It also makes the guest feel important. The housekeeping department can access the guest's name in a number of ways.

▷ the telephone system used in many venues has a display panel that reveals the guest's name and room number when they call

▷ the room allocation sheet issued to room attendants daily, lists room numbers and corresponding guests' name. If the guest request is face-to-face in the guest's room, you can look up the guest's name on this sheet (you will have this with you)

▷ if the request comes from another department, the guest's name can be asked for

▷ you can look up the guest's name on the computer

▷ ask the guest.

The room allocation sheet—the list of rooms to be cleaned by a room attendant. Includes the room number, room status and guest's name.

Always be courteous and polite

Courtesy means various things to each of us. In general terms, it means performing your role in a polite and friendly manner. Courtesy is demonstrated through positive body language and the use of the guest's name. It is also demonstrated by carrying out the request promptly and professionally.

Confirm request details

Some requests may be complex, while others may need to be passed on to someone else. Other requests may need to be completed at a later time. Any request that has any of these characteristics should be written down and repeated back to the guest. There are several reasons for this.

Meeting guest requests:
• use the guest's name
• be courteous
• confirm request details.

By writing the details down you will have a permanent record of the information for later reference if required. It will also help you remember the information—a written message is remembered better than a verbal message. To ensure you have all the details correct, repeat them back to the guest. This is difficult to do if it is not written down. By repeating the details to the guest, you are allowing them the opportunity to confirm what they have told you and make any adjustments if necessary.

Promptly locate and deliver requests

All requests should be promptly located and delivered. This means that the guest should not be kept waiting for their request, or worse, have to call a second time to find out what has happened to their request. Requests need to be delivered at the guest's convenience, not yours. For example, a request for fresh towels is probably wanted immediately. However, a request for dry cleaning may be able to wait until later.

Always check with the guest to determine when they would like the request met or let the guest know if a delay is expected in meeting their request. For example, advise the guest you will deliver the towels within ten minutes. Or ask the guest what time would be convenient for you to deliver their laundry. Whatever time frame you agree on with the guest, it is an important part of the service to ensure you do what you say you are going to do.

Collect items within an agreed time frame

The guest sometimes requests a service that requires you to collect items from their room. Examples of this include shoes to be polished and clothes to be laundered.

Laundry bags are provided by most venues in the guest room. The guest completes the accompanying laundry docket and either leaves the bag in their room when they go out (the room attendant will collect the bag when they service the room) or calls housekeeping for someone to come and collect the bag. When you are called to collect dry cleaning, ask the guest when it would be a convenient time for collection. The guest will let you know if they want you to collect the laundry bag now, or at a later time when they are out of their room.

For a shoe cleaning service, most venues will collect shoes to be cleaned, similarly to the collection of laundry items (ask the guest when they would like you to collect the items), or most guests know that by leaving their shoes outside their room door at night, the shoes will be collected during the night, cleaned, and returned by early morning.

Set up equipment for guests

Guests request the use of various pieces of equipment that housekeeping is both responsible for locating and delivering in a timely manner, and for setting up, such as a rollaway bed. When setting up equipment, always check with the guest where in the room they would like you to place it, and set it up according to manufacturer's instructions and so that it is ready for the guest's immediate use. Examples of equipment you may need to set up for the guest include:

▷ rollaway bed
▷ sofa bed
▷ cot
▷ iron and ironing board
▷ alarm clock.

Rollaway bed or foldaway bed

A rollaway bed is a bed that can be folded length-ways in half, has fold-up legs and is on castors. It may also be referred to as a trundle bed. These beds are designed this way for easy storage and manoeuvrability. Most venues have available rollaway beds for guest use on request, for example, when a guest requests a third bed in a double room. A sofa bed or foldaway bed is usually hidden inside a couch or sofa. Although the guests are able to access the bed themselves because it is part of the room fittings, it is housekeeping's responsibility to make up the bed for the guest and make certain it is safe for use.

Cot

Like a rollaway bed, a cot must be set up and made ready for the guest's use. Instructions for set up usually accompany the cot and must be strictly observed.

Iron and ironing board

Many venues today supply an iron and ironing board in all guest rooms. Even if this is the case, the guest may request someone to set it up for them. If it is not provided, then housekeeping must locate the items, deliver them to the guest room and set them up for the guest.

Alarm clock

An alarm clock is a standard feature in many guest rooms today. However, a guest may not know how to use it and request housekeeping set it for them. For those establishments that do not provide alarm clocks in the guest room, a wake up call service is usually available. A guest however, may still prefer an alarm clock and every effort should be made to locate one.

Because each venue will have a variety of equipment and a variety of brands of equipment, it is important to check first the correct way to set up each piece of equipment. Failure to do so could result in a safety hazard for the guest or for you.

SKILLS FOCUS

Guest requests are made in a number of ways: face-to-face, through another department or via the telephone. However they are made, respond to guests' requests efficiently, courteously and in a friendly manner.

Guest requests of housekeeping may be made any time throughout the cycle of service. Examples of requests include a cot, rollaway bed, fresh towels, additional linen, laundry services, local area information and set up of equipment.

When you fulfil guest requests never say no to unusual requests, but attempt to find out if the request can in fact be met. When possible always use the guest's name, be courteous and polite, confirm request details with the guest to determine accuracy and promptly locate and deliver requests within agreed time frames.

When guests request that items be collected from them, agree on a time for collection. When guests request use of equipment, such as a cot or rollaway bed, set these up in a location that is convenient for the guest.

FOCUS REVIEW

▷ *How are housekeeping requests received?*

▷ *If you can't say 'no' to even very strange requests, how should you handle them?*

▷ *Make a list of 10 local attractions or features that your guests may seek information about. If you have trouble coming up with 10, remember it's even less likely that your guests will know!*

▷ *List three ways you can find out a guest's name.*

▷ *Why is confirming the guest's request important? What advantages are there to writing down a guest's request?*

▷ *Why must requests be met in a timely manner?*

▷ *Why do you think it is important to ask the guest where they would like equipment set up?*

▷ *Why is it important to follow the manufacturer's instructions when setting up equipment for the guest?*

▷ *If you are currently working in an accommodation venue, make a list of all the services housekeeping provides and a list of the equipment available for guest use.*

APPLY YOUR KNOWLEDGE

You are responsible for managing guest requests today. It is 8.30 am and you have just received the following list of requests. It's clear from the length of the list that you can't perform all tasks yourself so you decide to seek the assistance of a houseperson.

> *Prioritise and allocate the various tasks to the houseperson or yourself to ensure that all tasks are performed in a timely manner. Indicate what action you would take to complete each task. All same day laundry and dry cleaning must be collected before 9.30 am.*

▷ *Mr Jones in 1205 wants a toothbrush and toothpaste before he leaves for his 9.00 am meeting.*
▷ *Ms DuMaine in 3506 has dry cleaning to be collected for same day return.*
▷ *Mr Thomson in 4501 needs his room serviced before 11.00 am. He is conducting interviews in his room today.*
▷ *Mr Lee in 2705 has dry cleaning for collection.*
▷ *Ms van Ingen in 1407 needs more juice in her mini-bar before her return tonight.*
▷ *Ms Pullman in 3607 wants to purchase a bathrobe and have it delivered to her room before she checks-out at noon.*
▷ *The iron isn't working in 1508 and Mr Brice is running late for an appointment.*
▷ *Reception needs the spare room amenities restocked. They have the room showing booked at 10.00 am.*
▷ *The child in room 1409 was sick in the cot this morning.*
▷ *Mr Green in 2801 broke a glass in the bathroom and has reported it to reception.*
▷ *Mr Abernethy has laundry, which must be back by 5.00 pm tonight.*
▷ *Mr Hedger needs his shoes polished for a function tonight.*
▷ *Ms Hunt needs a hem mended on a suit before tomorrow morning.*
▷ *Mr Carling thinks he left his diary in the bar last night and wants to know if it has been found.*

Advising guests on room and housekeeping equipment

Apart from the equipment that you may be requested to set up for the guest, there are a number of facilities and equipment that are standard features of most guest rooms. These may include:

▷ television and video
▷ air conditioning unit
▷ telephone system
▷ facsimile machine
▷ Internet access or computer modem
▷ in-room safe
▷ stereo system
▷ hair dryer
▷ iron and ironing board
▷ **murphy bed** (a bed that can be folded full length into a wall cavity or purpose-built cupboard)
▷ kitchen appliances (microwave, stove)
▷ alarm clock.

Working in housekeeping makes it necessary for you to know how to operate each piece of equipment so that you are able to demonstrate its use for the guest. There are a number of reasons why a guest may require assistance to use the equipment:

▷ no instructions, poor instructions or complicated instructions
▷ unfamiliar with the brand of equipment
▷ English language restraints
▷ disability.

Although the in-room equipment will vary between each venue it is important for you to be familiar with its use *before* you are asked to show a guest how to use it. As you do when meeting guest requests, when you are asked to demonstrate the correct use of equipment:

▷ be courteous and polite. Don't assume that everyone knows how to operate the equipment
▷ explain the instructions clearly. Don't use jargon or speak too fast
▷ ask the guest to show you how to operate the equipment after you have demonstrated its use, so that you can be sure they have understood
▷ ask the guest if there is anything else you can do for them.

The guest may be a little embarrassed, not being able to do something as seemingly simple as turning on the television. Put them at ease and reassure them that there is nothing to be embarrassed about.

Managing malfunctions of in-room equipment

Whether it is in-room equipment, such as the television or air conditioning unit, or equipment you are responsible for setting up, such as a cot or rollaway bed, occasionally a piece of equipment may break down (which may be why the guest couldn't get it to work in the first place!) or become damaged. You are likely to learn of damaged or malfunctioning items when either a guest complains, asks for assistance to operate the equipment, or you discover it while cleaning a guest room.

Most establishments have a procedure in place for managing malfunctions of in-room equipment. The procedure may simply be to call maintenance and then check later that the problem is fixed. But there are times when maintenance may not be available or the problem cannot be fixed immediately.

Always check with your supervisor if you are not sure what to do, but remember that as long as an item is not working, there is an inconvenience to the guest. Usually there are four ways of managing malfunctions in the guestroom.

FIX THE PROBLEM

There are many small malfunctions that you may be able to fix. For example, a guest complains that the lamp in his room isn't working. You can check that it is plugged in or you may need to replace the globe. If still it doesn't work, then you can replace the lamp (if a replacement is available) or call maintenance.

The first step in fixing all electrical appliances is to check that the item is plugged into the power supply. If it is and it still doesn't work then you need to call maintenance, especially if it is a large item such as a television. If it is a small item, such as a kettle or iron, you can replace the item. Give the damaged item to maintenance later so that it can be repaired. What is important is to make sure that the guest is not inconvenienced longer than is necessary.

Another important point to remember is not to attempt to fix something that you know little or nothing about. This can pose a danger to you and the guest and may result in even more damage. If, for example, an electrical appliance has a damaged cord or plug, do not attempt to use the item. Replace it immediately.

REFER THE PROBLEM TO MAINTENANCE

If you need to call maintenance, do so immediately and from the guest's room. Tell maintenance where you are (room number), what the problem is, for example, you cannot get the air conditioning to work and ask how long they expect to take to attend to the problem. You may need to confirm that this is acceptable to the guest.

If maintenance is going to attend to the problem immediately, then it is common practice for you to remain with the guest. If maintenance indicates that they cannot attend to the matter immediately, explain this to the guest, apologise for the inconvenience and let them know when they can expect maintenance to fix the problem. It is appropriate for you to call the guest later to determine that everything is now working satisfactorily.

REPLACE THE ITEM

Some items can be replaced quickly and with minimal disturbance to the guest. Sometimes this is a better option than calling maintenance. For example, it is common practice to have available in housekeeping a spare kettle, alarm clock, hair dryer, iron or other small electrical appliances. When you have determined that the equipment does not work, apologise to the guest for the inconvenience and offer to replace it immediately. When you return with the item, turn it on to ensure that this new one does work.

For larger pieces of equipment, such as a television, if maintenance is unable to fix the item in a timely manner, it is not unusual to replace the item. A television may be replaced with one from another (vacant) guest room.

When malfunctioning or damaged items need to be collected from a guest's room, agree on a time for collection that is suitable for the guest. Either you or a maintenance staff member may remove the item. If you or another housekeeping staff member removes the item, send it to maintenance to be fixed.

CHANGE THE GUEST ROOM

In some instances, fixing or replacing a piece of equipment is not an option. For example, if the toilet breaks and cannot be fixed until a plumber is called in the morning, then it may be appropriate to move the guest to another room. If a guest is to be moved to another room, you will need first to contact reception to determine if another room is available. Reception will then process the room move on the PMS and you may need to assist the guest with the actual move. Advise the guest to repack their luggage, while you collect the new room key. When you return, escort the guest to the new room. You may need to assist with carrying their luggage. When you arrive at the new room, open the door, allow the guests to enter and quickly inspect the room to determine that it is more suitable than the previous room.

Whatever arrangements are made for managing malfunctions of room and housekeeping equipment it must be in accordance with the venue's procedures and at the guest's convenience.

SKILLS FOCUS

A number of facilities and types of equipment are standard features in guest rooms and you may be requested to demonstrate their use for guests. Examples include the television, in-room safe, telephone system and air conditioning unit. You therefore need to know how to operate each of these items and demonstrate their use in a way that is clear, courteous, polite and timely.

On occasion you will find that the in-room equipment cannot be used because it is damaged or malfunctioning. There are four ways you can manage these situations: fix the problem yourself, but only if safe to do so, refer the problem immediately to maintenance, replace the item if practical, or move the guest to another room.

FOCUS REVIEW

▷ *Why might a guest need assistance to operate in-room equipment?*
▷ *When demonstrating the use of in-room equipment, what are the four key points to remember?*
▷ *There are four options available to you if in-room equipment is damaged or malfunctioning. Briefly explain each.*
▷ *Which option would you chose, and why, for managing in-room equipment malfunctions for the following items?*
   – *microwave*
   – *refrigerator*
   – *video*
   – *stereo*
   – *telephone*
   – *kettle.*

PUT YOUR KNOWLEDGE TO THE TEST

Robyn was excited about starting in housekeeping. It was the last stage of her traineeship and she was determined to do a good job. Although Robyn was familiar with most of the rooms at the Grand Central Hotel, Dion, the executive housekeeper, believed it was important to spend Robyn's first two days showing her around the guest rooms and public areas again and explaining the importance of the housekeeping functions and its role in meeting guest expectations.

Robyn had always imagined that working in housekeeping meant her interaction with guests would be considerably less than working in reception or on the porter's desk. She was surprised to learn that in fact housekeeping staff had considerable contact with guests, not just while cleaning, but also in meeting guests' requests.

Dion first assigned Robyn the responsibility of meeting guest requests before training her in other roles in housekeeping. He began by showing her the lost and found cupboard (where lost and found items are stored), then explained where she would find most of the items guests request, such as fresh towels, additional amenities, small electrical appliances.

Robyn's first job of the morning was to sort through all the lost property from the weekend and then check that what was recorded in the Lost Property Log matched what was in the cupboard. While she was doing that Ms Nelligan rang to say she had left her perfume in her room on Saturday. Robyn was able to locate the perfume and arrange for it to be sent back. Mr Girrard from France called and said he thought he had left his electric shaver in his room eight weeks ago. Robyn was also able to find this and return it.

Dion asked Robyn to go with him to assist Mr Malouf in moving to another room. The air conditioning in his room was broken and unable to be fixed until tomorrow. As the temperature was expected to reach 32°C he didn't want to stay in that room. Dion had already arranged a new room with reception.

Dion suggested to Robyn that it would be helpful for her to make a list of all the housekeeping services available in the Grand Central Hotel and how those services could be met. She could ask any of her colleagues for information. Dion explained that by writing down this information, it would help Robyn to remember. As an example, Dion explained that one housekeeping service was the provision of a cot on request. A cot would be placed in the room for the guest either before the guest arrived or on arrival, and set up according to the manufacturer's instructions.

Robyn's next task was to assist with linen control. She was required to check the quantity of dirty linen received from the various departments and issue clean linen in exchange.

The next day, Robyn assisted Aaron with room mini-bars. They worked from floor to floor, and room to room, checking, restocking and recording consumption of each mini-bar. Robyn found that the trolley was very heavy and difficult to push. She was also aware from working on reception that some people did not always pay for their mini-bar and the venue had to delay charge their credit cards or write some of the charges off. Other people complained of the high prices on the mini-bars. Robyn questioned in her mind the value of maintaining mini-bars in all the rooms.

1. When is a room move likely to happen? For Mr Malouf, was there another option that could have been offered before he was moved? What is housekeeping's responsibility in the room move procedure?

2. Write up the list of services you think Robyn would have included when Dion suggested she do this.

3. As you may imagine, offering most of these services is time-consuming for staff and therefore expensive for the venue in terms of wages. Which services, if any, do you think could be cut on the weekends to reduce wages? Justify your answer. What impact might this have on guest expectations? Remember to think of the needs of different target markets of the Grand Central.

4. What is the name of the system of linen control being used at the Grand Central Hotel? Why do you think this linen control system is popular? Why do you think it is not acceptable for staff to just help themselves to whatever linen they need to do their job? Can you think of any other systems that could work?

5. Why do you think venues have mini-bars? Do you think they are worth keeping? Why or why not?

Cleaning Premises and Equipment

LEARNING OUTCOMES

On completion of this chapter you will be able to:

▷ define public areas and explain the importance of cleaning these areas;

▷ select and set up cleaning equipment;

▷ correctly prepare for cleaning;

▷ select and use the appropriate personal protective clothing;

▷ identify hazards in public areas;

▷ clean dry and wet areas;

▷ correctly dispose of garbage;

▷ maintain and store cleaning equipment and chemicals;

▷ manage equipment maintenance requirements.

Introduction

When a guest arrives at your venue, one of the first things they are likely to do is form an opinion about the standard of cleanliness. It is not planned and it is not intentional, but it happens. People tend to notice either very clean environments or messy and dirty environments.

Imagine a friendly, courteous porter has just greeted a guest. The porter carries her bags inside, and places them on the floor next to the guest who is now standing at reception. The guest cringes as she realises that her bags have just been placed on what looks like mud carried in on someone else's feet. As the guest signs the registration form, her arms rest on a greasy patch on the desk. Looking around, she notices newspapers scattered around the foyer, scuffed and damaged furniture and dust on almost every surface. What sort of image has this establishment created? What expectations would this guest have of the room?

No matter how friendly and efficient the staff, this venue has created a poor moment of truth with its low cleaning standards, and failed to meet the expectations of this guest. This poor image is lasting. And throughout the guest's stay and even at departure, this guest is likely to be assessing the cleaning standards of the entire venue. If the cleaning standards continue to fail to meet expectations, it's probable that this guest will never return.

In this chapter you will learn the importance of public area cleaning and how to effectively carry out general cleaning duties to maintain the venue's cleaning standards and meet guests' expectations.

Public areas

Public areas are those parts of the establishment to which the public has access. Housekeeping staff clean these areas daily or more frequently. Public areas include:

▷ foyers and lobbies
▷ restaurants and bars
▷ function and conference rooms
▷ lounge areas
▷ public toilets
▷ lifts and stairways
▷ corridors and balconies
▷ guest facilities, such as the pool and gym.

WET AND DRY AREAS

Wet area—an area exposed to the presence of water or other liquids.

Public areas are classified as either wet or dry. As the name suggests, **wet areas** are so called due to the presence of water or other liquids, such as in a bar area, pool or external walkway. The surface of the floor in these areas such as tiles, concrete, slate and marble are designed to facilitate easy removal of water or other liquids.

Dry area—an area not meant to be exposed to water or other liquids.

Dry areas are those parts of the venue not meant to be exposed to water, for example, guest rooms and function areas. The floor coverings are likely to be carpet or rugs, but dry areas may also have hard floor surfaces usually found in wet areas. Of course, that is not to say that these don't get wet—spillages do occur. But these are isolated incidents and the spillage is always quickly removed.

Understanding the difference between wet and dry areas is important because of the way in which these areas are cleaned. Table 11.1 shows the public areas classified either wet or dry and the possible floor surface.

It is not only the floor surfaces you need be concerned with in public areas. The other surfaces to be cleaned in public areas include the furniture, walls, soft furnishings and fixtures and fittings, and all must be cleaned to meet the standards of the venue.

Table 11.1 ▷ **Wet and dry public areas**

PUBLIC AREA	DRY/WET	POSSIBLE FLOOR SURFACE
Foyers and lobbies	Dry	Tiles, marble, slate, carpet
Restaurant	Dry	Carpet, tiles
Bar	Wet	Non-slip tiles
Function areas	Dry	Carpet
Public toilets	Wet	Tiles, slate
Lifts	Dry	Carpet, tiles
Balconies and external walkways	Wet	Concrete, tiles
Internal corridors	Dry	Carpet
Pool area	Wet	Concrete, tiles
Gym	Dry	Tiles
Stairways	Dry	Carpet, tiles

The importance of cleaning public areas

Apart from maintaining the venue's cleaning standards, there are a number of other reasons why cleaning public areas is important:

▷ hygiene—hygiene regulations must be met to ensure the well-being of all guests and staff

▷ safety—occupational health and safety legislation stipulates a minimum standard required to protect the health and safety of everyone who uses the venue

▷ guest expectations of the venue—expectations are influenced by the guest's own experiences and the venue's star rating, reputation and location, among other things

▷ to extend the life of the items cleaned—correct cleaning procedures ensure that items are not damaged by the cleaning process (or lack of cleaning)

▷ to create a favourable appearance—first impressions are lasting. And throughout the guest's stay the venue is being judged on its cleaning standards.

Importance of cleaning:
• hygiene and safety
• to comply with legislation
• meet guest expectations
• extend the life of the items cleaned
• create a favourable appearance.

This suggests that if we don't clean, the venue will struggle to create a favourable impression, fail to meet the required high standard of hygiene and therefore guests' expectations cannot be met. It is also possible that the venue is in breach of hygiene and safety regulations and that the venue's fixtures and fittings will wear out more quickly.

SKILLS FOCUS

Public areas are those parts of the establishment to which the public has access. The cleaning standard of the venue's public areas create moments of truth for the guest from the point of arrival through to departure. This means a high standard of cleaning is important to create a good overall impression.

There are several other reasons why cleaning is important: for hygiene and safety reasons, to extend the life of items cleaned, to comply with legislation and to meet the venue's cleaning standards.

Public areas are classified as either wet or dry. Wet areas are those which are exposed to water or other fluids, such as the bar and external walkways. Dry areas are those areas not to be exposed to water, such as those areas that are carpeted.

FOCUS REVIEW

▷ Define 'public area'.
▷ Distinguish between 'wet' and 'dry' areas. Give three examples of each.
▷ Why is the cleaning of public areas important?

Selecting and setting up cleaning equipment

A variety of cleaning equipment is used in accommodation venues and each piece is designed to perform certain tasks. Used correctly, the equipment supplied helps make your job easier and protects the surfaces you are cleaning. To make the cleaning task easier:

▷ use the right equipment for each task
▷ check that the equipment is in safe working order before using it
▷ use equipment as intended by the manufacturer
▷ follow procedures for carrying out each task.

USING THE RIGHT TYPES OF EQUIPMENT

Before you use any piece of equipment, you need to know what each is used for and how to use it. If the wrong equipment is used to clean a particular surface, you risk damaging that surface, as well as the equipment. Table 11.2 explains the use of each piece of equipment used to clean public areas, the cleaning task it performs and the surface it may be used on.

CHECKING EQUIPMENT BEFORE USE

Clean and fault-free equipment performs cleaning tasks better than damaged and dirty equipment.

Before using any equipment, you need to check that it is in good working order and that it is clean. Faulty or dirty cleaning equipment, such as broken attachments or damaged working parts, pose potential safety hazards to you, the equipment and the surface being cleaned.

The only way to check your equipment is to physically inspect it. Inspect each of the working parts by lifting up each piece of equipment and looking at it. This may seem tedious and even unnecessary, but takes only a short time, and potentially saves time later (because you won't have to deal with problems caused by using faulty or damaged equipment). If you

Table 11.2 ▷ Types of equipment and their use

EQUIPMENT	USE	SURFACE
Vacuum cleaner (wet and dry)	▷ Carpet cleaning ▷ Removal of water	Carpet, some hard floor surfaces
French polisher/ dust mop	Removal of dust and loose dirt on hard surface floors before mopping	Tiles, marble, lino, parquetry, floor boards
Broom	Sweeping hard surface floor	Tiles, marble, lino, concrete, slate, floor boards, parquetry
Dust pan and brush	Sweeping up collected dirt off hard surface floor	Tiles, marble, lino, parquetry, floor boards, slate, concrete
Wet mop and bucket	For washing hard floor surfaces after dust mopping or sweeping (bucket carries the water and cleaning agent)	Tiles, marble, lino, floor boards, parquetry
Floor polisher	Polishing hard surface floors after sweeping and mopping	Tiles, marble, lino, parquetry
Toilet brush	Cleaning inside toilet bowel	Porcelain
Scrubbing brush	Cleaning floors and tiled areas, particularly grouting between tiles	Tiles
Fabric brush	Brushes lint and dust off fabrics	Furniture, curtains
Cleaning cloths	Various functions including: ▷ cleaning ▷ polishing ▷ rinsing ▷ wiping ▷ dusting	Tiles, marble, lino, parquetry, porcelain, glass, fabrics, plastic, stainless steel, painted surfaces
Hand caddy	For carrying chemical bottles and small cleaning utensils	

find damage to or fault with any equipment, do not use it. Report to maintenance so that it can be fixed or the item replaced.

Vacuum cleaners

Vacuum cleaners perform a range of tasks, most commonly the removal of dust and dirt from carpeted areas. However, various designs enable you to perform a range of other tasks, including hard floor vacuuming, the removal of water from carpet and fabric cleaning. When inspecting a vacuum cleaner, check that:

▷ the wheels turn, or, if a back pack variety, that the straps that attach it to your body are secure
▷ the dust bag is empty and in the right place
▷ the dust bag compartment is properly sealed
▷ there is no damage to the body
▷ the electrical cord is not damaged and that the outer casing is intact
▷ the plug is not loose or damaged
▷ the suction hose is not twisted or punctured
▷ there are no blockages in the suction hose
▷ the condition of the various hose attachments, such as the suction head, is in good working order.

French polisher

A French polisher is also referred to as a dust mop or dry mop (because it is used to collect dust, and is not used with water). A French polisher is used to sweep medium to large, open hard floor areas, such as the foyer. They are frequently double-headed or large-headed broom-like mops, with a long pole-like handle, and used by pushing forward, collecting rubbish and dust as they move across the floor. They can cover large areas much faster than a broom. You will need to check that:

▷ the head is clean and free from obvious dirt and grime
▷ the head is securely attached to the handle
▷ the handle is not splintered or cracked.

Mops and brooms

The size and style of the head of mops and brooms may vary, as might the bristles on a broom, depending on the task to be performed. For example, a 'soft' broom is used on tiles, parquetry and polished floorboards, while a 'hard' broom may be used for sweeping concrete areas and external walkways. Mops and brooms have a long wooden, plastic or fibreglass pole-like handle. A broom is used to remove dust and rubbish from small to medium sized hard floor areas, before the area is washed. Is it is easier to get into corners with a broom than with a dust mop, but the task takes longer to perform. A broom is pushed forward along the floor collecting dust and dirt in its path.

A mop is used for washing a hard floor surface in wet areas after sweeping. It is used in a sweeping motion across the floor as you move backwards.

When inspecting mops and brooms, check that:

▷ the head is securely attached to the handle
▷ the handle is not splintered or cracked
▷ the head is clean and free from obvious dirt and grime.

Dirt and bacteria build up easily on a mop head. If you notice that it is dirty, wash it with detergent and hot water and rinse thoroughly before using it; otherwise you risk spreading dirt and bacteria.

Dustpan and brush

The dustpan and brush are used for picking up the dirt and other rubbish collected with the broom or dust mop. They must be kept in good working order to ensure they effectively pick up dust and dirt.

Buckets

Buckets come in a range of shapes and sizes. Most buckets are used in conjunction with a wet mop and carry the water and detergent required for washing floors. The mop is put in the cleaning solution and 'wrung' out on the rollers attached to the bucket, to remove excess water. Before you fill it with the cleaning solution, check for:

▷ dirt and grime build up in the bucket—wash out thoroughly before use if this is the case
▷ holes—the bucket is no longer any use to you with a hole in it, so replace it
▷ loose handles—these can usually be reattached by maintenance
▷ working wheels/rollers—broken wheels may scratch floor surfaces. Have them repaired or replaced by maintenance.

Only half fill the bucket with water. This makes it easier to carry or push along the floor, and it also prevents spillage.

Floor polisher

Floor polishers can be large, cumbersome pieces of equipment. They are designed for use after sweeping and mopping floor surfaces such as slate, tiles, wood and granite. It gives the surface a high sheen as well as helps protect it from scratches and scuff marks. Although it is difficult to lift, you can check most of its parts as you would a vacuum cleaner. Also check that the pad or brush you are fitting is clean. If the pad is dirty, it will rub the dirt into the floor and possibly scratch the floor's surface.

Cleaning brushes

The varieties of cleaning brushes are designed to accomplish various cleaning tasks effectively. You can inadvertently spread bacteria or cause damage to objects by using the same brush for each cleaning task. Check your brushes for cleanliness before using them. Replace all brushes when they look shabby and scruffy.

The toilet brush is used to clean the inside of the toilet bowl. Clean your toilet brush daily using a disinfectant and boiling water, as a toilet brush carries a lot of bacteria.

The dust brush, or feather duster, is used to remove dust build up on ledges such as door frames and skirting boards.

The fabric brush is used to remove lint and dust from soft furnishings (furniture and curtains), which can then easily be removed from the brush by hand.

Cleaning cloths

The selection of cleaning cloths is quite important because of the types of surfaces to be cleaned. When wiping a surface, it is not desirable to leave smears or lint. Cleaning cloths should also be washed daily, and a different cloth used for cleaning the different surfaces (and chemicals used). If you do not keep your cloths clean, or if you continuously use the same cloth to apply different chemicals, you risk damaging the surface being cleaned. Your cleaning cloths should be:

▷ absorbent so that they can be moistened and collect the dirt and dust easily
▷ soft so that they do not scratch surfaces
▷ lint-free so that they do not leave fluff behind.

Chemical dispensers/spray bottles

Spray bottles or chemical dispensers are used to hold and dispense your chemicals. They are usually small clear plastic containers fitted with a spray trigger. This is a pump action attachment that allows you to apply the chemical in the same amount each time. Refill your chemical dispensers daily from the bulk storage facility, usually kept in housekeeping. Check that the outside of the bottle is clean and that the dispensing nozzle is not blocked or damaged. A damaged dispenser can be a safety risk, as the spray of chemical may not point in the direction you intend, or spray more or less than desired.

Hand caddy

The **hand caddy** is a small, hand-held container, similar to a bucket, which holds your cleaning chemical spray bottles, cleaning cloths and cleaning brushes. It is carried with you as you move from one area to the next.

Hand caddy— a small, hand-held container, similar to a bucket, which holds your cleaning chemical spray bottles, cleaning cloths and cleaning brushes.

USING EQUIPMENT AS INTENDED BY THE MANUFACTURER

All equipment you use has a specific purpose and should be used only for this purpose. Most of the equipment will come with manufacturer's instructions for use. On the job, you will also be trained in how to operate your equipment. Manufacturer's instructions must be followed so that the equipment and surfaces are not damaged by incorrect use.

Another reason it is important to follow the manufacturer's instructions for use is that many pieces of equipment have a warranty or maintenance contract. This means that if the equipment is damaged or faulty then the equipment or parts are replaced, usually free of charge.

FOLLOWING CLEANING PROCEDURES

Every task you complete in your housekeeping role will be accompanied by a procedure. A procedure, as you know, is a step-by-step instruction for completing tasks. You have a responsibility to follow procedures. By following procedures:

▷ tasks are completed correctly
▷ cleaning standards are maintained
▷ your job is made easier.

SKILLS FOCUS

To make your job easier, you need to be familiar with the different types of cleaning equipment used by housekeeping. You must use the right equipment for each task, check that it is safe to use and use it as intended by the manufacturer. All tasks are accompanied by procedures, which are step-by-step instructions that ensure all tasks are completed and a consistent standard is maintained.

The different surfaces you are required to clean require you to use the right equipment for the job; otherwise you risk damaging the surface and the equipment. The most common equipment you will use includes a vacuum cleaner, mop and bucket, floor polisher, a range of cleaning brushes and cleaning cloths and a dust pan and brush. A hand caddy is used to hold your chemical dispensers, cleaning brushes and small cleaning tools.

FOCUS REVIEW

▷ *What is the difference between a dry mop and a wet mop? What is a dust mop used for?*
▷ *Why is it important to check your equipment before using it?*
▷ *Why is a range of cleaning cloths preferred for each of the different cleaning tasks?*
▷ *What are the steps to checking the vacuum cleaner?*
▷ *What should you do if you find a fault with any equipment?*
▷ *Explain briefly the four things that makes your job easier.*

Preparing to clean

Knowing what equipment you need, what each is used for and checking it for safety is only the beginning of the process for cleaning public areas. Before you can begin to actually clean, you also need to:

▷ identify what is to be cleaned
▷ select equipment and chemicals for the task
▷ check that the area is safe.

IDENTIFY WHAT IS TO BE CLEANED

There are several systems used that let you know what you have to clean during your shift. The most common system used is a **cleaning schedule**. Another system is a **daily cleaning record**. It is also likely that your supervisor will advise you of other cleaning tasks to be performed at the beginning of your shift.

Cleaning schedule—a permanent list of all the cleaning tasks to be completed and how frequently each task is to be performed.

Cleaning schedules

A cleaning schedule, as shown in Table 11.3, is a permanent list of all the cleaning tasks to be completed and how frequently (daily, weekly) each task is to be performed. The schedule may also list the chemicals and equipment to use and protective clothing to be worn. A schedule helps control the frequency of cleaning and makes sure that nothing gets overlooked.

Daily cleaning record—a standard form or handwritten list of the cleaning tasks to be completed that day.

However, the usefulness of a cleaning schedule is sometimes limited for the purpose of cleaning public areas. The reason is that you may not always have access to the area to be cleaned, so flexibility is required. For example, a schedule may require you to mop the foyer at 3.00 pm each day. The front office has advised you that a tour group is due to arrive at 3.00 pm and cleaning at this time would be inconvenient for the registration of the tour group.

Daily cleaning record

Due to the need for flexibility, a daily cleaning record can be used as well as, or instead of, a cleaning schedule. It is similar to a daily running sheet used in front office or a room allocation sheet used in housekeeping, in that it will list the tasks (or areas) to be completed that day. The daily cleaning record may be a pre-printed standard form with each of the tasks to be completed checked off daily, or a handwritten list compiled by you or your supervisor.

The factors that can influence when you clean an area, such as the time of day, the volume of traffic, or the need to clean, are catered for with the use of a daily cleaning record, as it is more flexible than a cleaning schedule.

For example, there may have been a function last night and you will need to clean the function room by 8.00 am so that it can be reset for a lunchtime function. The public toilets are usually cleaned at 10.00 am but because of the function, they need to be cleaned at 7.00 am. Early morning is always a busy time at reception, so it is best to wait until after the majority of guests who are expected to check-out have departed before cleaning this high traffic area. Table 11.4 gives an example of a daily cleaning record. It also shows that on completion of the cleaning task, the time is recorded to indicate when it was last done.

Table 11.3 △ **Cleaning schedule: public area cleaning**

AREA	CHEMICAL/ EQUIPMENT	PROTECTIVE CLOTH-ING	DAILY	WEEKLY	MON	TUE	WED	THU	FRI
Foyer			△ 6.00 am △ 11.00 am △ 3.00 pm						
Cocktail bar			△ 8.00 am	△ Clean all glass/windows	8.00 am				
Bistro			△ 9.00 am						
Pool			△ 10.00 am						
Gym			△ 11.00 am △ 4.00 pm △ 9.00 pm						
Boardroom			As instructed	△ Wax table				4.00 pm	
Hotham Room			As instructed	△ Polish brass and chrome		3.00 pm			
Hudson Room			As instructed						
Harold Room			As instructed	△ Clean glass and mirrors					4.00 pm
Bistro toilets			△ 11.00 am △ 4.00 pm △ 11.00 pm △ and other times as instructed						
Function room toilets			As instructed						
Front steps			△ 7.00 am						
Other									

Table 11.4 ▷ **Daily cleaning record: Day shift 6.00 am–2.30 pm**

THURSDAY

TASK	TIME(S)	COMMENTS	TIME COMPLETED
Foyer	▷ 6.00 am		
	▷ 11.00 am		
Cocktail bar	▷ 8.00 am		
Bistro	▷ 9.00 am		
Pool	▷ 10.00 am		
Gym	▷ 11.00 am		
Boardroom	▷		
Hotham Room	▷		
Hudson Room	▷		
Harold Room	▷		
Bistro toilets	▷ 11.00 am		
Function room toilets	▷		
Front steps	▷		

Communication with the supervisor

It is usually your supervisor who gives you the daily cleaning record and who will communicate to you any special instructions for the day. The supervisor is in regular contact with other departments who require the services of the public area cleaner, and it is your supervisor who will advise you to clean particular areas in addition to what is shown on your daily cleaning record. For example, you may have just finished cleaning the public toilets an a hour ago but your supervisor asks you to do it again due to an accident which has made the floor slippery.

At the end of your shift, when all tasks are completed, the daily cleaning record is returned to your supervisor, who arranges to have the areas checked.

SELECTING EQUIPMENT AND CHEMICALS FOR THE TASK

Selecting the right equipment and chemicals to use for each task is as important as knowing which areas to clean. As you have learned, using the wrong equipment or chemical may damage the surface and/or the equipment, and may result in the surface not being cleaned properly. It can also take too long to perform each task.

Equipment selection

The selection of equipment depends on the task to be completed. When cleaning public areas, it is not necessary to carry with you all your cleaning equipment. The one item that will be with you most of the time is the hand caddy. The other equipment should be selected according to the task. Table 11.5 lists the equipment needed for each area to be cleaned.

Chemical selection

A variety of chemicals are used throughout hospitality venues. Different chemicals perform different tasks and different surfaces respond to different chemical actions so chemical selection is usually based on what surfaces are in the venue. When used properly, chemicals will help you to clean. The main function of a chemical in the cleaning process is the breakdown of soil and stains. Water alone is not sufficient, and not always appropriate.

Table 11.5 ▷ **Areas to be cleaned and the required equipment**

AREA TO BE CLEANED	EQUIPMENT REQUIRED
Foyer	▷ dust mop ▷ mop and bucket ▷ hand caddy
External walkways/balconies	▷ broom (hard bristles) ▷ mop and bucket ▷ hose
Lounge area	▷ vacuum cleaner ▷ hand caddy
Bar	▷ vacuum cleaner ▷ mop and bucket ▷ hand caddy
Restaurant	▷ vacuum cleaner ▷ mop and bucket ▷ hand caddy
Function rooms	▷ vacuum cleaner ▷ mop and bucket (for dance floor) ▷ hand caddy
Toilets	▷ mop and bucket ▷ hand caddy
Lifts and stairways	▷ vacuum cleaner ▷ mop and bucket ▷ hand caddy
Corridors	▷ vacuum cleaner ▷ hand caddy
Pool/gym	▷ mop and bucket ▷ hand caddy ▷ hose

Chemical types

Water—acts as a rinse solution to remove excess detergent left behind by the cleaning process.

▷ **Water.** Used on its own, water acts as a rinse solution to remove excess detergent left behind after the cleaning process. It is not very effective as a cleaning agent except under high pressure (such as hosing down external walkways), so it is usually mixed with other cleaning agents.

Types of detergents— neutral, alkaline, acid.

▷ **Detergents.** Detergents are designed to loosen dirt and grime. There are several detergents: neutral, alkaline and acid. A variety is needed because of the different surfaces and stain types. For example, a neutral detergent is an all-purpose detergent used on many surfaces and suitable for light cleaning duties. An alkaline detergent is used for heavier cleaning tasks, such as cleaning some floor types. However, it is corrosive and can easily damage some surfaces. An acid detergent is used to remove certain stains such as lime build up in toilets. Acid detergents can be very harmful (they are corrosive) if used incorrectly.

Abrasive cleaners— quite aggressive due to gritty particles that loosen stains from the surface being cleaned.

▷ **Abrasive cleaners.** These are quite aggressive due to the small gritty particles that loosen stains from the surface. They come in a variety of forms including liquid, powder, cream or paste and are used for cleaning enamel and ceramic such as the bath and toilet bowl. Due to their abrasive nature, these cleaning agents should not be used on surfaces that are easily scratched, such as plastic or marble.

▷ **Disinfectants.** Most disinfectants are designed to clean the surface and kill the bacteria and germs in the one action. Disinfectants are commonly used in toilet and bathroom areas on floors, basins, walls, urinals, showers, toilet bowls and tiles—anywhere bacteria grow readily. However, it is important never to use disinfectant on food surface areas, as it will contaminate food.

▷ **Sanitisers.** Sanitisers are used to kill bacteria and are typically used after the surface has been cleaned. Sanitisers are suitable for use on food surfaces and other items that may come into direct contact with food, such as eating utensils and food preparation utensils. For this reason sanitisers, rather than disinfectants, are used in kitchens.

▷ **Solvent cleaners.** Solvent-based cleaners are specifically designed to remove heavy grease, stains and soilage build up from surfaces such as stove tops and ovens, kitchen floors and concrete areas, such as driveways. Like all chemicals, these should only be applied according to the manufacturer's instructions; solvent-based cleaners represent the greatest health risk to users of all cleaners.

Handling chemicals

Chemicals are dangerous substances that can pose major occupational health and safety risks if not handled correctly. To reduce risk and ensure workplace safety, always follow the guidelines listed below:

▷ Always read the safety instructions before use.
▷ Dilute chemicals used to perform your duties according to the manufacturer's instructions.
▷ Wear personal protective clothing, such as gloves and an eye mask.
▷ Use the right chemical for the job.
▷ Wipe up spills or drips immediately.
▷ When filling up chemical dispensers from the bulk supply, ensure the area is well ventilated. Wear gloves, an apron and eye protection.
▷ Don't use old food containers to store chemicals.
▷ Do not use chemicals left behind by guests. Dispose of them as you would workplace chemicals.

Which chemical, which surface?

As we have said, cleaning public areas requires you to clean a variety of surfaces, and use a variety of chemicals. Table 11.6 lists the most common surfaces you will clean and the most suitable chemical to use.

Treating stains

Stains on surfaces to be cleaned can be caused in numerous ways such as from spillages, heavy guest traffic, in-ground dirt and scuffmarks. Some stains are light and easy to remove, such as coffee spills on tiled areas, while others are quite difficult to remove, such as grease, blood and red wine. All stains need to be treated as soon as possible, otherwise they become difficult to remove and may leave permanent marks. The following are some of the stains you may need to treat in an accommodation venue.

▷ **Alcohol.** Alcohol spilt on carpet should be sponged immediately with a clean dry cloth to remove the excess liquid. The carpet can be shampooed later. For hard surface floors, mop up immediately.

▷ **Food.** This depends on the food type. Beetroot (on fabric or carpet) should be treated with

Table 11.6 ▷ **Common surfaces and chemicals used to clean them**

SURFACE	ITEM TO BE CLEANED	CHEMICAL
Porcelain, ceramic	toilet bowl, bath, spa, vanity unit	detergents, abrasive cleaner, disinfectants
Marble	walls, floors, tables, fire surrounds	neutral detergent, special marble cleaner
Tiles	walls, floors	neutral detergent and some abrasive cleaners
Wood	walls, ornaments, furniture	wood polish, wax, some neutral detergents
Carpet	rugs, carpet	carpet shampoo
Glass	windows, mirrors, doors	window cleaner, methylated spirits
Fabrics	furniture, curtains, soft furnishings	laundry detergents
Painted surfaces	walls, ceilings, cupboards	neutral detergents
Stainless steel	lifts, fridges, kitchen benches	neutral detergents, stainless steel cleaners, sanitisers
Concrete	balconies, external walkways	solvent cleaners

cold water and a neutral detergent before it is allowed to dry. Most other spills (hard floor surfaces) should be mopped or swept up immediately so that the food item is not ground into the floor (making it harder to clean).

▷ **Dirt.** This is frequently brought in on people's shoes and is generally unavoidable. Clean the surface as soon as possible (according to the type of surface) so that the stain does not have time to set. If the surface is carpet, let the dirt dry before vacuuming. Do not try to wash the carpet, as this will cause a permanent stain.

▷ **Blood.** Treat with cold water. Wash the surface as usual then treat with a disinfectant. Blood is classified as contaminated rubbish.

▷ **Vomit.** Mop up immediately and treat the area with disinfectant. Vomit is classified as contaminated rubbish. The acid in vomit can damage the surface if not treated immediately.

CHECKING THAT THE AREA IS SAFE

Checking that the area to clean is safe requires a brief inspection of the surrounds. You are looking for things that may cause injury to yourself or others, or damage to the equipment you are using. You are also making sure that there are no obstacles in the way to hinder the cleaning process. Checking the area means that you:

▷ inspect the area and clear away any hazardous objects
▷ erect barricades or hazard warning signs
▷ move furniture if required.

Inspecting the area

The reason for inspecting the area is to ensure that there is no rubbish or any hazardous objects in your way. If there are hazardous objects, you must remove these before you can begin cleaning. Rubbish and hazardous objects include:

▷ sharp objects
▷ needles and syringes
▷ human waste and body fluids
▷ used condoms
▷ surgical dressings
▷ general non-contaminated rubbish.

All of these items, with the exception of general rubbish, are referred to as **contaminated rubbish** (rubbish that can cause an injury or illness). Contaminated rubbish needs to be handled and disposed of carefully as it has the potential to cause harm to you or others through the transmission of bacteria and disease. When handling contaminated rubbish:

▷ always wear gloves. Never pick up any contaminated rubbish with your bare hands
▷ pick it up with tongs or a dustpan and brush
▷ always bring the bin or other disposal unit to the rubbish—never carry contaminated rubbish to a bin (this reduces the chance of spilling it or dropping it)
▷ never pass contaminated rubbish from yourself to another person
▷ thoroughly wash all equipment and protective clothing after handling contaminated rubbish.

Contaminated rubbish includes anything that may cause you harm, such as syringes, surgical dressings, used condoms and used sanitary napkins.

SHARP OBJECTS

Sharp objects include items such as broken glass, skewers, bones, crustacean shells, and knives. When handling sharp objects remove them quickly and safely.

Wrap broken glass, crustacean shells and skewers securely in newspaper before disposing of them. Carry knives by the handle, with the blade pointing downwards, beside your body.

Needles and syringes

Needles and syringes are also referred to as sharps and pose a potential major risk to your health if you receive a prick from one. It is necessary to be alert for these in public areas on the ground, behind furniture, on ledges and in rubbish bins. Never handle them directly, and dispose of them only in a sharps container. There are various types of sharps containers but the type you are most likely to find in an accommodation venue is a hard yellow secure container with an opening at the top that allows you to put the needle in while preventing you from putting your hand in. On the side of the container is usually written 'Hazardous Material'.

Should you receive a needle stick injury, wash the area thoroughly and report immediately to your supervisor.

Human waste and body fluids

Human waste and body fluids include vomit, faeces, urine, saliva, semen and blood. All of these carry the potential for bacterial contamination that can harm you, a colleague or a guest. Clean these hazards quickly, thoroughly and with great care and remember:

▷ never touch human waste directly
▷ avoid contact between your eyes and hands and the waste
▷ thoroughly mop the area, and then disinfect the area.

Used condoms

These may be found in public toilet areas, guest rooms and elsewhere and should be removed quickly using a dustpan and brush or tongs. Never directly touch the condom.

Surgical dressings

Surgical dressings include band-aids, swabs, bandages and cotton balls, any of which may be contaminated with blood or other bodily fluids. These products pose a potential bacterial contamination hazard and should not be handled directly. Wear gloves when disposing of these items and always wrap the dressings in newspaper first.

General non-contaminated rubbish

General rubbish usually includes newspapers, bottles, food wrappings and other items of a general nature. This type of rubbish is generally considered non-contaminated rubbish, as it is not likely to harm you in any way.

Erecting barricades or hazard warning signs

As you know, accommodation venues have a legal responsibility for the health and safety of their guests as well as their staff. While cleaning is taking place, barricades and hazard warning signs are used to warn people of the potential danger in the area. The dangers are likely to be a slippery floor or the equipment in use. A barricade prevents people walking through those areas where injury may occur. It also prevents people from walking through areas you have just cleaned or are trying to clean. Examples of warning signs include:

▷ slippery floor
▷ wet floor
▷ cleaning in progress.

Display hazard warning signs in easy view of the public, generally in the entrance to the area being cleaned.

Moving furniture

As part of your preparation before cleaning, you may be required to move furniture. This allows greater access to some areas as well as ease of movement while performing cleaning tasks. Examples include stacking chairs in function rooms, moving tables to one side and lifting small items of furniture off the floor. Some furniture may not even belong in the area you are to clean. Return this to its correct location before commencing cleaning.

APPLY YOUR KNOWLEDGE

Accommodation venues should be able to maintain the same high standard of presentation at any time of the day. To test if this statement is true, visit a local accommodation venue first in the morning and then again in the afternoon (it doesn't have to be on the same day) and assess the standard of cleaning in all the public areas you are able to access. As you wander about these areas consider your first, second and overall impressions:

▷ *Is it clean and tidy?*
▷ *Is there any rubbish lying around?*
▷ *Is the public area cleaner doing a thorough job (can you see one working)?*
▷ *Does the venue smell clean?*
▷ *How do you think a guest might feel about the standard of cleanliness?*
▷ *How thorough is the standard of cleaning in the public toilets?*
▷ *Would you want to stay at this venue?*

After checking your equipment and preparing it for use, you then need to prepare the area for cleaning. This involves first identifying what is to be cleaned. This information is provided either on a cleaning schedule or daily cleaning record. Alternatively, your supervisor may instruct you which tasks to complete.

When you have identified what is to be cleaned, you need to select the equipment and chemicals you need to perform each task. The selection of these items depends on the tasks to be performed. Next you need to inspect the area quickly to help you identify things that could hinder the cleaning process. The inspection process requires you to identify and remove any items that may pose a danger to you including contaminated and non-contaminated rubbish.

It is important to erect barricades and hazard warning signs to alert guests and other staff to the potential dangers in the area. Sometimes you may be required to move furniture that may potentially hinder the cleaning process before you start cleaning.

FOCUS REVIEW

▷ *There are three main tools used for identifying what needs to be cleaned. Briefly describe them. Which do you think is (are) the most effective? Why?*

▷ *Why is it important to select the right equipment and chemicals for each cleaning task?*

▷ *Why is water alone not an effective cleaning agent?*

▷ *What is the difference between a disinfectant and a sanitiser? Why is a disinfectant not suitable for use on food surfaces?*

▷ *Why is an acid detergent not suitable for all surfaces?*

▷ *What cleaning equipment is required to clean the toilet? The restaurant?*

▷ *What are the general guidelines for handling chemicals?*

▷ *Which chemicals are suitable for cleaning porcelain and ceramics?*

▷ *Why is it important to check an area to be cleaned before commencing? What are you looking for?*

▷ *Explain the difference between contaminated and non-contaminated rubbish.*

▷ *What purpose do hazard warning signs serve?*

▷ *Why might you be required to move furniture before cleaning?*

Protective clothing and equipment

Personal protective clothing and equipment (PPC&E) is clothing and equipment designed to protect you from hazards that may cause injury and illness. It can only do this if you use it correctly. Legislation requires employers to make protective clothing and equipment available to employees and to make sure they wear this clothing and use this equipment. As an employee, you are required by law to wear what your employer provides.

PPC&E—it is in everyone's best interests to use the personal protective clothing and equipment provided in the workplace.

If a particular piece of personal protective clothing is not available in the workplace, ask your employer to get it for you. It is in everyone's best interests to use the protective clothing and equipment.

In the workplace, personal protective clothing and equipment includes:

▷ **Uniform, including appropriate shoes.** Most venues stipulate what uniform is to be worn or they provide it for you. Your uniform must be worn at all times when on duty. Uniforms are designed for ease of movement and to protect you from some of the hazards that may exist while performing cleaning duties. Appropriate shoes include anything that provide good support and protect your feet (in the event that something falls on them). It is also a good idea to have shoes with a non-slip sole.

▷ **Disposable and chemical resistant gloves.** Disposable gloves are worn when performing light cleaning duties and handling hazardous material. Chemical resistant gloves should be worn when handling chemicals and performing cleaning tasks that involve the use of corrosive chemicals.

▷ **Face masks.** Face masks used by cleaners in accommodation venues are not usually the full-faced versions, but cover only your mouth and nose. A face mask should be worn when you mix chemicals, to prevent inhalation of fumes.

▷ **Hair nets.** A hair net is usually worn by kitchen staff to keep their hair from falling onto food and food surfaces, and to discourage people from touching their hair while working with food. If you are cleaning in the kitchen, you may be required to wear a hair net.

▷ **Aprons.** A thick plastic apron should be worn when mixing chemicals. Aprons are also worn in the kitchen by chefs and other kitchen staff to protect against spills and other accidents. An apron is also often part of the female housekeeping staff's uniform.

▷ **Glasses/goggles.** There are several varieties of protective eyewear that are used. The best varieties provide protection at the side of your face as well as the front. Protective eyewear is worn when mixing/handling chemicals.

▷ **Tongs.** Long-handled tongs are used to pick up contaminated rubbish. The tongs are operated similarly to a pair of scissors. Squeeze the mechanism to open the tongs and release the mechanism to clasp the item being picked up. Tongs also serve another purpose—the use of long-handled tongs prevents the need for you to bend or stretch.

The protective clothing worn does depend on the cleaning task to be undertaken. For example, specific hazards, such as handling chemicals or cleaning the toilet bowl, require you to wear gloves. When handling a syringe or surgical dressing wear gloves and pick up the item with tongs or dustpan and brush.

Hazards in public areas

Hazards— anything that may cause harm to you (or a guest).

A **hazard** is anything that may cause harm to you (or a guest). That harm occurs as a result of a workplace accident or poor work practice. Most workplace accidents are preventable. Prevention of workplace accidents begins by having an understanding of what can cause you injury and how to avoid it; and you should always take responsibility for your actions.

Hazard prevention— this begins by having an understanding of what can cause you injury and how to avoid it and by taking responsibility for your actions.

In housekeeping, hazards exist from the way you work, such as bending, lifting and stretching (manual handling), from the equipment you use, the actions of other people and from lack of training. Hazards also exist from the items you clean up, such as sharp objects, needles and syringes, human waste, chemicals and other contaminated and non-contaminated rubbish. To reduce hazards always:

▷ check your equipment before use

▷ use equipment correctly

- ▷ use chemicals safely
- ▷ wear appropriate PPC&E
- ▷ handle all rubbish with care
- ▷ observe correct manual handling techniques
- ▷ follow procedures.

SKILLS FOCUS

Personal protective clothing and equipment is designed to protect you from injury and illness. It can only do this if used correctly. The wearing of personal protective clothing is required by law. It protects the wearer against specific hazards in the workplace. PPC&E includes your uniform, disposable and chemical resistant gloves, face masks, hair nets, eye protection, tongs and aprons. You are required to wear a uniform at all times while on duty. Other pieces of PPC&E are used depending on the task to be completed.

A hazard is anything that may cause you injury. In accommodation venues many hazards exist from the way you perform your tasks, manual handling, the actions of other people and from lack of training. Hazards also exist from the items you clean up. Prevention is the best tool for reducing hazards. Being aware of the dangers will help minimise your risk exposure.

To help reduce hazards, check your equipment before use, use equipment correctly, use chemicals safely, wear and use appropriate PPC&E, handle all rubbish with care, observe correct manual handling techniques and follow procedures.

FOCUS REVIEW

- ▷ *What is the purpose of PPC&E?*
- ▷ *What is the legal requirement for personal protective clothing for employers? Employees?*
- ▷ *Why might wearing a uniform be beneficial?*
- ▷ *Why would you need to wear a hair net while cleaning the kitchen?*
- ▷ *Briefly explain the danger that exists from equipment use.*
- ▷ *What dangers exist from handling chemicals?*

Cleaning public areas

As with all cleaning, cleaning public areas aims to achieve a high standard of hygiene, to create a good impression of the venue and to maintain the quality of the fixtures, fittings and furniture. You can only do this when the right chemicals and equipment are used, procedures are followed, the cleaning schedules are observed and when you are trained correctly. A systematic approach ensures that nothing gets overlooked. Always start with high surfaces and work down (because the dust falls downward) and begin in one corner of a room and work around in a clockwise manner (so that nothing gets overlooked). Vacuuming or wet mopping is always carried out last.

Cleaning systematically:
- start with high surfaces and work down
- begin in one corner of the room and work clockwise
- vacuum or mop a floor last.

While it is not possible or practical here to provide a step-by-step procedure for every cleaning task, we have attempted to provide a better understanding of the systematic approach required to achieve cleaning objectives. All procedures assume you have checked the area for hazards, placed hazard warning signs where appropriate and moved furniture as required.

PUBLIC TOILETS

To gain an overall impression of a venue's hygiene standard, we recommend you visit the public toilets (you possibly did this for the activity Apply your Knowledge on page 324). If care and attention to detail are evident here, it's probably a safe bet that other areas in the venue also maintain a high standard of hygiene. A bad impression here is a lasting impression.

Because of the number of people who use public toilets in commercial operations, a high standard of cleaning is required to ensure they are hygienically clean. The reasons this is so important are because:

▷ waste materials including general dirt from people's bodies and human waste products contain large amounts of bacteria. Correct and hygienic cleaning prevents the spread of this bacteria

▷ the warm and moist conditions in sanitary areas provide ideal breeding grounds for bacteria

▷ leaks, blockages and smells can go undetected if proper cleaning is not carried out regularly and cause damage to the sanitation system and other parts of the building.

The cleaning of public toilets is scheduled either twice a day, every four hours, as required, or at any other time. It is difficult to be too specific about cleaning toilets (and some other public areas) because of unforeseen accidents, higher than expected trade or other unexpected occurrence.

To clean a public toilet area:

1. Check and replace hand towels.
2. Remove all rubbish and replace bin liners.
3. Wash the vanity area, tiles and surrounds. Remove all signs of dirt build up around taps and plughole. There should be no residual watermarks on tiled areas.
4. Polish all mirrors.
5. Clean toilets and surrounds, commencing with the furthermost toilet cubicle and working along the row.
6. Check individual cubical walls, doors and tiles and clean as necessary. There should be no residual watermarks on tiled areas. Replace toilet paper. Leave toilet doors open when finished.
7. For male toilets, starting with the furthermost urinal, clean each urinal as for each toilet bowl. Flush when completed. Clean outside of unit, then check the surrounding walls and clean as required.
8. For disabled toilets, clean as for steps 5 and 6 then polish handrails and other fittings. If a separate vanity unit is provided in the cubicle, clean this as for other vanity units at this time.
9. Mop the floor. Starting at the furthermost cubicle, mop the floor working backwards towards the exit door.
10. Before leaving, check that no chemicals or cleaning cloths have been left behind.
11. Remove all cleaning equipment and other signage and rubbish.

BARS

Bars are usually cleaned either after each service period or early in the morning. The extent of cleaning will vary but as a general guide:

1. Remove all glasses, bottles, ashtrays and rubbish from the bar and tables.
2. Remove all bottles and rubbish from the bar area.
3. Wash and dry all bins and replace bin liners.
4. Working around the room, and from top to bottom, wipe over all furniture and fixtures (such as picture frames, light fittings, tables, skirtings etc).
5. Polish foot rail around outside of bar.
6. Sweep then mop hard surface floor areas (behind the bar then around the outside of bar).
7. Vacuum carpeted areas.
8. Put all furniture back in place.
9. Check that all chemicals and cleaning cloths are removed from the area before departing.

RESTAURANT AND FUNCTION ROOMS

It is most likely that cleaning the restaurant will be according to a cleaning schedule. However, because of the nature of hospitality, function rooms are cleaned after every function, and this may mean that there is no function for a week, or that there are three functions in one day.

Often, the public area cleaner is required to clean the floors, windows and fixtures and fittings as food and beverage service staff performs other cleaning duties such as wiping down tables and chairs. The following is a guide:

1. Clean windows according to the schedule. Wipe window sills daily (they readily collect dust and dead insects).
2. Working from top to bottom, wipe over all fixtures, such as picture frames, railings, lamps, ornaments and skirtings.
3. Starting at one end of the room and moving backward towards the door, vacuum the restaurant/function room floor in sections (for hard floor surfaces, mop the floor). Do not vacuum if a guest is in the room.
4. As you progress, put the chairs back in place.

Most cleaning in the restaurant is carried out between service times, that is, between breakfast and lunch, and lunch and dinner. During these times, usually only a light vacuuming or light mopping may be required. However, after dinner a thorough clean is expected.

PRIVATE LOUNGE AREAS

A private lounge area is any room made available by the venue for the guest's use. It can be a television room, a reading room, or a games room or have any other number of names or uses. Most lounge areas are decorated with chairs and sofas, a few coffee tables, a reading desk and may include a bar and food service area. Cleaning of these areas is usually done first thing in the morning, and then again after lunch and dinner.

Private lounge area—any room made available by the venue for the guest's use.

If the room has several parts—lounge, bar, food service area—each should be cleaned in turn as you would for other similar areas. The following suggested procedure assumes no guests are present when cleaning takes place.

1. Switch on all lights and open curtains.
2. Pick up any rubbish and other items lying around the room, such as crockery, glassware and newspapers.

3. Remove all rubbish from the room and bar and food areas.
4. Clean bar area first if there is one.
5. Clean food service area next. Make sure all food is removed from the area before spraying chemicals.
6. Clean all furniture, fixtures and fittings, ledges, skirtings and walls and doors.
7. Sweep and mop hard floor surfaces.
8. Starting at one end of the room, and working towards the door, vacuum all exposed carpeted areas including under tables and chairs.

If guests are present, cleaning should cause as minimal disruption as possible and vacuuming is usually done at a later time (when no one is present). Vacuuming is likely to disturb the guest.

FOYERS AND PASSAGEWAYS

Keeping the foyer clean and tidy is very important because this is often where the guest gets their first visual impression of the establishment. General tidying of the foyer is ongoing whereas more thorough cleaning takes place during slow traffic times, for example, after 11.00 am and after 3.00 pm. Because the foyer cannot be closed off completely for cleaning purposes, clean small sections at a time. Follow these guidelines:

1. Pick up any items lying around, such as newspapers and magazines.
2. Straighten furniture and soft furnishings according to workplace standards.
3. Wipe over fixtures and fittings including handrails, banisters, side tables and lamps.
4. French polish hard surface floors (sweep small areas with a standard broom).
5. For high traffic areas and areas with heavy soiling, mop or vacuum as required (usually during quiet times in the foyer area).
6. Polish hard surface areas during the night. Beginning at one end, polish the floor moving up and down the section being cleaned, until the entire floor has been polished.

BALCONIES AND EXTERNAL WALKWAYS

Balconies and outside walkways attract debris such as loose papers, leaves and general dirt. This can look both untidy and be a potential hazard so these areas must be cleaned frequently—at least daily and sometimes more often. Follow this procedure:

1. Sweep area to remove dirt, leaves and other debris. Sweep in the same direction as the wind is blowing.
2. Wipe over handrails on balconies and walkways.
3. If a hose is available, hose down walkway. Be sure there are no guests nearby.
4. Use a hard bristle broom to 'sweep' excess water off walkway.
5. Depending on the surface (tiles, slate, parquetry, concrete) mop the area and place 'Slippery Floor' sign in entrance to the balcony until area is completely dry.

LIFTS

The easiest way to clean a lift is to shut it down and leave the door open. The best time to do this is late at night. If cleaning the lifts is scheduled for during the day, it may not be practical to shut it down. It will therefore be necessary to clean the lift while it is still operating. However, if a guest gets in the lift, stop cleaning until they get out again. Follow these guidelines:

1. Clean and polish the mirrors, wall panels, display units, internal doors and handrails.
2. Vacuum or mop floor.
3. Clean the external lift doors.

STAIRWELLS AND STAIRWAYS

Hospitality venues usually have public access stairways and back of house stairwells (used only by staff). As a public area cleaner you may be responsible for cleaning both. Most back of house stairs have a concrete surface. Most of the time these are only swept. If they are mopped, do not use excess water as the stairs may be in constant use. Back of house stairwells may only be cleaned weekly, while public access stairways are usually cleaned daily or twice daily, depending on the extent of traffic. Here's the procedure:

1. Clean the banisters and balustrades.
2. Sweep then mop or vacuum the stairs (depending on the floor surface) beginning at the top and working your way down.

SKILLS FOCUS

Cleaning public areas is hygienically and effectively achieved by following a systematic approach. This ensures nothing is overlooked and that the establishment's cleaning standards are met. Always start with high surfaces and work downwards and begin in one corner and work clockwise around a room. Vacuuming or wet mopping is always carried out last.

FOCUS REVIEW

▷ *Do you think a systematic approach to cleaning public areas is important? Why? Why not?*
▷ *When cleaning, why do we start at the 'top' and work 'down' and work around a room?*
▷ *What are the reasons it is important to ensure that public toilet cleaning reaches a high standard?*
▷ *When are bars usually cleaned?*
▷ *Why is the restaurant usually cleaned between service times? To what extent are they cleaned at these times?*
▷ *Why is it preferable to shut down a lift while cleaning it?*
▷ *Why should you not vacuum a public area, such as a lounge, if a guest is present?*
▷ *Why is vacuuming or mopping always carried out last?*

Disposing of garbage

Accommodation venues generate enormous quantities of garbage. Garbage is collected from guest rooms, the restaurant and bars, front office and all back of house operations. It needs to be sorted, for environmental reasons, and it needs to be stored, for convenience, hygiene and safety reasons. It then needs to be disposed of.

When cleaning public areas, it is important to remove rubbish from general public view quickly. It should be removed to the service area during your shift, and, at the end of the day, stored in the external garbage disposal area. Do not leave rubbish overnight in the service area.

When cleaning public areas remove rubbish from general public view quickly.

ENVIRONMENTAL ISSUES

To efficiently manage all this rubbish it is sorted both to enable efficient disposal and for environmental reasons. Most accommodation venues make an effort to recycle as much garbage as possible to help protect our environment, that is, to prevent pollution and save on the finite resources we have. To aid with convenience, rubbish collection agencies provide appropriate receptacles to facilitate this process.

Most accommodation venues make provision for the various types of rubbish collected, including:

▷ glass (bottles, glassware)
▷ newspapers, magazines and other paper and cardboard products
▷ contaminated rubbish (surgical dressings, needles)
▷ non-contaminated rubbish (general rubbish)
▷ chemical containers (hazardous waste).

Failing to observe correct recycling of the rubbish collected can raise both safety and hygiene issues. For example, if you place unwrapped broken glass in a plastic garbage bag with other rubbish, it is possible that the glass may break the bag and the person carrying it may cut himself or herself. If contaminated rubbish is disposed of with non-contaminated rubbish a person may be unnecessarily exposed to health and hygiene risks.

SAFETY AND HYGIENE FOR HANDLING GARBAGE

By separating garbage according to type, such as contaminated, paper, bottles etc, it reduces the likelihood of hazards such as contamination and injury. Poorly stored garbage may attract pests, is malodorous and can cause accidents. Handle garbage with care and:

▷ always wear gloves (check for holes and tears)
▷ never handle contaminated objects directly—use tongs or a dustpan and brush
▷ do not put contaminated rubbish directly into rubbish bags—wrap it in newspapers and put needles in a sharps container
▷ do not over fill rubbish bags
▷ do not put your hands into rubbish bags
▷ always wash your hands after handling rubbish
▷ carry rubbish bags away from your body
▷ separate rubbish into correct containers
▷ observe correct manual handling techniques.

DISPOSING OF CHEMICALS AND CHEMICAL CONTAINERS

Chemicals have the potential to cause harm to you and the environment if not disposed of appropriately. All hospitality venues must make provision for the disposal of chemical waste created from the cleaning process. In the housekeeping service areas there is usually a sink or gully trap for the disposal of chemical products such as those used in buckets of water to clean the floor. Use this sink also for cleaning your equipment after use.

Empty chemical containers are stored separately from other containers because of the potential to contaminate. A separate storage facility in the external waste disposal area is provided for this purpose. Never use empty chemical containers to store other chemicals or food products.

STORING GARBAGE

Before garbage is collected from the venue it needs to be stored. In most cases, garbage is collected daily from venues, but even if this were true of all venues, it still needs to be stored first. Garbage is often stored in a service area before being removed to an external area.

Most accommodation venues maintain an external area for the storage of their garbage until it is collected. This area is usually out of the public view. Your guests do not want to see or think about the garbage generated as a result of their visit.

Even though the guest may not be able to see the garbage storage area, it is important that the area is properly maintained on a daily basis. This means that the area needs to be kept clean, and secure, so in many instances, the garbage area is lockable. Keeping the area clean:

▷ prevents odours
▷ keeps pests such as rodents, birds, flies and other insects away
▷ prevents health and safety issues from arising
▷ encourages others to keep it clean.

The area is arranged so that the various types of garbage (glass, paper products, contaminated rubbish etc) can easily be sorted, stored and collected.

SKILLS FOCUS

Accommodation venues generate large quantities of garbage that must be disposed of appropriately. Correct garbage disposal considers environmental, safety and hygiene factors. Garbage needs to be stored before it is collected. It is often stored first in a service area then in an external area. The external area is usually arranged so that the various types of garbage can be easily sorted, stored and collected.

When handling rubbish of any sort, observe correct handling procedures and always wash your hands afterwards.

The recycling of garbage is encouraged. It provides convenience for the venue (particularly in terms of storing garbage) and it helps protect the environment.

FOCUS REVIEW

▷ *Is it important for hospitality establishments to be environmentally aware when disposing of their garbage? Why? Why not?*
▷ *How may contamination and injury occur as a result of handling rubbish?*
▷ *Why is the correct storage of garbage important?*
▷ *Why is it important to keep external garbage storage areas clean?*

Maintaining and storing equipment and chemicals

Maintaining your equipment in good working order and storing it appropriately are important aspects of the public areas cleaner's job. Equipment that is not properly cared for will break down and potentially cause harm to you or the surfaces it is intended to protect. It will also shorten the life span of the equipment. Even though you checked your equipment at the start of your shift, it is important to take the time to check it again as you clean it at the end of your shift, because during the day, while you were using the equipment, it may have sustained damaged.

CLEANING AND STORING EQUIPMENT

At the end of your shift all equipment and cleaning utensils are returned to the storage or service area and cleaned. Cleaning will help prolong the useful working life of the equipment and prepare it for use again. It will also give you the opportunity to spot maintenance requirements. When cleaning your equipment, remember to wear your gloves.

Storing equipment and all chemicals correctly will prevent accidents or damage to the equipment. It also means that the items are easily located next time they are required. Store rooms are usually fitted with the requisite hooks, hangers and shelving and each piece of equipment will have its own home among these. The important things to remember when storing equipment are:

▷ don't store items in walkways, doorways or passages as this could pose a potential hazard to someone
▷ prevent damage by storing equipment according to manufacturer's instructions, for example, 'store upright'
▷ store in the same place each time (so that it is easily located next time it is required. This also helps keep track of all items)
▷ store everything neatly, so that it is easy to access
▷ store everything safely
▷ store similar items together, such as brooms, mops, cleaning cloths etc
▷ store chemical containers off the floor (so they don't get kicked over).

Table 11.7 provides an easy reference guide for cleaning and storing your equipment at the end of the day.

MAINTENANCE REQUIREMENTS

If you discover faulty or damaged equipment, replace the item or report it to maintenance.

As each piece of equipment is cleaned, it can be checked again for faults and damage. Remember, faulty or damaged equipment should not be used as it may pose a safety risk to the user. If you discover faulty or damaged equipment, there are two standard options to follow: replace the item or report it to maintenance. Do not try to fix faulty items yourself and don't leave the item for someone else to use.

Report to maintenance

A damaged piece of equipment (that can be fixed) should be reported to maintenance.

Examples include frayed electrical cords, punctured suction hoses, broken mop heads, broken handles, loose attachments.

The standard procedure is to complete a maintenance form or, if these are not used, make a note in the housekeeping diary or maintenance diary. It is important to note down the nature of

Table 11.7 ▷ **Cleaning and storing equipment**

EQUIPMENT	CLEANING AND STORAGE
Vacuum cleaner	▷ empty or replace dust bag ▷ wipe over body ▷ dismantle according to manufacturer's requirements ▷ wrap electrical cord according to manufacturer's instructions ▷ store upright, on the floor, against a wall
Brooms and dust mop	▷ remove lint from heads ▷ wash dust mop head at least monthly ▷ store upright, together
Dust pan and brush	▷ wash and dry dust pan ▷ remove excess lint from brush ▷ store together (with brooms)
Mop and bucket	▷ wash mop head in hot soapy water. Rinse thoroughly and stand upright to dry ▷ empty bucket and wash and dry thoroughly ▷ store upside down (excess water in buckets will corrode steel types)
Cleaning brushes	▷ clean toilet brush and scrubbing brush in a disinfectant solution then rinse thoroughly ▷ hang to dry ▷ remove excess lint from fabric brush ▷ store in hand caddy
Chemical dispensers	▷ wipe over with clean damp cloth
Hand caddy	▷ empty of contents and clean thoroughly ▷ replace chemical dispensers and cleaned brushes
Cleaning cloths	▷ send to laundry to be cleaned ▷ if washed in service area, hang to dry over sink
Personal protective clothing	▷ rinse gloves, aprons and goggles under hot running water ▷ hang to dry over sink

the problem, the date, how it was damaged, and your name. Take the item to the maintenance department with the maintenance request form or advise maintenance of the item's location.

Replace the item

Not all damaged equipment need be reported to the maintenance department. Some items, such as a broken toilet brush, ripped personal protective clothing or a bucket with a hole in it, will need to be replaced. The usual procedure for replacing small items is to requisition the item from the housekeeping department where a supply of such items is usually maintained.

SKILLS FOCUS

Caring for your equipment is an important part of your job. It helps sustain the life of the equipment, prevents injury to you and damage to the surfaces it is intended to clean. It also means that the item is easy to locate next time it is required and gives you an opportunity to spot maintenance issues. Faulty and damaged equipment should not be used but replaced or fixed.

Items that can be fixed should be reported to maintenance. The usual procedure is to complete a maintenance request form or enter the details in the maintenance diary. Items that need to be replaced should be requisitioned from housekeeping.

FOCUS REVIEW

▷ Why is it important to care for your equipment?

▷ Why is it a good idea to check your equipment again at the end of your shift?

▷ There are several important things to remember about storing your equipment. What are they?

▷ What is the correct procedure for caring for mops and buckets? Vacuum cleaner? Chemical dispensers?

▷ What are the two options available for managing faulty or damaged items?

PUT YOUR KNOWLEDGE TO THE TEST

Robyn has spent a few days working with the public area cleaner, Nathan, and learning how to use cleaning equipment and how to clean the various surfaces in the Grand Central Hotel. Nathan has been a public area cleaner for a number of years and is very familiar with his equipment and how to use it. He is methodical when checking his equipment and stocking up his chemicals, he follows procedures and uses his PPC&E. Nathan regularly gets angry and frustrated, when, after his rostered days off, he returns to work and finds that no one seems to take as much care as he does in maintaining the equipment or filling up the chemicals to his liking. He explains to Robyn the importance of these tasks.

During his holidays, Robyn is to take over Nathan's duties. She is conscious of doing a good job and keeping the public areas up to Nathan's high standard. She has performed all the cleaning tasks on numerous occasions, has a copy of all the relevant procedures and knows where everything is kept. Her supervisor has given her the daily cleaning schedule and advised Robyn of the groups arriving today.

1. It's 8.00 am and Robyn is starting her shift. She checks the vacuum cleaner and notices the cord is frayed and the vacuum dust bag full. What should Robyn do? What might happen if Robyn did not do this?

2. Maree, Robyn's supervisor, lets Robyn know that there is a large group checking out between 8.30 am and 10.00 am and another group is due to check in at 2.00 pm. When should Robyn clean the foyer? Why at this time? Should Robyn plan to vacuum at 10.00 am? Why or why not?

3. At 10.00 am Bryce, the concierge, calls because a guest has been ill in the public toilets. Robyn was busy vacuuming the restaurant and tells Bryce she was scheduled to clean the toilets at 10.30 am so will clean it up then. Do you agree with Robyn's response? Why or why not? What would you do?

4. Robyn works an eight-hour day. In this time she must clean two sets of public toilets (men's and women's), each taking 40 minutes and twice vacuum the restaurant and bar, each also taking 40 minutes. She must check her equipment and restock her chemicals at the start and finish of her shift (10 minutes each time), clean the foyer (30 minutes) and two function rooms (30 minutes each room). Robyn also needs to clean the three lifts (10 minutes each) and deal with any cleaning emergencies that may arise. Prepare a daily cleaning schedule for Robyn. Remember to consider high guest traffic times in all areas.

5. Make a list of equipment Robyn should take with her when she cleans each of the public areas. The bar floor is carpeted and the actual bar is marble with a mirrored backing wall. The function rooms and the restaurant have carpeted floors. The foyer has a tiled floor.

6. When Robyn is cleaning the foyer she notices mud on the floor. What chemicals and equipment will she need to clean this up?

Preparing Rooms for Guests

LEARNING OUTCOMES

On completion of this chapter, you will be able to:

▷ describe the activities and tasks undertaken at the commencement of the shift;

▷ correctly set up cleaning equipment required for room cleaning;

▷ correctly identify and access rooms requiring servicing;

▷ make beds and clean guest rooms;

▷ describe the procedures for replacing room amenities, reporting maintenance, resetting room equipment, reporting lost and found and managing pests in guest rooms;

▷ follow procedures for cleaning stay overs and checking vacant clean rooms;

▷ manage unusual or suspicious events;

▷ demonstrate how to clean and store equipment.

Introduction

Guests check-in and out of accommodation venues every day of the year. Some guests stay one night while others stay for days, even weeks. Whether staying overnight or longer, accommodation venues clean guest rooms daily. What may differ between venues is the extent (standard) to which the guest rooms are cleaned.

At the beginning of the last chapter you learned that one of the first things guests will do when they arrive at a venue is form an opinion about the standard of cleanliness. Guests may not consciously look for signs of poor cleaning standards, but will notice them just the same because they have expectations of the venue based on their own experiences and knowledge and the venue's star rating. This expectation of a high cleaning standard is even more important in the actual guest room.

Your guests will expect that the sheets on the bed are fresh, the bathroom hygienic, that the fixtures and fittings sparkle and that there are no signs of anyone else having previously used the room. Big expectations! Housekeeping's role is to ensure that all of these expectations are met.

Activities undertaken at the commencement of the shift

Room attendants clean guest rooms. At the beginning of the shift there are a number of tasks to be completed before you start cleaning guest rooms. In most venues you are required to:

▷ attend a briefing
▷ collect a room allocation sheet
▷ collect a master key
▷ collect a hand caddy and cleaning chemicals
▷ set up cleaning equipment.

THE BRIEFING

Briefing—a short informal meeting when important information about the day's activities is passed on to the room attendants.

A briefing is a short informal meeting (of about 10 minutes' duration) when important information about the day's events is passed onto the room attendants and public area cleaners. It is common for the housekeeping department to hold a briefing (usually conducted by the executive housekeeper or a supervisor) at the commencement of each shift. In some venues the laundry attendants and the housepersons may also attend.

The briefing is an opportunity for housekeeping staff to meet and discuss any problems (such as equipment failure) or follow up on issues raised at previous briefings. The briefing is also usually the time when cleaning staff receives:

▷ the room allocation sheet
▷ information about special events occurring in the establishment
▷ details about VIPs arriving
▷ details about other tasks cleaners may be required to perform
▷ their master key.

THE ROOM ALLOCATION SHEET

Every morning the housekeeping department receives a copy of the room status report from reception. In Chapter 5 you learned that the room status report lists the status of each room according to the number of guests (rooms) who have checked out or are due to check out, which guests are staying another night and the number of guests due to arrive. An example of this is shown in Figure 12.1. From this information (room status report) the executive housekeeper is able to determine the number and type of rooms each room attendant is required to clean for that shift.

Productivity

Productivity refers to the number of staff required to clean the rooms that need to be cleaned. The room status and the room type affect productivity. Different room types and different room status require different cleaning times. For example, a **departure** may take 30 minutes to clean while a **stay over** may take only 20 minutes to clean. A suite is likely to take longer to clean than a double room. Thus, the number of rooms to be cleaned in an eight-hour shift by one person will depend on the room status (departure or stay over) and room type (standard room or suite).

Figure 12.1 ▷ **Room status report**

Fidelio Version 7 for Windows

5 Housekeeping Rooms Status Report*

****Occupied—Dirty****

| D BKN 107 | D STW 108 | D BKN 127 | D BKN 131 | D BKN 137 | D BKN 138 | D BKN 207 | TTW 315 |

****Vacant—Clean****

SUI 101	DTW 102	DTW 103	DTW 104	DTW 105	BTW 106	SKN 109	SUI 110	DKN 111	SKN 112
STW 113 A	BKN 114	BTW 115	DKN 116	DKN 117 A	DKN 118	DKN 119	DKN 120	BTW 121	BTW 122
BTW 123	BTW 124	DTW 125	DKN 126	STW 128	SKN 129	BTW 130	SKN 132	STW 133	BTW 134
DKN 135 A	DTW 136	BKN 139	BKN 140	STW 141	STW 142	STW 143	STW 144	DTW 145	DKN 146
BTW 147	BKN 148	SKN 149	STW 150	SUI 151	SKN 152	SKN 153	SKN 154 A	DTW 155	DKN 156
BTW 157	STW 158	SKN 159	SUI 160	SUI 201 A	DTW 202	DTW 203	DTW 204	DKN 205	BTW 206
STW 208	SKN 209	SUI 210	DKN 211	SKN 212	STW 213	BKN 214	BTW 215	DTW 216	DKN 217
DKN 218	DKN 219	DKN 220	BTW 221	BTW 222	BTW 223	BTW 224	DTW 225	DKN 226	BKN 227
STW 228	SKN 229	BTW 230	BKN 231	SKN 232	STW 233	BTW 234	DKN 235	DTW 236	BKN 237
BKN 238	BKN 239	BKN 240	STW 241	STW 242	STW 243	STW 244	DTW 245	DKN 246	BTW 247
BKN 248	SKN 249	STW 250	SUI 251	SKN 252	SKN 253	SKN 254	DTW 255	DKN 256	BTW 257
STW 258	SKN 259	SUI 260	TSU 301	TKN 303	TKN 304	TKN 305	TKN 306	TKN 307	TKN 308
TSU 310	TSU 311	TKN 313	TKN 314	TTW 316	TTW 317	TTW 318	TTW 319	TTW 320	

****Due Out****

| BKN 107 | STW 108 | BKN 127 | BKN 131 | BKN 137 | BKN 138 | BKN 207 |

****Assigned****

| V BKN 114 | V DKN 118 | V DTW 136 | V DTW 155 | V DTW 202 |

C—Check Out/Dirty, D—Due Out, A—Assigned, V—Vacant, B—Blocked, L—Sleep, K—Skip

In most venues, a departure is cleaned more thoroughly than a stay over. However, some establishments clean all rooms every day as if they were departures. The extent to which a room is cleaned depends on the standards in place at each venue.

Room attendants are allocated a number of rooms to clean during their shift (according to productivity requirements). The rooms to be cleaned are indicated on the room allocation sheet (also referred to as a room assignment list).

The room allocation sheet lists rooms by room number as either:

Departure—the guest has already checked out.

▷ departure–the guest has checked out of the room and the room needs cleaning
▷ stay over–the guest is staying another night and the room needs cleaning
▷ due out–the guest is due to depart today and the room needs cleaning.

Stay over—the guest is staying another night.

Depending on the front office software used by the venue, the room allocation sheet may also list:

Due out—the guest is due to depart today but has not yet checked out.

▷ the guest's name
▷ VIP status
▷ special requests or conditions regarding room cleaning, such as 'Not before 10.00 am', 'Late departure', 'Early arrival'.

An example of a room allocation list is shown in Figure 12.2.

THE MASTER KEY

Master key—a key opening several locks, each of which has their own individual key.

A master key is a single key that opens several locks (guest rooms and storage areas) each of which has also its own separate key. Possession of a master key means that you do not need to carry a separate key to access every room. In some venues the master key will only give you access to the floor you are working on.

Figure 12.2 ▷ **Room allocation sheet**

Date of printing:
Thursday, November 23, 2000 11:59

Fidelio Version 7 for Windows

Rooms Allocation Sheets
Exclude Parlour Rooms/Summary Room Type—All Rooms
By Room Attendants/Printing Style 1

Room Attendant 1

Room		Status	Credit	Name	VIP	Arrival	Departure	Time	Persons
107	∧	DI	20	Harris		15/11/00	16/11/00		1
108	∧	DI	20	Mr/Sambora		15/11/00	16/11/00		1
127	∧	DI	20	Mr/Hinkley		15/11/00	16/11/00		1
131	∧	DI	20	Mr/Johnson		15/11/00	16/11/00		1
137	∧	DI	20	Kelleher		15/11/00	16/11/00		1
138	∧	DI	20	Mrs/Livingston		15/11/00	16/11/00		1
207	∧	DI	20	Mr/Higgins	2	15/11/00	16/11/00		1
315		DI	15	Yerondais		15/11/00	18/11/00		2

Notes: ∧ Departure   § Arrival Expected   @ Sleep & Skip   * Sharer

Possession of a master key raises several security issues. Because the master key gives you access to several rooms, it must be kept secure at all times. While you have a master key in your possession, you are responsible for the safety and security of the key and of the personal belongings of the guest to whose room you have access.

COLLECT HAND CADDY AND CLEANING CHEMICALS

The hand caddy holds the chemicals, cleaning cloths and cleaning brushes. You need to collect your caddy at the start of each shift and return it at the end of your shift. The caddies are usually kept in housekeeping for:

▷ safety—this prevents misuse or theft of the chemicals or other items
▷ convenience—a central location makes it easier to locate the hand caddy each time one is required. Also, the chemical spray bottles are usually filled from the bulk supply kept in housekeeping.

Depending on the venue, you may be required to top up your chemicals at either the beginning or the end of your shift.

Cleaning chemicals

In the last chapter you learned that there are a number of different surfaces to be cleaned:

▷ floors (tiles, wood, marble)
▷ furniture (fabric, wood, stainless steel, plastic)
▷ fixtures and fittings (wood, glass, painted surfaces, brass, chrome, ceramic, porcelain).

Because different chemicals perform different functions and because of the type of surfaces to be cleaned and extent of soilage, different chemicals are used in the room cleaning process. Each surface must be cleaned to meet the standards of the venue and also to protect the item being cleaned. Types and use of chemical varieties were discussed in Chapter 11.

The chemicals used by room attendants are often colour coded. These help you to quickly and easily identify the right chemical to use for each cleaning task. Also, most of your chemicals will serve more than one purpose:

▷ all purpose cleaner (detergent)—this cleans most surfaces, such as tables, bed heads, fixtures and fittings
▷ abrasive cleaner/disinfectant (detergent) (such as a cream cleanser)—this cleans baths, toilet bowls, vanity units
▷ glass cleaner (detergent)—used for cleaning windows and mirrors
▷ air freshener.

SETTING UP CLEANING EQUIPMENT

Not unlike cleaning public areas, you need a range of different equipment to perform the various cleaning tasks. All equipment needs to be checked (to ensure they are safe to use) and set up before you use them. The equipment you need includes:

▷ trolley
▷ vacuum cleaner
▷ mop and bucket
▷ cleaning brushes
▷ cleaning cloths
▷ feather duster.

With the exception of the trolley and feather duster, the set up and preparation for use of each of these was discussed in the last chapter. Remember to select the right equipment for each cleaning task and use each piece of equipment as it was intended.

The trolley

Trolleys are used to give you easy access to all your cleaning needs, as well as **room supplies** and **room amenities**. The trolley is a mobile store room that carries limited supplies of each of the items you need to service guest rooms. Because it is on wheels, the trolley is easy to manoeuvre. It has separate compartments for storing the various room supplies and amenities, which makes them easy to locate and safely stock.

A store room, service area or pantry is usually located on each floor of the venue. Most of your equipment and supplies are kept here. For example, in the store room you are likely to find:

▷ the trolley
▷ room supplies
▷ room amenities
▷ cleaning equipment (vacuum cleaner, mop and bucket)
▷ rollaway bed
▷ spare blankets and pillows.

Some venues now use hand baskets to carry room amenities because trolleys have the potential to cause physical damage to the premises and can look untidy. The main restraint of the basket is that you need to return to the store area to collect fresh linen for every room.

*Room amenities—*those items supplied by the venue for the guest's consumption or use, such as shampoo, conditioner, soap, bottled water, pen and paper, matches and tea and coffee.

*Room supplies—*those items supplied by the venue for the guest to use while using the room, such as towelling, cups and saucers, bathrobes and drinking glasses.

Preparing your trolley

It is in the store room that the trolley is stocked and other equipment is prepared for use. Before using your trolley:

▷ Check that it works properly. For example, check that the wheels turn correctly, handles are in place, and shelving is secure. If it is faulty, report it to maintenance to fix. A faulty trolley can create a safety hazard to you or a guest, or cause physical damage to the premises.
▷ On the top shelf neatly stock sufficient amenities to meet your needs.
▷ On the lower two shelves neatly stock a range of linen (sheets, pillow slips, doona covers, bath towels, bath mats, face washers, hand towels). The amount and type needed depends on the number and type of rooms to be cleaned.
▷ At one end of the trolley attach a garbage bag.
▷ At the other end of the trolley attach a linen bag (for dirty linen).

You will also need to stock a supply of tissues, toilet rolls and garbage bags.

Your trolley should be kept neat, tidy and safe at all times. It is used in a public area, which means your guests can see it. It is also easier to locate each item when required when the trolley is kept neat. An overloaded or poorly stacked trolley is an unsafe trolley; items may fall and injure you or a guest. And a trolley that is too heavy to pull or push may be difficult to manoeuvre and cause back strain or other injuries. Figure 12.3 shows a diagram of a trolley and indicates where each of your cleaning requirements is stored.

Room amenities and supplies

No two venues provide the exact same supplies and amenities. It is also common (and sometimes confusing) to find that in the one venue, room supplies and amenities may vary depending on the room type.

Figure 12.3 ▷ **Room attendant's trolley**

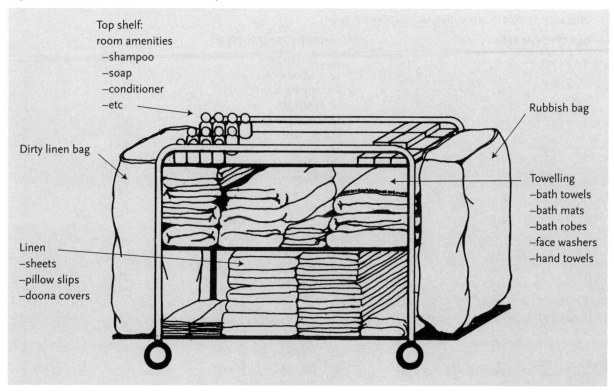

Table 12.1 lists examples of amenities venues are likely to supply in their guest rooms and where in the guest room they are likely to be located. You will need a supply of all these items on your trolley.

How much of what?

The quantity of supplies and amenities placed in each room depends on the number of sleeping spaces. A **sleeping space** is the bedding arrangement and how many people can be accommodated in that room. For example, a double (double bed) or twin (two single beds) room has sleeping spaces for two people. A suite may have sleeping spaces for four people (a queen size bed and a double sofa bed). It does not matter how many people actually stay in the room (up to the maximum sleeping spaces) but it does matter that sufficient amenities are provided for the maximum number of people who may stay in that room.

The feather duster

The feather duster is used to remove light dry particles of dust from a range of surfaces particularly in hard to reach places. The dust is dispersed onto the floor, which you later vacuum. The duster needs to be maintained in good working order so that is does not damage (scratch) the surfaces being cleaned and is effective. Store your feather duster either on the trolley or in the hand caddy.

Sleeping spaces—the bedding arrangement and how many people can be accommodated in that room.

Compendium—a handbook or information folder. It contains information about the venue, such as facilities and services available, operating times, contact numbers, etc. It often also contains local area information and stationery items such as letterhead and envelopes.

Table 12.1 ▷ Room amenities and location in room

GUEST ROOM AREA	AMENITIES AND SUPPLIES
Bathroom	▷ shampoo
	▷ conditioner
	▷ bubble bath
	▷ bath gel
	▷ shower cap
	▷ moisturiser
	▷ soap
	▷ sanitary pads
	▷ razor
	▷ drinking glasses
Bedroom	▷ ashtray and matches
	▷ stationery items (pen, paper)
	▷ tea, coffee, sugar, milk
	▷ sewing kit
	▷ laundry bags and laundry list
	▷ clothes brush
	▷ shoe shine kit
	▷ clothes hangers
	▷ bathrobes and slippers
	▷ room service menu
	▷ breakfast menu
	▷ Do Not Disturb signs
	▷ newspaper signs
	▷ make up my room signs
	▷ compendium inserts

SKILLS FOCUS

At the beginning of the your shift, you need to complete a number of tasks: attend the briefing, collect the room allocation sheet, master key and hand caddy, and set up your equipment.

A briefing is a short informal meeting providing important information about the day's activities. The room allocation sheet is a list of the rooms (and room status) you are required to clean for that shift. The master key gives you access to a number of predetermined rooms.

Cleaning equipment is set up prior to room cleaning. Your trolley is a mobile store room and is used to give you easy access to the room supplies and amenities and cleaning utensils needed. The trolley should be stocked in an orderly and safe manner to reduce the likelihood of accidents.

A range of room amenities is supplied in the guest room and the number of sleeping spaces determines the quantity provided. Sleeping spaces refers to the bedding arrangement in a guest room and how many people can be accommodated in that room.

▷ What activities must the room attendant undertake before cleaning rooms?
▷ What is a briefing? Who attends the briefing? Do you think the briefing is useful? Why? Why not?
▷ What information is contained on the room allocation sheet?
▷ What two factors most influence how long a room will take to clean?
▷ Where does the information on the room allocation sheet originate?
▷ What is the difference between a 'due out' and a 'departure'?
▷ What is a 'stay over'?
▷ How does the room status affect productivity?
▷ What is the hand caddy and what is it used for?
▷ There are usually four main chemicals the room attendant needs. What are they and on what types of surfaces would you use them?
▷ What is the difference between room supplies and room amenities?
▷ Describe the process for stocking the trolley.
▷ Why is it important to keep your trolley neat, tidy and safe?
▷ What determines the number of amenities placed in each guest room?
▷ What does 'sleeping spaces' mean?
▷ What is a compendium? What information might it contain?

Accessing guest rooms

The order in which you clean guest rooms depends on the room status. Check the room status before attempting to gain access to a guest room to minimise the likelihood of disturbing a guest. When you know the room status, you can access the room according to the procedure in that venue.

THE ORDER OF ROOM CLEANING

Departures are cleaned first, followed by stay overs, and then due outs. The reason for this is that it reduces the likelihood of disturbing guests not yet ready to check out and those guests staying another night (who may not want to be disturbed as early as you start work). By cleaning rooms in this order—departures, stay overs, due outs—you will use your time most efficiently (you are not hanging around waiting for someone to leave or losing time by disturbing people too early). The first departure rooms to be cleaned are those that are required for a guest arriving that day.

Order of cleaning
1. Departures
2. Stay overs
3. Due outs.

GAINING ACCESS

All rooms, irrespective of the status, are accessed following the same procedure:

1. Position your trolley and cleaning equipment immediately outside the room to be accessed. This alerts others to your presence and makes it easy for you to access what you need.
2. Knock on the door and announce that you are from 'Housekeeping'. (This lets the guest know who is at their door. Do this even if you are certain the guest has departed.)
3. Wait a few seconds to give the guest an opportunity to answer the door. If there is no response, knock again, wait briefly and then open the door slightly (using your master key)

to let yourself into the room. If the guest answers the door, ask when it would be a suitable time to clean the room.

4. As you open the door and step into the room, again say, 'Housekeeping' (in case a guest is in the room but did not hear you knock). If the guest is in the room but asleep or in the bathroom, quietly leave.

Dos and dont's

This procedure for accessing rooms is straightforward but there are a few other things to remember:

▷ don't block doorways or passages with the trolley. Guests and colleagues need to use the passageway
▷ don't take the trolley into the room with you. It is too cumbersome
▷ don't use your master key to knock on the door. It may damage the door
▷ don't assume the guest has departed. Following procedure will reduce the likelihood of disturbing the guest
▷ don't access rooms with a 'do not disturb' sign. These guests want privacy
▷ do take the basket into the room with you if you use one. These are less cumbersome than trolleys and therefore won't be in the way
▷ do take your hand caddy into the room with you. You need ready access to the items contained therein.

'Do Not Disturb' signs

A Do Not Disturb (DND) sign hanging on the outside of the guest room door means just that! Whenever you see a Do Not Disturb sign, respect the guest's wishes. Make a note of the room number and time and come back later. Clean the room when the guest removes the sign.

If, near the end of your shift the sign has still to be removed, most venues write a brief note to the guest explaining that they were unable to access their room today (because of the DND sign) and if they would like their room cleaned, to call housekeeping. The note is slipped under the guest's door.

Guests in the room

Even when you have correctly accessed a room, there are times when a guest may be present. For example, the person may not yet be ready to check-out or is a stay over. The way you handle this situation (when attempting to gain access) depends on whether the guest is a departure, a due out, or a stay over.

Departure and due out

If the guest is departing today but is obviously not yet ready to leave the room:

▷ access the room following the standard procedure
▷ apologise for disturbing them and explain you will come back later. For example, 'Good morning Mr Shoebridge. I'm sorry I disturbed you. I'll come back later.'
▷ leave the room, closing the door behind you.

Stay over

When you access a stay over, the guest will indicate whether they want you to clean now, while they are in the room, or want you to come back later.

▷ access the room following the standard procedure

▷ apologise for disturbing them

▷ ask whether they would like you to clean the room now or come back later. For example, 'Good morning Mrs Goldberg, I'm sorry I disturbed you. Would you like me to clean your room now or come back later?'

If, while you are cleaning a stay over, and the guest is not in the room but returns while you are cleaning, offer to come back later.

GUEST ROOM SECURITY

You play an important role in the security of the guest's belongings and the fixtures and fittings in guest rooms. Having gained access to a guest room, whether an occupied or vacant room, never leave the room unattended while the door is open. If you need to leave the room, lock the door behind you. This will ensure that the room and its contents are safe.

Access to a room should be limited to the guest registered to that room, yourself while cleaning it, and your supervisor while checking it. However, the guest should only be allowed access to their room with their own key. In other words, if a guest asks you to let them into their room with your master key, you must politely decline. Explain to the guest that you are unable to do this and refer them to reception for a key. The reason for this is that you may not know the guest asking to be let in to a room. And even if you do know that this is that guest's room, decline to give them access because this ensures consistency. Usually a policy exists that stipulates you cannot give access to anyone.

There may be other occasions when you need to be security conscious:

> Guest room security:
> • never leave room unattended
> • restrict access to key holders when they have a key with them.

▷ A guest follows you into another guest's room while you are cleaning, for example, to ask you a question. Escort the guest back out into the corridor before answering the question.

▷ You may be suspicious about a person hanging around the corridor or trying to get into a room while you are cleaning. Report the incident immediately to your supervisor or the security department.

▷ Although your trolley is left in the corridor, be alert to people attempting to remove items from it.

SKILLS FOCUS

Guest rooms are cleaned in a particular order according to the room status—departures, stay overs, then due outs—and accessed following a four-step procedure: position your trolley outside the room, knock on the door and announce yourself, open the door, again announce yourself as you enter the room.

A Do Not Disturb signs indicate that the guest is in the room but does not wish to be disturbed. You need to note this room number down and come later when the sign has been removed. When a guest is the room you want to clean, offer to come back later.

You play an important role in guest room security. It is your responsibility to ensure the guest's belongings and the room fixtures and fittings are kept safe and secure while cleaning is in progress. If you need to leave the guest room, lock the door behind you. Refusing access to anyone without a key, remaining vigilant to activities of others on that floor and reporting suspicious people are also your security responsibilities.

FOCUS REVIEW

▷ There are four steps to accessing the guest room. What is the point of each step?
▷ What is meant by the 'order of cleaning'?
▷ Why is it important to correctly follow the order of cleaning?
▷ What is a DND sign? What should you do if a room you need to clean has a DND sign on the door?
▷ What should you do if a guest is in the room when you want to gain access?
▷ What role do room attendants play in security?
▷ What action should you take if you notice a suspicious looking person hanging around the floor where you are cleaning?

Making beds and cleaning rooms

All guest rooms need cleaning and are cleaned to a predetermined standard (set by the establishment). Procedures are usually put in place for each of the tasks you need to perform. However, procedures may vary according to the star rating or type of venue, the expected productivity level, the training you receive and the equipment available. All room cleaning procedures should ensure that:

▷ safe work practices are observed
▷ nothing is overlooked
▷ presentation standards of the venue are met
▷ productivity levels are maintained
▷ maintenance is minimised.

SAFE WORK PRACTICES

The way in which you work has the potential to cause injury from accidents. You are particularly exposed because of the extent to which you bend, stretch, lift and pull objects. Accidents happen because of:

▷ poor work practices (not wearing gloves when handling chemicals, poor manual handling)
▷ failing to follow procedures (taking shortcuts)
▷ careless behaviours, or
▷ the actions of others.

All accommodation venues (indeed all workplaces) are required by law to provide a safe working environment. This means that the venue must have systems and procedures in place that help keep you safe. You also have a legal obligation to take reasonable care for your own and your colleagues' welfare. To help you do this:

▷ use equipment as intended
▷ don't use faulty equipment
▷ wear protective clothing
▷ observe correct manual handling
▷ don't leave objects where someone may trip over them
▷ follow procedures.

NOTHING IS OVERLOOKED

To ensure nothing is overlooked rooms are cleaned:

▷ from top to bottom
▷ clockwise (or anti-clockwise) around the room
▷ following the procedures in place.

An organised sequence also helps ensure presentation and productivity standards are maintained.

PRESENTATION STANDARDS

Presentation standards refer to the way in which a room looks. The room must look attractive and be functional. The bed is usually the central feature of the room and fixtures and fittings are arranged and designed for comfort and aesthetic appeal (those things that make the room look attractive). In other words, the room must look pleasant, smell clean and be welcoming.

Most venues have standardised room designs (all double rooms look the same, all suites look the same). What may vary are the fixtures and fittings but the layout will be similar. All rooms are likely to contain the following:

▷ bed (various sizes)
▷ bedside table and bedside lamp
▷ desk or table or fitted dressing table
▷ seating (chairs, couch)
▷ clothes storage
▷ mirror
▷ lamp
▷ rubbish bin
▷ pictures (on the walls) or other decorations
▷ telephone
▷ television
▷ air conditioning.

What is also likely to vary between rooms is the number of each item but there will always be a standard way in which the room is presented. For example, the furniture is always placed in the same location in each room.

Another important aspect of cleaning is achieving a high standard of hygiene. It is important to control the spread of bacteria by cleaning (using the correct chemical and equipment), which in turn reduces the likelihood of disease or infection, unpleasant odours or damage to surfaces.

PRODUCTIVITY STANDARDS

As we mentioned earlier, productivity standards refer to the number of rooms to be cleaned over a period of time, by one person. For example, if you are rostered to work an eight-hour shift with half an hour for lunch, you have 7.5 hours (450 minutes) allotted to cleaning. If a double room stay over takes 20 minutes to clean, then it is expected that one room attendant can clean three double rooms per hour (22.5 rooms, rounded down to 22 rooms in a 7.5 hour shift). If a departure suite takes 45 minutes to clean, then in a 7.5 hour shift, ten departure suites should be cleaned.

REDUCING MAINTENANCE

Cleaning carefully and regularly helps reduce maintenance problems. If fixtures and fittings are maintained properly there is less likelihood of damage occurring and this in turn will reduce replacement and maintenance costs.

Cleaning techniques

The cleaning of rooms requires different cleaning techniques or applications. This is because of the different surfaces, chemicals used and amount of soilage. The types of cleaning you are required to do includes:

▷ **Dusting**—dusting removes build up of dust but redistributes it to another place (usually the floor).

▷ **Damp dusting**—a dampened cleaning cloth (with water and a chemical) removes dust and soil build up. It doesn't redistribute the dust as the dust is collected on the damp cloth. A different cloth should be used for each chemical used (depending on the surface).

▷ **Scrubbing**—applying a water and chemical solution with a scrubbing brush to remove soil build up on some surfaces, such as the toilet bowl.

▷ **Sweeping**—using a broom to collect the dirt and dust on a hard surface floor such as tiles, marble and wood.

▷ **Mopping**—for cleaning (removing soilage) hard surface floors applying water and a suitable chemical agent.

▷ **Vacuuming**—removal of dust and particles from carpeted areas.

▷ **Polishing**—usually done after cleaning. Apply a chemical and then remove with a clean cloth or rub with a clean cloth only.

▷ **Brushing**—removing dust and particles from fabrics such as drapes and furniture.

▷ **Washing**—either submerging in a water and chemical solution or applying the solution directly onto the surface then rinsing.

Cleaning procedures

As you know, by following procedures nothing gets overlooked and standards are maintained. The following is one room cleaning procedure for a room with a status of departure. And while it lists the steps to follow, it does not provide specific detail on *how* to perform each task.

After accessing the guest room the procedure for cleaning is:

1. Switch on the lights.
2. Open the curtains. This helps you see all surfaces to be cleaned.
3. Put the hand caddy in the bathroom.
4. Collect all rubbish (from the bedroom and the bathroom) and remove it to the trolley. Remove any room service trays or trolleys from the room and place them out of the way in the corridor.
5. Place all used glassware, crockery and cutlery that belong in the room in the bathroom (or kitchen) sink.
6. Clean the rubbish bins and replace bin liners.
7. Strip and remake the bed.
8. Clean all surfaces in the bedroom (top down—dusting and damp dusting) including:
   ▷ furniture (tables, chairs, bedhead, bedside table)
   ▷ fixtures and fittings (lamps and lamp shades, windows and window sills, mirrors, dressers, telephone, inside drawers, door knobs, skirtings, walls).
9. Check that the room equipment is working by switching on and off and replace in usual position.
10. Return all equipment and in-room facilities to the correct position.
11. Brush down fabrics on furniture.
12. Check cupboards and drawers are empty (guests often leave personal items) or have in them what the venue provides. Close all cupboard doors and drawers.
13. Check room supplies and amenities and replace as required (according to the establishment's standards and the number of sleeping places in the room).
14. Arrange soft furnishings according to standard procedure.
15. Wash all dishes and arrange according to standard procedure.
16. Clean the kitchen (in self-contained apartments and some suites a small kitchen is built into the room design).
17. Clean the bathroom.

18. Vacuum the carpeted floors.
19. Arrange curtains and drapes according to standard procedures.
20. Spray room with air freshener.
21. Return all cleaning equipment and chemicals to your trolley.
22. Inspect the room a final time to make sure nothing has been overlooked or any cleaning items left behind.
23. Switch off all lights at the door and lock the door behind you.
24. Mark the room as cleaned on your room allocation sheet.

MAKING BEDS

Making beds, like all tasks, follows a standard procedure, ensuring a consistency in the way a bed is made and in presentation. Some rooms may have more than one bed and in some instances different sized beds.

Strip the bed

1. Pull the bed out from the wall or bedhead (most beds are on castors).
2. Remove the bed covers (blankets and bedspread or doona) from the bed and place on a chair.
3. Remove the sheets and pillowcases and bundle them in the centre of the bed (place the pillows on top of the bed covers).
4. Remove the dirty linen to the trolley (and bring back required clean linen).
5. Check the mattress and mattress protector for stains and damage.
6. Check under the bed for rubbish and guest's belongings.

   If there is more than one bed in the room, repeat the process for all other beds.

Checking for stains and damage

As you strip the bed, check for stains and damage on the bed covers, pillows, mattress and mattress protector. Damaged items need to be replaced. In some instances, these items are sent to the laundry to be mended (pillows, blankets, doonas and bedspreads). Bed bases and mattresses may need to be replaced altogether. Report to maintenance damage such as broken bed legs or a damaged mattress, so that they can be mended.

   If the bed covers, mattress protector, or pillows are stained, send them to the laundry to be cleaned. If the damaged items or soiled items cannot be fixed or replaced immediately, the room status must be recorded as out-of-order so that the front office knows not to check a guest into that room.

Remake the bed

Although there may be variations in the bed making process between establishments, following the standard procedure will minimise the likelihood of injury (from bending and stretching) and ensure consistency. To save time (and unnecessary walking), start making the bed on one side and complete every step on that side before moving around to the other side.

1. Spread the bottom sheet (right side up) over the mattress first. The sheet should hang evenly on both sides and at each end.
2. Beginning at the top corner on one side and working around the bed, tuck the bottom sheet under the mattress using a **mitre fold** at the sides.

3. Spread the top sheet on the bed, wrong side up. Straighten the sheet so that the edge is level with the mattress at the top end. The sheet should hang evenly on each side.
4. Place blankets over the top sheet. Straighten the blankets so that the top end is 20 centimetres lower than the top sheet. The sides of the blankets should hang evenly over the mattress.
5. Tuck in the sheet and the blankets under the mattress together at the base of the bed.
6. At the top of the bed, fold back the top sheet over the blankets, and then fold over the sheet and blankets together 20 centimetres.
7. Mitre fold the top sheet and blankets together at the bottom side of the bed then tuck in along one side of the bed; then repeat for the other side.
8. Centre the bedspread over the bed and straighten ensuring an even hang on both sides.
9. Fold the bedspread down from the head of the bed, leaving enough room to cover the pillows.
10. Put pillowcases on the pillows. Neatly arrange the pillows side by side with open ends facing inwards on the bed at the top end and fold the top end of the bedspread back over the pillows.
11. Push the bed back into place against the wall or bedhead.

Mitring a corner

The term 'mitring' refers to the fold used at the sides of the bed when tucking in the blankets and sheets (it is also sometimes referred to as 'hospital corners'). Figure 12.4 is a step-by-step diagram of how you mitre a corner. A mitre fold gives a smooth, professional finish and holds the sheets and blankets firmly in place.

Doonas

Many venues now use doonas in place of blankets and bedspreads. One advantage of this is that there is less physical work required in making the bed. Another advantage is that it can save time. However, a disadvantage of doonas is that they are more likely to harbour mites and dust than blankets. For this reason, doonas must be regularly changed and washed. They must also be checked regularly for stains and damage and replaced as required. The doona cover should always be changed when cleaning a departure.

CLEANING THE KITCHEN

As we said earlier, many accommodation venues offer self-contained rooms or suites that include a kitchen. Some will have a full range of kitchen facilities while others may only have a microwave oven and refrigerator. We also mentioned earlier that achieving a high standard of hygiene is important in room cleaning. This is particularly true of cleaning kitchens and bathrooms.

When cleaning the kitchen, if the guest has left behind any food or beverage items, these must be thrown away and not recycled or consumed (for health and hygiene reasons). To clean the kitchen:

1. Half fill the sink with warm soapy water.
2. Empty the fridge of any foodstuffs and dispose of them.
3. Wash and dry all the dishes and return them to their correct place.
4. Check each cupboard and drawer (for foodstuffs) and clean them.
5. If there is a microwave check that it works then clean it.
6. If there is a stove check that each element works then clean it.

Figure 12.4 ▷ **Mitring a corner**

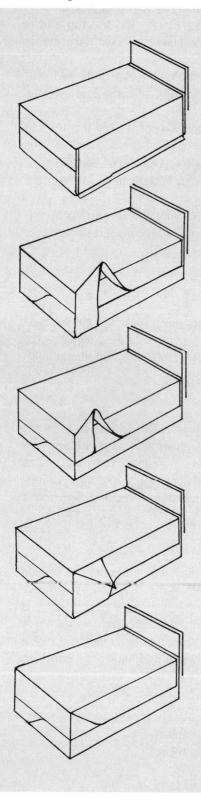

1. Tuck in the sheets and blankets along the sides and foot of the mattress.

2. At the side of the bed, take the loose end of the sheet and blanket, about 30 centimetres from the corner, and pull it straight out, forming a flap.

3. Tuck in the free part of the sheet.

4. Pull the flap out towards you and down over the side of the bed.

5. Drop the flap down and tuck in under the mattress ensuring the corner is smooth and snug.

7. If there is an oven check that it works, remove each of the oven racks and wash them in the sink then clean the rest of the oven.
8. Clean the fridge. Remove each of the racks and wash them then clean first the inside of the fridge then the outside. Do not turn the fridge off.
9. Check the freezer compartment and clean as required. Re-fill the ice cube containers and return to the freezer.
10. Wipe over all cupboard surfaces, bench tops, and walls and skirtings.
11. Empty the sink of water and wipe over with a dry clean cloth. Polish the taps and stainless steel.
12. Mop the floor. Start at the far end of the kitchen and work backwards toward the door.
13. Switch off the lights and close the door.

CLEANING THE BATHROOM

If there isn't a kitchen, the bathroom is cleaned after cleaning the rest of the guest room. Again, hygiene plays an important role. One of the most common complaints about the cleaning standard of a guest room relates to the bathroom. Specifically:

▷ hair strands (for example, in the shower and on the floor)
▷ soap scum (around the taps and basin and on the soap dish)
▷ mould and mildew (on grouting between tiles, particularly in corners)
▷ water marks (on tiles, the shower screen and mirrors)
▷ grime build up (in nozzles and taps, particularly in spa baths, and on the back of the cistern, which also poses a health hazard).

Each of these problems has the potential to allow for bacterial growth, which can become odorous or cause other problems such as the spread of disease. Each of these problems is likely also to lead to guest complaints.

Because you are using strong chemicals in a relatively confined space, work with the door open, extractor fan on and wear gloves. To clean the bathroom:

1. If the room does not have a kitchen, wash all crockery, cutlery and glassware in the hand basin and dry with a clean cloth before replacing.
2. Remove all dirty towelling to the trolley (bring back required towelling and bathroom amenities).
3. Clean the shower recess and shower screen.
4. Clean the bath and spa, including the taps and plug hole inside and out.
5. Clean the toilet bowl and surrounds.
6. Clean the mirrors.
7. Clean the bathroom door, walls and skirtings and any other fittings or fixtures.
8. Clean the vanity unit and surrounding areas.
9. Polish all fixtures and fittings, such as the soap dish, towel hooks, and hand rails.
10. Replace all amenities (do not recycle used amenities) and arrange according to the venue's standards.
11. Replace toilet paper and tissues.
12. Replace all towelling.
13. Mop the floor. Begin in the far corner of the room and work back towards the door.
14. Check over the bathroom to make sure all tasks are complete and no chemicals or cleaning cloths have been left behind.
15. Switch off the lights. The bathroom door is usually left ajar.

VACUUMING THE FLOOR

Vacuuming the floor of the guest room is usually the last task to be completed. The reason for this is that while cleaning other areas (dusting, wiping, polishing) dust and dirt will have fallen onto the floor and now need to be removed. There are a few important points to remember when vacuuming:

▷ don't vacuum wet areas (such as the bathroom floor)
▷ don't run over the cord as you pull the vacuum along
▷ don't pull the vacuum along by the cord
▷ don't use a damaged vacuum
▷ don't bump into furniture or walls with the vacuum (it will cause damage).

When vacuuming the guest room:

1. Start in the far corner of the room and work in sections around the room.
2. Vacuum all exposed areas of carpet, including under furniture.
3. Vacuum each corner of the room and along the edges of the wall.
4. As each section of the room is vacuumed, arrange the furniture according to the venue's standards.

SKILLS FOCUS

Guest rooms are cleaned to a predetermined standard set by each venue. Procedures are established to help ensure safe work practices are observed, nothing is overlooked, presentation standards are met, productivity levels achieved and maintenance reduced.

There are various techniques used in servicing guest rooms including dusting, damp dusting, scrubbing, polishing, sweeping, mopping, washing and brushing.

When beds are made they are checked for stains and damage. Clean the rest of the guest room after making the bed then clean the kitchen, if there is one, followed by the bathroom. The last cleaning task you will perform is the vacuuming.

FOCUS REVIEW

▷ *Who determines the procedure for servicing guest rooms? Why do you think the procedure may vary between venues?*
▷ *What are the four main causes of accidents while cleaning guest rooms? Give an example of each.*
▷ *How can risks in the workplace be reduced?*
▷ *What is meant by presentation standards?*
▷ *What are productivity standards?*
▷ *Describe the cleaning techniques used in servicing rooms.*
▷ *What should you do with damaged and soiled bedding?*
▷ *What is 'mitring' a corner? Why is it used?*
▷ *When cleaning the kitchen, why should you dispose of all food left behind by guests?*
▷ *List the most common complaints guests have about the cleaning standard in the bathroom.*
▷ *What should you not do when vacuuming?*

Replacing room amenities and reporting maintenance

Each venue has different standards in the arrangement, type and quality of the room supplies and amenities used in the guest rooms. Table 12.2 provides an indication of the most likely 'home' for each of the room supplies and amenities. Each item must be replaced in its home to maintain standards and consistency. Remember too that most room supplies should match the number of sleeping places.

REPORTING MAINTENANCE

Another responsibility you have while cleaning guest rooms is the reporting of faulty and damaged equipment and facilities. The items that are most frequently found to be faulty or damaged are the:

▷ television
▷ air conditioning
▷ iron and board
▷ kettle

Table 12.2 ▷ **Replacing room amenities and supplies**

LOCATION	AMENITIES AND SUPPLIES
Bedside table	▷ Bible
	▷ telephone books
	▷ note pad and paper and pen
	▷ telephone
	▷ lamp
	▷ compendium
	▷ stationery items
	▷ ashtray and matches (smoking rooms only)
Wardrobe	▷ hangers
	▷ bath robe and slippers
	▷ iron and ironing board
	▷ spare blankets and pillows
Drawer	▷ laundry bags and laundry list
	▷ clothes brush
	▷ shoe shine kit
	▷ sewing kit
Bathroom vanity	▷ bathroom amenities (shampoo, soap etc)
	▷ hair dryer
	▷ towelling
	▷ tissues/toilet paper
Cupboard	▷ tea and coffee making facilities
	▷ mini-bar
Back of door	▷ breakfast menu
	▷ do not disturb sign
	▷ emergency procedures
	▷ Innkeepers Act

▷ light fittings and light globes
▷ fixtures and fittings (table, chair, lamp, mirror, pictures, etc)
▷ glassware and crockery.

With the exception of broken glassware and crockery, which you can replace from the supply kept in the store room, all maintenance issues are reported to the maintenance department while you are still in the guest room. These items need to be fixed or replaced immediately otherwise a guest cannot use the room. When maintenance issues arise:

1. Call maintenance from the guest room. Advise them of the room number and the nature of the problem.
2. Keep a written record (room number, nature of the problem, date, time it was reported to maintenance).
3. Advise your supervisor (who will follow up the problem to make sure it is fixed).

RESETTING EQUIPMENT

Part of the room attendant's responsibility while cleaning rooms is to reset the equipment and facilities in the guest room. Table 12.3 lists the most common items that need to be reset and how to do it.

LOST AND FOUND

Guests frequently leave behind personal items such as jewellery and clothing. The most common places you will find these items are in cupboards and drawers and under the bed. These items are referred to as 'lost and found' or 'lost property'. You need to report any guest

Table 12.3 ▷ **Resetting equipment**

EQUIPMENT	PROCEDURE
Lights	▷ Turn all lights on when entering the room and off when leaving.
	▷ Note any lights not working and report to maintenance.
Television	▷ Switch on and turn to preferred channel (for example, some venues have their own channel with a welcoming message displayed when switched on. It may also provide information about how to use the television and the services available in the venue, such as regular channel viewing, on-demand videos, Internet access, and check-out facility), then switch off.
Air conditioning	▷ If the air conditioning unit has been used, switch it off and leave the temperature gauge at 0°C.
Alarm clock	▷ Switch alarm off (no one likes to wake up to an alarm set by the previous guest).
	▷ Don't disconnect it from the power.
Hair dryer	▷ Replace in the cradle provided (if there is one) or neatly wrap the cord around the handle after disconnecting from the power supply.
Kettle	▷ If it has been used, switch on to check that it is working, then switch off again.
	▷ Unplug it from the power source and empty the water.
	▷ Wrap the cord around the kettle and replace it in the cupboard.
Iron and ironing board	▷ Disconnect the iron and allow to cool.
	▷ Empty the iron of water and wrap the cord neatly around the handle.
	▷ Store in the wardrobe (or other designated area).
	▷ Dismantle the ironing board and store upright in the wardrobe (or other designated area).

items you find in the room and hand them in to housekeeping (or to the security department in some venues) for safekeeping. Where housekeeping is responsible for lost and found:

1. Secure the item by returning immediately to the housekeeping office so that it can be safely locked away. Do not leave lost and found items on the trolley (as they may be stolen) and do not put them in your uniform pocket (as you may forget that they are there).
2. Report the item to your supervisor.
3. Record the details in the lost and found book. The following information is recorded:
   ▷ room number
   ▷ description of item(s) found
   ▷ where the item was found (room number and location in the room)
   ▷ date and time found
   ▷ finder's name.
4. Number the item (that corresponds with the record in the lost and found book) and place the item in the lost and found safe or cupboard.

   If the item isn't claimed within three months, you have the legal right to keep it.

PESTS IN GUEST ROOMS

A wide range of pests finds their way into guest rooms, and while a high standard of cleaning reduces the likelihood of pest infestation, pests still manage to get in, in a number of ways:

▷ windows
▷ ventilation systems
▷ poorly sealed or damaged walls
▷ accidentally by a guest.

Pests are more frequently found in rooms that have not been used for a while and in locations that are more prone to infestation, such as in the tropics (because of the hot and damp weather). Pests include:

▷ flies
▷ ants
▷ cockroaches
▷ silverfish
▷ moths
▷ spiders
▷ beetles
▷ mice and rats
▷ fleas.

Controlling pests

Of course, restricting access is the best way to prevent pest infestations but this is not always possible (even when the venue is suitably designed and built). Pest control is also achieved by a high standard of cleaning, early detection and identification, and destruction and elimination.

While cleaning rooms, be alert to signs of pests (such as droppings, webs, small holes in fabrics) and take steps to manage the situation. For example, if pests (or signs of their existence) are found they must be removed immediately by:

▷ using a pesticide

▷ using a pest control agent, or

▷ cleaning and disinfecting the area.

A pest control agent is usually only necessary for the removal of mice, rats and cockroaches. Pesticides should kill most other pests, but these can leave strong smells and stains on furniture.

SKILLS FOCUS

The arrangement, types and quality of room supplies and amenities vary between venues. Each room supply and amenity has a 'home' and must be replaced in its 'home' to maintain standards and consistency.

During the servicing of a guest room, you are responsible for identifying equipment faults and damage, which need to be reported to maintenance.

Equipment supplied in the guest room, such as the television, alarm clock and air conditioning unit, needs to be reset and returned to the usual location.

Lost and found are those items left behind by guests when they have vacated the room. Secure the item and record the details in the lost and found book, usually located in housekeeping.

Pests, although not common, are sometimes found in guest rooms, particularly rooms that have not been occupied for some time. Pests get in a number of ways and must be controlled by preventing access, using a pesticide, using a pest control agent or cleaning and disinfecting the area.

FOCUS REVIEW

▷ *Why is it important to replace all amenities and supplies in the same place each time?*

▷ *What are the most frequently damaged or faulty pieces of guest room equipment?*

▷ *What is the procedure for reporting maintenance issues?*

▷ *Why do you think it is important to reset equipment?*

▷ *Describe the procedure for managing lost and found items.*

▷ *What should you not do with lost and found items?*

▷ *What pests are most likely to be found in your town? What factors, if any, do you think influences infestations of these pests?*

▷ *How can you control pests in the guest rooms?*

Cleaning stay overs

So far this chapter has focused on cleaning departures. And as we said earlier, many venues clean all guest rooms every day as though they were departures. However, there are a few variations to observe when cleaning stay overs. The most important thing to remember when cleaning a stay over is that the guest's personal belongings are in the room and you are responsible for their safety and security. Never touch a guest's belongings and if the guest is in the room while you are cleaning, try to minimise the disruption to that person's privacy.

WHEN THE GUEST IS NOT IN THE ROOM

If the guest is not in the room, access the room in the usual manner and:

▷ don't leave the room unattended with the door open
▷ don't touch any personal belongings (although on occasion you may need to put them neatly out of the way while you finish a task, such as making the bed)
▷ don't touch any personal papers or use equipment (such as a computer)
▷ don't throw anything away that is not in the rubbish bin (except empty food and beverage containers)
▷ if the iron and ironing board have been used, leave them set up.

Bed linen is not necessarily changed every day for a stay over. It may be changed every second or third day or as required.

WHEN THE GUEST IS IN THE ROOM

Sometimes the guest is in the room while you clean, and at other times may return while you are cleaning. The guest expects to be disturbed for as short as time as possible. Proceed to clean as you would if the guest was absent. Remember, however, that there are things you should *not* do if the guest is present, including:

▷ switching lights on or off or opening or closing curtains
▷ touching the guest's personal belongings (unless they need to be moved to perform a task, such as making the bed. Ask the guest for permission)
▷ spraying air freshener
▷ standing around chatting or disturbing the guest
▷ checking or resetting any equipment. If anything in the room does not work or is damaged, the guest will tell you
▷ dismantling the iron and ironing board.

You should, however, ask the guest if they mind you vacuuming and if you are told not to bother cleaning something, do not do it.

Checking vacant clean rooms

Guest rooms that have not been occupied (vacant clean) for some time need to be checked for cleanliness when a guest is due to be registered to that room. This is because over time, dust will build up and there is the possibility that pests have made a home in these rooms. By checking the room, you are making sure it meets the establishment's usual high standards of cleanliness.

WHAT TO CHECK

It won't be necessary to completely clean the room again or change the linen, but make sure to check:

▷ dust and grime build up on surfaces (clean as required)
▷ signs of pests (remove as necessary)
▷ lights and equipment are working
▷ supplies and amenities are adequate and in the right place.

Managing unusual or suspicious events

What takes place in the privacy of a guest room is the guest's business. However, there may be times when cleaning the room that you notice something unusual or suspicious such as:

▷ people behaving strangely or suspiciously
▷ serious damage (smashed furniture)
▷ illicit items such as guns or drugs
▷ large quantities of valuables (money, jewellery)
▷ contaminated rubbish (syringes, surgical dressings)
▷ animals
▷ excessive bodily fluids (for example, blood).

For safety and security reasons you must report these events. If you are suspicious about anything, leave the room immediately and lock the door. Call your supervisor and, if the venue has a security department, contact them as well.

Because in some instances it may be necessary to contact the police, and in other instances it will be considered a breach of the guest's privacy:

▷ do not touch anything
▷ do not attempt to clean around items
▷ do not discuss what you have seen with other staff or guests.

Your supervisor will tell you when you can return to clean the room and may ask you to complete an incident report.

CONTAMINATED RUBBISH

Of all the items listed, contaminated rubbish is the most commonly experienced event. Contaminated rubbish includes anything that may cause you harm, such as syringes, surgical dressings, used condoms and used sanitary napkins.

Handling contaminated rubbish

With the exception of syringes, all contaminated rubbish is disposed of in a yellow contamination waste bag. Do not place any of these items in the non-contaminated rubbish disposal unit as this may then contaminate that rubbish. When handling contaminated rubbish:

▷ Check the contaminated rubbish bag for holes and tears.
▷ Wear gloves.
▷ Take the bag to the rubbish, not the rubbish to the bag.
▷ Use a dustpan and brush or tongs to pick the item up.
▷ Never place your hands in the bin.

After disposing of the items, clean the area with disinfectant or bleach, and always wash your hands, gloves and the utensils used to pick up the objects.

Contaminated rubbish should be disposed of in the external contaminated rubbish bin. Do not put it in the usual rubbish bin.

Handling syringes

Syringes are most often left in the bin but may also be found in the bedding, on the floor or in the toilet. Because of the potential risk involved from a needlestick injury, when stripping the bed, don't shake the linen or covers vigorously. Be conscious of items discarded on the floor. When handling syringes:

▷ always wear gloves
▷ pick up the item with a dust pan and brush or tongs
▷ place the syringe in a sharps container (yellow hard plastic puncture-proof container that is designed to allow you to put the item in without removing the lid)
▷ bring the container to the syringe, not the syringe to the container
▷ never pass a syringe from one person to another.

In some venues, each trolley will have its own sharps container. If this is not the case, you will need to contact the housekeeping office and ask someone to bring you a container. If a proper sharps container is not available, place the syringe in a glass jar and seal it. The jar should be disposed of in the external contaminated waste bin. Do not put it in the usual rubbish bin.

Syringes should be reported to the supervisor. Remember however, that where several syringes are found, it is unlikely that security need to be involved. Syringes are used every day for medical purposes (such as diabetes) and their presence therefore does not always involve the use of illegal drugs.

Cleaning up bodily fluids

Bodily fluids have the potential to cause you harm. When cleaning up bodily fluids remember:

▷ wear protective gloves and eye wear (to avoid splashes)
▷ use a mop (or cleaning cloth) and a solution of hot water and bleach to clean the fluid

▷ wash all protective clothing and cleaning utensils with hot water and a disinfectant after use.

If it is a large blood spill, you should not attempt to clean it but contact the supervisor. It is possible that contract cleaners will need to be called to clean the spill.

SKILLS FOCUS

Unusual or suspicious events are those things that cause concern about safety and security. These events should be reported to your supervisor. If you are suspicious about anything, leave the room immediately and lock the door, contact your supervisor and do not touch anything in the room or attempt to clean up around the items. Do not discuss what you have seen with other staff or colleagues.

Contaminated rubbish is any rubbish that has the potential to cause you or others harm. All contaminated rubbish is disposed of separately from non-contaminated rubbish. Follow procedures for handling contaminated rubbish for your own safety.

Syringes or sharps are disposed of in a puncture-proof container. Handle sharps with care; wear gloves and pick up the needle with a dustpan and brush or tongs. Take the container to the syringe, not the syringe to the container.

Bodily fluids include vomit, urine, faeces, semen and blood, all of which have the potential to cause harm. Remember to wear protective clothing when cleaning up bodily fluids and wash thoroughly afterwards.

FOCUS REVIEW

▷ *What is meant by an unusual or suspicious event? Give three examples.*
▷ *What is the first thing you should do if you are suspicious about something? Then what should you do?*
▷ *How should you handle contaminated rubbish? Why should it not be mixed with non-contaminated rubbish?*
▷ *What are 'sharps'?*
▷ *What is the procedure for handling sharps? How should you dispose of them?*
▷ *How should you dispose of a syringe if a yellow sharps container is not available?*
▷ *Why should you wear eye protection when cleaning up bodily fluids?*

Activities undertaken at the end of the shift

After cleaning all your allocated rooms, there are a number of tasks still to be completed:

▷ return your trolley and spare supplies to store room
▷ clean and store all of your equipment
▷ dispose of rubbish collected during your shift (in the external waste disposal area)
▷ replenish your store room stocks
▷ return the hand caddy, master key and room allocation sheet to housekeeping.

RETURN YOUR TROLLEY AND SUPPLIES

When the trolley is returned to the store room, it is usually restocked in readiness for the next day. However, the problem with stocking your trolley at the end of the day rather than at the beginning, is that at the end of your shift there may not be sufficient supplies yet available. Only restock your trolley if there are sufficient supplies.

Remaining supplies are never unloaded from the trolley. At the end of the shift:

▷ wipe down your trolley with a damp cloth
▷ straighten (and restock) supplies
▷ remove all rubbish and soiled linen.

CLEAN AND STORE EQUIPMENT

All of the equipment used during your shift needs to be cleaned and correctly stored, as you are not the only person who may use cleaning equipment. Equipment must be cleaned because:

▷ during the day it becomes scuffed and dirty
▷ it helps keep it in good working order
▷ it helps you to spot maintenance problems.

At the end of your shift:

▷ wash out the mop and bucket
▷ empty the hand caddy and clean it
▷ wipe over the chemical containers (to remove residues and drips) with a damp cloth (then replace in the hand caddy). Rinse off the scrubbing brushes and disinfect the toilet brush
▷ empty the vacuum bag (and put it back in the vacuum)
▷ wipe over the vacuum cleaner with a damp cloth
▷ check all equipment for faults and report faults to maintenance
▷ send the cleaning cloths to the laundry with the dirty linen (a houseperson may be responsible for collecting dirty linen from the store area)
▷ rinse out and correctly store any personal protective clothing (such as gloves) used
▷ clean any other cleaning utensils used.

After cleaning the equipment, return it to its correct storage area. The correct storage area for most of equipment, such as your trolley and vacuum cleaner, is the service area (store room) on each floor. It is important to store equipment correctly because it:

▷ prevents loss
▷ prevents theft
▷ prevents damage
▷ keeps it in good working order
▷ prevents tripping accidents from occurring
▷ makes it easier to locate each item (when needed).

DISPOSING OF RUBBISH

The rubbish bag (which is full by the end of the day) is removed from the trolley and tied off. Place the bag beside the service lift for the houseperson to collect. In some venues, you may be responsible for removing the rubbish to the external rubbish area. Never leave rubbish stored inside overnight.

REPLENISHING ROOM AMENITIES AND SUPPLIES

Bulk supplies of room amenities and supplies are usually kept in the main housekeeping area. And as you know, small quantities are kept in the store room on each floor. When your supplies in the store room get low, you will need to re-order the items needed (except for linen and towels as the houseperson is usually responsible for re-stocking these).

The systems in place vary and may require you to re-order weekly, monthly, as required or in some other time frame. You may be required to complete a **requisition form** that indicates the amount and types of supplies you need, or simply take what you need as you need it. In either case, it is your responsibility to keep an eye on stock levels to avoid having to order supplies halfway through your shift.

Requisition form—standard form for reordering stock requirements. It requires you to list stock items required, quantity, delivery details, date and name of person ordering.

RETURNING TO HOUSEKEEPING

When everything else is complete, you need to return to housekeeping to hand in your room allocation sheet and master key to the supervisor and return the hand caddy. This time also gives you an opportunity to communicate to your supervisor any relevant events or issues that occurred during your shift such as following up on maintenance, any difficulties you experienced, faulty equipment or pests found in a room.

SKILLS FOCUS

At the end of the day, when all rooms have been cleaned, a number of tasks need completing. The trolley is returned to the store room, tidied and cleaned, and the rubbish and dirty linen removed. All equipment is cleaned and correctly stored. The rubbish and linen are placed next to the service lift ready for collection or removed to the external rubbish area. You need to check your stock of room supplies and re-order items as you need them. A procedure is usually in place to manage restocking room supplies and amenities. Finally, you need to return your room allocation sheet, master key and hand caddy to the housekeeping office. This provides you with the opportunity to discuss the day's events with your supervisor.

FOCUS REVIEW

▷ *What five things must the room attendant do after cleaning all his or her allocated rooms? Briefly explain what is involved for each task.*
▷ *Why is the equipment cleaned at the end of each shift?*
▷ *Describe the main reasons for correctly storing equipment.*
▷ *Whose responsibility is it to restock room supplies and amenities in the store room on each floor? How is this achieved?*
▷ *What is a requisition form?*
▷ *What should you return to the supervisor at the end of the shift?*

PUT YOUR KNOWLEDGE TO THE TEST

Robyn was assigned 12 double room and two suite departures to clean. It had taken longer than planned to set up her trolley because it was left in an awful state. Whoever had used it last had left it in a mess; all the room amenities were mixed up and there was dirty linen still on it from yesterday. To make matters worse, her allocated rooms were spread over two floors. This meant that either she had to try to take the trolley in the lift down to the next floor, or hope the trolley on that floor was in a better state.

Arriving at the first suite, Robyn was pleased to see that the departing guest had made hardly any mess. She knew she could save time here. The floor looked OK so may be she wouldn't need to vacuum. She also noticed that this guest had left some fruit in the fridge. That would do for her lunch! Robyn managed to clean six of the double rooms as well as the suite before going to lunch. However, she was late getting back from lunch and as she rushed into the room she tripped over the linen she'd left in the doorway.

Robyn managed to finish on time. This was important, as she knew that as this was the last stage of her traineeship, her final assessment rested on her success in housekeeping.

1. Assuming a double room departure takes 30 minutes to clean and a suite departure takes 45 minutes to clean, how long will it take Robyn to clean all her allocated rooms?

2. How should the trolley be left at the end of a shift? Who is responsible for this?

3. If Robyn doesn't follow all room cleaning procedures (such as vacuuming the floor) what impact do you suppose this may have on the guest's expectations of the venue? What other problems might arise if procedures are not adhered to?

4. What should Robyn have done with the fruit she found in the fridge? Why?

5. How might Robyn's accident been prevented? What is the proper procedure for handling dirty linen?

6. What tasks must Robyn complete at the end of shift?

CHAPTER 1

Dealing with Conflict Situations

LEARNING OUTCOMES

At this end of this chapter you will be able to:

▷ define conflict and recognise the different types and causes of conflict;

▷ resolve conflict situations within the scope of your responsibility;

▷ describe the various conflict resolution techniques;

▷ demonstrate effective communication skills in managing conflict;

▷ implement conflict resolutions;

▷ respond to customer complaints sensitively, courteously and discreetly;

▷ turn complaints into opportunities.

Introduction

Most people tend to view conflict in a negative light: something to be avoided, something they would rather not deal with, something that is someone else's problem. And while conflict has the potential to be negative, it can also be positive. You have a responsibility to manage conflict in your work environment. Your responsibility is to turn conflict into positive opportunities for the establishment, colleagues and yourself.

The concept of conflict as being negative and something to be avoided, is a traditional view and assumes that all conflict is harmful to the organisation. If conflict remains unresolved or is ineffectively resolved, then certainly it can be harmful. However, a more current view of conflict is that it is both inevitable and potentially positive for the organisation. Conflict is seen as inevitable because no two people can agree on absolutely everything, and positive because it presents opportunities to improve the way in which we do things.

Conflict, when handled appropriately, can also lead to improved working relationships and customer service, increased productivity and opportunities for you to develop your interpersonal skills. The conflicts that present themselves on a daily basis in a hospitality environment can leave you feeling either exhausted and frustrated, or challenged and relieved. The skills you have to manage conflict will determine the outcome resulting from the experience.

In this chapter we aim to give you the skills and knowledge necessary to manage conflict to achieve a positive result every time.

What is conflict?

Conflict—any situation that leads to a disagreement between two or more individuals.

Conflict in the workplace is any situation that leads to disagreement between two or more individuals. The disagreement usually flows from a misunderstanding about people's expectations and needs. Conflict in the workplace can occur between colleagues, staff and guests and staff and management. What is important about conflict is that it must be identified before it can be resolved.

Types of conflict

When we think of conflict, we usually only associate it with a disagreement between two people. However, there are in fact several types of conflict for you to be aware of and these are briefly discussed below.

CONFLICT WITHIN YOURSELF

This type of conflict arises when you are 'in two minds' about something. It could be as simple as having difficulty in prioritising the completion of one task versus another. Or the conflict could be more serious and have ethical or legal implications that may impact on others, such as taking the credit for work you didn't do or not employing someone because of your racial bias.

CONFLICT BETWEEN YOU AND A COLLEAGUE

In the workplace, conflict between colleagues is a frequent and common occurrence. It is important to recognise that it exists and to learn how to manage it. Unresolved conflict between colleagues can be disruptive and potentially damaging to the standard of service delivered and the well-being of the establishment. (It can also upset other colleagues.) Many of these conflicts are role related, while others are personality related (also referred to as the 'cause of conflict').

Types of conflict
• within yourself
• between colleagues
• with a guest
• between organisations.

CONFLICT BETWEEN YOU AND A GUEST

Another frequent occurrence of conflict is that between staff and a guest. As a service industry, hospitality venues are concerned with providing their guests with the best possible service within their means. However, many venues frequently find they have failed to meet the guest's expectation of service, and this results in an area of conflict.

CONFLICT BETWEEN ORGANISATIONS

Conflict between organisations arises because each organisation is striving to achieve its own goals (of profit, success, growth, market share) and this may sometimes be to the detriment of similar organisations. Perhaps a more appropriate term for this type of conflict is competition. This form of conflict (competition) is generally perceived as good, as it contributes to the well-being of the economy (and will therefore benefit your guests). It can lead to the development of better services and products and often, lower prices.

Throughout this chapter we will focus on conflict between you and your colleagues and you and your guests.

Causes of conflict

Now that you know the different types of conflict and that conflict is generally considered a form of misunderstanding, it is important that you be aware of the main causes of conflict that arise in the workplace.

▷ **Different expectations.** Throughout this book we have talked about guests' expectations of you and your venue's products and services. Failing to meet guests' expectations may lead to conflict.

▷ **Communication barriers.** Conflict between colleagues as well as guests may result from communication barriers. Communication barriers are those things that get in the way of effective communication, for example, language differences, an inability to express the proper meaning of information, poor communication due to poor systems or failure to follow procedure, poor listening skills, preconceived ideas, poor verbal skills, prejudices and a range of other factors.

▷ **Motivation factors.** In Chapter 2, we talked about the factors that motivate you to do something. These factors vary between each of us and will influence how we respond to others. For example, if in the workplace you believe you are highly motivated to do a good job and your colleague is not as motivated as you are, then this could lead to conflict.

▷ **Cultural values.** The many people you encounter in hospitality come from an enormous cultural pool. Our cultural influences lead us to behave and react in certain ways. For example, cultural values will influence work ethics, how we respond to people from other

Communication barriers—those things that get in the way of effective communication such as language, poor listening skills, preconceived ideas, poor verbal skills and prejudices.

Causes of
conflict:
• misunder-
  standings
• different
  expectations
• communica-
  tion barriers
• motivation
  factors
• cultural values
• personality
• safety and
  security
  issues
• organisational
  structure
• change.

cultures and how we deal with authority. It is not reasonable to expect that we all would behave in the same way or react to the same event in the same way, and so conflict inevitably arises.

▷ **Personality.** Personality is made up of your individual characteristics. Even those from the same cultural background will experience conflict that may be personality related. Sometimes you may find you just don't like someone. You may even think this irrational because you can't pinpoint what it is about this person that you don't like. But this is a very real, and frequent, cause of conflict in the workplace and may relate to a colleague or a guest. Personality traits are not something you can do anything about, but you can and should learn to live (and work) with others' 'irritating' ways.

▷ **Safety and security issues.** Where a person feels his or her safety or security is compromised (whether real or imagined) conflict will arise. Safety usually relates to a person's physical well-being. Security may also relate to a person's physical well-being but also that person's state of mind. For example, if a colleague feels intimidated or insecure about her position in the workplace, conflict may arise as she may feel she can't fully undertake her duties.

▷ **Organisational structure.** In Chapter 1 you learned that some hospitality establishments have clearly defined roles and responsibilities while in other venues, roles tend to overlap. A potential cause of conflict with roles and responsibilities (organisational structure) lies in the fact that many people feel 'that's not my job' when confronted with a request that is usually performed by someone else. In hospitality, all requests are everyone's responsibility where the guest is concerned—even if it means that you take the request and then refer it to a colleague for completion.

▷ **Change.** Whenever change occurs in the workplace, conflict is sure to arise. This is because many people are resistant to change. 'What's wrong with the way we do it now?' 'We've always done it this way!' People are resistant to change because it forces them to adapt to new situations and conditions. It forces them to deal with things they would rather not deal with.

Of course there are numerous other potential causes for conflict, such as your attitude (and the attitude of others), stress levels, experience, training, frame of mind and skill level, just to name a few. These will all potentially cause conflict and affect how you manage conflict with both your guests and colleagues.

IDENTIFYING POTENTIAL FOR CONFLICT

As we have said, identifying the potential for conflict is the necessary first step to managing it. How do you identify potential conflict? Think of it in the context of your workplace. Because conflict is any disagreement between two or more people, in a hospitality environment, the most likely cause of conflict arises from differences in expectations. In other words, what are the expectations of your guests? Your colleagues? Your employer?

Guest expectations

Your guests expect you to:

▷ be able to do your job
▷ do your job efficiently
▷ be professional in dealing with them
▷ solve their problems.

If at any point you are unable to meet these expectations, you have a potential conflict.

Colleague expectations

Whether you consider it reasonable or not, colleagues have expectations of each other. These expectations extend beyond your immediate work group to include colleagues in other departments. For example, if you recommend to a guest they dine in the restaurant of your venue because the service and food are excellent, you expect that the food and the service will live up to the expectation you have created in your guest's mind. If the restaurant service turns out to be poor, there is potential for conflict between you and restaurant staff (you will be reluctant to recommend the restaurant again) and potentially between you and the guest, as their expectations have not been met. Colleagues also expect you to:

▷ have similar work-related goals
▷ do your job well
▷ pull your weight (do your fair share of the work)
▷ be reliable
▷ meet guests' expectations
▷ meet the establishment's expectations.

If you (or a colleague) are unable to meet all of these expectations, then there is the potential for conflict to arise.

Establishment expectations

The venue you work for tries very hard to establish and maintain standards of service in order to attract and retain its targeted market. The venue relies on its staff to meet the expectations it has created in its guests. This means that the venue relies on you to provide a standard of service that reduces the likelihood of conflict between the venue and its guests. The establishment also expects you to:

▷ have good interpersonal skills
▷ do your job well (following established procedures)
▷ meet guest expectations
▷ be well presented
▷ be motivated (to do a good job)
▷ be reliable
▷ be consistent (in performing your tasks)
▷ be professional.

Already you are able to identify a number of events that may lead to conflict. If you don't live up to all the expectations listed, there may be conflict. Having an awareness and understanding of these expectations will help you to take action quickly, diplomatically and professionally to prevent a major incident.

Body language

Body language is another way to identify potential conflict situations. Guests and colleagues communicate thoughts and feelings using body language. Recognising potential conflict through body language presents an opportunity for you to address the problem. The following examples are a few of the body language signals you may encounter:

▷ someone tapping their fingers or feet (impatience)
▷ a frown or a snarl (anger)

$\triangleright$ arms crossed (defensive)
$\triangleright$ poor eye contact (not listening to you)
$\triangleright$ aggressiveness, like finger pointing or arm waving
$\triangleright$ shrugging the shoulders (not interested)
$\triangleright$ shaking of the head, eyes closed (indicating they do not agree with what you are saying).

Of course there are many more examples, but it is important to remember that body language signals are not universal. Cultural factors may influence the message being sent using body language, so body language signals should not be considered in isolation. Listen to what the other person is *saying* as well as indicating. Their arms may be crossed because they are cold, they may be pointing at something unrelated to you, they may be tapping their feet to a tune they can hear.

The spoken word

What someone is saying and how that person is saying it can clearly indicate potential (or actual) conflict. For example:

$\triangleright$ the pitch of the voice may be rising
$\triangleright$ the rate (speed) of speech may increase or slow down
$\triangleright$ the tone of voice may be sarcastic or condescending ('Perhaps I should speak with your supervisor who *would* understand what I'm saying?')
$\triangleright$ you might be accused of something ('*You're* the one who messed this up, *you* fix it')
$\triangleright$ you might be told how to behave ('Perhaps you should get a better attitude').

Or any number of other things. A couple of examples will help demonstrate how to identify potential conflict and stop it in its tracks before it becomes a major incident.

Example 1

A guest is standing at reception. It's late at night and the guest is obviously tired and grumpy and looking very untidy after driving all day. You can see he is anxious to get to his room. He is tapping his fingers and looking around. You cannot find his reservation, several other guests keep staring at this untidy person and the phone is ringing. What should you do?

Answer: Already you have identified that this person is tired and grumpy. It's probable that he is beginning to feel quite uncomfortable at the way other people are looking at him. In Chapter 6 you learned that the check-in procedure should not take more than a couple of minutes. This is your priority at this point. Ask a colleague to answer the telephone. If you have followed the correct procedure for checking a guest in, you will have passed a blank registration form to the guest, continued to process the guest's registration and roomed him without delay.

But what would have happened if you had not roomed him quickly?

While you look around for his reservation, explained you can't find it, suggested he is at the wrong venue or ignored his discomfort, you would have created a delay in the registration process and a poor first impression. You would have increased his discomfort and given him good reason to complain (about you and the venue).

Example 2

You overhear a colleague in reception explaining to a guest that it's not reception's fault that his dry cleaning is not back yet and that he should take the problem up with housekeeping. The guest is shaking his head and saying that all he wants is to get his suit back. This colleague has been known to be unhelpful before and you feel that this is not the sort of service standard expected by your guests. What should you do?

Answer: There are several possible approaches here. The conflict is really within you (and potentially within the guest as the guest may feel he should complain about the poor service and attitude at reception). You don't like the way this colleague sometimes deals with guests. If the guest doesn't complain, should you?

If you step in and resolve the problem (about the dry cleaning) yourself, your colleague may feel embarrassed in front of the guest, creating a whole new conflict. If you ignore the problem, your colleague isn't to know that service standards in the venue are not being met. If you confront your colleague later, he or she may resent your interference. If you tell your supervisor, your colleague is going to feel that you are a back stabber and you should have confronted the colleague. All options seem to lead to a lose-lose situation. But this is not the case. The outcome will depend on how you approach the situation and the relationship you have with the other person.

▷ If you have a good working relationship with this colleague, you can diplomatically interrupt and offer to follow up the dry cleaning. This approach will also work if the colleague is new and not fully trained.
▷ If your relationship with this colleague is strained to begin with, it may be appropriate to speak with the supervisor (and probably time you fixed this additional conflict!).
▷ You may feel it appropriate to speak with your colleague later and explain the standard of service expected in the venue and offer your assistance if required in the future.

Whatever you do, **do not ignore it**. This will only lead to you feeling resentful which in turn will lead to greater conflict. It will also potentially lead to further complaints from guests (about the venue and your colleague).

SKILLS FOCUS

Conflict is a form of disagreement between two or more people. However, conflict may occur within the individual. In the workplace, conflict may result from disagreements between guests or colleagues. Causes of conflict include different cultural values, personality, motivating factors, different expectations (of colleagues, guests and your employer), security and safety issues and communication barriers.

Early identification of potential conflict situations can prevent a major incident. By being aware of the expectations of others in the workplace and signs that indicate a problem may arise (body language, words used), you can reduce the likelihood of conflict.

FOCUS REVIEW

▷ *What is conflict?*
▷ *Why is it important to manage conflict in the workplace?*
▷ *In what ways can conflict be positive for the workplace?*
▷ *Explain three causes of conflict. Give an example of each.*

Resolving conflict situations

How each of us resolves conflict is different. Some of us are good at it, while others shy away from it. Some of us will become aggressive when confronted with conflict, while some of us will take the opportunity to learn from it. Because each of us has a preferred way of managing conflict, it's as equally important to be aware of conflict management styles as it is to identify potential causes.

Our response to conflict in the workplace will determine whether the outcome is constructive or destructive. An important goal of all conflict management should be resolution that satisfies *all* parties. Because the outcome is so important, we begin this section with a discussion on the possible outcomes before moving onto the actual techniques that can be used to resolve conflict.

FINDING A SOLUTION

Conflict outcomes:
• lose-lose
• win-lose
• win-win.

Finding a solution to conflict is not necessarily an easy task. It frequently requires us to explore areas we would sometimes rather avoid. But avoiding the conflict (by pretending it doesn't exist, hoping it will go away or ignoring the problem altogether) escalates the problem in the long run. The goal should be to resolve the conflict quickly and satisfactorily.

Lose-lose conflict

This outcome results in everyone being unhappy and dissatisfied. Everyone walks away feeling resentful and frustrated. Take the example of a guest who complains about the length of time that it took for reception to acknowledge him. Reception replies that 'we are very busy and I'll get to you when I can'. Who wins here? Nobody. The guest certainly lost and the receptionist resents the guest for the negative feedback.

Win-lose conflict

In this situation, one party loses and the other party wins. For example, when two colleagues disagree about how to perform a procedure, if the conflict is resolved by declaring one entirely right and the other entirely wrong, then you end up with a win-lose situation. In the workplace, this outcome fails to consider at least part of the underlying cause of the conflict in the first place—it may be poor communication, a personality clash or cultural differences, among others. This means that further conflict is likely to arise.

But a win-lose situation can have a positive outcome if indeed one person was wrong (or incorrect) and is able to acknowledge this. Getting people to understand that they were wrong about something (without blame or accusations) requires exceptional interpersonal skills.

Win-win conflict

As the title suggests, win-win aims to satisfy all parties. It involves collaboration between the parties and consideration of all the underlying influences that caused the conflict in the first place. For example, a guest complains about the standard of cleaning in his room. Housekeeping acknowledges the guest has a right to complain and inspects the room so that the guest is able to point out what he considers to be the problem. Housekeeping apologises for the inconvenience and immediately arranges for the room to be cleaned again to the guest's expected standard. The guest feels satisfied that quick and appropriate action was taken to resolve his problem (his services expectations have been met). Housekeeping knows that they have done the right thing to effectively resolve the problem. The venue is more likely to retain the guest.

To get to a win-win situation, several things must happen:

1. You must be willing to acknowledge that different people have different expectations and perceptions.
2. You must be willing to accept that people have a right to complain.
3. You must be willing to cooperate in the conflict resolution strategy.
4. You must be able to assert what you want (if you cannot do this, the outcome will be win-lose. You lose because you were unable to say what you wanted).
5. You must be able to accept and respect others' points of view.
6. You must be able to identify and practise appropriate conflict resolution techniques based on your judgment of the situation.

RESPONSIBILITY FOR RESOLVING CONFLICT

Responsibility for resolving conflict usually begins with those directly involved. Other factors however, may influence who is responsible for resolving some types of conflict.

Your position in the workplace

You may or may not be expected, or allowed, to resolve all conflict situations. Your ability to manage conflict in the workplace may be limited by the scope of your responsibility. For example, if the conflict is about locating a guest's lost dry cleaning you can take the responsibility for doing so. The guest needs to feel that whoever he deals with in the venue has the authority to solve simple problems like finding his dry cleaning.

If, on the other hand, a guest is extremely aggressive and demanding something of you that you do not have the authority to grant, such as that you pay for the lost suit, then you need to call in your supervisor or manager. Some people may only be satisfied when dealing with a higher authority anyway. If this is the case, give the guest what he or she wants: call your supervisor.

The people involved

The example above deals specifically with a guest. Sometimes, as you know, conflict may be with a colleague. Most workplaces have a procedure in place for conflict resolution (grievance procedure). Usually, your workplace will require you to attempt to resolve a conflict with a colleague before following formal procedures. For example, your colleague who told the guest it wasn't reception's responsibility to find his dry cleaning was very aggressive when you approached him about what you had overheard. A couple of days later when he had calmed down, you decided to bring up the matter again. This time he becomes even more aggressive and says things that frighten you. At this stage it would be appropriate to follow formal grievance procedures.

Nature of the conflict

Some conflict, by its very nature, requires intervention by others. For example, any incident that results in potential or actual safety or security breaches requires the involvement of management. An example may be a guest being assaulted in the bar, or a guest complaining about theft from the room. Because both these incidents may require police involvement, it is appropriate to include management in resolving the conflict.

During any conflict situation where you do not feel totally comfortable or in control in resolving it, it is important that you involve your supervisor. If you don't, there is a possibility that the conflict outcome may be other than win-win.

SKILLS FOCUS

Conflict is managed differently by each of us and will result in one of three outcomes: lose-lose, lose-win, win-win. Win-win is the most desirable outcome in the workplace whether the conflict is between colleagues or guests. Our ability to manage conflict is influenced by the position we hold (our level of authority), the people involved and the nature of the conflict. Sometimes it is appropriate to seek outside assistance, such as from your supervisor or manager.

FOCUS REVIEW

▷ *Why is a win-lose outcome not acceptable in conflict situations?*
▷ *To get to win-win, six things must happen. What are they? Why do you think they are so important to the outcome?*
▷ *How does your position affect your ability to manage conflict situations?*
▷ *When would it be appropriate to ask for your supervisor's intervention in a conflict?*

Conflict resolution techniques

Now that you know the possible outcomes resulting from conflict, obviously you will agree that a win-win situation is the most preferred, and most of the time this is what you will achieve. But to get to win-win, you need to be aware not only of those techniques that achieve it, but also those techniques that fail to achieve it. The following techniques demonstrate what is required to get a certain result and when it is and isn't appropriate to use.

GETTING TO WIN-WIN

Many conflict resolution techniques are available. The one used will depend on the factors discussed earlier (the nature of the conflict, the people involved and your position in the workplace). Remember the outcome you are trying to achieve is win-win. But not all approaches to conflict resolution result in win-win.

Compromising

This conflict resolution technique attempts to find a 'middle' ground between the conflicting parties. The idea is that both parties achieve a few 'wins' and both parties make a few sacrifices. Of course, it is hoped that the 'wins' and the sacrifices counter-balance each other so that the final outcome is win-win. But this rarely occurs. Most of the time the outcome is lose-lose. A compromising technique usually requires the input of a third party or 'mediator'. This allows both parties the opportunity to express their viewpoints without being overpowered by the other, so assertiveness skills and cooperation are required.

The disadvantage of this technique is that sometimes the solution is only partially acceptable to both parties. While the conflict appears to be settled now, be aware that this technique leaves itself open to recurrence later.

Compromising is usually used between conflicting colleagues, although it may be used in a conflict with a guest. For example, if two colleagues can't work together, and both insist they are 'right' (and the other wrong) the solution may be that they are rostered on different shifts. This way, no one loses their job or feels that they have to leave. However, the new rosters may not suit; the two parties still have a conflict and the other 'loser' may be the organisation.

Using a compromising technique with a guest may be appropriate when a guest, for example, is demanding a total refund for his stay in your venue because the tap dripped all night disrupting his sleep. It is not likely the venue will want to give a total refund for the room, but may offer a free meal in the restaurant or another night in the venue during off peak season. This way, the venue has the opportunity to turn a negative moment of truth into a positive one (by resolving the conflict to the guest's satisfaction and getting a second chance at creating a good impression when the guest returns).

Accommodating

Accommodating, or smoothing things over, involves playing down the real issues at hand (the reason for the conflict). It also plays up the similarities between the parties and focuses on these to achieve a resolution. The recognition of common interests serves to establish a peaceful coexistence long enough to develop a genuine resolution.

This conflict technique can work and achieve win-win only if the conflict is addressed early. If the conflict has been allowed to fester, then it won't work as it has a tendency to force a submissive approach because the parties need to put the other person's needs before their own. The other disadvantage is that accommodating can potentially lead to one party taking advantage of the other. This means it is more likely to result in a win-lose or lose-lose outcome.

Accommodating is frequently used when managing some forms of conflict with a guest. For example, a guest is checked into a room that he insists is not what he booked. He says that he explicitly remembers requesting a room with a view and a spa bath. Even though you remember taking this booking and that these things were *not* requested when you offered them, you agree to move the guest immediately. There is no point served in arguing with this guest.

Competing

A **competing** conflict resolution technique frequently means that there is a clear cut winner and loser. This may be from force, authority, domination or superior skill. To successfully use this technique (whatever the parties are competing for), *both* parties need to be assertive and uncompromising.

A **competing** technique results in victory for one through force, authority, domination or superior skill.

The competition may be about who is right and who is wrong or who did what better; it may be about supervisor and subordinate roles ('I'm the boss so you have to do what I say'). It frequently requires the intervention of a third party to impose a solution (you win, you lose) or recommend a compromise. It is rare that both parties are right (at least in the eyes of the other). If a competing technique is used, it's only going to be effective if the conflict is over something trivial in the first place (who checked in a guest the fastest!). If it is over a (perceived) major issue ('I'm the most efficient worker on reception') then this technique won't work. It is clear to see that this technique mostly results in win-lose outcomes.

The only time that this may be appropriate when guests are involved is when immediate action needs to be taken. For example, you have a large, rowdy and drunken group of sports fans in the foyer. Other guests' safety is at risk. Another guest complains about the group's behaviour and she is concerned for her family's welfare. Immediate action must be taken to ensure the well-being of others. The action you take must also be diplomatic and assertive to ensure that you don't make the matter worse by offending the group.

This technique is used when the issue is more important than the relationship. The disadvantage, of course, is that there is the potential to cause damage to the relationship.

Avoiding

Avoiding means that all parties ignore the conflict issues in the hope that they will go away.

Avoiding frequently results in a lose-lose situation. This is an extreme case of not dealing with the problem at all. For example, if the guest who complained about the rowdy sports group saw that you did nothing to allay her concerns, then she will feel you have failed in your duty to protect her and her family. The venue has probably lost a guest. Neither party got what they wanted.

This is a poor technique to use in a hospitality environment. Whether you feel a guest's complaint is reasonable or not, some form of resolution must be sought. Avoiding is also uncooperative because essentially, the conflict is brushed aside, or 'swept under the carpet' in the hope that it will go away. But the conflict will not go away—the rowdy group may eventually leave but the poor image left on the complaining guest is still there.

Avoiding does not work either when dealing with conflict between colleagues. If the issues remain unresolved, there is the potential for it to simmer and grow and eventually manifest as an even bigger problem at a later stage.

Sometimes temporary avoidance is appropriate if the timing to address the problem is not right (in the middle of a busy check-out) or if the conflicting parties need time to think about the issue and 'cool off'. However, be sure to tackle the conflict soon, before it gets out of hand.

Collaborating

Collaboration iis the most effective and direct technique for achieving win-win conflict resolution. It uses problem-solving techniques to meet the expectations of each of the conflicting parties.

Collaboration is the most effective and direct approach to getting to win-win. It is a positive approach that involves recognition by all that something is wrong and needs to be resolved. Only through collaboration can both parties constructively present their points of view and have all of their expectations met.

Collaboration works by working through the stages of problem solving, that is, by gathering and evaluating all the relevant information, then identifying possible solutions and agreeing on the most appropriate solution. Collaboration takes time and problem solving skills and well developed interpersonal skills. But in many instances, whether colleague or guest related, it is well worth the effort and the most effective means by which everyone is satisfied.

As you can see, there are several techniques for managing conflict. Being aware of each gives you the opportunity to avoid the pitfalls and take advantage of the benefits (and correct application) of each.

SKILLS FOCUS

There are several techniques that can be used to manage conflict. Not all will result in a win-win outcome. Compromising is when each party involved in the conflict is required to give up something they value. This frequently results in a lose-lose outcome. Accommodating plays down differences and plays up similarities between the conflicting parties in the hope of smoothing things over. Most of the time the accommodating technique will result in a win-lose or lose-lose outcome. A competing technique results in a clear winner and loser (win-lose) through the use of force, authority, domination or superior skill. Avoiding frequently results in a lose-lose situation. Avoiding means that all parties ignore the conflict in the hope that it will go away.

The only technique that can result consistently in a win-win outcome is collaborating. It uses problem solving techniques to meet the expectations of each of the conflicting parties.

FOCUS REVIEW

▷ *Why does a compromising technique frequently end up with a lose-lose outcome? Give an example of when you think it may be appropriate to use this technique.*
▷ *What is the usual outcome of an accommodating technique? Do you think it is appropriate to use this technique to resolve conflict between colleagues? Why? Why not?*
▷ *When is using a competing technique appropriate for conflict resolution? Why?*
▷ *If the avoiding technique results in lose-lose, what benefit is there in knowing it exists? When might avoiding be appropriate?*
▷ *Why is the collaborating technique the most preferred method for getting to win-win? Explain briefly how it works.*

Using communication skills in conflict resolution

Whichever conflict resolution technique is used, to be effective requires excellent communication skills. You will need to be able to express yourself clearly, assertively and diplomatically. Here we take a brief look at each to help you understand their application in the conflict resolution process.

INTERPERSONAL SKILLS

Interpersonal skills are those skills relating to how we interact with other people. These skills also help us work and communicate with others. Everyone has interpersonal skills. What varies is how well developed these skills are and how we use them in a work context. Success in conflict resolution requires highly developed interpersonal skills, which means you are able to:

Interpersonal skills—those skills relating to how we interact with other people.

▷ communicate thoughts and ideas clearly
▷ communicate using appropriate words and gestures
▷ demonstrate effective listening skills

- ▷ display empathy and sympathy
- ▷ display understanding
- ▷ be assertive
- ▷ demonstrate integrity
- ▷ act appropriately for the situation
- ▷ be attuned to others' needs and wants.

Good interpersonal skills take time to develop and increase the likelihood of success in resolving conflict. It means that you need to think about what you say, before you say it, consider how the other person may feel about your words and actions and you need to be open to others' ideas and views.

ASSERTIVENESS

Assertiveness
—the ability to confidently express thoughts and feelings with regard to the other person's point of view.

Assertiveness is the ability to express your own concerns and needs in a direct and honest manner, yet tactfully and with concern for the other person's feelings. Assertive people have high self-esteem, respect for others' viewpoints and clear and strong values that they are able to clearly express.

In a communication context, assertiveness is demonstrated both verbally and non-verbally. That is, what you say and how you say it, is supported by your body language. What assertive people communicate is a clear explanation of their views and needs without feeling guilty or selfish and with due consideration for the other party's needs and views. Assertive people are flexible, constructive in their feedback and confident in their opinion. Their body language is likely to be open and they take responsibility for how they feel. For example, '*I* feel frustrated when I am unable to assist you with the problems I think you sometimes have communicating with guests'. In this example, the assertive person is not accusing or blaming the other person, but letting him know how he feels in response to the actions of the other.

Aggressiveness
—forcefully imposing your views and ideas without regard for the other person.

By contrast, **aggressive** people are likely to forcefully impose their point of view on others, fail to respect the other person's views, ideas and opinions and are not only dominating but also demanding. Aggressive people put their own wants and needs before others'. Their body language will reflect their aggression too. They may stare (or glare) a lot, they may be inclined to poke their fingers and invade others' personal body space. During conflict, aggressive people are likely to 'accuse' their opponent of causing them to feel the way they do, for example, '*You* make me very angry when . . .'.

Passiveness—
submissive behaviour that demonstrates a willingness to allow others to dominate and impose their viewpoints without consideration for their own.

The behaviour of **passive** people is fairly submissive. A passive person is likely to be eager to please and reluctant to 'make waves'. This person often lacks the ability to confidently express his or her opinion and usually defers to the other person. The passive person is likely to cast his eyes down and slump his shoulders during conflict situations and agree to just about everything. For example, 'You're right, it is my fault . . .'.

In a conflict situation, assertiveness is a more desirable attribute (and communication technique) than either passiveness or aggressiveness. However, it is useful to be aware of all three styles as this helps you to manage the situation more effectively when dealing with each type. It is also useful to help you identify traits *you* may demonstrate during conflict that may hinder the resolution process.

DIPLOMACY

Diplomacy is the ability to tactfully and intelligently manage personal relations. By this we mean you use your assertiveness to express your ideas and opinions, show sympathy, respect and **empathy** to others (by placing yourself 'in their shoes') when they are expressing their views, and demonstrate understanding through positive body language and listening (which allows you to ask relevant questions).

Having **tact** (an intuitive perception to say and do the right thing) is possibly the key to maintaining effective diplomatic relations during a conflict. We all like to feel that we are being listened to and that our version or complaint is taken seriously and duly considered. If this does not happen ('You're not listening to what I'm saying . . !') the conflict resolution process can be frustrated and will stall. The result will be a lose-lose situation.

As you can see, your good communication skills are vitally important in conflict resolution. Think about what you are saying, think about the impact of your words on the other person, think about your body language and think about solving the problem. Don't think about who is right and who is wrong.

Diplomacy—the ability to tactfully and intelligently manage personal relations.

Empathy—putting yourself in someone else's shoes.

Tact—an intuitive perception to say and do the right thing.

SKILLS FOCUS

To be effective, conflict resolution requires excellent communication skills. Interpersonal skills are those skills that relate to how we interact with other people. They help us work and communicate with others.

Assertiveness is the ability to confidently express thoughts and feelings with regard to the other person's point of view. By contrast, aggressiveness is forcefully imposing a point of view on another, failing to respect the views, ideas and opinions of others and is dominating and demanding. Passiveness is fairly submissive and means a person is likely to be eager to please and not make waves. In a conflict situation, assertiveness is the more desirable attribute.

Diplomacy is the ability to manage personal relations tactfully and intelligently.

FOCUS REVIEW

▷ *From the list of interpersonal skills, what do 'display empathy and sympathy' mean?*
▷ *Why is it important to be attuned to others' needs and wants?*
▷ *Explain the difference between assertiveness, aggressiveness and submissiveness. During which conflict resolution technique might you be aggressive? Submissive?*
▷ *Why is diplomacy important with resolving a conflict with a guest?*

Implementing conflict resolutions

You now have the knowledge and understanding of conflict resolution techniques. You also have the knowledge that allows you to effectively communicate in conflict resolution situations. What you now need is the skill to implement a conflict resolution. Any of the techniques can be used but different outcomes for the same problem may result. Whichever technique you choose, there are five steps in the implementation process. These are the steps to follow:

1. Collect and discuss the facts.
2. Clarify your position.

3. Identify alternative solutions.
4. Solve the problem.
5. Implement the decision.

But before this can take place, both parties need to acknowledge that there is a conflict! This may seem obvious but frequently one or both sides pretend there isn't a conflict (avoidance) so that they don't need to confront the problem. It is not uncommon to find that one person thinks that the problem is not theirs but the other person's or that they feel they are blameless in the conflict. This creates a problem in getting to the first step. Both parties should be willing participants. Both parties need to accept that for conflict to exist there are at least two sides. Once this is achieved, you need to decide whether a mediator is needed or if you are able to resolve the conflict between yourselves. This is possible as long as you both respect the implementation process.

1. COLLECT AND DISCUSS THE FACTS

Now that you have both acknowledged there is a conflict, you need to collect and present the facts. This means initiating an open and honest line of communication. It means allowing first one person to state their side then the other to state theirs, without interruption, judgment or accusation.

Using phrases that begin 'I believe . . .', 'I feel . . .' or 'My understanding is . . .' are far more effective (and assertive) than saying 'You did this . . .', or 'You make me feel . . .' or 'It's your fault because . . .' which are aggressive and unhelpful. Deliver the facts without embellishment and without unnecessary dramatic effects.

Example

Jill: 'Jenny, there is a procedure in place for depositing guests' valuables in the safety deposit box. For security reasons it should always be followed. I feel at times you may be cutting corners and not following procedure.'

Jenny: 'That's not true, I always follow procedure. But it gets so busy at reception sometimes and when I'm on my own.'

2. CLARIFY YOUR POSITION

This is your opportunity to respond and question the other person. You can only do this if you have actively listened to the facts as they were presented. When the other person has stated their side of the conflict, you can ask questions to clarify what you don't understand. At this point, try to put yourself in their shoes. How would you feel if you were that person? Are you being unreasonable or unfair? Is that person being unreasonable or unfair?

Jill: 'OK. So you're saying that it gets so busy on reception that sometimes it's hard to follow all procedures to the letter?'

Jenny: 'Well, yes.'

Jill: 'So the problem as I see it then, isn't that you don't know the procedure but that sometimes you're too busy to follow procedure?'

Jenny: 'That's right. But I don't think you fully appreciate how hard it is when I'm out there on my own with no support during the busy periods.'

Jill: 'Jenny, I do understand what it's like but it is important that procedures be followed.'

3. IDENTIFY ALTERNATIVE SOLUTIONS

Once all the facts are clearly stated, it would help to summarise the problem to ensure you both have the same understanding of the issues. How does each person feel about the facts? For example, if the conflict is a work-related issue, make sure you are both talking about the same procedure or policy.

Jill: 'So, the real issue here is that there are times when you need additional help on reception? Is that right?'

Jenny: 'Basically, yes. There are times when I'm on my own and some procedures can't be followed correctly because there are other, more important things to do at the time.'

Jill: 'How do you think we could deal with this problem?'

Jenny: 'Well, we can either change some of the procedures to reduce the time it takes to do them, or we can get an additional staff member to cover the busy periods, because that's when most of the problems arise.'

Jill: 'Most of the problems arise when you're on your own and the busiest times are when staff take their lunch. What about if we reschedule lunch breaks so that they don't conflict with those busy periods?'

4. SOLVE THE PROBLEM

Now you have a few alternative solutions, it's time to solve the problem. You do this by evaluating each alternative solution in turn until you find one best solution that is going to meet the needs of all. You need to consider what the advantages and disadvantages of each solution are. Is one solution the best solution? Does a compromise need to be agreed to? Is one person right, the other wrong? Is a win-win solution achievable, or does someone have to lose? Given a limited knowledge of Jill and Jenny's conflict, it's possible that all solutions may work. However, it is probable that one solution is better than the other.

Jill: 'Unfortunately it's not likely that management will agree to give us another staff member just to cover the busy lunch period. And procedures for the safety deposit box are there to ensure the safe keeping of the guests' valuables, so I don't think it's possible to adjust the procedure. Unless you have an idea for adjusting the procedure without compromising security?'

Jenny: 'Afraid not. And you're right about not getting another staff member. But I do think your idea about moving lunch breaks is workable.'

This solution was achieved by collaboration. Both were able to walk away feeling satisfied.

5. IMPLEMENT THE DECISION

This is the final stage of resolving the conflict. Now that a solution has been found it is important to implement it (change the lunch times so that Jenny has help on reception during the busy times) and later you will need to evaluate its success (is Jenny now able to follow established procedures?). Failure to implement the decision will compound the problem and make it even more difficult to resolve later.

Before implementing the decision, however, you need to consider whether or not you have the authority to, or whether the decision has to be presented to a 'higher authority' for approval. Sometimes this can stall the process, but generally, by including management in solving the problem and implementation stages, it is easier to implement (remember many people are resistant to change, but may accept it more readily when it comes from higher up).

The successful ingredients of this conflict resolution scenario were that each person listened to the other, the problem was clarified, and neither party's needs or values were compromised. The solution was achieved by collaboration.

SKILLS FOCUS

The implementation of a conflict resolution technique is a five-step process: collect and discuss the facts, clarify and empathise, offer alternative solutions, solve the problem and implement the decision. Following these five steps allows everyone the opportunity to discuss openly their perspective of the problem and enable a win-win outcome.

FOCUS REVIEW

▷ *Why is it important for both parties to the conflict to acknowledge there is a conflict?*
▷ *What do you think is likely to happen if you skip any of the steps to conflict resolution?*
▷ *Why are alternative solutions necessary?*
▷ *What would be the consequence of failure to implement the decision?*

APPLY YOUR KNOWLEDGE

Until recently, you and a colleague have enjoyed a good working relationship. Since your colleague was promoted to supervisor, you feel that the relationship has deteriorated. She always expects you to work late, asks you to do things no one else wants to do and takes credit for things you did. You have avoided confronting her until now but feel it's time to let her know how you feel.

Working with two other people, role play the above scenario with the third person observing how each of you deal with the conflict resolution process. At the end of the role play, the third person is to provide feedback on your technique, communication skills and outcome, noting which technique was used, whether or not the five steps to conflict resolution were observed and what communication styles were used.

Responding to customer complaints

You learned earlier that guests have expectations of you and your ability to perform your job. Guests expect you to be professional, meet their needs and to solve their problems. If you are unable to meet any of these expectations, the guest may complain. We say 'may' complain, because not every guest who has a problem will complain. It is not uncommon for guests to choose not to complain when something goes wrong. Instead they leave the venue feeling disappointed and frustrated and rather than confront the issue, tell several of their friends and colleagues about the experience and vow never to return. You never get a chance to find out why you have lost a guest, nor get the opportunity to fix the problem.

Of the guests who do complain, many will be left with a negative attitude towards the business if the complaint is not handled correctly. Complaints need to be viewed as an opportunity for you to:

▷ create a positive impression
▷ retain the guest's business
▷ improve the processes that caused the problem in the first place.

GUEST EXPECTATIONS AND COMPLAINTS

The expectations of your guests will vary depending on their needs and wants. For example, some guests will be satisfied with a particular standard of service while others will not be. Some guests will understand that a dripping tap is 'one of those things' while for others it will ruin their whole stay. Some guests may seem impossible to please or rude and ungrateful, while others will be exceedingly appreciative of your help and concern. Because of this variability of guests' expectations all guest complaints must be:

▷ handled sensitively, courteously and respectfully
▷ handled professionally
▷ taken seriously
▷ immediately acted upon
▷ followed up.

HOW GUESTS EXPRESS THEIR COMPLAINTS

Guests will complain in a number of ways and at different times:

▷ immediately the problem arises
▷ after they have left
▷ to another department
▷ aggressively or pleasantly.

Most complaints are directed at reception. This is because reception, for many guests, represents the 'face' of the venue and accordingly is perceived as the solver of all problems. Whether the complaint is about the awful food last night in the restaurant, the leaking tap, or the porter who dropped their bags, complaints frequently land at reception. Another reason this happens is that many people prefer to complain to someone other than the one who caused the problem as this avoids direct confrontation. This is also why so many complaints leave the establishment without the establishment knowing it, although friends and colleagues get to hear all about it.

For immediate and appropriate action about a bad meal in the restaurant, the guest needed to tell the waiter, who could have done something about it at the time. There isn't much the venue can do if, at check-out, the guest tells the cashier that the food was awful.

Immediately the problem arises

For most simple problems, guests will call reception immediately the problem arises. For example, housekeeping forgot to change the guest's towels. Some guests may call housekeeping, and request that fresh towels be brought to their room. For another guest, this may be a serious matter. They will call reception and complain that housekeeping has failed in its duty. Either way, the guest complains immediately. By complaining immediately, the venue has the opportunity to fix the problem immediately, thereby ensuring the rest of the guest's stay meets their expectations.

After they have left

Complaining after departure is a useful way of avoiding confrontation. For many guests it is also a useful way to express their disappointment about something that they don't consider fatal to their relationship with the venue. For example, a guest may have had a bad experience with room service. The order took too long and when the food arrived it was cold and greasy. The guest did not consider this too dramatic at the time, but thought the venue should be aware of the problem with room service. The guest may either complete the venue's in-house feedback questionnaire or write a letter.

However the concern is communicated after departure, the venue should use this opportunity to investigate the complaint and thank the guest for bringing it to their attention.

To another department

As you have already seen, many guests prefer to complain to someone other than the person who caused the problem. If there is a problem with the food, why not tell the waiter? Why wait until check-out to mention it? If there is a problem with the standard of cleanliness in the room, why call reception and blame them?

Apart from wanting to avoid direct confrontation with the person who can actually fix the problem, the guest has often formed a comfortable relationship with reception staff. You checked them in, you arranged the hire car for them, and you always use their name. This rapport may not exist with other departments. Telling reception about a problem in another department may indicate that the guest is not actually looking for a resolution, but simply wants the problem acknowledged and an apology.

Aggressively or pleasantly?

A seemingly minor problem ('I didn't get my newspaper this morning') may be conveyed aggressively or pleasantly. Similarly, a major incident ('I slipped in the shower and hurt myself') may be conveyed aggressively or pleasantly. Whether you think the problem is minor or major is irrelevant. And whether you think the attitude and behaviour of the guest is rude or aggressive or inappropriate is also irrelevant. However, an aggressive and rude complaint can sometimes get in the way of solving the problem. You are left wondering why this person is being so rude instead of thinking clearly about what the problem is and how you can fix it.

What the guest really wants (and expects) is to be taken seriously, have the problem fixed promptly and receive a courteous response. If the guest is being rude and aggressive in a public area, that may potentially draw attention from other guests, try to calm the guest down and remove the person to a more private area. For example, 'Ms Hanson, I can appreciate that you are upset and I am sorry that this happened. If you would like to take a seat over here, we can talk about it'.

It is very difficult for someone to continue being aggressive when you are calm, pleasant and concerned. Because of your immediate attention and concern, it is likely that the guest will be willing to sit and more quietly talk about her problem. Once you have gained some control over the situation, you will be able to implement a complaint handling strategy.

COMPLAINT HANDLING STRATEGY

Whatever the complaint is about, it should be managed within a standard framework that will ensure no steps in the process are omitted. Whether the complaint is the result of a simple error (by you or a colleague) or a more serious event, focus on a solution that satisfies the guest. Most of you will develop your own style for handling complaints, but you should not ignore any of the steps that ensure successful outcomes.

The complaint handling strategy follows these steps:

1. Listen to the guest and acknowledge the problem.
2. Express concern and empathise.
3. Take responsibility for resolving the complaint.
4. Indicate what action will be taken.
5. Take action to resolve the complaint.
6. Follow up.

Listen and acknowledge

Guests make complaints about all sorts of things. Some of these things are easy to fix (a blown light globe) while others are complicated (the guest believes someone has entered her room and gone through her belongings). Some complaints may seem petty and unimportant, while others will require immediate action and incur a cost to the venue.

Always allow the guest time to explain the problem, without interruption, then acknowledge the problem. It is important for you to find out the exact nature of the problem and all of the related details. Take the problem seriously. Ignoring it won't make it go away, it will just compound it.

Don't take it personally

It's not uncommon for guests to blame you for their problem even when it has nothing directly to do with you. You are the 'face' of the establishment, and as far as the guest is concerned, his problem *is* your problem. Don't get upset or defensive when the guest is accusing you of sabotaging their romantic weekend away. Remain calm, attentive and focused.

Concern and empathy

Your concern must be sincere and appropriate to the complaint. For example, if a guest tells you that the light globe is still not fixed, they don't expect you to behave as though it is the end of the world. They just want you to fix it. Now. If a guest has told you they have slipped over in the shower, you need to express concern for their well-being and empathise with their discomfort.

Take responsibility

Even though you didn't cause the problem, you must take responsibility for it. This means that you immediately and sincerely apologise on behalf of the venue. Don't blame someone or something for the complaint. It is not appropriate to say 'It's not my fault the shower is slippery'. It is appropriate to let the guest know that you take responsibility for the accident, by apologising, even if there is nothing you can do to fix the problem except refer the matter on to your supervisor.

A guest wants someone to take responsibility and the person they complain to is usually the one. The responsibility they expect of you extends beyond just apologising to offering a solution. Sometimes, however, an apology is all the guest expects.

Indicate what action you will take

The action you take will depend on the nature of the incident.

Fix it yourself

Whether you can fix a problem yourself or not will depend on the extent of your authority in the venue. If the problem is simple, like a blown light globe, let the guest know you will call maintenance immediately. Where legal or financial concerns may be involved, it is common to refer the matter on to your supervisor. If you constantly receive complaints of a recurring nature, for example, the newspaper is frequently not delivered, then this too may need to be referred to your supervisor.

Refer the problem on

The problem of the woman who slipped in the shower may need to be referred to your supervisor and maintenance or housekeeping. There may be legal repercussions from the fall. Let the guest know that you will ask housekeeping to provide a non-slip mat for the shower, but that you will also refer the complaint to your supervisor.

You would also refer the matter of the complaint about the guest's luggage (that someone had gone through her things) to your supervisor. This complaint has potential legal implications (breach of security) that need to be considered.

Take action

Now that you have indicated what you are going to do, do it. If you need to call your supervisor, call the supervisor. If you need to contact other departments, for example, maintenance, or housekeeping, call them. If you say 'I'll look into that for you' the guest is not likely to feel very confident. The guest wants you to act now, not later.

Follow up

A complaint doesn't go away just because you have listened, empathised and apologised. Most complaints need to be followed up. You need to make sure that what you said would be done has, in fact, been done. Even if someone else is going to fix the problem, the guest expects you to follow up.

Call maintenance or housekeeping and check that they have done what you asked them to do for the guest. Check with your supervisor what the outcome was of the complaint that you referred on. In many cases it is also appropriate to follow up with the guest. For example, you may call the guest in their room and ask if everything is now OK. This gives them an opportunity to express satisfaction (or dissatisfaction) with how the complaint was handled.

Record the incident

Some complaints may need more than a quick call to the guest's room to make sure the problem has been resolved. The nature of the complaint, and the policy in your establishment, may mean that you document the incident. The incident that resulted in a guest sustaining an injury after slipping in the shower and the incident of the guest whose bags were rifled through both need recording. The complaint about the light globe doesn't need to be recorded (except in the maintenance book or front office diary).

Most venues will have in place an incident report form. Even if your workplace doesn't have a standard form, the following information needs to be recorded:

▷ name and address of guest
▷ date of the incident
▷ nature of the incident

▷ how the incident occurred (exact and specific details)
▷ witnesses to the incident
▷ action taken
▷ venue representative who dealt with the situation.

This information may be required later, particularly if legal action results. The report should include, when relevant, conversations, diagrams and results of subsequent investigations. Complete the report as soon as possible after the complaint was made. The next day may be too late as relevant details may be forgotten.

Turning complaints into opportunities

While it's easy to conclude that all complaints create a negative impression (a bad moment of truth) this doesn't have to be the final outcome. You will remember earlier that we said complaints are an opportunity for the venue to improve the way it does things. This is only true if complaints are taken seriously and handled properly. By following the complaint handling strategy, being aware that each of your guests is different, developing your interpersonal skills and managing conflict with win-win in mind, complaints will give the venue the opportunity to:

▷ convince the guest it is a professional operation
▷ convince the guest that they are important to the venue
▷ persuade the guest to return
▷ demonstrate its high standard of customer service
▷ highlight the ability of its staff
▷ create positive moments of truth.

SKILLS FOCUS

Complaints from guests are an opportunity for you to create a positive impression, retain the guest's business and improve the processes that caused the problem in the first place. Guests expect that their complaints will be handled sensitively, courteously and respectfully. They also expect you to take complaints seriously no matter what the complaint or how they express it.

Some guests will complain immediately while others will do so after they have left the venue. Others will not complain at all. Some guests will complain aggressively while others will be polite. However a guest complains, there is a complaint handling strategy that needs to be followed: listen to the complaint and acknowledge the problem, express concern and empathise, take responsibility and indicate what action will be taken. Take action to resolve the problem then follow up to ensure the guest is now satisfied.

Don't take complaints personally and record in detail those complaints that may have legal or financial implications for the venue.

Every opportunity should be taken to turn complaints into a positive moment of truth for your guest.

FOCUS REVIEW

▷ Why do you think some guests do not even bother to complain?

▷ What opportunities arise for the venue from a complaint?

▷ Why do you think some guests are more likely to complain to another department than to the department that caused the problem?

▷ The complaint handling strategy follows six steps. Why should each of the steps be followed when resolving guest complaints?

▷ Why should you take responsibility for a problem when you weren't the one who caused it?

▷ What sorts of complaints are you likely to be able to fix yourself?

▷ Why is the follow up stage important in complaint handling?

▷ Under what circumstances would you need to complete an incident report?

PUT YOUR KNOWLEDGE TO THE TEST

Robyn was working the swing shift last Tuesday when a guest came storming over to reception demanding to know why this venue was so incapable of providing decent service. 'Since my arrival two days ago, I've had nothing but problems with this place,' he said. 'First of all, the porters lost my luggage, then housekeeping took all day to clean my room and when they got around to it they forgot to change the towels! To make matters worse, the room service food last night was atrocious.' As he related each new problem, his voice grew louder and his tone became more aggressive. 'What,' he demanded to know, 'are you going to do about these problems?'

'First of all', said Robyn, as she glared at the guest. 'I'd like to help you but as I'm not the one who caused all your problems, why scream at me? Second, since your problems are with departments other than reception, I'll get my supervisor who may be able to help you.'

1. What should have been Robyn's first response?

2. What did Robyn do right?

3. What did Robyn do wrong?

4. Following the complaint handling strategy, write the responses Robyn should have given for each of the guest's complaints.

5. What should Robyn's supervisor say to the guest?

6. Who should take responsibility for the guest's problem?

7. What impression would another guest in the foyer get on hearing the guest's complaint and Robyn's response?

Glossary

Accommodating

A conflict resolution technique which plays down the differences and plays up the similarities between the conflicting parties in the hope of smoothing things over.

Accommodation services

Also referred to as 'rooms division'. Refers to the department(s) responsible for selling and maintaining guest rooms and associated services for guests while in-house.

Account posting machine

This is a machine that allows you to record financial transactions to individual guest's accounts and keeps track of the total revenue for each service available in the venue.

Account settlement

Settlement of the guest account, usually at the time of departure.

Accounts receivable

Total of all moneys owed to the venue by entities other than in-house guests.

Active document

Document or file currently in use.

Actual arrivals

Guests who have arrived at the venue and who are already checked into their rooms.

Actual departures

Guests who have already checked out of their rooms.

Add ons

Additional products and services that can be attached to the base product to make it more desirable and also to promote use of other areas in the venue. Sometimes referred to as cross selling or extras.

Adjustment

An adjustment is made when the total charge for an item is altered to change the amount recorded to the guest account.

Advance deposits

Prepayments made by the guest usually to secure a reservation for a room.

Advertising

Any paid promotion of the establishment in the mass media such as television, radio and print mediums.

Agenda

List of the points or topics to be discussed at a meeting.

Aggressiveness

The forceful imposing of your views and ideas without regard for the other person.

Allotment

An agreed number of rooms allocated on specified dates. The hotel cannot sell these rooms to anyone else before the release back date.

Anti-competitive agreement

Arrangements (or contracts) that are likely to, or have the purpose of, reducing competition in the market place.

Anti-competitive behaviour

The behaviour of businesses to reduce competition in the market place.

Archiving

The practice of removing a file or record from everyday use and storing it in another location (because the file or document is now inactive).

Arrival

Second stage of the cycle of service. Refers to the guest's arrival at the venue (check-in).

Assertiveness

The ability to confidently express thoughts and feelings with regard to the other person's point of view.

Auditing

The process of checking and reviewing all financial and non-financial transactions to determine their accuracy.

Australian Business Number (ABN)

An exclusive identification code that enables businesses to deal not only with the Australian Taxation Office, but also with a range of other government departments and agencies.

Australian Competition and Consumer Commission (ACCC)

The main regulatory body responsible for overseeing compliance with the *Trade Practices Act 1974*.

Automated system

This system contains a minimal amount of handwritten information. Rather, information is entered into a computer where it is compiled and processed.

Avoiding

A conflict resolution technique, which occurs when all parties ignore the conflict issues in the hope that they will go away.

Back office

Provides support for front office services. Responsible for reservations and switchboard. The back office is physically located directly behind front office.

Banking report

The summarised amounts for the cash, credit cards, cheques, foreign currency and EFTPOS taken for the day and compiled in one report.

Batching

Putting all the same charges (source documents) together.

Black list

A list of guests who have stayed previously at the venue but are now banned from doing so. This could be because they didn't pay their account last time or they were drunk or displaying undesirable behaviour.

Blanket authority

An agreement between the venue and certain companies that allows that company's staff to charge back to the company some or all charges without written authority every time the guest stays at the venue.

Briefing

Short informal meeting when important information about the day's activities is passed on to the room attendants.

Bulk check-out

Groups that have all their accommodation and meals charged back to the tour company are checked out at once.

Bump

The arrangement to transfer the guest to another venue because of overbooking at your venue. This is sometimes referred to as *walking* a guest.

Butler services

Services provided by the housekeeping department. A butler service is very personalised service to certain guests, including unpacking and packing the guest's luggage, laundering and dry cleaning clothing, ironing the newspaper, shining shoes, maintaining the guest room in an orderly manner, running the bath, personal shopping for the guest, and a range of other services.

Buying signals

Unintentional signs that customers give to signal their interest to 'buy', although they may need help making the decision. Buying signals can be the words spoken or body language.

Cash folio

Used for recording all cash transactions not linked to a guest room. The cash folio must always be at zero.

Central Reservation System (CRS)

A reservation system capable of receiving, controlling and maintaining the reservations for several venues (within a chain) in one location and automatically redirecting the reservation to the required venue accordingly.

Charge back facility

The ability to charge some or all of the account back to a company.

Check-in

The procedure of registering at a venue.

Check-out

The procedure of settling the account and departing the venue.

City ledger

A collection of accounts receivable held for non in-house guest accounts.

Clean for dirty exchange

The exchange of one clean item of linen for each dirty item. The system helps reduce linen loss and control stock supplies.

Cleaning schedule

A permanent list of all the cleaning tasks to be completed and how frequently each task is to be performed.

Close of day

Final stage of the night audit procedure. It is the procedure to close the trading day and rollover to a new trading day.

Closed questions

Questions that usually begin with 'would' and make it easy for a guest to say yes or no.

Collaboration

A conflict resolution technique. It is the most effective and direct technique for achieving a win-win solution. It uses problem solving techniques to meet the expectations of each of the conflicting parties.

Commercial venues
Hospitality establishments in business to make money and hence a profit.

Company charge back
The ability to charge some or all of the account back to a company.

Computerised accounts system
An accounting system whereby all transactions are processed by a computer.

Conference groups
A group of guests staying in the venue and participating in a conference, whether the conference is held in the accommodation venue or elsewhere.

Conflict
Any situation that leads to a disagreement between two or more individuals.

Contaminated rubbish
Any rubbish that is contaminated with something that may cause you harm, such as syringes, surgical dressings, used condoms and used sanitary napkins.

Contra transactions
Transactions involving the exchange of a service for a service.

Communication barriers
Those things that get in the way of effective communication, such as language, poor listening skills, preconceived ideas, poor verbal skills and prejudices.

Compendium
Handbook or information folder containing information about the venue, such as facilities and services available, operating times, contact numbers, etc. It often also contains local area information and stationery items such as the venue letterhead and envelopes.

Competing
A conflict resolution technique resulting in victory for one through force, authority, domination or superior skill.

Compromising
A conflict resolution technique, in which each party to the conflict is required to give up something they value in order to resolve the conflict.

Concierge
Person in charge of the porters. The concierge department is responsible for providing a range of guest services.

Corporate client
Guests whose employers, usually companies, pay the venue's charges.

Correction
Total charge for an item removed from the account.

Correspondence
Written communication between the venue and external entities.

Credit payment
A transaction that decreases the balance owed by a guest.

Credit check report
A report that lists all the accounts whose totals are near to or in excess of their limit.

Credit limit
The maximum amount that a company or individual can charge to their account.

Cross-selling

Selling other services and products available in the venue in addition to the base product (room) to make it more desirable and also to promote the use of other areas in the venue. Sometimes referred to as extras or add ons.

Cross-training

Training in more than one job or department in a hospitality venue to enable you to perform in more than one role.

Cycle of service

The four stages of the guest's experience with the venue: pre-arrival, arrival, occupancy, and departure.

Daily cleaning record

A standard form on which each of the tasks to be completed are listed and checked off daily, or a handwritten list compiled by a supervisor daily.

Daily running sheet

A checklist for, and reminder about, the duties to be completed on a particular shift in the front office.

Day use room

A guest room used usually between 9.30 am–4.30 pm. These rooms are then cleaned and can be resold that night.

Debit charge

A transaction that increases the balance owed by a guest to a venue.

Debtor

Any business or individual who owes the venue money for services rendered.

Delay charge

Charge(s) made to the guest's account after departure.

Demographics

A list of characteristics of potential guests such as their age, education, income, occupation, marital status and where they live.

Departure

1. The final stage of the cycle of service. 2. A room status, meaning that the guest has departed and the room needs cleaning.

Deposit ledger

A ledger that holds advanced deposits received from guests (to secure their reservations).

Diplomacy

The ability to tactfully and intelligently manage personal relations.

Direct dial telephone

A telephone that allows the user to make outgoing calls and to receive incoming calls without the assistance of an operator.

Directory

A book that is maintained alphabetically, listing attractions, places of interest, services, costs, directions and a list of contacts and telephone numbers. Used and maintained by the porters.

Disclaimer

Limits the liability amount payable by the venue in the event of theft, loss or damage to guest's personal belongings while on the premises.

Disturbance

Any event or occurrence that interrupts the normal activities in the venue.

Do Not Disturb (DND)

A sign hanging on the outside of the guest room door means the guest does not wish to be disturbed.

Double room

Guest room with sleeping spaces for two people.

Down selling

Selling technique that begins by suggesting the highest priced item and working down through the price and quality levels.

Drop box

A drop chute situated in a safe for the depositing of floats and takings received from different departments within the venue.

Dry area

Those areas in the venue not meant to be exposed to water or liquids, for example, carpeted areas.

Due out

The guest is due to depart today (but is not yet ready to leave) and the room needs cleaning.

Early departures

Guests who were meant to stay longer but checked out earlier instead.

EFTPOS

Electronic Funds Transfer at Point of Sale.

Empathy

Putting yourself in someone else's shoes.

End of day projection

The total number of rooms in the venue minus expected occupied rooms and OOO rooms.

Expected arrivals

Guests due to check-in.

Expected departures

Guests due to leave today.

Express check-out

Guests fill in a form with their credit card details and address for all charges to be charged and sent to them. They leave the key in the room and don't go to reception to check-out, thus facilitating the check-out process.

Extended stays

Guests who were meant to depart today but decided to stay longer.

External use documents

Those documents that are coming into or being sent out of the venue, for example invoices and confirmation letters to guests.

Extras

Services and products that can be sold in addition to the base product to make it more desirable and also to promote use of other areas in the venue. Sometimes referred to as cross-selling or add ons.

Extras account

A guest account that records all the charges payable by the individual (whose company is paying for at least accommodation).

Extrinsic motivation

Motivation that is related to the receiving of rewards.

False representations

Any misleading claims or representations a venue makes about the price, benefits, standard, quality, value or grade of goods or services, that may unfairly influence guests' purchasing decisions.

Family room

A guest room designed to accommodate a family. Usually has a double bed and two single beds. May also have kitchen facilities and a separate living area.

Fast track machine

Machine that allows the venue to process charge and credit card transactions the day the transaction occurred. The money is deposited directly into the venue's bank account. A fast track machine is linked to the EFTPOS machine.

Filing

The process of arranging and storing documents according to a particular classification.

Financial control

Management of revenue received, and expenses incurred, by the venue.

Financial transactions

The exchange of something of value, usually money, in return for a service or product.

Flag reports

A list of activities/guest requests to be completed during the shift.

Float

Starting 'bank' to enable financial transactions.

Floor limit

The limit credit card companies set on how much a venue can allow a guest to charge to the card before authorisation by the credit card company must be sought.

Foreign exchange

Exchanging currency from another country into the local one.

Formal research

The systematic gathering and analysis of information from primary and secondary sources relating to a product or service or even the industry in general.

Franking machine

A machine that stamps and dates envelopes by printing the correct amount of postage required according to the envelope's weight and size.

Free independent travellers (FITs)

Free or fully independent travellers are those guests who make reservations directly with the accommodation venue, are not part of a group, and make their own travel arrangements.

Front office

The 'face' of the hotel. Provides reception services. The term 'front office' is frequently used to imply both front office and back office operations.

Full-board

Three meals a day included in the tariff.

Gift voucher

Voucher for the supply of services or goods. The voucher is paid for but the value is not usually indicated. What is indicated is what the holder of the voucher is entitled to, such as one night's accommodation.

Goods and Services Tax (GST)

Broad based tax of 10 per cent on the supply of most goods and services.

Group booking
Indicates that a reservation is for a group of people.

Group inclusive tours (GITs)
A group of people travelling together on a package arrangement. This means their transport, accommodation, meals (some or all) and side trips are usually inclusive in the price paid. Everyone will arrive together, eat together and check-out together.

GST exclusive
The GST applicable is not included in the rate or the price quoted, but listed separately.

GST inclusive
The GST applicable is included in the rate or the price quoted.

Guaranteed booking
The guest has agreed to pay for the room whether they arrive or not and the venue agrees to keep the room available until the check-out time the day following the day of arrival.

Guest accounting cycle
The processing of financial transactions throughout the cycle of service resulting in the three stages of accounts: creation, maintenance and settlement.

Guest accounting system
Means of controlling the financial transactions by following the guest accounting cycle. This can be either computerised or manual.

Guest accounts
The record of all financial transactions between the venue and the guest during the guest's stay. Also referred to as the guest folio.

Guest folio
The record of all financial transactions between the venue and the guest during the guest's stay. Also referred to as the guest account.

Guest profile
Also called a guest history or guest history profile. It is a record of personal details of each guest and maintains records of their stays, preferences and other details relating to their use of the venue.

Guests
The people who pay for the services and facilities provided by a hospitality establishment.

Half-board
Two meals included in the rate of the accommodation, usually breakfast and dinner.

Hand caddy
A small, hand held container, similar to a bucket, which holds cleaning chemical spray bottles, cleaning cloths and cleaning brushes.

Hand over
Communication about what is happening in the venue from one shift to the next.

Hazards
Anything that may cause you or a guest harm.

High season
Those times when room availability is low. Often referred to as peak period.

Honour system
A system of relying on the guest, during the check-out process, to advise reception of additional charges incurred since that morning or last night (such as mini-bar consumption).

Hospital corners
The fold used at the sides of the bed when tucking in the blankets and sheets (it is also sometimes referred to as 'mitring').

Hospitality industry
A sector of the broader tourism industry providing a range of accommodation, food, beverages and associated services to meet the needs of people while away from home.

Hospitality sectors
The various types of establishments offering hospitality services, for example, hotels, motels, caravan parks, restaurants and bars.

Housekeeping
The department responsible for maintaining the cleanliness of the guest rooms and public areas of the establishment.

House limit
The amount the venue will allow a guest to charge to their account before some form of payment must be made. The house limit is set by the venue.

House status report
Reporting providing details of the status of all rooms in the venue.

IDD (international direct dialing)
A telephone feature that allows the user to make international calls without the assistance of an operator.

Inactive document
A document or file not currently in use. Is likely to be archived.

Inbound tourist
Visitors travelling to Australia whose main place of residence is outside Australia.

Incoming calls
Telephone calls received from external and internal sources.

Informal research
The collection of information from sources that have already formally researched the products and services (secondary sources).

In-house guest
A guest who is currently staying in the venue.

In-house entertainment
Includes all the activities available to guests while they stay in the venue, for example videos, swimming pool, sauna, gaming.

In-house extensions
Telephone extension numbers used within the venue.

In-house guest ledger
The ledger that holds all in-house guest accounts.

Interconnecting room
Two guest rooms next to each other with a door giving access between them.

Internal use documents
Those documents used within the venue such as the front office diary and memos.

Interpersonal skills
Those skills relating to how we interact and communicate with other people.

Interstate visitors
Visitors who live in Australia travelling within Australia but outside their home state.

Intrastate visitors
Visitors who live in Australia travelling within their home state.
Intrinsic motivation
Motivation related to the personal satisfaction at having achieved something.
Invoice
A document requesting payment for services or goods supplied. Provides a detailed account of the actual goods or services bought by the venue, date supplied, cost per unit and settlement details.

Late arrivals
Guests with reservations who have made arrangements for a late check-in.
Late charge
Charges for services used by a guest, the details of which do not arrive at reception until after the guest has departed (they are then posted to the guest's account).
Lead time
Minimum amount of time allowed for a cancellation to be accepted without incurring a penalty.
Leisure market
People travelling on holiday, visiting friends or relatives, taking a short break, such as a weekend getaway, or long term visitors such as backpackers.
Log on
Entering the computer program by entering a password or your name, which registers you in the computer and allows it to keep track of all entries made by you during your shift.
Lose-lose conflict
A conflict outcome resulting in both parties losing.
Lost and found
Personal belongings of a guest which are left behind in the venue. These are usually stored in housekeeping until claimed.
Lost property
Personal belongings of a guest which are left behind in the venue.
Low season
Those times when room availability is high. Often referred to as off peak.
Loyalty programs
A program that recognises and rewards frequent user guests.

Mail merge
Merging of the standard documents you create with the database of names and addresses.
Mail out
Term used to describe a sales letter sent to a large number of existing or potential guests on the venue's mailing list.
Manual system
Manual completion of all tasks relating to guest and venue activities. The only automation is possibly a typewriter and a calculator. The most common system is known as the Whitney system.
Marketing
All of the activities carried out by the establishment which are aimed at identifying its target market and promoting the venue to attract that target market.

Marketing mix

A combination of strategies that are selected to achieve the establishment's marketing goals of attracting their targeted markets by using a combination of the 4Ps of marketing (product, price, place promotion).

Marketing strategies

Activities the venue undertakes to attract potential guests. Includes developing products and services, positioning its products and services in the market place and developing the marketing mix.

Market segment

Group of customers, or guests, with similar traits, needs and wants.

Market research

Research carried out by sales and marketing staff in order to know what the venue's target markets want, to identify opportunities in the market place and the best way to promote the venue.

Master account

Main guest account. Includes all the charges paid for by a company or group.

Master key

A single key that opens several locks, each of which has also its own separate key.

Meal plans

The meals that individuals or groups may have booked as part of their room rate. A meal plan may include breakfast, half-board or full-board.

Media release

An informative newsworthy article written to promote a new service or product or the venue itself.

Memorandum (memo)

An internal document used for communicating a brief message to many people at once.

Minutes

The record of a meeting; what was discussed and by whom, decisions made, date the meeting was held, who was in attendance and who wasn't and anything else relevant to the particular meeting.

Mitring

The fold used at the sides of the bed when tucking in the blankets and sheets (also sometimes referred to as hospital corners).

Moment of truth

Impression created by each experience the guest has in the venue. It may be positive, negative or neutral.

Motivation

The force that induces us to do certain things.

Movement

The number of rooms and people who are coming and going today.

Movement marker

A system of recording the movement of a file.

Multi-skilled

Possessing skills in more than one area.

Murphy bed

A bed that can be folded full length into a wall cavity or purpose-build cupboard.

Mystery customer

A customer paid to evaluate a venue to assist with market research.

Needlestick

A syringe.

Needlestick injury

An injury sustained from the prick of a syringe.

Negative moment of truth

Occurs when a bad impression is left on the guest.

Neutral moment of truth

Occurs when a moment of truth fails to make any impression at all.

Non-commercial businesses

Establishments providing hospitality services but not for profit.

Non-contaminated rubbish

General rubbish including newspapers, bottles, food wrappings and other items of a general nature that are not likely to harm you in any way, (that is, they are not contaminated).

Non-guaranteed booking

A reservation not secured with a deposit or credit card. The reservation is held until 6.00 pm or an otherwise agreed time, then released.

Non-income transactions

Transactions posted to guest accounts that display a credit or debit that will be a direct substitute for services rendered.

No-show

A reservation who does not arrive or who cancels their booking.

No-show report

A list of all guests who didn't turn up for their reservations.

Occupancy

The third stage in the cycle of service. Refers to the actual stay in the venue.

Occupancy level

The number of rooms booked in the venue. Usually expressed as a percentage of the total number of rooms available in the venue.

Occupied clean

Guest is in the room and the room doesn't need to be serviced as the guest may have just arrived, or the room has just been serviced.

Occupied dirty

Guest is in the room and housekeeping hasn't cleaned the room yet.

Off peak periods

Those times when room availability is high (low occupancy). Often referred to as low season.

Open-ended questions

Questions that make a yes or no answer difficult. Open-ended questions assume the guest is going to purchase and usually begin with 'why', 'which', 'how', 'what' and 'who'.

Operator assisted calls

Calls where the operator is required to place national and international calls for guests.

Organisational chart

A graphic representation of the division of labour, levels of authority and lines of communication in a business.

Organisational structure

How the services and facilities of a venue are organised and grouped in order to conduct its business so as to meet guests' needs and expectations.

Out of order (OOO)

Rooms listed as out of order and which are not available for sale. Out of order rooms reduce the number of rooms an establishment has to sell for that day.

Out of service (OOS)

Rooms that cannot be used for a brief time during the day.

Over-stay

A guest who stays beyond the original date of departure.

Overbooking

Practice of accepting more reservations than actual rooms available in an attempt to maximise occupancy.

Package

Refers to the inclusion of several services in a deal or room rate, such as room and breakfast.

Paging system

Internal communication tool used to maintain contact with staff whose place of work is not in one location. The staff member wears a pager, which registers a message sent through the paging system control panel, alerting that person to the fact that he or she is needed somewhere in the venue.

Paid out

A charge incurred by the guest that has been paid for by the venue on behalf of the guest.

Passiveness

Submissive behaviour that demonstrates a willingness to allow others to dominate and impose their viewpoints without consideration for their own.

Peak period

Those times of the year when room availability is low (high occupancy). Often referred to as high season.

Personal protective clothing and equipment (PPC&E)

Clothing and equipment designed to protect the wearer from hazards that may cause injury and illness.

Personal selling

Face-to-face promotional selling activities designed to inform targeted markets of the venue or about new products and influence them to buy the service. Personal selling is often referred to as sales calls.

Place

One of the 4Ps of the marketing mix. It refers to how the products and services (or information about them) are distributed.

Policy

A statement about the venue's position on an issue.

Point of Sale (POS)

Recording of the transaction at the time it occurred.

Porterage

A service fee charged to the guest when storage and/or delivery of luggage is required.

Porters

Accommodation services position in concierge. Responsible for guest services such as valet parking, luggage and general information.

Position

Refers to how guests perceive the product in relation to similar products in the market place.

Positioning

Positioning is the determination of where a venue fits in the market place in relation to its competitors and in conjunction with communicating the benefits of their products and services to their guests.

Positive moment of truth

Occurs when a good impression has been made.

Posting

The posting of charges means recording the details of the financial transaction on the account of the guest who used the service.

Pre-arrival

First stage of the cycle of service. This stage occurs before the guest stays at the venue, for example reservation.

Pre-assigned rooms

Rooms already blocked for a guest as per their request, for example high floor rooms, quiet rooms, fold-out sofa bed or a room near the lift.

Pre-authorised

To gain authorisation for a specified amount on a credit card and held by the venue as a means of ensuring the account is paid.

Prepayment

Money paid by the guest to the venue before the guest arrives to guarantee their booking. Also called advance deposit.

Pre-registered guest

This happens when a guest is registered in the PMS and assigned a room before arrival.

Presentation standards

Refers to the way in which a room looks.

Price

One of the 4Ps of the marketing mix. Price refers to the pricing structure of products and services designed to attract the target market.

Price differentiation

Occurs when the same products and services are offered by otherwise similar venues but the price differs.

Price fixing

When a business enters into an agreement with its competitor(s) to fix the price of a good or service.

Primary source

Information collected through interviewing (one-on-one or group sessions) or questionnaires (for example, completed by the guest) or by chatting to colleagues.

Private lounge area

Any room made available by the venue for the guest's use. It can be a television room, reading room, games room or have any other number of names or uses.

Procedure

A step-by-step guide to performing a task.

Product

One of the 4Ps of the marketing mix. Managing the products and services so they are beneficial and desirable to the guest.

Product differentiation

Occurs when a guest chooses a product based on the comparison between two similar products.

Product knowledge

Being familiar with all aspects of the products and services available in the venue.

Productivity

The number of rooms to be cleaned by one person in a given time frame.

Promotion

One of the 4Ps of the marketing mix. The way in which the market is informed about the products and services offered.

Promotional materials

Any printed matter such as brochures and leaflets produced for the venue promoting its products and services.

Proofing

To read a document, look for errors and correct them.

Property Management System (PMS)

A system that helps coordinate the flow of information required to control the transactions and activities that take place in a hospitality establishment. It is a means of collecting, storing and manipulating data.

Public areas

Those areas in a hospitality venue to which the public has general access, for example, a bar, restaurant, or foyer.

Publicity

Free communication to the public about the venue (services) in the media.

Public relations

A range of activities designed to promote the venue in a positive light through publicity.

Rack rate

The standard rate charged for a particular room type. It is the maximum rate usually charged for any given room type and several factors influence its determination and subsequent adjustments to them.

Receipt

Detailed record of the transaction indicating what the transaction was, the amount paid and the method of payment.

Reception

The front office, or front desk of the venue.

Receptionist

Person who works on the front desk.

Record maintenance

Retrieval, modification, updating and re-filing of documents.

Record utilisation

Accessing and using documents.

Registration

Refers to the procedure for checking a guest into the venue.

Release

Make a guest room available for resale.

Release time

If the guest has not checked in by a pre-determined time (usually 6.00 pm), then the room is released, so that it can be sold to another person.

Requisition form

A standard form for reordering stock requirements. Requires you to list stock items required, quantity, delivery details, date and name of person ordering.

Reservation

A booking for accommodation in a hospitality venue.

Reservations clerk

Person who records guest reservations.

Rollaway bed

A bed that can be folded length-ways in half, has fold-up legs and is on castors. These beds are designed this way for easy storage and manoeuvrability.

Rollover

Night audit function requiring the close of the current business day and the opening of the new business day.

Room allocation sheet

A list of rooms, room status and room types that a room attendant is required to clean in a shift.

Room amenities

Those items supplied by the venue for the guest's consumption or use, such as shampoo, conditioner, soap, bottled water, pen and paper, matches and tea and coffee.

Rooming list

List of all the guests included on a conference, detailing: arrival date and time, departure date and time, payment details and all guests' names (and who will be sharing a room with whom).

Rooming the guest

Procedure for issuing the guest with a key, instructing the guest on how to find their room and if applicable escorting the guest to their room.

Rooms division

See also 'accommodation services'. The rooms division is responsible for the front and back office, housekeeping and concierge services in an accommodation venue.

Room move

The guest is moved from the allocated room to a new room.

Room night

Occupancy of one room per night irrespective of the number of guests in the room.

Room rack

Manual or computerised record indicating the status of a room and therefore room availability.

Room only rate

Rate charged for a room only (inclusive of GST).

Room rate variance report

A listing of all occupied rooms sorted by room rate code, guest name, dates of stay and remarks relevant to the rate charged.

Room summary

Indicates the total number of rooms to sell and the total number of out of order rooms.

Room supplies

Those items supplied by the venue for the guest to use while occupying the room, such as towelling, cups and saucers, bathrobes and drinking glasses.

Room yield management

A technique used to maximise the number of rooms sold, on a specific day, at the highest possible rate.

Safety boxes

Safety boxes, or safety deposit boxes, are a means of securing guests' valuables (at the front office).

Sales calls

Face-to-face promotional activities designed to inform targeted markets of the venue or new products or services and influence them to buy. Sales calls are often referred to as personal selling.

Sales forecasts

Estimates of the number of rooms the reservations department expects to sell on specific dates.

Same day reservations

Reservation for guests who book their room the same day they are arriving.

Same chain referral

Reservations received for guests from venues that belong to the same group or chain.

Screening

Procedure for asking the caller's name and sometimes why they are calling before transferring the call.

Semi-automated system

One in which the data is processed manually but there is some automation in the accounting area of front and back office.

Service differentiation

A guest chooses a venue based on the difference in service standards or services offered.

Seasonality

The time of year. Likely to influence occupancy levels in the venue.

Secondary source information

Information gathered from already published data.

Services

Something that cannot be touched, seen or felt. Services have the potential to lack consistency and demonstrate a great potential for variability.

Sharps

A syringe.

Sleeping space

The bedding arrangement and how many people can be accommodated in that room.

Skipper

Person who departs without settling his or her account.

Source documents

Documentation detailing the charges made by the guest.

Special interest tour (SIT)

Group of people travelling together because of a mutual interest. Other features are similar to GITs.

Special offers

Any deals that the venue has to increase occupancy over the low periods such as packages and special rates.

Specials report
A list of all requests by guests such as a particular room, rollaway bed, fruit and champagne, and anything else that makes this reservation special.

Staffing levels
The number of staff required to serve the expected number of guests.

Standard letter
Business letter that conveys the same information to many recipients and is merged with a database to personalise it.

Status
The state of each room, for example occupied, vacant, clean or dirty.

Stay over
The guest is staying another night and the room needs cleaning.

STD (subscriber trunk dialing)
Telephone calls to or from a number outside the metropolitan area (long distance calls).

Suggestive selling
The selling of products or services by suggesting alternatives in a way that creates desire.

Suite
A guest room with separate living and sleeping areas. May also have kitchen facilities.

Suspicious person
Any person who is behaving in a way that seems unusual.

Swing shift
A shift rostered on in the middle of the day to cover breaks over the busy periods. Usually rostered on from 11.00 am–7.30 pm.

Switchboard
A piece of equipment that allows a venue to connect all the telephone lines and extensions.

Tabular ledger
A manual financial transaction record keeping system. Guest charges are tallied in columns and corresponding rows tally departmental revenues.

Tag
An identification label attached to the handle of luggage.

Target markets
The venue's potential guests. Categories of people with similar characteristics and buying habits that the venue wants to attract.

Tariff
Rate charged for a guest room. Usually rack rate.

Telephonist
The person who operates and manages the telephone system in the back office.

Template
A blueprint for text, graphics or layout, or a combination of all three.

Toll free line
Telephone line whereby the venue pays for the cost of the incoming call. Usually only available for long distance calls.

Touch up
When a guest has been in the room and then is quickly moved to another room, housekeeping needs to check the room and generally remove any evidence of someone having been in there.

Tourists

People travelling away from home for pleasure, either for a day, a night or longer but not for business.

Track

Finding out where a financial transaction error exists by checking and recalculating entries made during the shift until the error is located and then making the necessary adjustment to fix the problem.

Trade Practices Act 1974

This Act regulates business dealings between consumers, competitors and suppliers operating in the Australian market place.

Travel agent commissions

An amount of money paid to travel agents as payment for making the booking. Usually 10 per cent.

Turn down service

An evening service provided by housekeeping to prepare the guest's room for use. May include simply folding over the covers or, remaking the bed including changing the linen. Will usually include tidying the bathroom and straightening up the guest's room.

Under-stay

A guest who checks out of the venue before their planned departure date.

Unfair trading

The behaviour of businesses that may mislead or deceive consumers or be dishonest or unfair. It relates particularly to advertising and promoting the venue and applies regardless of how the promotion took place.

Upselling

Selling technique that starts at the lowest priced product or service and progressively moves up the price and quality levels.

Vacant clean

Room is vacant and clean (ready for the guest to check into).

Vacant dirty

Room is vacant but not yet cleaned.

Wake up call

A call placed to the guest room to wake the guest up.

Walk

Arrange to transfer the guest to another venue because of overbooking at your venue. This is sometimes referred to as bumping a guest.

Walk ins

Guests who arrive at the venue seeking accommodation without a reservation.

Wet area

An area that maybe exposed to the presence of water or other liquids.

Whitney system

This is a type of manual PMS. This system uses booking diaries and conventional charts to keep track of reservations, colour coded room racks to keep track of room types, room status and room occupancy. Most transactions are processed manually.

Win–lose conflict
A conflict outcome resulting in one party winning and the other losing.
Win–win conflict
A conflict outcome resulting in both parties achieving a satisfactory outcome.

Index